Research Ideas for the Classroom

High School Mathematics

Research Ideas for the Classroom

High School Mathematics

PATRICIA S. WILSON, *Editor*

**National Council of Teachers of Mathematics
Research Interpretation Project**

SIGRID WAGNER, *Project Director*

MACMILLAN PUBLISHING COMPANY
NEW YORK

Maxwell Macmillan Canada
TORONTO

Maxwell Macmillan International
NEW YORK   OXFORD   SINGAPORE   SYDNEY

Dedicated to

William F. Burger
in appreciation for his contributions
to his students and to mathematics education

Macmillan Publishing Company
866 Third Avenue
New York, NY 10022

Maxwell Macmillan Canada, Inc.
1200 Eglinton Avenue East, Suite 200
Don Mills, Ontario M3C 3N1

Macmillan Publishing Company is part of the Maxwell
Communication Group of Companies

Library of Congress Catalog Card Number: 92-11551

Printed in the United States of America

Printing number
    4   5   6   7   8   9   10

Library of Congress Cataloging-in-Publication Data

High school mathematics / Patricia S. Wilson : National Council of
    Teachers of Mathematics. Research Interpretation Project. Sigrid
    Wagner, project director.
        p.   cm. — (Research ideas for the classroom)
    Includes bibliographical references and index.
    ISBN 0-02-895793-8. — ISBN 0-02-895796-2 (pbk.)
    1. Mathematics—Study and teaching (Secondary) I. Wilson,
Patrica S. II. Wagner, Sigrid, 1942– . III. National Council of
Teachers of Mathematics. Research Interpretation Project.
IV. Series.
QA12.H54   1993
510′.71′2—dc20   92-11551
                                                        CIP

The paper used in this publication meets the minimum requirements of American National
Standard for Information Sciences—Permanence of Paper for Printed Library Materials.
ANSI Z39.48-1984. ∞™

Contents

Series Foreword

*R*esearch *Ideas for the Classroom* (RIC) is a three-volume series of research interpretations for early childhood, middle grades, and high school mathematics classrooms. These books reflect the combined efforts of well over two hundred researchers and teachers to produce a comprehensive and current compilation of research implications in mathematics education. We hope these volumes will serve as a useful sequel to the popular *Research Within Reach* published a decade ago by the National Council of Teachers of Mathematics (NCTM). Much research activity has transpired in the past few years and whole new lines of inquiry have emerged, particularly in the area of technology. It is time to look again at what research has to offer in the way of ideas for the classroom.

The ultimate goal of research in mathematics education is to improve learning and teaching, and from this perspective the RIC volumes serve as a valuable complement to the NCTM Research Agenda Project (RAP) monographs published in 1988 and 1989. The RAP monographs provide syntheses of several strands of existing research, as well as recommendations for future directions. The RIC volumes link the existing research to the classroom and provide ideas for teachers to explore with their own students.

From still another perspective, the RIC volumes should serve as an important supplement to the NCTM *Curriculum and Evaluation Standards* and *Professional Teaching Standards*. Chapter authors were asked to indicate where research supports recommendations in the *Standards* and where a research base is lacking. We hope these frequent citations will help guide implementation of the *Standards* and inform future recommendations.

A subtitle for the RIC volumes might be *Learning from Students*. Part of the value of research in mathematics education lies in the process itself, the process by which we learn from our students what they understand and how that understanding develops, how they feel about mathematics, and what factors affect those feelings. Any teacher who has ever asked a question or noticed an expression of puzzlement or delight has engaged in informal research. What we learn from students may cause us to question our assumptions, fortify our knowledge, investigate our reasoning, or rethink our methods of teaching.

Because research is a learning process, interpreting research becomes a multilayered process of construction in which objective phenomena are filtered through the subjective inferences of researchers, editors, and readers. Yet, as with most learning, this individual process of construction leads, over time, to shared systems of beliefs that influence our behavior in remarkably similar ways. We may tend to regard the key elements of these belief systems as "truths" even though we know that truth is a function of the times, context, and people involved.

The authors of the chapters in *Research Ideas for the Classroom* have attempted to convey the key points suggested by research in their areas of specialization. We hope that you, the reader, will be intrigued enough by ideas described in these pages to do two things: (a) go to the source of the authors' inspiration, the research reports listed at the end of each chapter (especially those marked with an *), and (b) go to the source of the researchers' inspiration, to students, and try some of these research activities yourself. By so doing, you can peel away several layers of subjective interpretation and come that much closer to learning the "truth" from your own students.

The NCTM Research Interpretation Project began in 1988 with a proposal to the National Science Foundation (NSF) to produce an updated and comprehensive set of research interpretations for the mathematics classroom. The project was funded under NSF Grant No. MDR-8850572. The editorial panel and advisory board met in the spring of 1989 to structure the volumes and identify chapter topics. To enhance communication between teachers and researchers, as well as insure the readability and practicality of the books, it was decided that chapters would be co-authored by a researcher and a teacher.

Without a doubt, the most crucial step in any writing project is picking the right authors. Researcher co-authors were chosen by the editorial panel for their knowledge of the research literature and their ability to interpret findings for the classroom. The researchers selected teacher co-authors for their expertise in teaching and the creativity of their ideas.

Authors agreed to an imposing array of requirements designed to guarantee comprehensive coverage, minimum overlap, and uniform format. They were given a long list of subtopics to be included in their chapters and then were told that they had to address all these topics in only twenty manuscript pages of text and five pages of references! They were asked to give some preference to easily accessible research reports, including research-based articles in *Mathematics Teacher*, *Arithmetic Teacher*, and *School Science and Mathematics*. They were asked to identify (*) articles that are especially rich in ideas for teaching.

Chapter development was a four-stage process. Editors and advisory board members reacted to chapter outlines and preliminary bibliographies from the standpoint of coverage and structure of the total volumes. First drafts of chapters were reviewed by researchers for breadth of coverage and balance of treatment within each chapter. Second drafts were reviewed by teachers for clarity of writing and practicality of suggestions for the classroom. Third drafts went to the publisher.

Each volume looks at research from the perspective of the learner, the content, and the teacher. Two chapters in each volume focus on the learner—one on cognition and one on affect. The content chapters vary according to the level, but each volume includes chapters on problem solving and technology. Four or five chapters in each volume focus on teaching—models of instruction, planning curriculum, classroom interaction, and evaluation. Each volume concludes with a chapter on teachers as researchers, which includes descriptions of research activities conducted by teachers within the constraints of the typical classroom environment.

The chapter structure makes each book easy to read selectively. References to accompanying chapters are included wherever appropriate, yet each chapter is quite comprehensible by itself. It is our sincere hope that most readers will enjoy an entire volume for its wealth of useful information and interesting ideas.

As comprehensive as the editors, authors, and reviewers have tried to be in a limited number of pages, the astute reader will surely note that some important themes are underrepresented. Some content topics (e.g., discrete mathematics, statistics, integers, inequalities), despite their importance in the mathematics curriculum, lack a substantial research base related to teaching and learning. Some themes, perhaps most notably that of gender and mathematics, have such a substantial research base that numerous books and monographs have been devoted to those single themes. Gender and mathematics is addressed in RIC in the chapters on affect, but we encourage the interested reader to consult other publications for further information. Other themes (e.g., multiculturalism or communication) have long histories of research but only recently within the field of mathematics education. We leave it to the next edition of NCTM research interpretations to report on these areas.

On behalf of the editorial panel, we thank the National Science Foundation, and especially Raymond J. Hannapel, for encouraging and supporting the project and for supplying copies of these books to mathematics supervisors across the country. We thank Lloyd Chilton for his help in launching the volumes and arranging for publication. We thank James D. Gates and Cynthia Rosso at NCTM and Philip Friedman and Michael Sander at Macmillan for helping in many ways throughout the project. We thank the advisory board—John A. Dossey, Mark J. Driscoll, Fernand J. Prevost, Judith T. Sowder, Douglas B. Super, and Marilyn N. Suydam—for their enthusiastic vision and willingness to share ideas. We thank the reviewers whose thoughtful comments and suggestions helped improve the quality of the final product. Most especially, we thank the authors for their considerable talents, their cheerful willingness to meet impossible constraints, and their patience in awaiting the final outcome.

I personally want to thank the volume editors—Robert J. Jensen, Douglas T. Owens, and Patricia S. Wilson—for the exceptional skills and tireless efforts they devoted to the project. It was an honor and a pleasure to work with them—they made a big job a lot of fun!

Sigrid Wagner

Introduction: Becoming Involved with Research

Patricia S. Wilson

Throughout this volume of *Research Ideas for the Classroom*, High School Mathematics, a familiar theme appears frequently: Students must be involved in their own learning. Research suggests that carefully planned activities and efforts to involve students lead to understanding. Since individual learners have different ways of making sense out of ideas, it is not sufficient for a learner to listen to and practice the teacher's ideas. Each student must be actively involved in the learning process. Building on this wisdom, each reader needs to become an active participant in interpreting the research in mathematics education for his or her own classroom. Rather than just reading this volume, teachers are encouraged to *use* it. Teachers must become involved in their own learning! We have designed the volume to inform classroom practice, stimulate collegial discussions, and encourage teachers to conduct investigations in their classrooms.

In an effort to support individual and varied use of the high school volume, the introduction provides information about it, including an explanation of why and how it was written, comments on research in general, an analysis of what is included and excluded, a brief summary of the contents, and suggestions for use.

Why and How Was the High School Volume Written?

Numerous journals, books, and periodicals report research in mathematics education. Examples include *Journal for Research in Mathematics Education*, *For the Learning of Mathematics*, *Educational Studies in Mathematics*, and *Journal of Mathematical Behavior*. Likewise there are several respectable journals, books, and periodicals that focus on teaching high school mathematics in the classroom. Examples are the *Mathematics Teacher*, various methods books, the NCTM yearbooks, *Every Minute Counts*, and *Computing Teacher*. However, there are very few efforts to interpret bodies of research for the purpose of informing mathematics teachers in the high school classroom. Mark Driscoll wrote the helpful *Research within Reach, the Secondary School* in 1980, which interpreted research selected to address specific questions that teachers asked. In contrast, the *Research for the Classroom* has attempted to interpret a more comprehensive selection of mathematics education research that surveys the field of mathematics education. All three volumes, elementary, middle, and high school, provide a current selection of research that reflects what has been accomplished since 1980. At the high school level, there has been significant research in the areas of technology, representations, and teacher beliefs as well as new research in such familiar areas as algebra and geometry.

Like the other volumes in *Research Ideas for the Classroom*, each chapter was written as a partnership between a researcher and a classroom teacher. In addition to the teacher/researcher authors, the book received the input of a board of ten classroom teachers, who critiqued early drafts, met as a group to discuss research and classroom implications, and designed classroom investigations that they implemented in their own classrooms. The last chapter, "Teacher as Researcher," describes their experiences and contributions.

Each chapter went through numerous revisions in an attempt to include as much research and interpretation as possible in an extremely limited space. Without exception, each author team struggled as it interpreted a large quantity of research but of necessity had to limit that research to a few exemplary studies. In some cases the authors also acknowledged a need for research to investigate existing policy, beliefs, and practice.

What Is Research?

Although a definitive answer is not provided in these pages, you should keep this important question in mind. A classroom teacher is both a consumer of research and someone with the opportunity to make research-based decisions every day. A teacher must read research critically and constantly be investigating in his or her classroom.

Mathematics education research studies address a great diversity of topics. Different topics require different methods of investigation, and a variety of methodologies in mathematics education research has been refined over the last ten years. Some studies have employed an experimental design using quantitative data and statistical procedures to analyze and report findings. Other studies have used interviews, observations, and ethnographic approaches to gather qualitative data and have reported findings with thick descriptions. Some studies involve hundreds of subjects while others focus on one individual in a case study. Research is done both in and outside the classroom, with increased attention to research from other fields such as psychology, anthropology, sociology, and history.

All research contains bias from multiple sources. First the bias of the researcher is woven into the proposed design and approach of the study. The subjects, situation, and content introduce a culturally established bias. The analysis of the data is biased by the type of data and the analysis procedures used. The authors of each chapter have introduced their biases by the studies chosen and the themes established in their chapters. The editor and reviewers have introduced additional influences. Finally, your reading and interpreting are influenced by your own biases. The point is that research does not uncover the truth. Clearly it is important to look at a body of research rather than at one study, and to continue to seek multiple answers.

Research does analyze and report events that reflect the researcher's view of the world. More important, research provides a foundation for interpreting the multitude of events that are happening in our mathematics classrooms every day. Research allows us to make informed decisions and to ask better questions. Research allows us to advance the field of mathematics education based on an analysis of the past rather than on myth.

What Should I Expect to Read and What Is Missing?

The chapters report a survey of existing research in mathematics education, but they can only report a sample of studies. The authors have synthesized numerous studies and have focused their scholarly interpretation of the research for the high school classroom. The analyses have often identified important constructs of learning and teaching as well as holes in our existing research base. In many instances, the authors have gone beyond interpreting research and provided examples of practice and activities that are suggested by a particular body of research. The authors have also posed questions and suggested investigations that you may want to use in your classroom.

Authors have made an effort to show how research relates to both the the NCTM *Curriculum and Evaluations Standards* and the *Professional Standards For Teaching Mathematics.* In many cases research supports suggestions and positions provided in the documents. The authors have also pointed to areas where we lack studies that address concerns raised by the *Standards.* The high school volume does offer valuable, research-based information that will help you apply NCTM's recommendations wisely. For example, the *Standards* recommends active student involvement in learning and this volume offers research on how and why to involve students.

This volume was not intended as a comprehensive report of all research in mathematics education. It is not a critique of the literature, and does not discuss theoretical or philosophical foundations of various studies. In many cases, the research is painted with a broad brush in order to highlight significant classroom applications. Readers interested in a particular area of research are encouraged to read original studies, which are cited in the reference lists. There was an effort to include sources available to classroom teachers. In some instances it may be necessary to consult university libraries or to make use of materials through interlibrary loans.

This volume was not intended as a methods book or a discussion of theories of teaching. Although several activities are suggested, action on the interpreted research is left to the creative, competent reader. Using research findings in the classroom is a very personal matter. Nina Kay Lankford discusses related issues in the chapter, "Teacher as Researcher."

This volume was organized so that it would be useful to the practicing mathematics teacher, but any given organization influences the selection and presentation of research. If the body of research in mathematics education had been organized differently, other topics would have gained more visibility. For example, the extensive body of research on gender and mathematics is not specifically addressed but is scattered through the chapters on learning and teaching and in some content areas. A new body of research that is giving attention to the influence of culture on learning and teaching mathematics is not well represented. Other examples of research not specifically addressed include language and mathematics, writing in mathematics, out-of-school mathematics, discrete mathematics, philosophy of mathematics, and policy studies.

How Is This Volume Organized?

The first section of the high school volume focuses on the learner. Stiff, Johnson, and Johnson interpret research on cognition. They provide a brief historical trip through the literature and focus on the current trends in constructivism and information processing. McLeod and Ortega look at the affective domain interpreting research on beliefs, attitudes, and emotions and how these components influence mathematical learning.

Chapters 3 through 5 focus on the processes of reasoning, problem solving, and representing mathematical ideas. O'Daffer and Thornquist emphasize practical classroom ideas based on research. They address critical thinking, mathematical reasoning, and proof. Wilson, Fernandez, and Hadaway have integrated problem-solving research with Polya's problem-solving model to offer valuable ideas related to using problem solving in the mathematics classroom. Janvier, Girardon, and Morand present an extensive body of research on using representations such as diagrams, graphs, and tables. The chapter is rich with examples and analysis of different forms of representation.

Research on specific mathematical content is interpreted in Chapters 6 through 10. Schoen and Hallas offer insights into the general mathematics students and the content of general mathematics curricula. Examples of classroom activities used in research are discussed. Wagner and Parker discuss research in teaching algebra including many common errors made by students. They describe the importance of addressing the structural aspects of algebra. Burger and Culpepper discuss the van Hiele levels of understanding geometry and provide research-based instructional guidelines. Ferrini-Mundy and Lauten interpret research related to precalculus and calculus learning. They raise issues related to representations and technology as well as specific concepts such as functions. Shaughnessy and Bergman include wonderful problems that have been used in probability research and classify the types of problems students have with probabilistic thinking.

Research related to technology is integrated with content in most of the chapters, but Heid and Baylor, in Chapter 11, take a look at the broader implications for the mathematics classroom based on research in using computers and calculators. They have categorized their interpretations by looking at technology as tool, tutor, and tutee.

Chapters 12 through 15 interpret research on teaching. Prichard and Bingamon present a collection of models of instruction and interpret research that will help you make informed choices. They also include research on cooperative learning and instructional aids. Brooks and Suydam interpret research on planning and preparing before entering the classroom, including such topics as homework, textbooks, and curriculum. Brown and Baird discuss research related to the classroom teacher. They interpret studies investigating teachers' knowledge, attitudes, and beliefs, as well as teachers' views of mathematics learning and mathematics teaching. The chapter on evaluation, by Badger, Cooney, and Kanold, has collected research on both formative and summative evaluation including teacher-made tests and standardized tests. Alternatives to testing are discussed.

The last chapter captures the theme of the *Research Ideas for the Classroom* volumes. Lankford writes on the teacher as researcher in the classroom, sharing her personal experiences of using research studies in her teaching and conducting her own classroom investigations. She outlines how to add researcher to the many hats that teachers wear and explains why she thinks it is critical for teachers to be involved in research.

How Can I Get the Most Out of My Limited Reading Time?

A quick scan of the table of contents and the index will give you a good idea of the diversity of topics and the wealth of ideas contained in the high school volume. Several topics will probably catch your attention and you will want to turn to them right away. Spot reading can be valuable and should be easy to accomplish. If you have particular areas of interest, you should be able to find specific information quickly and will find related research referenced. While such a dictionary-use of the volume may be useful, the authors have contributed to a much more valuable experience. The reader is encouraged to read entire chapters in order to place individual studies in a context, to identify trends in research, and to see how one body of research relates to another. Indeed, there are even studies that appear to contradict each other!

Most likely, if you are an algebra teacher you will want to read the algebra chapter first. The geometry teacher or general mathematics teacher will turn enthusiastically to the corresponding chapter. These chapters serve to organize the research in a specific content area and will provide a wealth of information, but a word to the wise is in order. Just as the reader is likely to be a mathematics teacher rather than simply an algebra teacher, students are learners, problem solvers, and reasoners as well as geometry students. Many chapters will contribute to your knowledge about your algebra students. The chapters on problem solving, representations, reasoning, and technology cut across all areas of content. The chapters on learning have implications for teaching, and likewise, the chapters on teaching provide insight into learning.

You may want to read the last chapter both first and last. The chapter on teachers as researchers provides an overview of the entire book and serves as a useful summary. It provides practical steps to conducting investigations in your own classroom. In fact, it argues that you will gain as much from investigating your classroom as you will from reading about other investigations.

This book can easily be read by yourself, but the benefits are increased if you can discuss your ideas with someone else. Encourage a colleague or your entire mathematics department to use the high school volume as a stimulus for discussion of program reform or improvement. Being informed should be the first step to taking action.

The bottom line is that this volume can be put to many uses. It can be read cover to cover, or in an altered order, but it is designed to be useful to you. Teachers and researchers have collaborated to offer an interpretation of current research in mathematics education that can make a difference in your practice in the high school classroom.

PART I

Learning

CHAPTER 1

Cognitive Issues in Mathematics Education

Lee V. Stiff, Janet L. Johnson, and Mary R. Johnson

> *As a parent, I wondered if the geometry course was going to serve the needs of my daughter. Several of the teachers with whom I spoke indicated that Mr. Peterson didn't really teach the kids. They said he just turned them loose to explore ideas on their own with "little or no direction." After six weeks of class and observing a lot of learning taking place, I asked my ninth grader how she enjoyed her math class. "It's okay," she said, "Mr. Peterson lets us find out things on our own . . . it's different . . . I like it! Anyhow, he helps us when we get stumped. But ya' know, Dad, I hate to say this, but he seems to like the boys better than he likes the girls."*

Teaching mathematics is a complex task. Many factors influence the process of communicating mathematical skills, concepts, and principles successfully to students. Perhaps the most significant factor in the teaching process is an understanding of intellectual development, or cognition. How a student learns or acquires new skills and information has a direct and significant impact upon how teachers should teach mathematics. But no one theory of learning completely describes how students acquire mathematical understanding. In part, this is a result of how different learning theorists view the goals of mathematics instruction. Some regard the learning of mathematics as the acquisition of algorithmic skills, others see it as the understanding of concepts and relationships that define the structure of mathematics, and many view it as the development of problem-solving skills. As we move into the twenty-first century, we face the challenge of adapting our teaching methods and classroom practices to meet the needs of students. The National Council of Teachers of Mathematics (NCTM), in its *Curriculum and Evaluation Standards for School Mathematics* (26) and *Professional Standards for Teaching Mathematics* (27), offers a vision of mathematics education and a perspective of cognitive development that can help teachers serve all students.

No theory of learning is a prescription for instruction. Nevertheless, there are several theories of learning from which high school teachers perhaps can fashion effective methods for promoting the learning of mathematics, or at least understand why current teaching practices exist. Indeed, the variety of learning theories might be seen as a reservoir from which teachers can draw ideas about methods of instruction suitable to their topics, the learning environment, and the needs of their students.

The Influence of Theories of Cognition and Intellectual Development

The development and maintenance of such mathematical skills, as completing the square, balancing a checkbook, bisecting an angle, or graphing a system of inequalities is a significant component of most mathematics instruction. Students may experience difficulty in solving rational equations because they are unable to manipulate rational expressions. A decision to review operations with rational expressions by practicing appropriate techniques reflects Thorndike's (44) theory of connectionism in which bonds between stimuli and responses are established and stengthened through the use of reinforcements or repeated application of the stimuli. Skinner (39) maintained that learning could be completely defined in terms of observable behaviors. Behavioral objectives such as "Students will be able to compute the sum of the measures of the interior angles in a convex polygon" would be used to describe the type of learning outcomes expected of students. The works of Thorndike and Skinner form the basis of the "drill-and-practice" approaches to teaching and learning seen throughout mathematics instruction in the United States and Canada. Algebra flash cards, computer-assisted instructional programs, and back-to-basics textbooks, with their repetitive approaches to instruction and skill development, are other examples of the influence that the behavorist theories of learning exert over mathematics instruction. Unfortunately, such theories ignore the structure of mathematics by treating mathematics as a collection of isolated skills.

Using available instructional technologies in the development and maintenance of algorithmic skills frees students and teachers to place greater emphasis on reasoning, making connections, communication, and problem solving as foci of instruction and learning. Heid (18) found that calculus students who used the graphics and symbolic-manipulation capabilities of a computer (some hand-held calculators have similar capabilities) to perform algebraic computations for the first twelve weeks of the course and spent the last three weeks on skill development showed better understanding of the course concepts than—and performed almost as well on a final exam of routine calculus skills as—a class that practiced skills for the entire fifteen weeks. This is an example of how the availability of calculators and computers diminishes the importance of practicing computational and algorithmic skills.

Have you ever asked, when planning a mathematics lesson or unit, "Where do I begin?" Robert Gagne's (15) theory of learning may suggest some ideas about how to start. Gagne's work is based on the assumption that the correct sequence of experiences, practiced sufficiently, will result in the desired learning. He asserts that higher-order tasks can be mastered, provided they are first decomposed into the elementary building-blocks that represent a hierarchy of subordinate and prerequisite abilities. For example, to find the roots of the polynomial

$$4x^2 + 6x - 6 = 0$$

using the quadratic formula, students must be able (among other competencies) to identify given coefficents of a general quadratic expression, recall the quadratic formula, evaluate algebraic expressions, extract square roots, and simplify rational expressions.

Evidence that students often learn procedures with little or no understanding of the mathematics involved comes from a National Assessment of Education Progress (NAEP) report (8). Students did much better on questions requiring exact answers to fraction problems than on those requiring estimates, indicating that although they had learned procedures for working with fractions, they had little understanding of their meaning.

William A. Brownell (5) was one of the first to promote a theory of "meaningful learning" in mathematics (arithmetic) instruction. Brownell argued that effective mathematics instruction must promote an understanding of the concepts, relationships, and processes that define arithmetic. Research indicates that students often learn procedures in algebra without understanding the meaning of what they are learning. Reed (31) found that alternate presentations of algebra word problems made all problems easier for students to complete. If students understand the underlying structure of problems, the wording of problems has less effect on students' ability to solve them or construct alternative solutions. An important strategy for helping students understand problems in a meaningful way is to have them rewrite and reformulate problems before attempting to answer them (20). Such computer software as the *Geometric Supposer* offers students the opportunity to go even further, by allowing them to formulate and then solve original problems—or at least problems not posed in the textbook (48).

Which problem is easier to solve?

1. Flying east between two cities that are 300 kilometers apart, a plane's speed is 150 kph. On the return trip, it flies at 300 kph. Find the average speed for the trip.
2. A plane flies 150 kph for 2 hours and 300 kph for 1 hour. Find its average speed.

The teaching and learning theories of Brownell (5), Bruner (6), Ausubel (2), and Gagne (15) focus more on the nature of the mathematics content than on how students learn. In fact, Gagne's view of learning has helped perpetuate the view that students cannot learn more advanced mathematics until they are computationally proficient. This prespective persists even though calculators and computers *can* be used to compensate for computational and algebraic deficiencies. A consequence of this view is that we needlessly require general mathematics students to study the same mathematical topics year after year in pursuit of computational excellence. They become bored and discouraged by the repetition, instead of challenged and excited by topics from such areas as algebra, geometry, statistics, probability, and discrete mathematics.

> "High school mathematics instruction must adopt broader goals for *all* students. It must provide experiences that encourage and enable students to value mathematics, gain confidence in their own mathematical ability, become mathematical problem solvers, communicate mathematically, and reason mathematically."
> *Curriculum and Evaluation Standards* (26, p. 123)

The best-known theory of intellectual development comes from the work of Jean Piaget (30). His early work identified four stages of cognitive development: the sensorimotor, the preoperational, the concrete operational, and the formal operational. Students seldom reside exclusively at one stage of development, however. High school students will frequently move between the concrete operational stage and the formal operational stage when faced with learning new skills, concepts, and principles. They need experiences that incorporate concrete operations and abstractions.

Piaget's theory of intellectual development centers around the processes of assimilation and accommodation of information into the mental schema of learners. *Assimilation* is the process by which new experiences and information are placed into the cognitive structure of the learner, and *accommodation* is the product of any restructuring of that cognitive schema. For example, acquiring the skills associated with solving systems of equations may mean that students have to work with matrices for the first time, which practice may result in a restructuring of their understanding of solving linear and quadratic equations.

The implementation of Piaget's theory of developmental stages illustrates that it is often difficult to translate a theory into a prescription for teaching. His work stresses the importance of human interaction and physical manipulation in the acquisition of knowledge. Many educators, however, inappropriately believe they are applying Piaget's theories when they merely show objects to students, instead of letting them manipulate the objects and make their own mathematical connections. (See [36] for a discussion of the implementation of Piaget's theory in the classroom.)

Geometry is an area of mathematics in which students often lack the necessary schema to understand new skills, concepts, and principles. The van Hiele model (14) of geometric thought addresses the problem of student readiness for learning by providing a guide to effective geometric instruction. Influenced by Piaget's work, the van Hiele model consists of sequential levels of understanding influenced by both instruction and the maturity of students. A recognition of the mismatch between students' readiness and course objectives is a first step toward providing better geometry instruction. Teachers must afford concrete experiences in geometry to bridge the gap between knowledge and skills, and proof. (See Chapter 8 for more information about the van Hiele model.)

Information processing is a current approach to the study of cognition, a view of it influenced by the way modern electronic computers process data. Emphasis is given to the mental processing of symbol manipulations, the processing and representation of information, and the simulation of cognition by "intelligent" machines. According to Ashcraft (1), there are three assumptions governing this view of cognition: Mental processes exist; people are active information processors; and mental processes and structures can be revealed by means of time and accuracy measures. Ashcraft outlines the following seven themes in cognitive psychology.

1. Attention is responsible for transferring information from the sensory memories to short-term memory and is a limited mental resource.
2. Mental processes fall along a continuum, from "fully conscious" to "fully automatic."
3. Some mental operations may occur serially and other mental processes occur in parallel or simultaneously.
4. Some mental processes are "data-driven," that is, they rely on information presented in the environment, while "concept-driven" mental processes rely on information already stored in memory.
5. The manner in which information is represented or stored in memory is critical.
6. Comprehension involves knowledge that is not stated, as well as inferences drawn from memory.
7. Metacognition is a key mechanism by which we assess our level of comprehension and plan strategies for improving performance. Metacognition refers to monitoring one's own cognitive system and its functioning.

The constructivist theory of learning asserts that students construct knowledge to "fit" what they already know (or believe) about the world. Sometimes the "fit," or adaptation, cannot be easily achieved. When students cannot readily assimilate new data into existing mental structures, they construct new relationships or schema in order to accommodate the new knowledge. For students to experience cognitive growth, they must be actively involved in the restructuring of that knowledge. Just as several keys may fit a single lock, different learners may create different mental schema that unlock information. What matters is that the knowledge they construct empowers them to understand their world.

Bruner (6) formulated four "theorems" about learning mathematics that support the constructivist view of cognition. The *construction* theorem states that students should be given the opportunity to construct their own representation of mathematical concepts, rules, and relationships. This often means that teachers must provide concrete models or use manipulatives in their instruction to assist in the process. The *notation* theorem asserts that the use of good notation simplifies the cognitive process through which students must reconcile new concepts, rules, and principles. For example, the concept of "variable" might be better understood if iconic representations, such as $12 = \underline{} + 5$, were used with seventh graders instead of the standard notation $12 = x + 5$.

The *constrast and variation* theorem says that the progression from concrete representations of concepts to abstract ones depends on experiences during which students contrast the attributes of certain concepts with those of similar concepts, and thus encounter a variety of examples thereof. The *connectivity* theorem states the need for teachers to demonstrate connections between and among the skills, concepts, and principles of mathematics. The establishment of these connections promotes higher levels of both mathematical reasoning and intuition—simultaneously promoting meaningful mathematical learning, because mathematics topics then do not exist in isolation. Few will argue the power of relating the process of solving systems of equations to matrix operations, for example.

Connections between mathematical topics empower students.
System of equations:

$$
\begin{array}{l}
5x + 3y = 3 \\
10x + 7y = 8
\end{array}
\quad \text{becomes} \quad
\begin{array}{rr}
-10x - 6y = & -6 \\
10x + 7y = & 8 \\
\hline
y = & 2
\end{array}
$$

$$
\text{giving} \quad
\begin{array}{r}
5x + 3(2) = 3 \\
5x = -3 \\
x = -3/5
\end{array}
$$

Matrices:

$$
\begin{pmatrix} 5 & 3 & | & 3 \\ 10 & 7 & | & 8 \end{pmatrix} \rightarrow
\begin{pmatrix} 5 & 3 & | & 3 \\ 0 & 1 & | & 2 \end{pmatrix} \rightarrow
\begin{pmatrix} 5 & 0 & | & -3 \\ 0 & 1 & | & 2 \end{pmatrix} \rightarrow
\begin{pmatrix} 1 & 0 & | & -3/5 \\ 0 & 1 & | & 2 \end{pmatrix}
$$

The implications derived from the constructivist view of teaching mathematics are important. As teachers alone, we cannot transfer mathematical concepts and relationships to the minds of students simply by telling them what we know. The constructivist approach to instruction tells us to become facilitators of learning as well. Classroom interactions must let students build upon what they already understand, explain why teachers handle the mathematics as we do, allow students to reconcile misconceptions, and offer different schema from which to view or interpret information. Indeed, the constructivist perspective accounts for why it is so difficult to remove misconceptions that students have about mathematical knowledge (25, 34). As Kuhn (22) suggested, the only way to remove a misconception based on an errant theory is to replace that theory with one that does a better job of explaining.

Of course, students can either construct knowledge or just accept information (4). Students who construct their own knowledge focus on the underlying structure of problems, often ignoring specific details of a problem. The way they solve problems is analogous to the way they construct information: They look for organizing information such as patterns, related but simpler problems, models, and so on. Students who simply accept information typically focus only on the details of problems, attempting to relate the superficial features to procedures they have memorized. Mistakes often reflect confusion over problems with similar surface structures but different underlying structures (19). For example, students frequently confuse the algorithms for adding and multiplying rational expressions, or the procedures for factoring trinomials and solving factorable quadratic equations. "Distributing exponentiation" is another example of how students often recognize only surface-feature similarities between exponentiation and multiplication of a quantity.

A common student error:

$$(x + y)^3 = x^3 + y^3$$

Carnine (7) points to the faulty construction of knowledge as another source of misunderstandings. According to Carnine, learners categorize and recategorize knowledge according to the similarities they see. They may construct untaught rules based upon perceived similarities or differences. Repeated reinforcement of the similarities they observe further validates these rules. To explain, Carnine observes that students may first learn to write equivalent fractions by comparing the shaded parts of circles (see Fig. 1.1). Later, if asked to find equivalent fractions *without* the use of shaded parts of circles, students will tend to seek other similarities in order to create new rules about writing equivalent fractions—such as adding the difference between denominators to both the numerator and denominator of the fraction to be rewritten in equivalent terms. Carnine suggests that students be taught to write equivalent fractions by multiplying a given fraction by a fraction equal to 1. This device often

FIGURE 1.1   Students may construct incorrect rules for writing equivalent fractions when shaded circles are not used

Comparing equivalent fractions using shaded circles.

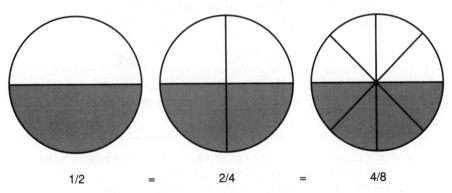

$$1/2 \qquad = \qquad 2/4 \qquad = \qquad 4/8$$

Comparing equivalent fractions without using shaded circles.

$$\frac{1}{2} = \frac{3}{4} \qquad\qquad \frac{1}{2} = \frac{7}{8}$$

$$\frac{3}{4} = \frac{7}{8}$$

leads to an understanding of the process that would prove even more useful in algebra. It also usually helps students to see that the rules governing algebraic fractions are connected to the rules governing numeric fractions. Students will be less likely to make errors in algebra such as adding the same number to both numerator and denominator when writing equivalent fractions.

One error made by students creating their own rules for deriving equivalent fractions.

$$\frac{x}{y} + \frac{z}{y + 3} = \frac{x + 3}{y + 3} + \frac{z}{y + 3}$$

To illustrate how students' perception of unintended similarities may lead to misconceptions, consider the similarities between mathematical units and algebraic variables. Sims-Knight and Kaput (38) found that a common source of error among students is their inability to distinguish between the symbolizations of an algebraic statement and a statement of equivalence. For example, 1,000 grams are equivalent to 1 kilogram, and this is symbolized by 1,000 g = 1 kg, where "g" and "kg" are units. Many students would similarly symbolize "There are six students for every professor" as $6S = P$, where S is the number of students and P is the number of professors. It is important to note that even students who have successfully learned computational skills involving units and variables may be confused about differences in their meanings.

Beyond pointing out surface-feature similarities that might lead to misunderstandings about mathematics, we should emphasize underlying structures and identify similarities among problems. This involves teaching alternative methods for solving problems and alternative perspectives for categorizing problems. This method will, in turn, reduce students' needs to memorize procedures. For example, we could teach uniform motion, work, and mixture problems as weighted-average problems (31). Then, summarizing solution strategies for these problems as weighted averages would provide the students with a perspective that emphasizes similarities among problems and helps students to construct cognitive structures that should be useful in handling unfamiliar problems later.

How many gallons of an A%-acid solution and a B%-acid solution should be mixed to produce N gallons of a C%-acid solution?
If the constant C is between constant values A and B, there are:

$$\left(\frac{C - B}{A - B}\right) \bullet N \quad \text{gallons of the A\% solution, and}$$

$$\left(\frac{A - C}{A - B}\right) \bullet N \quad \text{gallons of the B\% solution.}$$

Another important goal of mathematics instruction is the development of good problem-solving skills. When looking for ways to teach and enhance these skills, we must consider how students think, how experts solve problems, and how teachers and students alike view problem solving and its relationship to intelligence. There are similarities among problem-solving strategies that experts from different fields employ. These similarities include breaking problems into simpler ones, looking for analogous problems, rethinking or reformulating problems in terms of general principles, and proposing several solutions for consideration (24, 46, 3). In fact, it may be useful to identify other content areas (e.g., biology, political systems, and English) in which students have developed good problem-solving skills, and help them apply those skills in mathematics.

Positive correlations among measures of cognitive abilities suggest that all cognitive processes, including problem solving, are related to some level of general ability (32). Teachers and students who view cognitive abilities as sets of skills that can be expanded and enriched through applying those skills, and see the teaching/learning process as a way to provide intellectual growth, have a perspective on learning that will facilitate the development of problem-solving skills (10). In contrast, teachers and students who believe that intelligence and general cognitive abilities are innate and cannot be developed will have difficulty believing that problem solving can be taught and learned. Students who view cognitive abilities as being fixed, and see learning as merely an opportunity to display cognitive abilities that either do or do not exist, will try to avoid situations that might reveal a lack of ability (12).

My grandfather's pocket watch runs fast. It gains 6 minutes every hour. If Grandpa correctly set it at 3:00 P.M. today, what time will it show when the correct time is 7:30 P.M.?
A solution:

Step 1. From 3:00 P.M. to 7:30 P.M. is 4.5 hrs.
Step 2. The clock gains 6 min. every hour. In 4 hrs. it will gain 24 min. and in 0.5 hrs. it will gain 3 min. So in 4.5 hrs. it will gain 27 min.
Step 3. 7:30 P.M. plus 27 min. is 7:57 P.M.

Another solution:
Keeping track of the time with a table:

True Time	Time Shown by Clock
3:00	3:00 (at the start)
4:00	4:06
5:00	5:12
6:00	6:18
7:00	7:24
7:30	7:57

Teachers who think that problem-solving abilities and intelligence are equivalent and innate characteristics should consider the findings of Resnick (32), who reviewed problem-solving instructional programs. The evidence suggests that problem solving can be taught, and indeed is transferable across different instructional settings. Whimbey and Lockhead's work, *Problem Solving and Comprehension* (47), is designed to improve students' analytical thinking skills. It makes students aware of their thinking habits, discusses common errors in reasoning, and outlines the techniques of good problem solvers. Students practice their problem-solving skills by stating their solutions to a variety of problems and comparing their solutions to those of good problem solvers. In a related fashion, Davis (11) views problem solving as consisting of two processes. One process utilizes detailed and specific information in the building of representations while the other, meta-analysis, involves planning and monitoring problem-solving attempts. The two processes occur simultaneously and require practice if they are to be used effectively. Moreover, Schoenfeld (35) stresses the importance of metacognition (or meta-analysis) in mathematical problem solving as an organization technique for thinking about problems. (Chapter 4 provides more research related to problem solving.)

Individual and Group Differences Related to Cognition

Individual Differences

If all students were the same, all day, every day, a teacher's job would be simple—and boring. Researchers would develop one comprehensive theory of learning and prescribe the one most effective model for instruction. Teachers would simply follow the recipe to produce high levels of success for all their students. The reality, however, is that students are different, one from the other. Teachers have many teaching strategies that they can implement, but the challenge is to find the combination of strategies that will enable all students to reach their full potential. Individual differences can be cognitive or affective in nature. (In this section, individual differences in cognition will be discussed. Refer to Chapter 2 for a discussion of differences in the affective domain.)

Intelligence is one of the first things that comes to mind when thinking of how children differ cognitively. However, focusing on differences in intelligence can be unproductive. Instead of being useful information in the design of instruction, the knowledge of intelligence scores frequently becomes the reason for a breakdown in instruction. Intelligence tests and achievement tests are only measures of students' present accomplishments. Nevertheless, they are frequently used to place students in below-average, average, or above-average tracks, although "study after study, including randomized experiments of a quality rarely seen in educational research, finds no positive effect of ability grouping in any subject or at any grade level, even for the high achievers most widely assumed to benefit from grouping" (41). Tracking high school students into the low track in mathematics usually leads to poor performance simply because of the inferior academic experiences in that track (16).

When planning instruction, we should consider the cognitive factors field-dependence/field-independence, reflectivity/impulsivity, and sensory modalities. Field-dependent students are holistic in their perspectives and social in their interactions with others. They tend to prefer people-oriented teaching/learning activities such as cooperative learning groups. Field-independent students are more analytical and impersonal, more accepting of independent or individualized teaching/learning activities such as lectures (17, 45).

The typical mathematics instruction favors field-independent learners. However, although these students may experience more success in the typical mathematics classroom, all students benefit from instructional strategies that expose both mathematical structure and relationships. Overviews of lectures, flowcharts of algorithms (Fig. 1.2), diagrams of word problems, and problem-solving cooperative groups are a few ways to modify instruction in order to benefit not only field-dependent students (21, 37), but all students.

All of us have had students whose apparent goal when taking tests is to finish as quickly as possible. They turn in the exam without ever checking their answers. Or we have had students who agonize, seemingly for hours, before completing a single test item! The first type of student is impulsive. We can teach impulsive students to be more deliberate in their actions by teaching them to wait a few seconds before giving a response, by requiring that answers be checked on the test, or by asking them to explain their answers. The second type of student is reflective. We should, on a regular basis, provide reflective students with feedback about their mathematics performance. Too, these students should be encouraged to discuss their learning with others, as a means of achieving greater confidence about what they know.

Whimbey and Lockhead (47) describe a problem-solving technique called "paired problem solving" that might be useful to both reflective and impulsive students. In this technique, one student plays the role of listener while the other is the problem solver. The problem solver thinks aloud through the solution of a problem while the listener continually checks for accuracy and demands vocalization. In the appropriate role setting, this activity would force a reflective student to await feedback and an impulsive student to take the time to think.

Another cognitive trait that affects school instruction and learning is sensory modality—which includes visual, auditory, and kinesthetic modalities. We suggest that teachers address sensory-modality differences among students by using a combination of teaching modes that includes all of these modalities. On one day outlines, models, or diagrams could be fundamental to the teacher's presentation; on another day, instruction could center around cooperative learning groups in which communication is emphasized; on a third day, manipulatives or games could be used; and so on. For example, the effects of constants on the graph of a basic function can be introduced, using computer or calculator graphics. Visual learners benefit from "seeing" the effects of constants upon the basic graph (Fig. 1.3). Later, small-group discussions about the effects of constants upon the basic graph would appeal to the auditory nature of other students.

FIGURE 1.2 Flowcharts are one way to modify instruction to benefit field-dependent learners

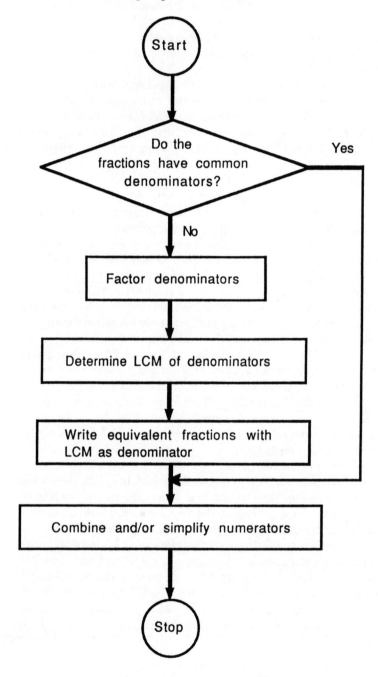

Adding Algebraic Fractions

FIGURE 1.3 Graphs are a useful way to tap into students' visual modality

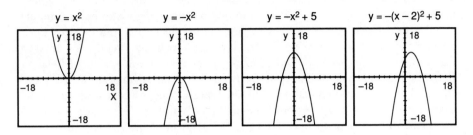

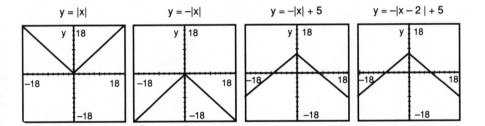

Group Differences

Both *Curriculum and Evaluation Standards* (26) and *Professional Standards for Teaching Mathematics* (27) describe a mathematics environment that encourages variety in instructional methods and materials. To address the needs of culturally diverse students, we may need to employ teaching methods different from those that have become the norm. Although more research is needed, there is evidence that poor and non-white students exhibit field-dependent learning styles and are better motivated in cooperative rather than competitive learning environments (37, 42). It has been observed that female students also benefit from cooperative learning environments (29).

> "To reach the goal of developing mathematical power for all students requires the creation of a curriculum and an environment in which teaching and learning are to occur, that are very different from much of current practice." *Professional Teaching Standards* (27, p. 1)

General mathematics classes contain a disproportionate number of African American, Hispanic, and American Indian students. The typical instructional approach in general mathematics is individual drill and practice designed to build computational skills. In fact, review topics constitute most of the curriculum in many mathematics classes labeled as low algebra and low geometry tracks, pre-algebra, and general mathematics. The topics are primarily skill-oriented and taught in isolation. Both teachers and students know that today's skills will be taught again in tomorrow's classes (16). This instructional approach is, however, inconsistent with our knowledge of the learning styles of non-white (and poor) students. Instruction based only on behaviorist learning theories is not sufficient to meet the needs of the diverse populations we serve in the schools (33).

Students in advanced mathematics classes are also taught from a behaviorist perspective. Although lessons are organized so that topics relate to one another and build upon previous topics in a logical manner, individual skills are frequently developed using the drill and practice instructional style. Ironically, once the hierarchy of skills and concepts has been acquired, advanced mathematics students are more likely to work cooperatively to identify commonly used problem-solving strategies or to compare the effect of changes to the argument of different functions than are students for whom cooperation and exploration would have the most benefit. The legacy of the behaviorists' theories of learning is the perspective that students must construct mental schema of the world in the order and manner in which textbooks are written. There is, however, a variety of ways that knowledge may be obtained. The history of mathematics itself suggests that the discovery of mathematical knowledge has seldom been sequential or uniformly understood. The constructivist approach to teaching and learning accommodates the way people learn and the manner in which mathematics is acquired.

The use of instructional technologies in the classroom is one way to take advantage of different teaching methods. If we allow students to use calculators (e.g., fraction calculators, graphics calculators, or scientific calculators) and computer software such as spreadsheets, plotters, and hypothesis testing software (e.g., *Geometric Supposer*), the average mathematics curriculum can incorporate a variety of activities for students with diverse backgrounds and learning styles. Teachers can use spreadsheets, for example, to promote problem solving. By entering formulas into a spreadsheet and allowing students to evaluate them within it, they can explore relationships among variables that describe phenomena such as uniform motion or measures of central tendency. Students, working in groups, could make conjectures about uses of the formulas and how the variables are related.

Vygotsky's theory of learning supports this type of mathematical discourse by stressing the importance of peer interaction to facilitate concept formation (13). This theory contends that higher mental functions originate in social relationships. According to this theory, all students would benefit from the verbalization of ideas and the social interactions that take place in cooperative learning environments. The increased use of cooperative learning during mathematical discourse leads to improved student achievement, provided that cognitive conflicts arise, inadequate reasoning is exposed, disequilibrium occurs, and higher-order understandings emerge (40). Females and most minorities, however, may have fewer opportunities than white males to verbalize their ideas in school mathematics classes because of sexual and cultural biases and teacher expectations (43, 28). As the daughter in our opening remarks observed about her geometry teacher, "But ya' know, Dad . . . he seems to like the boys better than he likes the girls." Cooperative learning groups are an effective means by which we can include all students in the learning process.

Looking Ahead . . .

Promoting the idea that every student can have a rich and productive school mathematics experience depends upon convincing parents, teachers, and administrators that this is, in fact, possible. The evidence may reside in the answers to such questions as: How is students' mathematical power affected by constructivist teaching strategies, classroom uses of technology, students' learning preferences, and teacher beliefs about cognition among and within categories of students? And: How should we assess cognitive abilities in mathematics? (Ideas for assessment are explored by Collis, Romberg, & Jurdak [9].) Research will play a critical role in addressing such questions, and in the final analysis, will likely cast the deciding vote!

Lee V. Stiff
Janet L. Johnson

More research in cognition in mathematics at the high school level is needed. Teachers want to know more about the implications of research in cognition, for teaching purposes. Can research assist teachers in convincing parents, teachers, and administrators that a variety of instructional approaches is desirable? How does a constructivist approach to instruction affect the manner in which teachers evaluate students? What should be the role of textbooks, inservice workshops, and preservice programs in determining classroom practices? Researchers should work closely with classroom teachers both in developing and conducting research agendas, and in developing curriculum materials based on research findings.

Mary R. Johnson

About the Authors

Lee V. Stiff is an associate professor of mathematics education at North Carolina State University, Raleigh. His research focuses on instructional computing in secondary and college mathematics and the mathematics education of African American children.

Janet L. Johnson is a recent Ph.D. graduate in mathematics education from North Carolina State University. A veteran of seven years of classroom experience teaching secondary school mathematics, she is currently an evaluation specialist for the Wake County Public School System in Raleigh, NC.

Mary R. Johnson has a Master of Education degree in mathematics education. She has taught secondary school mathematics for six years and has been a computer laboratory coordinator. Ms Johnson enjoys teaching geometry because its mathematical richness supports the use of hands-on activities and real-world models.

References

1. ASHCRAFT, M. H. (1989). *Human memory and cognition*. Glenview, IL: Scott, Foresman.
2. AUSUBEL, D. P. (1963). *The psychology of meaningful verbal learning*. New York: Grune & Stratton.
3. BEREITER, C., & SCARDAMALIA, M. (1982). From conversation to composition: The role of instruction in a developmental process. In R. Glaser (Ed.), *Advances in instructional psychology, 2*, 1–64.
*4. BLAIS, D. M. (1988). Constructivism—a theoretical revolution for algebra. *Mathematics Teacher, 81*(8), 624–631.
*5. BROWNELL, W. A. (1935). Psychological considerations in the learning and the teaching of arithmetic. In W. D. Reeve (Ed.), *The teaching of arithmetic* (pp. 1–31). Reston, VA: National Council of Teachers of Mathematics.
*6. BRUNER, J. S. (1963, April). Observations on the learning of mathematics. *Science Education News*, pp. 1–5.
*7. CARNINE, D. (1990). New research on the brain; implications for instruction. *Phi Delta Kappan, 71*(5), 372–377.
8. CARPENTER, T. P., CORBITT, M. K., KEPNER, K. S., LINDQUIST, M. M., & REYS, R. (1980). Results of the second NAEP mathematics assessment: Secondary school. *Mathematics Teacher, 73*(5), 329–338.
*9. COLLIS, K. F., ROMBERG, T. A., & JURDAK, M. E. (1986). A technique for assessing mathematical problem-solving ability. *Journal for Research in Mathematics Education, 17*(3), 206–221.
10. COVINGTON, M. V. (1985). Strategic thinking and the fear of failure. In J. W. Segan, S. F. Chipman, & R. Glaser (Eds.), *Thinking and learning skills: Vol. 1. Relating instruction to research* (pp. 389–416). Hillsdale, NJ: Erlbaum.
*11. DAVIS, R. B. (1984). *Learning mathematics—the cognitive science approach to mathematics education*. Norwood, NJ: Ablex.
12. DWECK, C. S., & ELLIOT, E. S. (1983). Achievement motivation. In E. M. Hetherington (Ed.), P. H. Mussen (Series Ed.), *Handbook of child psychology; Vol. 4. Socialization, personality, and social development* (pp. 643–992). New York: Wiley.
*13. FORMAN, E. A. (1988). Learning through peer instruction: A Vygotskian perspective. *The Genetic Epistemologist, 15*(2), 7–15.
*14. FUYS, D., GEDDES, D., & TISCHLER, R. (1988). The van Hiele model of thinking in geometry among adolescents. *Journal for Research in Mathematics Education, Monograph Number 3*, 1–196.
*15. GAGNE, R. M. (1985). *The conditions of learning and a theory of instruction* (4th ed.). New York: Holt, Rinehart.
16. GAMORAN, A., & BERENDS, M. (1987). The effects of stratification in secondary schools: Synthesis of survey and ethnographic research. *Review of Educational Research, 57*(4), 415–435.
*17. GILBERT, S. E., II, & GAY, G. (1985). Improving the success in school of poor Black children. *Phi Delta Kappan, 67*(2), 133–137.
*18. HEID, K. M. (1988). Resequencing skills and concepts in applied calculus using the computer as a tool. *Journal for Research in Mathematics Education, 19*(1), 3–25.
19. HOLYOAK, K. J., & KOH, K. (1987). Surface and structual similarity in analogical transfer. *Memory and Cognition, 15*(4), 332–340.
*20. KILPATRICK, J. (1987). Problem formulating: Where do good problems come from? In

A. H. Schoenfeld (Ed.), *Cognitive science and mathematics education* (pp. 123–147). Hillsdale, NJ: Erlbaum.

*21. KORNBLUTH, J. A., & SABBAN, Y. P. (1982). The effects of cognitive style and study method on mathematical achievement of Black students. *School Science and Mathematics*, 82(2), 132–140.

22. KUHN, T. J. (1970). *The structure of scientific revolutions* (2nd ed.). Chicago: University of Chicago Press.

23. LACHMAN, R., LACHMAN, J. L., & BUTTERFIELD, E. C. (1979). *Cognitive psychology and information processing: An introduction*. Hillsdale, NJ: Erlbaum.

24. LARKIN, J. H., MCDERMOTT, J., SIMON, D. P., & SIMON, H. (1980). Expert and novice performance in solving physics problems. *Science*, 208(4450), 1335–1342.

*25. MAURER, S. B. (1987). New knowledge about errors and new views about learners: What they mean to educators and more educators would like to know. In A. H. Schoenfeld (Ed.), *Cognitive science and mathematics education* (pp. 165–187). Hillsdale, NJ: Erlbaum.

*26. NATIONAL COUNCIL OF TEACHERS OF MATHEMATICS (1989). *Curriculum and evaluation standards for school mathematics*. Reston, VA: Author.

*27. NATIONAL COUNCIL OF TEACHERS OF MATHEMATICS (1991). *Professional standards for teaching mathematics*. Reston, VA: Author.

*28. PARTINGTON, G. (1985). The same or different? Curriculum implications of feminism and multiculturalism. *Journal of Curriculum Studies*, 17(3), 275–292.

*29. PETERSON, P., & FENNEMA, E. (1985). Effective teaching, student engagement in classroom activities, and sex-related differences in learning mathematics. *American Educational Research Journal*, 22(3), 309–335.

30. PIAGET, J. (1970). *Science of education and the psychology of the child*. New York: Orion.

*31. REED, S. K. (1984). Estimating answers to algebra word problems. *Journal of Experimental Psychology: Learning, Memory, and Cognition*, 10(4), 778–790.

*32. RESNICK, L. B. (1987). *Education and learning to think*. Washington, DC: National Academy Press.

33. ROMBERG, T., & CARPENTER, T. P. (1986). Research on teaching and learning mathematics: Two disciplines of scientific inquiry. In M. C. Wittrock (Ed.), *The third handbook of research on teaching* (pp. 850–873). New York: Macmillan.

34. SCHOENFELD, A. H. (1987a). Cognitive science and mathematics education: An overview. In A. H. Schoenfeld (Ed.), *Cognitive science and mathematics education* (pp. 1–31). Hillsdale, NJ: Erlbaum.

*35. SCHOENFELD, A. H. (1987b). What's all the fuss about metacognition? In A. H. Schoenfeld (Ed.), *Cognitive science and mathematics education* (pp. 189–215). Hillsdale, NJ: Erlbaum.

*36. SCHWEBEL, M., & RAPH, J. (1973). *Piaget in the classroom*. New York: Basic Books.

*37. SHADE, B. (1982). Afro-American cognitive style: A variable in school success? *Review of Educational Research*, 52(2), 219–244.

*38. SIMS-KNIGHT, J. E., & KAPUT, J. (1983). Misconceptions of algebraic symbols: Representations and component processes. In *Proceedings of the misconceptions in science and mathematics* (pp. 477–487). Ithaca, NY: Cornell University.

*39. SKINNER, B. F. (1968). *The technology of teaching*. Englewood Cliffs, NJ: Prentice–Hall.

*40. SLAVIN, R. E. (1988). Developmental and motivational perspectives on cooperative learning: A reconciliation. *The Genetic Epistemologist*, 15(2), 17–28.

*41. SLAVIN, R. E. (1990). Achievement effects of ability grouping in secondary schools: A best-evidence synthesis. *Review of Educational Research*, 60(3), 471–499.

*42. STIFF, L. V. (1990). African-American students and the promise of the *Curriculum and Evaluation Standards*. In T. J. Cooney (Ed.), *Teaching and learning mathematics in the 1990s* (1990 Yearbook, pp. 152–158). Reston, VA: National Council of Teachers of Mathematics.

43. STONE, N. A. (1988, January/February). Thank heaven for gifted girls. *Mensa Bulletin*, 10–12.

44. THORNDIKE, E. L. (1922). *The psychology of arithmetic*. New York: Macmillan.

*45. VALVERDE, L. A. (1984). Underachievement and underrepresentation of Hispanics in mathematics and mathematics-related careers. *Journal for Research in Mathematics Education*, 15(2), 123–133.

46. VOSS, J. F., GREENE, T. R., POST, T. A., & PENNER, B. C. (1983). Problem solving in the social sciences. In G. H. Bower (Ed.), *The psychology of learning and motivation: Advances in research theory* (Vol. 17, pp. 165–213). New York: Academic Press.

*47. WHIMBEY, A., & LOCKHEAD, J. (1986). *Problem solving and comprehension*. Hillsdale, NJ: Erlbaum.

*48. YERUSHALMY, M., & HOUDE, R. A. (1986). The geometric supposer; Promoting thinking and learning. *Mathematics Teacher*, 79(6), 418-422.

CHAPTER 2

Affective Issues in Mathematics Education

Douglas B. McLeod and Michele Ortega

> *A student was trying to solve the "chickens and pigs" problem, an old favorite of her mathematics teacher. Her comments describe both the problem and her feelings about it. "OK, there're 30 animals . . . figure out how many pigs . . . and chickens . . . there're 86 feet . . . OK. . . . Do I have to solve this totally? . . . OK . . . [several minutes later] OK, 12 pigs and 18 chickens, I have 84 [feet], with 13 pigs . . . 85 . . . [long pause]. I'm lost. I did something wrong. . . .[Later] I was frustrated . . . I hate word problems!*

Students often enjoy the chickens and pigs problem. One version goes like this: A farmer has chickens and pigs in her barnyard. She counts 30 heads and 86 feet. How many chickens and how many pigs does she have?

$\mathbf{A}$ffect is an important factor in teaching and learning mathematics. When you talk with teachers and/or students about mathematics, the teachers more often discuss student enthusiasm (or apathy), and the students usually talk about classes that are interesting (or boring). And as the anecdote above indicates, problem-solving activities can cause students to have quite intense affective responses.

The National Council of Teachers of Mathematics (NCTM) puts considerable emphasis on affective issues in its recent publication of *Curriculum and Evaluation Standards for School Mathematics* (30). Two of the major goals of the *Standards* deal with helping students understand the value of mathematics and with developing student confidence. In the standard on mathematical disposition the assessment of student confidence, interest, perseverance, and curiosity all are recommended. People in the United States, however, have a tendency to believe that learning mathematics is a question more of ability than of effort. The National Research Council's (31) report on the future of mathematics education (*Everybody Counts*) emphasizes the need to change the public's beliefs and attitudes about mathematics. If students are going to be active learners of mathematics who willingly attack nonroutine problems, their feelings about mathematics are going to be very important.

The NCTM *Curriculum and Evaluation Standards* (30) lists the following "five general goals for all students: (1) that they learn to value mathematics, (2) that they become confident in their ability to do mathematics, (3) that they become mathematical problem solvers, (4) that they learn to communicate mathematically, and (5) that they learn to reason mathematically" (p. 5). Affect is a central part of these goals, especially the first two.

A variety of large-scale studies provide a substantial amount of data that indicate we have good reason to be concerned about affective factors. The Second International Mathematics Study (36) shows that there are large differences among countries on measures of mathematical beliefs and attitudes, just as there are large differences in achievement. Various national assessments have also included data on affective issues. Dossey, Mullis, Lindquist, and Chambers (11) report that students in the United States become less positive about mathematics as they proceed through school; both confidence and enjoyment of mathematics appear to decline as students move from elementary through secondary school.

Efforts to evaluate mathematics programs and to promote the reform and improvement of mathematics education usually take a very traditional approach to affective issues, using questionnaires to gather commonsense data on beliefs and attitudes toward mathematics. In this chapter we consider how some of this traditional research on affect (and some that is not so traditional) could be useful to secondary school mathematics teachers.

Describing the Affective Domain

Beliefs, attitudes, and *emotions* are terms that reflect the range of feelings and moods that make up our affective responses to mathematics. These terms vary from cold to hot in the level of intensity of the affect that they represent. They also vary in stability: Beliefs and attitudes are relatively stable and resistant to change, but emotional responses to mathematics may change rapidly. For example, students who say they dislike mathematics one day are likely to express the same attitude the next day. However, a student who is frustrated and upset when working on a nonroutine problem may express joy and enthusiasm just a few minutes later when the problem is solved.

Beliefs, attitudes, and emotions also differ in the ways that cognition is involved in the affective response. Although it is not possible to separate student responses into discrete affective and cognitive categories, some of these terms involve thoughts (cognition) as much as feelings. For example, beliefs are mainly cognitive in nature, built up over a relatively long period of time. Emotional responses, however, have a much stronger affective component, and they can appear quite suddenly. So the terms *beliefs*, *attitudes*, and *emotions* are listed in order of increasing affective involvement, decreasing cognitive involvement, increasing intensity, and decreasing stability.

The Tenth Evaluation Standard (30) discusses students' mathematical disposition in terms of their: "confidence in using mathematics . . .; flexibility in exploring mathematical ideas . . .; willingness to persevere in mathematical tasks; interest, curiosity, and inventiveness in doing mathematics; inclination to monitor and reflect on their own thinking and performance; valuing of the application of mathematics . . .; [and] appreciation of the role of mathematics in our culture." (p. 233)

In mathematics education, feelings and moods like anxiety, confidence, frustration, and satisfaction are all used to describe responses to mathematical tasks. Frequently these feelings are discussed in the literature as attitudes, although that term does not seem adequate to describe some of the more intense emotional reactions that occur in mathematics classrooms. For example, we recognize the "Aha!" experience in mathematical problem solving as a joyful event quite different from traditional definitions of attitude.

To further complicate the task of describing the affective domain, terms sometimes have different meanings in psychology than they do in mathematics education. Even within a given field, studies that use the same terminology often are not studying the same phenomenon. For example, Hart (18) notes that anxiety is sometimes described as fear, one of the more intense emotions, and in other studies as dislike, a less intense attitudinal response.

There have been many reviews of the literature related to affective factors and mathematics education, including those by Kulm (20), Leder (21), and Reyes (35). These reviews have generally focused on attitudes toward mathematics as their major concern, rather than on trying to describe and analyze all components of the affective domain. In this chapter we will try to broaden the view of affect by emphasizing those beliefs and emotions related to mathematics learning.

Psychological Theories and Affect

Changes in psychological theories have had a major impact on how affect is treated in mathematics education research. Frequently researchers have treated affect as an avoidable complication of modest significance. In recent years, however, we have made considerable progress in developing our knowledge of affective issues.

In the past, for example, some researchers have claimed that negative attitudes result in poor achievement in mathematics, while others have said that poor achievement in mathematics has produced negative attitudes. However, data suggest that *neither* of these statements is likely to be completely correct; rather, attitude and achievement interact with each other in complex and unpredictable ways. For example, data from the Second International Mathematics Study indicate that Japanese students had a greater dislike for mathematics than students in other countries, even though Japanese achievement was very high (27). There is a growing appreciation for the complexity of the affective domain: The original attempts to measure attitude toward mathematics seem exceptionally primitive, given our current knowledge and experience in the area (21).

In recent years affect has emerged as an important part of some cognitive theories. One of the most interesting of these theories for mathematics education is that of George Mandler (22, 23). Mandler's view is that most affective factors arise out of the emotional responses to the interruption of plans (see Fig. 2.1). In Mandler's terms, plans arise from the activation of a schema (see Chapter 1). The schema produces an action sequence, and if the anticipated sequence of actions cannot be completed, the blockage or discrepancy is followed by a physiological response. This physiological arousal is typically felt as an increase in either heartbeat or muscle tension. The arousal serves as the mechanism for redirecting the individual's attention. At the same time the arousal occurs, the individual attempts to evaluate the meaning of this unexpected or otherwise troublesome blockage. The evaluation of the interruption might classify it as a pleasant surprise, an unpleasant irritation, or perhaps even a major catastrophe. The cognitive evaluation of the interruption provides the *meaning* to the arousal.

Analyzing the meaning of the interruptions has several parts. First, the meaning comes out of the cognitive interpretation of the arousal. This meaning will be dependent on what the individual knows or assumes to be true. Second, the arousal that leads to the emotion generally doesn't last. Individuals normally adjust to the unexpected event, interpret it in the context in which it occurs, and try to find some other way to carry out their plan and achieve their goal. Third, repeated interruptions

FIGURE 2.1   Affect and problem solving

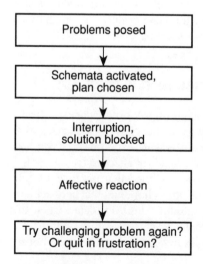

in the same context usually result in emotions that become less intense. We reduce the demand on cognitive processing by responding more automatically and less intensely as interruptions recur. Our responses in this situation become more stable and predictable, and begin to resemble the kinds of attitudes that have been the emphasis of past research on affect in mathematics education.

To help clarify the situation, consider the affective responses of a ninth-grade student to a typical story problem. Suppose that the student believes that story problems should make sense and should have a reasonable answer that can be obtained in a minute or two. Suppose also that the student has been reasonably successful in mathematics. If the student is unable to obtain a satisfactory answer in a reasonable time, the failure to solve the problem (an interruption of the plan) is likely to lead to some arousal. The interpretation of this arousal is likely to be negative; students usually describe it as frustration. If the students are able to overcome the blockage and find a solution to the problem, they may report positive reactions to the experience. If they are not successful, and negative reactions to story problems occur repeatedly, the negative response will eventually become automatic and stable. In this situation the student would have developed a negative attitude toward story problems. For further examples, see Marshall (24).

Teachers may be able to help students improve their affective responses to problem solving in a variety of ways. For example, teachers can help students expand their views of how much time a problem should take by assigning some tasks that are obviously meant to be completed over days rather than minutes. Problems such as those that involve gathering, graphing, and analyzing data can take a considerable amount of time.

In summary, there are three facets of the affective experience of mathematics students that seem particularly important:

- Students hold certain beliefs about mathematics and about themselves that play an important role in their affective responses.
- As interruptions and blockages are an inevitable part of the learning of mathematics, students will experience both positive and negative emotions as they learn mathematics. These emotions are likely to be more noticeable when the tasks are unfamiliar.
- Students will develop positive or negative attitudes toward mathematics as they encounter the same or similar mathematical situations repeatedly.

These three aspects of affective experience correspond to the three previously cited areas of research in mathematics education (beliefs, attitudes, and emotions) that we will now examine further.

Beliefs

Research on beliefs in mathematics education has become an important thread linking a number of studies of both teachers and students. Data have typically been gathered through observations of students and teachers, as well as through questionnaires and interviews. In this chapter we discuss several different kinds of beliefs.

Beliefs about Mathematics. Research on student beliefs about mathematics has received considerable attention over recent years. Data from the National Assessment of Educational Progress (2) suggest that students generally believe that mathematics is important, difficult, and based on rules. These beliefs about mathematics, although not emotional in themselves, tend to generate more intense affective reactions. For example, students who believe that mathematics is important are more likely to get emotional about problem solving than those who think mathematics is unimportant.

The NCTM *Curriculum and Evaluation Standards* (30) notes that "Teachers implicitly provide information and structure experiences that form the basis of students' beliefs about mathematics. These beliefs exert a powerful influence on students' evaluation of their own ability, on their willingness to engage in mathematical tasks, and on their ultimate mathematical disposition." (p. 233)

A variety of other major evaluation studies have also dealt with beliefs about mathematics. Dossey and colleagues (11) report that students in the United States (grades 3, 7, and 11) believe that mathematics is useful, but involves mainly memorizing and following rules. McKnight and colleagues (27) found similar results in the U.S. data from the Second International Mathematics Study (grades 8 and 12).

Research on beliefs has been a major focus in studies of problem solving. As Schoenfeld (38) has pointed out, students may hold beliefs about mathematics that weaken their ability to solve nonroutine problems. If students believe that mathematical problems should always be completed quickly, they may be unwilling to persist in trying to solve nonroutine problems that take substantially longer. Also, students may believe that only geniuses can be creative in mathematics, or that proof just confirms the obvious (38). Even though teachers do not necessarily share these beliefs, the traditional curriculum in the traditional classroom often provides support for the development of such beliefs.

A teacher comments on the importance of parental beliefs: "Many, even *parents*, really believe that math ability is *genetic*. . . . Parents tell their kids that they don't expect them to succeed in math because they, themselves, were unsuccessful."

Another important area of research on beliefs comes out of the work on gender differences in mathematics education. Most of the data has come from studies that used the Fennema/Sherman scales, and especially the scale on the perceived usefulness of mathematics (12). In summarizing this research, Fennema (12) notes that males in general rate mathematics higher on usefulness than females. These kinds of beliefs are important for gender differences in mathematics achievement, in enrollment, and in affective responses to mathematics.

Stodolsky (41) describes how beliefs about mathematics influence how students (and teachers) perform in mathematics classrooms, especially as compared to social studies classrooms. In social studies, students are much more likely to work in groups, to develop their research skills, and in general to work on tasks that are compatible with the development of higher-order thinking skills. In mathematics classrooms, on the other hand, students spend a lot of time doing individual seatwork. Other writers have noted how students view mathematics as a skill-oriented subject, and how such limited views of the discipline lead to anxiety about mathematics (16) and more generally interfere with higher-order thinking in mathematics (14).

Beliefs about the Self.   Much of the research on affective factors in mathematics education tends to focus on beliefs about the self. Some aspects of beliefs about the self have been researched quite thoroughly, especially in the area of research on gender differences. Other aspects are only beginning to be investigated. For example, there has been a substantial amount of data gathered on confidence in doing mathematics, but very little on how students develop a belief in themselves as independent learners of mathematics (13).

Major evaluation studies provide useful background data on confidence. National assessment data from the United States (11) asked children in grades 3, 7, and 11 if they were good at doing mathematics. The percentage of students who responded positively dropped from 65% in grade 3 to 53% in grade 11, providing at least a rough measure of how confidence declines as students progress through school.

Research on confidence in learning mathematics indicates that there are substantial differences between males and females on this dimension. Reyes (35) and Meyer and Fennema (29) summarize the relevant literature. In general, males tend to be more confident than females, even when females may have better reasons (based on their performance) to feel confident.

Another set of beliefs about the self that has been investigated quite thoroughly is the area of causal attributions—the reasons that students give for their successes and failures. Weiner (43) presents the central themes (see Table 2.1). The three main dimensions of the theory deal with the locus (internal or external), the stability (e.g., ability vs. effort), and the controllability of the cause of success and failure. For example, a student who fails to solve a mathematics problem could attribute the cause to the difficulty of the problem—a cause that is external, stable, and uncontrollable by the student. In contrast, a student who succeeds in solving a problem might attribute that success to effort—a cause that is internal, unstable, and controllable.

TABLE 2.1.   Attributions of Success and Failure

	Internal		External	
	Stable	Unstable	Stable	Unstable
Not controllable	Ability	Mood	Task difficulty	Luck
				Unusual help from others
Controllable	Typical effort	Immediate effort	Teacher bias	

(Adapted from 43)

Research on the nature of the attributions of female and male students has been an important theme in recent research in mathematics education, and the results provide some of the most consistent data in the literature on the affective domain. For example, males are more likely than females to attribute their success in mathematics to ability, and females are more likely than males to attribute their failures to lack of ability. In addition, females tend to attribute their successes to extra effort more than males do, and males tend to attribute their failures to lack of effort more than females do. We see the consequences of these differences in the way that more males than females have traditionally chosen mathematically related careers (12, 13, 29, 35).

A related area is research on learned helplessness. Diener and Dweck (10) describe learned helplessness as a pattern of behavior whereby students attribute failure to lack of ability. Such students tended to demonstrate a low level of persistence and to avoid challenges whenever possible. A contrasting pattern, referred to as a mastery orientation, was characterized by students who concentrated on monitoring their performance, making adjustments and trying new strategies as they solved problems. Mastery-oriented students usually saw intelligence as malleable rather than fixed, and knew that they could add to their knowledge through hard work.

Beliefs and the Social Context.   Recent research on mathematics learning has given increased attention to the social context of instruction in particular, and more generally to cultural issues in mathematics education (7, 33). Student beliefs about the social context appear to be another area that is closely related to affective concerns. For example, Cobb, Yackel, and Wood (6) found that explicit teaching of social norms in the classroom was directly related to the kinds of affective reactions that the students expressed: They observed a teacher who insisted that students not describe problems as "easy." The teacher's point was that describing a problem as easy was demoralizing to students who had not yet been able to solve the problem. That kind of talk, so common in most classrooms, was strongly discouraged by this teacher. The rest of us might want to consider how classroom conversations can undermine student confidence and how we might establish new social norms in our classrooms to change that kind of talk.

Similarly, at the secondary level, Grouws and Cramer (17) found that the classrooms of effective teachers of mathematical problem solving were characterized by a supportive classroom environment where social norms encouraged students to be enthusiastic and to enjoy mathematical problem solving. From a broader perspective, the social context provided by the school and the home also can have an effect on student beliefs. Parsons, Adler, and Kaczala (34), in their study of parental influences on student attitudes and beliefs, noted that affective reactions of students (particularly females) often reflect social norms as expressed by the parents. Research in crosscultural settings also points out the influence of the broader social context. Holloway (19), in her analysis of research on effort and ability, compared data from Japan and the United States. Some of the major findings from this report suggest that effort is believed to be of primary importance in determining achievement in Japan, but ability is seen as the primary factor in the United States. Apparently Japanese homes encourage task involvement in ways that promote attributions to effort. Related research (40) suggests that mathematics students in other countries expect mathematics to involve hard work on nontrivial problems; Chinese and Japanese parents expect their children to work hard at mathematics, and the children generally respond positively to this expectation. The culture promotes certain beliefs about education, and these beliefs can be powerful forces in children's affective responses to mathematics.

"Myth: Learning mathematics requires special ability, which most students do not have.
"Reality: Only in the United States do people believe that learning mathematics depends on special ability. In other countries, students, parents, and teachers all expect that most students can master mathematics if only they work hard enough." (31, p. 10)

Individual Differences in Beliefs.   As noted above, there are substantial differences in beliefs about mathematics between males and females, as well as across different cultures. Other differences in beliefs can be traced to other subgroups of the student population.

Although minority students, like females, tend to be underrepresented in mathematical careers, there is not much research that investigates affective responses of minority students to mathematics (26). The data that are available suggest that black students express positive beliefs about the usefulness and importance of mathematics, but this pattern of beliefs does not result in high levels of participation in mathematics (32). Although affective factors are likely to be important to persistence in mathematics for all groups, other issues apparently are influential in reducing the participation rate for minority students.

Research is also lacking on the affective factors that influence students with learning disabilities in mathematics. Chapman (5) reports that learning-disabled students have low academic self-concepts, and research suggests that these negative beliefs about the self persist from elementary through secondary school. Special programs (like mainstreaming) do not seem to have a major effect on the self-concepts of learning-disabled students. More research in this area could be useful to mathematics teachers.

Attitudes

Research on attitudes toward mathematics has a relatively long history. For recent reviews and analyses, see Kulm (20), Leder (21), and Reyes (35). Many of these reviews use attitudes as a general term that includes beliefs about mathematics and about the self. Here we use *attitude* to refer to affective responses that involve positive or negative feelings that are relatively stable. Liking geometry, disliking story problems, being curious about topology, and being bored by algebra all are examples of attitudes.

Attitudes toward mathematics appear to develop in two different ways. As we mentioned earlier, attitudes may result from the automatizing of a repeated emotional reaction to mathematics. For example, if a student has repeated negative experiences with geometric proofs, we might theorize that the emotional reaction will eventually become more automatic, there will be less physiological arousal, and the response will become a stable one that can probably be measured through use of a questionnaire. A second source of attitudes is the assignment of an already existing attitude to a new but related task. A student who has a negative attitude toward geometric proof may attach that same attitude to proofs in algebra. See Marshall (24) for more discussion.

Many cartoons about mathematics show the special role of affect in mathematics learning. One of our favorites is a "Far Side" cartoon (by Gary Larson, a graduate of Washington State University!) that shows "Hell's library" complete with a horned devil, flaming fire, and a bookcase full of titles like *Story Problems, More Story Problems, Story Problems Galore*, and *Big Book of Story Problems*.

Most major evaluation studies provide data on attitudes toward mathematics. In national assessment data (11) a positive correlation between attitude and achievement was found at all three grade levels assessed (grades 3, 7, and 11), but the percentage of students who say they enjoy mathematics declined from 60% in grade 3 to 50% in grade 11. Similar results appear in the Second International Mathematics Study (27).

Data from the Second International Mathematics Study indicate that that there are substantial differences in attitudes between different countries. When twelfth-grade students were asked if they liked mathematical activities such as checking answers and proving theorems, the Japanese students were much more negative than the students from Sweden and the United States. Students from Hong Kong were the most positive. (27)

Some studies have assessed attitude toward various subdomains that are part of or related to mathematics. For example, McKnight and colleagues (27) report that students generally like to use calculators, but dislike memorizing. Checking answers fell somewhere between. Corbitt (8) interviewed students in grade 8 regarding how much they liked fifteen different mathematical topics and found that many students reported being bored with the typical review of computation in eighth grade.

The study of mathematics anxiety has received more attention than any other area that lies within the affective domain (35). Yet the concepts underlying the research continue to be murky, and the terminology remains unclear. Anxiety has sometimes been characterized as fear, a "hot" emotion, and sometimes as dislike, an attitude (18). Conceptions of mathematics anxiety seem to overlap with test anxiety (37) as it applies to mathematics.

National assessment data from the United States (11, p. 96) indicate that over half of the students in grade 7 agree with the statement "I enjoy mathematics." The data are less positive for students in grade 11, but black and Hispanic students still tend to be reasonably positive.

Population	Percent agreeing	
	Grade 7	Grade 11
Nation	55	50
Male	54	51
Female	57	49
White	54	47
Black	63	62
Hispanic	53	56

Programs to reduce mathematics anxiety, in addition to providing instructional help in mathematics, generally use the same kind of strategies that occur in programs to reduce test anxiety. Students typically learn relaxation techniques, and often there is an attempt to change students' beliefs about both mathematics and themselves (9).

Emotions

The emotional reactions of students have not been major factors in research on affect in mathematics education. This lack of attention to emotion is probably due in part to the fact that research on affective issues has mostly looked for factors that are stable and can be measured by questionnaire. However, a number of studies have looked at how the emotions are involved in learning mathematics.

One of the early studies of problem-solving processes was conducted by Bloom and Broder (1). In this work they noted how students' engagement in the task led them into periods of tension and frustration, especially when they felt that their attempts to reach a solution were blocked. Once the block had been overcome, the students would relax and report very positive emotions. This study, conducted before the current focus on cognition became common, provides a useful model for integrating research on cognition and affect.

Reports of strong emotional reactions to mathematics do not appear in the research literature very often. An important exception is the work of Buxton (4). His research deals with adults who report their emotional reaction to mathematical tasks as panic. Their reports of panic are accompanied by a degree of physiological arousal so difficult to control that they find it disrupts their ability to concentrate on the task. The emotional reaction is variously described as fear and embarrassment, as well as panic.

A number of other researchers have investigated factors related to the influence of emotions on cognitive processes in mathematics. Wagner, Rachlin, and Jensen (42) report that algebra students who were stuck on a problem would sometimes get upset and grope wildly for any response, no matter how irrational, that would get them past the blockage. On a more positive note, Brown and Walter (3) suggest that making conjectures can be a source of great joy to mathematics students. Similarly, Mason, Burton, and Stacey (25) talk about the satisfaction of the "Aha!" experience in mathematical problem solving, and make suggestions about how students can be encouraged to savor and anticipate that positive emotional experience.

The studies mentioned above were generally focused on cognitive rather than affective issues, and reports of students' emotional responses frequently were sidelights, rather than highlights, of the research. However, some investigations have focused directly on the role of the emotions in mathematics learning. In a report on the emotional reactions of experts (research mathematicians) and novices (college students) to problem solving, McLeod, Metzger, and Craviotto (28) found that the emotional reactions to the frustrations and joys of solving problems are basically the same for each group: Even experts get frustrated! The experts, however, are better able to control their emotions: They stay flexible, trying a variety of strategies even when they are stuck.

In another study of experts, Silver and Metzger (39) interviewed research mathematicians and asked them to solve nonroutine problems while thinking aloud. Rather than viewing problems from a strictly utilitarian perspective, these experts frequently spoke about the elegance, harmony, and coherence of various solutions (or attempted solutions) to problems. The aesthetic aspects of the problem-solving experience were clearly linked to the experts' emotional responses, and especially to their enjoyment of the problem.

Although comments about emotion do appear in the research literature from time to time, it is fairly unusual for research on mathematics education to include measures of physiological changes that accompany the emotions. However, in a recent study Gentry and Underhill (15) gathered data on muscle tension while students solved problems; they also administered paper-and-pencil measures of anxiety toward mathematics. As one might expect, there was little correlation between the two measures, suggesting that traditional measures of anxiety may be quite different from the emotional responses that influence students in the classroom. Similar results were obtained by Dew, Galassi, and Galassi (9).

Summary

Many studies of affect are not directly applicable to classroom instruction, but one study (17) provides a useful summary of what might constitute good practice in dealing with affect in mathematics teaching. Grouws and Cramer observed six expert teachers of problem solving at the junior high school level. The focus of the study was on identifying the affective characteristics of the classrooms of these teachers during problem-solving lessons. The observations revealed that students in these classes enjoyed problem solving, persevered on problem-solving tasks, and worked willingly on problem-solving assignments. Observations and interviews with teachers revealed that teachers appeared to work hard to establish a good relationship with students, to be friendly rather than formal, and to share personal anecdotes about their own problem solving that illustrated their own strengths and weaknesses as problem solvers. In addition, the teachers held students accountable for their performance in problem solving. Student work was assessed, and credit was given for oral presentations and for the kinds of strategies used, as well as for the answer. The teachers also made frequent use of cooperative groups. Although no single factor appeared to be the cause of the success of these expert teachers, the strategies that they used suggest patterns that other teachers might try.

In summary: Students' beliefs, attitudes, and emotions are important factors in mathematics teaching and learning. If we help students develop positive beliefs and attitudes toward mathematics, their performance should improve. If we encourage students to think of mathematical problems as challenges rather than frustrations, they should be better able to control their emotions. If students' affective responses improve, our mathematics classrooms can be much more inviting places for both teaching and learning.

Looking Ahead . . .

Many teachers have great success in addressing affective issues with certain kinds of students, but few of us would claim to be completely successful with all kinds of students. If research could document what teachers do in situations where they are successful, we could all learn about strategies that we might try. This kind of research could be conducted by individual teachers working together or with other researchers; video equipment could be used to record classroom activities for repeated analysis. Careful observations would allow us to see the effects of student beliefs, attitudes, and emotions in our classrooms.

Douglas B. McLeod

The chapter invites further research that examines how students' awareness of their emotional responses can influence their performance as problem solvers. Is there a correlation between students' awareness of their emotional responses and their ability to solve problems? Is it possible to change a student's attitude toward problem solving by making the student aware that affect is part of the natural process of solving problems? The evidence before us indicates that the answer to both questions is *yes*. Our dual challenge as teachers is to prepare students to expect some frustration and anxiety during problem solving and to learn how to deal with these feelings as the expert problem solvers do.

Michele Ortega

About the Authors

Douglas B. McLeod is professor of mathematics and education at Washington State University, Pullman. A graduate of the Universities of North Dakota and Wisconsin, he is also affiliated with the Center for Research in Science and Mathematics Education at San Diego State University.

Michele Ortega teaches mathematics and computer science at Santa Fe High School, Santa Fe, NM. She is a graduate of Santa Fe High School, the University of New Mexico, and Washington State University. Ms. Ortega also teaches flamenco dance.

34   LEARNING

References

1. BLOOM, B. S., & BRODER, L. J. (1950). *Problem-solving processes of college students.* Chicago: University of Chicago Press.
2. BROWN, C. A., CARPENTER, T. P., KOUBA, V. L., LINDQUIST, M. M., SILVER, E. A., & SWAFFORD, J. O. (1988). Secondary school results for the Fourth NAEP Mathematics Assessment: Algebra, geometry, mathematical methods, and attitudes. *Mathematics Teacher, 81,* 337–347, 397.
3. BROWN, S. I., & WALTER, M. (1983). *The art of problem posing.* Philadelphia: Franklin Institute Press.
4. BUXTON, L. (1981). *Do you panic about maths?* London: Heinemann.
5. CHAPMAN, J. W. (1988). Learning disabled children's self-concepts. *Review of Educational Research, 58*(3), 347–371.
6. COBB, P., YACKEL, E., & WOOD, T. (1989). Young children's emotional acts during mathematical problem solving. In D. B. McLeod & V. M. Adams (Eds.), *Affect and mathematical problem solving: A new perspective* (pp. 117–148). New York: Springer–Verlag.
7. COCKING, R. R., & MESTRE, J. (Eds.) (1988). *Linguistic and cultural influences on learning mathematics.* Hillsdale, NJ: Erlbaum.
8. CORBITT, M. K. (1984). When students talk. *Arithmetic Teacher, 31,* 16–20.
9. DEW, K. M. H., GALASSI, J. P., & GALASSI, M. D. (1984). Math anxiety: Relation with situational test anxiety, performance, physiological arousal, and math avoidance behavior. *Journal of Counseling Psychology, 31,* 580–583.
10. DIENER, C. I., & DWECK, C. S. (1978). An analysis of learned helplessness: Continuous changes in performance, strategy, and achievement motivation cognitions following failure. *Journal of Personality and Social Psychology, 36,* 451–462.
*11. DOSSEY, J. A., MULLIS, I. V. S., LINDQUIST, M. M., & CHAMBERS, D. L. (1988). *The Mathematics Report Card: Trends and achievement based on the 1986 National Assessment.* Princeton: Educational Testing Service.
*12. FENNEMA, E. (1989). The study of affect and mathematics: A proposed generic model for research. In D. B. McLeod & V. M. Adams (Eds.), *Affect and mathematical problem solving: A new perspective* (pp. 205–219). New York: Springer–Verlag.
13. FENNEMA, E., & PETERSON, P. (1985). Autonomous learning behavior: A possible explanation of gender-related differences in mathematics. In L. C. Wilkinson & C. Marrett (Eds.), *Gender influences in classroom interaction* (pp. 17–35). Orlando: Academic Press.
14. GAROFALO, J. (1989). Beliefs, responses, and mathematics education: Observations from the back of the classroom. *School Science and Mathematics, 89,* 451–455.
15. GENTRY, W. M., & UNDERHILL, R. (1987). A comparison of two palliative methods of intervention for the treatment of mathematics anxiety among female college students. In J. C. Bergeron, N. Herscovics, & C. Kieran (Eds.), *Proceedings of the Eleventh International Conference for the Psychology of Mathematics Education* (Vol. 1, pp. 99–105). Montreal: University of Montreal.
16. GREENWOOD, J. (1984). My anxieties about math anxiety. *Mathematics Teacher, 77,* 662–663.
*17. GROUWS, D. A., & CRAMER, K. (1989). Teaching practices and student affect in problem-solving lessons of select junior high mathematics teachers. In D. B. McLeod & V. M. Adams (Eds.), *Affect and mathematical problem solving: A new perspective* (pp. 149–161). New York: Springer–Verlag.
18. HART, L. E. (1989). Describing the affective domain: Saying what we mean. In D. B.

McLeod & V. M. Adams (Eds.), *Affect and mathematical problem solving: A new perspective* (pp. 37–48). New York: Springer–Verlag.

19. HOLLOWAY, S. C. (1988). Concepts of ability and effort in Japan and the United States. *Review of Educational Research, 58,* 327–345.

20. KULM, G. (1980). Research on mathematics attitude. In R. J. Shumway (Ed.), *Research in mathematics education* (pp. 356–387). Reston, VA: National Council of Teachers of Mathematics.

21. LEDER, G. C. (1987). Attitudes towards mathematics. In T. A. Romberg & D. M. Stewart (Eds.), *The monitoring of school mathematics* (Vol. 2, pp. 261–277). Madison: Wisconsin Center for Education Research.

22. MANDLER, G. (1984). *Mind and body: Psychology of emotion and stress.* New York: Norton.

23. MANDLER, G. (1989). Affect and learning: Causes and consequences of emotional interactions. In D. B. McLeod & V. M. Adams (Eds.), *Affect and mathematical problem solving: A new perspective* (pp. 3–19). New York: Springer–Verlag.

24. MARSHALL, S. (1989). Affect in schema knowledge: Source and impact. In D. B. McLeod & V. M. Adams (Eds.), *Affect and mathematical problem solving: A new perspective* (pp. 49–58). New York: Springer–Verlag.

*25. MASON, J., BURTON, L., & STACEY, K. (1982). *Thinking mathematically.* London: Addison–Wesley.

26. MATTHEWS, W. (1984). Influences on the learning and participation of minorities in mathematics. *Journal for Research in Mathematics Education, 15*(2), 84–95.

27. MCKNIGHT, C. C., CROSSWHITE, F. J., DOSSEY, J. A., KIFER, E., SWAFFORD, J. O., TRAVERS, K. J., & COONEY, T. J. (1987). *The underachieving curriculum: Assessing U.S. school mathematics from an international perspective.* Champaign, IL: Stipes.

28. MCLEOD, D. B., METZGER, W., & CRAVIOTTO, C. (1989). Comparing experts' and novices' affective reactions to mathematical problem solving: An exploratory study. In G. Vergnaud (Ed.), *Proceedings of the Thirteenth International Conference for the Psychology of Mathematics Education* (Vol. 2, pp. 296–303). Paris: Laboratoire de Psychologie du Développement et de l'Education de l'Enfant.

*29. MEYER, M. R., & FENNEMA, E. (1988). Girls, boys, and mathematics. In T. R. Post (Ed.), *Teaching mathematics in grades K–8: Research-based methods* (pp. 406–425). Boston: Allyn & Bacon.

30. NATIONAL COUNCIL OF TEACHERS OF MATHEMATICS (1989). *Curriculum and evaluation standards for school mathematics.* Reston, VA: Author.

31. NATIONAL RESEARCH COUNCIL (1989). *Everybody counts: A report to the nation on the future of mathematics education.* Washington, DC: National Academy Press.

32. OAKES, J. (1990). Opportunities, achievement, and choice: Women and minority students in science and mathematics. In C. B. Cazden (Ed.), *Review of research in education* (Vol. 16, pp. 153–222). Washington, DC: American Educational Research Association.

33. ORR, E. W. (1987). *Twice as less: Black English and the performance of black students in mathematics and science.* New York: Norton.

34. PARSONS, J. E., ADLER, T. F., & KACZALA, C. M. (1982). Socialization of achievement, attitudes, and beliefs: Parental influences. *Child Development, 53,* 310–321.

*35. REYES, L. H. (1984). Affective variables and mathematics education. *Elementary School Journal, 84,* 558–581.

36. ROBITAILLE, D. F., & GARDEN, R. A. (Eds.) (1989). *The IEA Study of Mathematics II: Contexts and outcomes of school mathematics.* Oxford: Pergamon.

37. SARASON, I. G. (1987). Test anxiety, cognitive interference, and performance. In R. E.

Snow & M. J. Farr (Eds.), *Aptitude, learning, and instruction: Volume 3. Conative and affective process analyses* (pp. 131–142). Hillsdale, NJ: Erlbaum.

*38. SCHOENFELD, A. H. (1985). *Mathematical problem solving.* Orlando: Academic Press.

39. SILVER, E. A., & METZGER, W. R. (1989). Aesthetic influences on expert mathematical problem solving. In D. B. McLeod & V. M. Adams (Eds.), *Affect and mathematical problem solving: A new perspective* (pp. 59–74). New York: Springer–Verlag.

*40. STIGLER, J. W., & PERRY, M. (1988). Cross-cultural studies of mathematics teaching and learning: Recent findings and new directions. In D. A. Grouws & T. J. Cooney (Eds.), *Effective mathematics teaching* (pp. 194–223). Hillsdale, NJ: Erlbaum; Reston, VA: National Council of Teachers of Mathematics.

41. STODOLSKY, S. S. (1985). Telling math: Origins of math aversion and anxiety. *Educational Psychologist, 20,* 125–133.

42. WAGNER, S., RACHLIN, S. L., & JENSEN, R. J. (1984). *Algebra learning project: Final Report.* Athens: University of Georgia.

43. WEINER, B. (1986). *An attributional theory of motivation and emotion.* New York: Springer–Verlag.

PART II

Processes and Content

CHAPTER 3

Critical Thinking, Mathematical Reasoning, and Proof

Phares G. O'Daffer and Bruce A. Thornquist

It must be remembered that the purpose of education is not to fill the minds of students with facts . . . it is to teach them to think, if that is possible, and always to think for themselves.

—*Robert Hutchins*

The work titled *Curriculum and Evaluation Standards for School Mathematics* (25), developed by the National Council of Teachers of Mathematics (NCTM), calls for critical thinking, mathematical reasoning, and proof for all students—as suggested by the following statements.

> A climate should be established in the classroom that places *critical thinking* at the heart of instruction. . . . To give students access to mathematics as a powerful way of making sense of the world, it is essential that an emphasis on *reasoning* pervade all mathematical activity. . . . *Inductive and deductive reasoning* are required individually and in concert in all areas of mathematics.

To interpret research as it relates to the NCTM standards for reasoning, we will clarify the terms "critical thinking," "mathematical reasoning," and "proof," and report related research findings. Then we will suggest implications of these findings for helping students develop their critical thinking, mathematical reasoning, and proving abilities.

Critical Thinking

What Is Critical Thinking?

Critical thinking has often been described so generally that it seems to encompass almost any type of thinking activity we might mention. To provide a clearer focus, we will use a description of critical thinking synthesized from meanings used in research (4, 7).

> *Critical thinking* is a process of effectively using thinking skills to help one make, evaluate, and apply decisions about what to believe or do.

Some *thinking skills*, mentioned in this description of critical thinking and commonly used in research, are comparing, contrasting, conjecturing, inducing, generalizing, specializing, classifying, categorizing, deducing, visualizing, sequencing, ordering, predicting, validating, proving, relating, analyzing, evaluating, and patterning.

The process mentioned in the above description was given meaning by Fawcett, in research reported in *The Nature of Proof* (11, pp. 11–12). He observed that a student using critical thinking will:

1. Select the significant words and phrases in any statement that is important and ask that they be carefully defined
2. Require evidence supporting conclusions he/she is pressed to accept
3. Analyze that evidence and distinguish fact from assumption
4. Recognize stated and unstated assumptions essential to the conclusion
5. Evaluate these assumptions, accepting some and rejecting others
6. Evaluate the argument, accepting or rejecting the conclusion
7. Constantly reexamine the assumptions which are behind his/her beliefs and actions

The critical thinking process is further explicated by the following model, synthesized from the above ideas and those from other research (4, 7). Note that the model is not intended to suggest a specific sequence of steps for critical thinking.

The Process of Critical Thinking

- Understand the situation
- Deal with evidence/data/assumptions.
- Go beyond the evidence/data/assumptions.
- State and support conclusions/decisions/solutions.
- Apply the conclusions/decisions/solutions.

Using the Critical Thinking Process. Matt's steady girlfriend, Jordan agreed on a date tomorrow and told him that she was going to do something with her aunt tonight, so Matt decided to go to a movie. Approaching the theater, he saw Jordan entering with another boy. How should Matt deal with this situation? How would the process for critical thinking help?

Research on Critical Thinking

Norris (28) and Nickerson (26) synthesized research on critical thinking. Some of their conclusions are paraphrased below.

- High school students do not perform very well on the tasks that have been used to indicate critical thinking competence.
- The disposition to think critically—a "critical spirit"—is a crucial component of effective critical thinking.
- There is some evidence that attempts to teach critical thinking can be effective, but little is known about what specifically causes the observed improvement in critical thinking.
- The effective application of critical thinking abilities involves having developed these abilities as well as having a knowledge of the subject matter and experience in the area in which the thinking is taking place.

Can Mathematics Content Be Used to Develop Critical Thinking Skills That Can Be Transferred to Everyday Situations?   Fawcett (11) asserted: "It is the purpose of this study to describe classroom procedures by which geometric proof may be used as a means for cultivating critical and reflective thought and to evaluate the effect of such experiences on the thinking of the pupils."

Fawcett used real-world examples in an attempt to help students transfer critical approaches used in understanding geometric proof to everyday situations. He remarked about interviews with parents at the end of the course: "The parents appear to believe that through this course the thinking of their children has become more critical, and their only concern is that it should not become too critical" (11, p. 109).

Student Comment. "This year's work in geometry has had more effect on what I have done and thought outside of school than any other class this year. It has made me critical of things I read and hear that I have never noticed before. It has made me critical of the statements I make and the things I do" (11, p. 112).

Lewis (22) also tried to develop critical thinking by teaching logic and proof in a geometric setting, using applications to everyday situations. He found statistically significant gains in the experimental group over the control groups in critical thinking ability.

Price (33) investigated the effect of a discovery approach, and specific teaching for transfer of thinking skills, on the critical thinking development of tenth-grade general mathematics students. The transfer class scored significantly higher on the Watson–Glaser Critical Thinking Test than did either the control or discovery group.

Teaching Suggestions from Critical Thinking Research

Critical thinking is widely regarded as necessary for effective functioning in our society, but research evidence indicates that high school students have difficulty thinking critically. This suggests that we need to give greater attention to helping students use this process.

The early research regarding transfer of critical thinking skills from mathematics to the real world suggests the following.

Teach mathematics from a critical thinking perspective when possible. Integrate real-world decision-making situations into your mathematics classes to help students transfer critical thinking abilities from situations in mathematics to situations in the real world.

Sample Activity. After discussing the meaning of proof in geometry, ask students to discuss the following: A scientist gave a compound he had invented to 20 people for a period of two months. None of the people contracted a cold during the two months. Do you think the scientist *proved* that the compound prevented colds? How does this relate to the meaning of proof?

Sample Activity. After studying the converse, inverse, and contrapositive, ask students to decide if a reasoning error has been made in the following and support their conclusion: Katy's mother told her, "If you don't keep your room clean, then you won't get new wallpaper next spring." Katy kept her room clean, and felt her mother had broken a promise when she did not get new wallpaper.

The following, reflecting approaches used in reported research studies, describes a classroom focus to develop a "critical spirit."

Help students develop a critical spirit by creating a classroom climate where students feel comfortable questioning, challenging, suspending judgment, and demanding reasons and justification as they deal with mathematical and real-world content. Ask questions that stimulate students to monitor, evaluate, and act upon their own thinking.

Sample Activity. Ask students to work in groups to (a) discuss the situation below, (b) brainstorm ideas for resolving it, (c) find a solution acceptable to all, or present minority reports, and (d) discuss their thinking to arrive at a decision: Three highways intersect to enclose an equilateral triangular area. Where do you think is the best place inside the triangle to build a factory?

Note that none of the research reported earlier addresses the question of how to help students develop critical thinking abilities in *mathematics*. Some action research might involve creation, trial, and evaluation of *mathematical situations* (a) to help teach different critical thinking skills, such as evaluating assumptions, or (b) in which students are stimulated to use critical thinking to decide what to believe or do.

Mathematical Reasoning

What Is Mathematical Reasoning?

Although examples of mathematical reasoning are given in the NCTM Standards, it is not clear how mathematical reasoning differs from logical reasoning, mathematical thinking, or critical thinking. Mathematical thinking involves using mathematically rich thinking skills to understand ideas, discover relationships among the ideas, draw or support conclusions about the ideas and their relationships, and solve problems involving the ideas. Mathematical reasoning can be characterized as one part of the process of mathematical thinking. The following description is a synthesis of meanings used in research.

> *Mathematical reasoning* is a part of mathematical thinking that involves forming generalizations and drawing valid conclusions about ideas and how they are related.

Two important types of mathematical reasoning are inductive and deductive reasoning.

Insight from Polya. "A mathematical proof is demonstrative (*deductive*) reasoning, but the inductive evidence of the physicist, the circumstantial evidence of the lawyer . . . and the statistical evidence of the economist belong to plausible reasoning . . . *Inductive reasoning* is a particular case of plausible reasoning." Polya (37)

While Polya (32) includes *inductive* and *analogical reasoning* as particular cases of *plausible reasoning* and *proportional reasoning* as a case of *analogical reasoning*, we will deal primarily with inductive and deductive reasoning in this chapter. See Sternberg (39) for more on analogical reasoning.

The following description is consistent with the way in which inductive reasoning is interpreted in most research.

> *Inductive reasoning* is a mathematical reasoning process in which information about some members of a set is used to form a generalization about other or all members of the set.

Inductive Reasoning Example. A student saw the examples $16/64 = 1/4$ and $19/95 = 1/5$ and reasoned inductively that a common first and last digit in a fraction can be canceled. She tried $17/76$ and learned that generalizations formed in inductive reasoning aren't always true.

See Polya (32) for additional examples of inductive reasoning.

The following description of deductive reasoning is in keeping with the ideas from sources such as Smith and Henderson (38), and is consistent with meanings used in current research.

Deductive reasoning is a mathematical reasoning process in which valid inference patterns are used to draw conclusions from premises.

Note that *conditional reasoning* is the use of an if–then or conditional statement in the process of deductive reasoning.

As a great deal of the research on mathematical reasoning deals with student facility with logical inference, the basic valid and invalid inference patterns used in conditional reasoning are reviewed below.

Valid Patterns	Modus Ponens	Modus Tollens (Contrapositive)	Syllogism (Chain Rule)
	$p \rightarrow q$ is true p is true	$p \rightarrow q$ is true q is false	$p \rightarrow q$ is true $q \rightarrow r$ is true
	Therefore, q is true.	Therefore, p is false.	$p \rightarrow r$ is true

Using Modus Tollens. A tennis coach told a player, "If you win more tryout games than Burns, you will play second singles today." The player was not on the list to play second singles. He concluded that he had not won more tryout games than Burns.

Using the Chain Rule. A student knew that if the base angles of a triangle are congruent, then two sides of the triangle are congruent. She also knew that if two sides of a triangle are congruent, the triangle is isosceles. She concluded that if the base angles of a triangle are congruent, then the triangle is isosceles.

Invalid Patterns	Inverse	Converse
	$p \rightarrow q$ p is false	$p \rightarrow q$ q is true
	Therefore, q is false.	Therefore, p is true.

Invalidly Assuming the Converse. Carol knew that "if a number is divisible by 4, then it is divisible by 2." When given a number known to be divisible by 2, Carol concluded that it was divisible by 4.

Invalidly Assuming the Inverse. An advertisement stated: "If you take Vitamin B daily, then you will stay healthy." Terry thought, "If I don't take Vitamin B daily, then I won't stay healthy." He felt a need to buy some Vitamin B.

The term *class reasoning* is used to refer to use of the deductive inference in class inclusion rather than to conditional settings.

Class Inclusion Modus Ponens. All *As* are *B*

x is an *A*

Therefore, x is a *B*

Research on Mathematical Reasoning

What is the Nature of Deductive Reasoning Research? Much of the research on deductive reasoning is concerned with the growth in student ability to understand, detect, or use valid and invalid reasoning patterns.

Do Deductive Reasoning Abilities Improve Naturally Over Time? Inhelder and Piaget (16) theorized that children in the concrete operational stage (ages 7–11) are capable of class reasoning, but conditional reasoning is accessible to them only when they reach the formal operations stage (12 and over). Contrary to this, some research indicates that young children can recognize valid conclusions deduced from premises, and that this ability increases steadily from ages 6 to 8 (8, 15, 29).

Findings on the growth in student ability to infer valid conclusions or to detect invalid inference patterns are summarized below (5, 8, 18).

• Children, as early as age 6, can recognize valid conclusions.
• The ability to reason deductively and to detect invalid arguments in both class and conditional form generally improves with age.
• Growth in the ability to recognize the invalid conditional inference patterns is very slow until about age 16, or grade 10.

Are Some Deductive Reasoning Skills Easier Than Others for Students? O'Brien (30) investigated the status of subjects' performance on the four basic inference patterns. The percentages of correct test responses were 95% for modus ponens, 63% for contrapositive, 32% for inverse, and 11% for converse. Causal items were easier than nonsense items, and hypothesis negation items were most difficult.

Conclusions about relative difficulty of deductive reasoning skills, derived from several studies, are summarized below (8, 17).

• Class reasoning is generally easier than conditional reasoning.
• The inference patterns, from easiest to most difficult for students to use or in which to detect a fallacy, are *modus ponens, contrapositive, inverse,* and *converse.*
• With only a few exceptions, the difficulty of applying an inference pattern decreases as the meaningfulness of the content increases.

What Are Some of the Major Difficulties High School Students Have with Deductive Reasoning? It is clear that high school students have noticeable difficulties using valid inference patterns (6, 19, 30, 31).

- Many high school students have difficulty applying formal reasoning to detect necessary conclusions in inference patterns that involve if–then statements, other than modus ponens.
- They often interpret an if–then statement as if *and only* if. Many do not recognize the validity of the contrapositive inference pattern.
- Most do not recognize invalid converse and inverse reasoning patterns.
- They have difficulty dealing with negations in conditional statements.

What Are the Main Causes of Deductive Reasoning Errors?   The research of Wason and Johnson-Laird (45) gives impressive evidence for the case that errors in logic account for only part of the errors in deductive reasoning. They may also be a result of difficulty in keeping track of information, and the absence of semantic cues signaling a certain interpretation. J. St. B. T. Evans (10), when interpreting the errors made in deductive reasoning, also makes a strong case for considering not only the subjects use of formal logic, but the mental operations needed for the task.

Causes of errors in deductive reasoning, from several studies, are summarized below (5, 10, 17, 30, 31, 45).

- Errors in deductive reasoning often are caused by adding to, altering, or ignoring items from the premise.
- Errors are caused by allowing factual content to supersede the inference pattern. Traditional patterns of everyday discourse often override logic.
- Other causes of errors are language difficulties, number and location of negations, sentence and word length, and cognitive overload.
- Inability to accept the hypothetical also causes errors.

Can Deductive Reasoning Abilities Be Improved through Instruction?   In some studies, exposure to instruction through the use of selected manipulative materials had a positive effect on the development of the logical reasoning ability of second- and third-grade children (23). Suppes and Binford (42) reported that the upper quartile of fifth- and sixth-grade students can master elementary logic at a level 85% of that achieved by university students, using equal study time but spread over a longer period. Ennis and Paulus (8) indicated that class logic could be taught with success to eleven- and twelve-year-olds, but that instruction did not help students detect invalid inference patterns. Shipman (37) found that natural teacher use of conditional language and ideas in the classroom seemed to influence positively students' growth in reasoning ability.

- Preadolescent children can begin to develop some types of deductive reasoning abilities through carefully planned experiences.
- Class reasoning can be taught to early adolescents, but significant instructional success in improving the abilities of pre–sixteen-year-old adolescents to recognize invalid deductive arguments is not reported.
- There is a positive correlation between growth in reasoning ability and being in a mathematics class where a teacher often naturally uses if–then reasoning language and ideas.

Is It Possible to Teach Deductive Reasoning Skills in the Classroom in Such a Way That They Will Be Transferred to Everyday Situations?   There seem to be few definitive answers to this question, but an interesting recent study by Cheng, Holyoak, Nisbett, and Oliver (3) suggests promising directions. In this study, the naturally acquired idea that one may not do action *p* without first securing permission *q* (called the permission schema) helped subjects learn the modus ponens and contrapositive inference patterns and apply them to abstract and real-world situations.

- Students may have the necessary reasoning rules, but may fail to view situations in such a way as to be able to use or apply those rules. The use of students' natural schemas may facilitate both learning and transfer.

What is the Status of Inductive Reasoning Research?   Researchers have studied various aspects of the discovery of, or inductive approach to, *teaching* mathematics, but there is little research that focuses specifically on *improving students' ability to use inductive reasoning in mathematics.* Wason (44) gave subjects number triples (such as 2, 4, 6) and asked them to discover the rule by which these were formed. He found that subjects tend not to test initially workable hypotheses for validity, look for a more inclusive rule, or eliminate them, even in the face of clearly contradictory evidence. Other research suggests the following (27, 44).

- Students often make inductive inferences from limited samples.
- Students tend to cling to their inductive hypothesis, once it is formed, and aren't prone to subject it to sufficient tests for invalidity.
- Students use more-or-less intuitive rules of thumb that resemble formal statistical procedures for their inductive reasoning tasks. These often are appropriate, but sometimes are insufficient.
- Statistical training positively influences everyday inductive reasoning.

Teaching Suggestions from Mathematical Reasoning Research

The research suggests the following for teachers.

Teachers of younger children can use attribute blocks and other logic materials to help children begin to develop deductive reasoning abilities. At around age 11, more instructional activities helping students use valid class and conditional reasoning might be included.

Sample Activity. A school policy stated that athletes must have permission from their doctor to participate in sports. All students had been examined, and a school official had a short list of those denied permission and a much longer list of those granted permission. If she did not want to check all sports participants, what other method could she use to see if the policy had been carried out correctly? Discuss in groups. Support your conclusions.

From ages 12 to 15, more emphasis on helping students use the contrapositive inference pattern to draw conclusions might be in order.

Use the students' natural reasoning patterns and real-world examples to help insure transfer.

Because research indicates the value of if–then statements in the classroom, the following suggestion is given.

Plan to use if–then statements in class discussion, assignments, and tests, on a regular basis. Create opportunities to illustrate the idea that an if–then statement is not the same as an if-and-only-if statement.

Creative attempts to help students recognize invalid inference patterns more effectively are in order, and the following is recommended.

At least by age 16, provide significant experiences to help students learn to recognize the invalid converse and inverse inference patterns, in both mathematics and everyday situations.

Plan instruction based on the idea that the inverse inference pattern is easier for students to deal with than is the converse pattern. Instruction on invalid reasoning could be emphasized in geometry or integrated courses.

Sample Activity. As you work with the idea of converse and inverse of a statement in geometry, ask small groups of students to discuss situations like the following, and if possible draw a conclusion the group can agree upon: Allan's teacher said, "If you get As on all four tests, then you will get an A in the course." Allan did get an A in the course, but Glyn said this was not fair, since he knew that Allan received a B on one of the tests. Do you agree with Glyn? Why or why not?

Research on inductive reasoning suggests the following.

Provide inductive experiences where incorrect generalizations can be formed if too few examples are tested to extend understanding of inductive reasoning.

Give emphasis to statistical concepts and the role of sampling, correlation, and laws of large numbers in everyday inductive reasoning.

It should be recognized that many of these suggestions will require substantial curriculum development. You can become involved in action research in which you develop, use, and evaluate innovative materials designed to help promote reasoning abilities.

Proof

What Is Proof?

We know that both the concept of proof and the ability to prove are important, but to understand the implications of research for improving instruction on developing proofs, we need to clarify the meaning of the process of proving, and what constitutes a valid proof.

The following description synthesizes ideas from research (12, 38).

> *Mathematical proving* is a process that uses definitions, postulates, previously proven statements, and deductive reasoning to produce a sequence of true statements providing a valid argument that a statement to be proved is true.

Types of Proof

To understand the research on proof, we must first understand the following proof types or strategies.

Proof by counterexample involves finding at least one example in which a generalization is false, thus disproving the generalization or proving its negation.

Proof by Counterexample. A student makes the conjecture, "A negative number plus a positive number is always a negative number." Another student concludes, "That isn't true. Look at a problem such as $-3 + 7 = 4$."

Direct proof involves showing that a given statement is deducible through using basic inference patterns directly from given information and previously studied definitions, postulates, or theorems. *Two-column* or *paragraph* formats are traditionally used to show direct proofs. Attempts to better show the structure and the use of the inference patterns in a direct proof have involved the use of a *flow-proof* format. In this format, a sequence of conditional statements is given, with hypotheses and conclusion statements numbered. Later, a reason is stated for each numbered statement. See McMurray (24) for examples and further explanation of flow proofs.

Indirect proof involves assuming that the negation of the statement to be proven is true, and showing that this assumption leads to a contradiction.

An Indirect Proof. On arriving at the darkened store, Jimmy thinks: "The store must be closed." The logic behind this thought is: Suppose the store were open—then it would have the lights on. The lights are not on. Therefore, the store must be closed.

This proves that the assumption must be incorrect and the statement is true. Proof of a statement by proving the contrapositive of the statement can be thought of as a special case of indirect proof through contradiction. Paragraph formats often are used to show indirect proofs.

The Logic of Indirect Proof. To prove a statement p (such as "The number of primes is infinite") true, assume that p is false. Reason from $\sim p$ to show that some statement r is true, when it is known that r is false. Since r and $\sim r$ is a contradiction, we know that the assumed statement $\sim p$ is false, and the original statement p must be true.

Proof by induction is by far the most complex type of proof, as illustrated by the analysis of the process into behavioral skills given by Ernest (9). The Principle of Induction is the basis for proof by induction, and can be paraphrased as follows: "If a property is true for 1, and if for all $n > 1$, the property being true for n implies it is true for $n + 1$, you can conclude that the property is true for all natural numbers."

Real-World "Induction." Imagine lining up one domino for each natural number, fairly close together. If we know that (a) we can topple the first domino, and (b) the nth domino will topple the $(n + 1)$th domino, we confidently conclude that all the dominos will fall.

It should be understood that *proof by induction* and *inductive reasoning* are distinctly different ideas. Inductive reasoning might be used to discover a generalization about natural numbers, while mathematical induction would be required to prove it.

Research on Proof

Much of the research on proof deals with student abilities to plan and write proofs, and the nature of the difficulties they encounter. The major findings are presented below.

How Well Are Students Doing with Proof?   Senk (35) reports: "At the end of a full-year course in geometry in which proof writing is studied, about 25% of the students have no competence in writing proofs; another 25% can do only trivial proofs; about 20% can do some proofs of greater complexity; and only 30% master proofs similar to the theorems and exercises in standard textbooks."

In a study by Williams (46) involving 255 eleventh-grade students, less than 30% of the sample population exhibited an understanding of the meaning of proof. The other students did not realize the significance of hypotheses and definitions in mathematical arguments, and also did not understand indirect proof. Too, they did not always realize that inductive reasoning is inadequate to prove generalizations. Approximately 50% of these students did not even see any need to prove a mathematical proposition they intuitively considered to be obvious. Summarizing, then:

- Only about 20% to 30% of the students who have had tenth-grade geometry have a basic understanding of proof.

What Are the Major Difficulties Students Have with Proofs?   Senk (35) sampled 1,520 geometry students from five states and reported on students' difficulties with geometry proofs. Below are her major findings and those of Ernest (9).

- Students have logical and language difficulties with proofs, and find it difficult to begin a proof. They often use the theorem to be proved as a reason in its proof, and use invalid inference forms in writing proofs.
- Proofs with diagrams that contained several sets of embedded triangles or required auxiliary lines were among the most difficult. Similarity proofs were more difficult than congruence proofs requiring the same number of deductions.
- Students have difficulty with the complexity of the mathematical induction principle.
- No sex-related differences in proof-writing achievement are evident.

Are There Levels of Development that Affect Student Proof Writing?   Research on the van Hiele levels, described in Chapter 8 and reviewed below, addresses this question.

Level 1. *Holistic.* Student learns vocabulary and can identify a shape.
Level 2. *Analytic.* Student is able to identify properties of figures.
Level 3. *Abstract.* Student can logically order figures and relationships.
Level 4. *Deductive.* Student understands the role of postulates, theorems, and proof. Also, the student is able to prove theorems deductively.
Level 5. *Rigorous.* Student understands the necessity for the rigor of a deductive system and is able to make abstract deductions.

After analyzing test results from 241 students in eleven schools in five states, Senk (36) reports the significant results summarized below.

- The higher the van Hiele level on entering, the greater the probability that the student mastered proof writing later in the year, and the lesser the likelihood that he or she failed to learn to write proofs.
- Level 2 appears to be the critical entry level. A beginning student at level 2 had a 50–50 chance of mastering proof writing by the end of the year. A student at level 3 or 4 had a significantly greater chance of mastering proof writing.

For additional discussion of the van Hiele levels as they relate to proof, refer to Burger and Shaughnessy (1).

When Should We Introduce Proof?   There are differences of opinion as to when proof should be introduced in the mathematics curriculum. Suppes (41) states: "The ability to write a coherent mathematical proof does not develop naturally even at the most elementary levels and must be a subject of explicit training." King (20) conducted a study with capable sixth-grade students and found they were able to demonstrate an understanding of proof. The work of Suppes and Binford (42), Hill (15), and Lester (21) seems to suggest the following.

• Mathematical activities closely related to proof should be introduced, and can be understood by students in upper elementary grades.

Which Format and Approach to Writing Proofs Is Best?   Harbeck (14) and Summa (40) investigated the effect of the flow-proof versus the two-column proof format. Although students using the flow format had significantly more favorable attitudes toward that format, there were no significant differences in achievement or critical thinking ability. Van Akin (43) studied the paragraph format verses the two-column format and also discovered no significant difference in achievement on geometry facts or ability to reason logically.

Carroll (2) attempted to determine which is the best method of planning proofs. He used synthesis (begin with hypothesis and reason to conclusion), analysis (begin with conclusion and work back to hypothesis), or a combination of both. Research suggests the following.

• The format used for writing proofs—flow, paragraph, or two-column—does not significantly affect the achievement in either proof writing or development of deductive reasoning.
• Either synthesis or a combination of analysis and synthesis appeared to be better than analysis alone in planning proofs.

Teaching Suggestions from Research on Proof

Senk (36) states: "Much of a student's achievement in writing geometry proofs is due to factors within direct control of the teacher and curriculum." She suggests that research in mathematics education needs to identify cognitive and affective prerequisites for doing proofs, and techniques for helping students acquire the prerequisites.

> To develop student readiness for proof, elementary or junior high teachers should create activities or select texts with geometric/proof readiness activities that help students move through the van Hiele levels.

Student Activity. Ask junior high school students to give a convincing argument that "if the area of a rectangle with base *b* and height *h* is *bh*, then the area of a parallelogram with base *b* and height *h* is *bh*." Allow use of cardboard and scissors, and give hints if needed.

Reported research that points out difficulties students have with proof suggests that the following might help teachers improve their instruction.

Design situations that contrast everyday proof with the meaning of proof in mathematics. Continue to discuss and develop key ideas of logic and proof throughout geometry and other courses.

Develop readiness activities in geometry that help students to deal better with situations that have imbedded figures and auxiliary lines.

Focus on helping students to learn to begin proofs, combining both analysis and synthesis in the planning stages.

Studies of classrooms in which students have developed effective proof-writing abilities will provide guidance for developing useful methods and materials. Teachers and others should test, evaluate, and share materials and methods they find to be effective in teaching proof.

Summary

The sections of this chapter have presented meanings, research findings, and teaching implications for critical thinking, mathematical reasoning, and proof. The vintage and lack of mathematical research on some topics, and the caution with which the teaching suggestions must be received, are among the limitations to be noted. Some of the newer findings lend credence to Fischbein's (13) emphasis on the need to build on student intuitive reasoning patterns. The findings also clearly support Resnick's (34) comment: "We need both practical experimentation in schools and more controlled instructional experimentation in laboratories to discover ways of incorporating our new understanding of the knowledge–reasoning connection into instruction."

> "A fourth 'R'—reasoning—might be considered a candidate for a new enabling discipline in the school curriculum" (34).

We feel that the research, as reported and interpreted, can provide stimulation for creative ways to implement the NCTM *Standards* as we all work together to help students improve their ability to reason.

Looking Ahead . . .

For a long time, reasoning has been considered crucial for mathematics students and citizens—but our success in improving reasoning abilities has been limited. Now, as the NCTM *Standards* call for a greater emphasis on reasoning in all areas of mathematics, we have a new opportunity for progress. Quality research on reasoning is needed to help implement the NCTM recommendations. We must all cooperate in providing the best instructional settings possible to help students develop their reasoning abilities. We must devise effective ways to build on students' natural reasoning patterns and help them develop a critical thinking spirit. It is time for a massive effort toward making critical thinking and reasoning an integral, effective part of students' approach to mathematics and everyday life.

Phares G. O'Daffer

When you consider the difficulty that students have with critical thinking, mathematical reasoning, and proof, a number of questions arise. Should we try to teach students younger than 16 to detect invalid reasoning patterns? Is the average student capable of understanding the intricacies of proof, or should much less emphasis be given to this process? What would be an effective method for helping students better employ critical thinking or reasoning in everyday situations? It might help if researchers could provide better models for how students reason. Also, teachers could develop and use activities based on the teaching implications in this chapter and evaluate the results.

Bruce A. Thornquist

About the Authors

Phares G. O'Daffer is professor of mathematics, emeritus at Illinois State University. Besides concentrating on publishing his writings, he also is active in curriculum development, in consulting, and in state and national professional organizations. An author of texts and articles for teachers and students at a variety of levels, his areas of research interest are geometry, mathematical reasoning, and problem solving.

Bruce A. Thornquist teaches mathematics at Downers Grove South High School in Downers Grove, Illinois. His writing includes material for both a pre-algebra and a geometry textbook. Interested in teaching geometry, Mr. Thornquist was a consultant on a recently published geometry textbook. His presentations at NCTM and state conferences include a talk on motivational techniques for geometry lessons.

References

1. BURGER, W., & SHAUGHNESSY, M. (1986). Characterizing the van Hiele levels of development in geometry. *Journal for Research in Mathematics Education, 17*, 31–48.
2. CARROLL, D. C. (1977). The relative effectiveness of three geometric proof construction strategies. *Journal for Research in Mathematics Education, 8*(1), 62–67.
3. CHENG, P. W., HOLYOAK, K. J., NISBETT, R. E., & OLIVER, L. M. (1986). Pragmatic vs. syntactic approaches to training deductive reasoning. *Cognitive Psychology, 18*, 293–328
*4. COSTA, A. L. (Ed.) (1985). *Developing minds: A resource book for teaching thinking.* Alexandria, VA: *Association for Supervision and Curriculum Development.*
5. DONALDSON, M. (1963). *A study of children's thinking.* London: Tavistock.
6. EISENBERG, T., & MCGINTY, R. L. (1974). On comparing error patterns and the effect of maturation in a unit on sentential logic. *Journal for Research in Mathematics Education, 5*(4), 225–237.
*7. ENNIS, R. H. (1985). Goals for a critical thinking curriculum. In A. L. Costa (Ed.), *Developing minds: Adolescence book for teaching thinking.* (pp. 54–57). Alexandria, VA: Association for Supervision and Curriculum Development.

8. ENNIS, R. H., & PAULUS, D. H. (1965). *Critical thinking readiness in grades 1–12: Phase I: Deductive logic in adolescence.* Ithaca, NY: Cornell University.
*9. ERNEST, P. (1984). Mathematical induction: A pedagogical discussion. *Educational Studies in Mathematics, 15*(2), 173–189.
10. EVANS, J. ST. B. T., (1972). On the problems of interpreting reasoning data: Logical and psychological approaches. *Cognition, 1* (4), 373–384
*11. FAWCETT, H. (1938). *The nature of proof* (1938 NCTM Yearbook). New York: Columbia University Teachers College Bureau of Publ.
12. FETISOV, A. I., (1954). *Proof in geometry.* Boston: D.C. Heath.
13. FISCHBEIN, E., & KEDEM, I. (1982). Proof and certitude in the development of mathematical thinking. In A. Vermandel (Ed.), *Proceedings of the Sixth International Conference for the Psychology of Mathematics Education* (pp. 128–131). Antwerp: Author.
14. HARBECK, SISTER CAROL ANN. (February 1973). *Experimental study of the effect of two proof formats in high school geometry on critical thinking and selected student attitudes.* (Doctoral dissertation, Ohio State University). *Dissertation Abstracts International, 33,* 4243A.
15. HILL, S. A. (1961). A study of logical abilities in children. Unpublished doctoral dissertation, Stanford University.
16. INHELDER, B., & PIAGET, J. (1958). *The growth of logical thinking.* New York: Basic Books.
17. JANSSON, L. C. (1974). *The development of deductive reasoning: A review of the literature* (Preliminary Version). Winnipeg, Canada: University of Manitoba. (ERIC Document Service No. 090 034)
18. JANSSON, L. C. (1978). A comparison of two approaches to the assessment of conditional reasoning abilities. *Journal for Research in Mathematics Education, 9*(3), 175–188.
19. JANSSON, L. C. (1986). Logical reasoning hierarchies in mathematics. *Journal for Research in Mathematics Education, 17*(1), 3–20.
20. KING, I. L. (1973). A formative development of an elementary school unit on proof. *Journal for Research in Mathematics Education, 4*(1), 57–63.
21. LESTER, F. K. (1975). Developmental aspects of children's ability to understand mathematical proof. *Journal for Research in Mathematics Education, 6*(1),15–25.
22. LEWIS, H. (1950). *An experiment in developing critical thinking through the teaching of plane demonstrative geometry.* New York: New York University. [Reviewed in J. J. Kinsella (1950), Research in mathematics education, *Mathematics Teacher, 43*(8), 411–413.]
23. McGINTY, R. L. (1977). The effects of instruction in sentential logic on selected abilities of 2nd and 3rd grade children. *Journal for Research in Mathematics Education, 8*(2), 88–96.
*24. McMURRAY, R. (1978). Flow proofs in geometry. *Mathematics Teacher, 71*(11), 592–595.
*25. NATIONAL COUNCIL OF TEACHERS OF MATHEMATICS (1989), *Curriculum and evaluation standards for school mathematics,* Reston, VA: Author.
26. NICKERSON, R. (1988). On improving critical thinking through instruction. In *Review of research in education,* pp. 3–58. Washington, DC: American Educational Research Association.
27. NISBETT, R. E., KRANTZ, D. H., JEPSON, C., & KUNDA, Z. (1983). Use of statistical heuristics in everyday inductive reasoning. *Psychological Review, 90*(4), 339–363.
28. NORRIS, S. P. (1985). Synthesis of research on critical thinking. *Educational Leadership, 42*(8).

29. O'BRIEN, T. C., & SHAPIRO, B. J. (1970). Logical thinking in children ages six through sixteen. *Child Development, 41*, 823–829.

30. O'BRIEN, T. C. (1972). Logical thinking in adolescents. *Educational Studies in Mathematics, 4,* 401.

31. O'BRIEN, T. C., SHAPIRO, B. J., & REALI, N. C. (1971). Logical thinking—language and context. *Educational Studies in Mathematics, 4,* 201–219.

*32. POLYA, G. (1954). Induction and analogy in mathematics. In G. Polya, *Mathematics and plausible reasoning*, Vols. 1, 2. Princeton: Princeton University Press.

33. PRICE, J. (1967). Discovery: Its effect on critical thinking and achievement in mathematics. *Mathematics Teacher, 60*(8), 874–876.

34. RESNICK, LAUREN B. (1987) *Education and learning to think.* Washington, DC: National Academy Press.

35. SENK, S. L. (1985). How well do students write geometry proofs? *Mathematics Teacher, 78*(6), 448–456.

36. SENK, S. L. (1989). Van Hiele levels and achievement in writing geometry proofs. *Journal for Research in Mathematics Education, 20*(3), 309–321.

37. SHIPMAN, J. R. (1975). Structural and linguistic variables that contribute to difficulty in the judgement of deductive arguments of the conditional type. Annual meeting of the AERA, Washington, DC.

*38. SMITH, E. P., & HENDERSON, K. B. (1959). Proof. In *The growth of mathematical ideas: Grades K–12* (24th Yearbook of the National Council of Teachers of Mathematics). Washington, DC: NCTM.

39. STERNBERG, R. J. (1977). *Intelligence, information processing, and analogical reasoning: The component analysis of human abilities.* New York: Wiley.

40. SUMMA, D. (January, 1982). The effects of proof format, problem structure, and the type of given information on achievement and efficiency in geometric proof. (Doctoral dissertation, Pennsylvania State University, 1981.) *Dissertation Abstracts International, 42,* 3084A.

41. SUPPES, P. (1966). The axiomatic method in high school mathematics. *The role of axiomatics and problem solving in mathematics.* The Conference Board of the Mathematical Sciences, Washington, DC: Ginn.

42. SUPPES, P., & BINFORD, F. (1965). Experimental teaching of mathematical logic in the elementary school. *Arithmetic Teacher, 12*(3), 187–195.

43. VAN AKIN, F. (October 1972). An experimental evaluation of structure in proof in high school geometry. (Doctoral dissertation, University of Minnesota, 1972.) *Dissertation Abstracts, 33,* 1425A.

44. WASON, P. (1974). The psychology of deceptive problems. *New Scientist, 63,* 382–385.

45. WASON, P. C., & JOHNSON–LAIRD, P. N. (1972). *Psychology of Reasoning,* Cambridge, MA: Harvard University Press.

46. WILLIAMS, E. (1980). *An investigation of senior high school students' understanding of the nature of mathematical proof.* (Unpublished doctoral dissertation.) Edmonton: University of Alberta.

CHAPTER 4

Mathematical Problem Solving

James W. Wilson, Maria L. Fernandez, and Nelda Hadaway

> *Your problem may be modest; but if it challenges your curiosity and brings into play your inventive faculties, and if you solve it by your own means, you may experience the tension and enjoy the triumph of discovery. Such experiences at a susceptible age may create a taste for mental work and leave their imprint on mind and character for a lifetime. (26, p.v.)*

$\mathbf{P}$roblem solving has a special importance in the study of mathematics. A primary goal of mathematics teaching and learning is to develop the ability to solve a wide variety of complex mathematics problems. Stanic and Kilpatrick (43) traced the role of problem solving in school mathematics and illustrated a rich history of the topic. To many mathematically literate people, mathematics is synonymous with solving problems—doing word problems, creating patterns, interpreting figures, developing geometric constructions, proving theorems, and so forth. On the other hand, persons not enthralled with mathematics may describe *any* mathematics activity as problem solving.

Learning to solve problems is the principal reason for studying mathematics.
National Council of Supervisors of Mathematics (22)

Chances are that any two people talking about mathematics problem solving are not talking about the same thing. The rhetoric of problem solving has been so pervasive in the mathematics education of the 1980s and 1990s that creative speakers and writers can put a twist on whatever topic or activity they have in mind and call it problem solving! Every exercise of problem-solving research has gone through some agony of defining mathematics problem solving. Yet, words sometimes fail—most people resort to a few examples and a few nonexamples. Reitman (29) defined a problem as a situation in which you have been given the description of something but do not yet have anything that satisfies that description. Reitman's discussion described a problem solver as a person perceiving and accepting a goal without an immediate means of reaching that goal. Henderson and Pingry (11) wrote that to be problem solving there must be a goal, a blocking of that goal for the individual, and acceptance of that goal by the individual. What is a problem for one student may not be a problem for another—either because there is no blocking or no acceptance of the goal. Schoenfeld (33) also pointed out that defining what is a problem has always been relative to the individual involved.

How long is the groove on one side of a long-playing (33⅓ rpm) phonograph record? Assume there is a single recording and the outer (beginning) groove is 5.75 inches from the center and the inner (ending) groove is 1.75 inches from the center. The recording plays for 23 minutes.

Mathematics teachers talk about, write about, and act upon many different ideas subsumed under the heading of problem solving. Some have in mind primarily the selection and presentation of "good" problems to students. Some think of mathematics program goals in which the curriculum is structured around problem content. Others think of program goals in which the strategies and techniques of problem solving are emphasized. Some discuss mathematics problem solving in the context of a method of teaching—that is, a problem approach. Indeed, discussions of mathematics problem solving often combine and blend several of these ideas.

In this chapter we review and discuss research on how students in secondary schools can develop the ability to solve a wide variety of complex problems. We also address how instruction can best develop this ability. A fundamental goal of all instruction is to develop skills, knowledge, and abilities that transfer to tasks not explicitly covered in the curriculum. Should instruction emphasize the particular problem-solving techniques or strategies unique to each task? Will problem solving be enhanced by providing instruction that demonstrates or develops problem-solving techniques or strategies useful in many tasks? We are particularly interested in tasks that require mathematical thinking (34) or higher-order thinking skills (17). Throughout the chapter we have chosen to separate and delineate aspects of mathematics problem solving when in fact the separations are pretty fuzzy for any of us.

Although this chapter deals with problem solving research at the secondary level, there is a growing body of research focused on young children's solutions to word problems (6, 30). Readers should also consult the problem-solving chapters in the Early Childhood and Middle School volumes.

Research on Problem Solving

Educational research is conducted among a variety of constraints—isolation of variables, availability of subjects, limitations of research procedures, availability of resources, and balancing of priorities. Various research methodologies are used in mathematics education research, including a clinical approach that is frequently used to study problem solving. Typically, mathematical tasks or problem situations are devised, and students are studied as they perform those tasks. Often they are asked to talk aloud while working, or are interviewed and asked to reflect on their experience, especially their thinking processes. Waters (48) discusses the advantages and disadvantages of four different methods of measuring strategy use involving a clinical approach. Schoenfeld (32) describes how a clinical approach may be used with pairs of students in an interview, indicating that "dialog between students often serves to make managerial decisions overt, whereas such decisions are rarely overt in single student protocols" (p. 350).

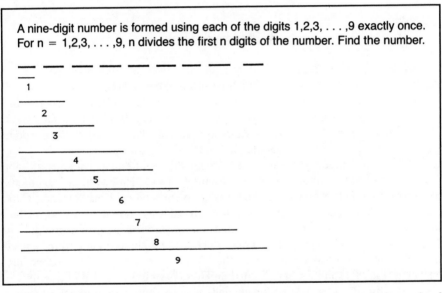

A nine-digit number is formed using each of the digits 1,2,3, . . . ,9 exactly once. For n = 1,2,3, . . . ,9, n divides the first n digits of the number. Find the number.

The basis for most mathematics problem-solving research for secondary school students since 1960 can be found in the writings of Polya (26, 27, 28), in the field of cognitive psychology, and, more specifically, in cognitive science. Cognitive psychologists and cognitive scientists seek to develop or validate theories of human learning (9), whereas mathematics educators attempt to understand how their students interact with mathematics (33, 40). The area of cognitive science has particularly relied on computer simulations of problem solving (25, 50). If a computer program generates a sequence of behaviors similar to the sequence for human subjects, then that program is a model or theory of the behavior. Newell and Simon (25), Larkin (18), and Bobrow (2) have provided simulations of mathematical problem solving. These simulations may be used to better understand mathematics problem solving.

Constructivist theories have received considerable acceptance in mathematics education in recent years. In the constructivist perspective, the learner must be actively involved in the construction of one's own knowledge, rather than in passively receiving knowledge. The teacher's responsibility is to arrange situations and contexts within which the learner constructs appropriate knowledge (45, 48). Even though the constructivist view of mathematics learning is appealing and the theory has formed the basis for many studies at the elementary level, research at the secondary level is lacking. Our review has not uncovered problem-solving research at the secondary level that has its basis in a constructivist perspective. Constructivism, however, is consistent with current cognitive theories of problem solving and mathematical views of problem solving involving exploration, pattern finding, and mathematical thinking (36, 15, 20). We thus urge that teachers and teacher–educators become familiar with constructivist views and evaluate these views with an eye toward restructuring their approaches to teaching, learning, and research dealing with problem solving.

A Framework

It is useful to develop a framework for thinking about the processes involved in mathematics problem solving. Most formulations of a problem-solving framework in U.S. textbooks attribute some relationship to Polya's (26) problem-solving stages. It is important, however, to note that Polya's "stages" were more flexible than the "steps" often delineated in textbooks. These stages were described as understanding the problem, making a plan, carrying out the plan, and looking back.

To Polya (28), problem solving was a major theme of doing mathematics, and "teaching students to think" was of primary importance. "How to think" is a theme that underlies much of genuine inquiry and problem solving in mathematics. Care, however, must be taken so that efforts to teach students "how to think" in mathematics problem solving do not become transformed into teaching "what to think" or "what to do." This is, in particular, a byproduct of an emphasis on procedural knowledge about problem solving as seen in the linear frameworks of U.S. mathematics textbooks (Fig. 4.1) and the very limited problems/exercises included in lessons.

Clearly, the linear nature of the models used in numerous textbooks does not promote the spirit of Polya's stages and his goal of teaching students to think. By their nature, all of these traditional models have the following defects:

1. They depict problem solving as a linear process.
2. They present problem solving as a series of steps.
3. They imply that solving mathematics problems is a procedure to be memorized, practiced, and habituated.
4. They lead to an emphasis on answer getting.

These linear formulations are not very consistent with genuine problem-solving activity. They may, however, be consistent with how experienced problem solvers *present* their solutions and answers after the problem solving is completed. In an analogous way, mathematicians present their proofs in very concise terms, but the

FIGURE 4.1 Linear models of problem solving found in textbooks that are inconsistent with genuine problem solving

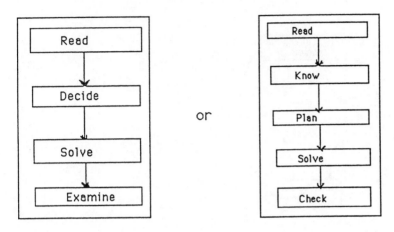

most elegant of proofs may fail to convey the dynamic inquiry that went on in constructing the proof.

Another aspect of problem solving that is seldom included in textbooks is problem posing, or problem formulation. Although there has been little research in this area, this activity has been gaining considerable attention in U.S. mathematics education in recent years. Brown and Walter (3) have provided the major work on problem posing. Indeed, the examples and strategies they illustrate show a powerful and dynamic side to problem-posing activities. Polya (26) did not talk specifically about problem posing, but much of the spirit and format of problem posing is included in his illustrations of looking back.

A framework is needed that emphasizes the dynamic and cyclic nature of genuine problem solving. A student may begin with a problem and engage in thought and activity to understand it. The student attempts to make a plan, and in the process may discover a need to understand the problem better. Or, when a plan has been formed, the student may attempt to carry it out and be unable to do so. The next activity may be attempting to make a new plan, or going back to develop a new understanding of the problem, or posing a new, possibly related, problem to work on.

The framework in Figure 4.2 is useful for illustrating the dynamic, cyclic interpretation of Polya's (26) stages. It has been used in a mathematics problem-solving course at the University of Georgia for many years. Any of the arrows could describe student activity (thought) in the process of solving mathematics problems. Clearly, genuine problem-solving experiences in mathematics cannot be captured by the outer, one-directional arrows alone. It is not a theoretical model. Rather, it is a framework for discussing various pedagogical, curricular, instructional, and learning issues involved with the goals of mathematical problem solving in our schools.

Problem-solving abilities, beliefs, attitudes, and performance develop in contexts (36), and those contexts as well as specific problem-solving activities must be studied.

FIGURE 4.2   Framework emphasizing the dynamic and cyclic nature of problem-
solving activity

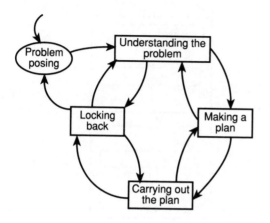

We have chosen to organize the remainder of this chapter around the topics of problem solving as a process, problem solving as an instructional goal, problem solving
as an instructional method, beliefs about problem solving, evaluation of problem
solving, and technology and problem solving.

Problem Solving as a Process

Garofalo and Lester (10) have suggested that students are largely unaware of the
processes involved in problem solving and that addressing this issue within problem-
solving instruction may be important. We will discuss various areas of research pertaining to the process of problem solving.

Domain-Specific Knowledge

To become a good problem solver in mathematics, one must develop a base of mathematics knowledge. How effective one is in organizing that knowledge also contrib-
utes to successful problem solving. Kantowski (13) found that those students with a
good knowledge base were most able to use the heuristics in geometry instruction.
Schoenfeld and Herrmann (38) found that novices attended to surface features of
problems, whereas experts categorized problems on the basis of the fundamental principles involved.

Silver (39) found that successful problem solvers were more likely to categorize
mathematics problems on the basis of their underlying similarities in mathematical
structure. Wilson (50) found that general heuristics had utility only when preceded
by task-specific heuristics. The task-specific heuristics were often specific to the problem domain, such as the tactic that most students develop in working with trigono-

metric identities to "convert all expressions to functions of sine and cosine and do algebraic simplification."

Algorithms

An algorithm is a procedure, applicable to a particular type of exercise, which, if followed correctly, is guaranteed to give you the answer to the exercise. Algorithms are important in mathematics and our instruction must develop them, but the process of carrying out an algorithm—even a complicated one—is not problem solving. The process of creating an algorithm, however, and generalizing it to a specific set of applications can be problem solving. Thus problem solving can be incorporated into the curriculum by having students create their own algorithms. Research involving this approach is currently more prevalent at the elementary level within the context of constructivist theories.

> The creation of an algorithm may involve developing a process for factoring quadratic expressions, as well as developing a process for partitioning a line segment using only Euclidian constructions.

Heuristics

Heuristics are kinds of information, available to students in making decisions during problem solving, that are aids to the generation of a solution, plausible in nature rather than prescriptive, seldom providing infallible guidance, and variable in results. Somewhat synonymous terms are strategies, techniques, and rules-of-thumb. For example, admonitions to "simplify an algebraic expression by removing parentheses," to "make a table," to "restate the problem in your own words," or to "draw a figure to suggest the line of argument for a proof" are heuristic in nature. Out of context they have no particular value, but incorporated into situations of doing mathematics they can be quite powerful (26, 27, 28).

> Many a guess has turned out to be wrong but nevertheless useful in leading to a better one. Polya (26, p. 99)

Theories of mathematics problem solving (25, 33, 50) have placed a major focus on the role of heuristics. Surely it seems that providing explicit instruction on the development and use of heuristics should enhance problem-solving performance, yet it is not that simple. Schoenfeld (35) and Lesh (19) have pointed out the limitations of such a simplistic analysis. Theories must be enlarged to incorporate classroom contexts, past knowledge and experience, and beliefs. What Polya (26) describes in *How to Solve It* is far more complex than any theories we have developed so far.

Mathematics instruction stressing heuristic processes has been the focus of several studies. Kantowski (14) used heuristic instruction to enhance the geometry problem-solving performance of secondary school students. Wilson (50) and Smith (42) examined contrasts of general and task-specific heuristics. These studies revealed that task-specific heuristic instruction was more effective than general heuristic instruction. Jensen (12) used the heuristic of subgoal generation to enable students to form problem-solving plans. He used thinking aloud, peer interaction, playing the role of teacher, and direct instruction to develop students' ability to generate subgoals.

Managing It All

Even an extensive knowledge base of domain-specific information, a plethora of algorithms, and a repertoire of heuristics are not sufficient during problem solving. The student must also construct some decision mechanism to select from among the available heuristics, or to develop new ones, as problem situations are encountered. A major theme of Polya's writing was to do mathematics, to reflect on problems solved or attempted, and to think (27, 28). Certainly Polya expected students to engage in thinking about the various tactics, patterns, techniques, and strategies available to them. To build a theory of problem solving that approaches Polya's model, a manager function must be incorporated into the system. Long ago, Dewey (8), in *How We Think*, emphasized self-reflection in the solving of problems.

Recent research has been much more explicit in attending to this aspect of problem solving and the learning of mathematics. The field of metacognition concerns thinking about one's own cognition. Metacognition theory holds that such thought can monitor, direct, and control one's cognitive processes (4, 41). Schoenfeld (34) described and demonstrated an executive or monitor component to his problem-solving theory. His problem-solving courses included explicit attention to a set of guidelines for reflecting on the problem-solving activities in which the students were engaged. Clearly, effective problem-solving instruction must provide the students with an opportunity to reflect, in a systematic and constructive way, during problem-solving activities.

The Importance of Looking Back

Looking back may be the most important part of problem solving. It is the set of activities that provides the primary opportunity for students to learn from the problem. Polya identified this phase (26) with admonitions to *examine* the solution by such activities as checking the result, checking the argument, deriving the result differently, using the result, or the method, for some other problem, reinterpreting the problem, interpreting the result, or stating a new problem to solve.

Teachers and researchers report, however, that developing the disposition to look back is very hard to accomplish with students. Kantowski (14) found little evidence among students of looking back, even though the instruction had stressed it. Wilson (51) conducted a year-long inservice mathematics problem-solving course for secondary teachers in which each participant developed materials to implement some aspect of problem solving in their ongoing teaching assignment. During the debriefing session at the final meeting, a teacher put it succinctly: "In schools, there is no looking back." The discussion underscored the agreement of all the participants that getting students to engage in looking-back activities was difficult. Some of the reasons cited were entrenched beliefs that problem solving in mathematics is answer-getting; pressure to cover a prescribed course syllabus; testing (or the absence of tests that measure processes); and student frustration.

The importance of looking back, however, outweighs these difficulties. Five activities essential to promote learning from problem solving are (1) developing and exploring problem contexts, (2) extending problems, (3) extending solutions, (4) extending processes, and (5) developing self-reflection. Teachers can easily incorporate the use of writing in mathematics into the looking-back phase of problem solving. It is what you learn *after* you have solved the problem that really counts.

Problem Posing

Problem posing (3) and problem formulation (16) are logically and philosophically appealing notions to mathematics educators and teachers. Brown and Walter offer suggestions for implementing these ideas. In particular, they discuss the "what-if-not" problem-posing strategy that encourages the generation of new problems by changing the conditions of a current problem. For example, given a mathematics theorem or rule, students may be asked to list its attributes. After a discussion of the attributes, the teacher may ask, "What if some or all of the given attributes are not true?" Through this discussion, the students generate new problems.

Brown and Walter provide a wide variety of situations implementing this strategy, including a discussion of the development of non-Euclidean geometry. After many years of attempting to prove the parallel postulate as a theorem, mathematicians began to ask, "What if it were not the case that through a given external point there was exactly one line parallel to the given line? What if there were two? None? What would that do to the structure of geometry?" (p. 47). Although these ideas seem promising, there is little explicit research reported on problem posing.

Given the Pythagorean Theorem where $a^2 + b^2 = c^2$. An attribute of the Pythagorean Theorem is that the variables are related by an equals sign. "What if" the variables are related by "$<$," i.e., $a^2 + b^2 < c^2$. (3).

Problem Solving as an Instructional Goal

What Is Mathematics?

If our answer to this question uses such terms as exploration, inquiry, discovery, plausible reasoning, or problem solving, then we are attending to the *processes* of mathematics. Most of us would also make a content list of words like algebra, geometry, number, probability, statistics, or calculus. Deep down, our answers to questions such as What is mathematics? What do mathematicians do? What do mathematics students do? Should the activities for mathematics students model what mathematicians do? can affect how we approach mathematics problems and, indeed, how we teach mathematics.

The National Council of Teachers of Mathematics' (NCTM) (23, 24) recommendations to make problem solving the focus of school mathematics posed fundamental questions about the nature of school mathematics. The art of problem solving is the heart of mathematics. Thus, mathematics instruction should be designed so that students experience mathematics as problem solving.

The National Council of Teachers of Mathematics recommends that—
    1. problem solving be the focus of school mathematics in the 1980s. *An Agenda for Action* (23)

We strongly endorse the first recommendation of *An Agenda for Action*. The initial standard of each of the three levels addresses this goal. *Curriculum and Evaluation Standards* (24)

Why Problem Solving?

The NCTM (23, 24) has strongly endorsed the inclusion of problem solving in school mathematics. There are at least five good reasons for its doing this. First, problem solving is a major part of mathematics. It is in fact tantamount to the sum and substance of our discipline, and to reduce that discipline to a set of exercises and skills devoid of problem solving is misrepresenting mathematics as a discipline and shortchanging the students. Second, mathematics has many applications often representing important problems in the field. Our subject is used in the work, understanding, and communication within other disciplines. Third, there is an intrinsic motivation embedded in solving mathematics problems. We include problem solving in school mathematics because it can stimulate the interest and enthusiasm of the students. Fourth, problem solving can be recreational: Many of us have continued to do mathematics problems just for the fun of it. Fifth, problem solving must be in the school mathematics curriculum in order to allow students to develop the art of problem solving. This art is so essential to understanding and appreciating mathematics that it *must* be an instructional goal.

Teachers often provide strong rationales for *not* including problem-solving activities is school mathematics instruction. These include arguments that problem solving is too difficult; it takes too much time; the school curriculum is very full, and so there is no room for problem solving; problem solving will not be measured and tested; because mathematics is sequential, students must master facts, procedures, and algorithms; appropriate mathematics problems are not available; problem solving is not in the textbooks; and basic facts must be mastered through drill and practice before attempting the use of problem solving. We should note, however, that—as discussed above—student benefits from incorporating problem solving into the mathematics curriculum outweigh this entire line of reasoning. Also, we should caution against claiming an emphasis on problem solving when in fact the emphasis is on routine exercises. As Suydam (44) concluded from various studies involving problem-solving instruction:

> If problem solving is treated as "apply the procedure," then the students try to follow the rules in subsequent problems. If you teach problem solving as an approach, where you must think and can apply anything that works, then students are likely to be less rigid. (p. 104)

Problem Solving as an Instructional Method

Problem solving as a method of teaching may be used to accomplish the instructional goals of learning basic facts, concepts, and procedures, as well as goals for problem solving within problem contexts. For example, if students investigate the areas of all triangles having a fixed perimeter of 60 units, the problem-solving activities should provide ample practice in computational skills and use of formulas and procedures, as well as opportunities for the conceptual development of the relationships between area and perimeter. The "problem" might be to find the triangle with the most area, the areas of triangles with integer sides, or a triangle with area numerically equal to the perimeter. Thus problem solving as a method of teaching can be used to introduce concepts through lessons involving both exploration and discovery.

The creation of an algorithm, and its refinement, also is a complex problem-solving task that can be accomplished through the problem approach to teaching. Open-ended problem solving often uses problem contexts wherein a sequence of related problems might be explored. For example, the problems on page 68 evolved from considering gardens of different shapes that could be enclosed with 100 yards of fencing.

Many teachers in our workshops have reported success with a "problem of the week" strategy. This is often associated with a bulletin board on which a challenge problem is regularly presented (e.g., every Monday). The idea is to capitalize on intrinsic motivation and accomplishment, to use competition in a constructive way, and to extend the curriculum. Some teachers have used schemes for granting extra credit to successful students. The monthly calendar found in each issue of *The Mathematics Teacher* is an excellent source of problems.

Whether students encounter good mathematics problems depends on the skill of the teacher to incorporate problems, often not found in textbooks, from various sources. We encourage teachers to begin building a resource book of problems oriented specifically to a course in their ongoing workload. Good problems can be found in the *Applications in Mathematics* (AIM Project) materials (21) consisting of videotapes, resource books, and computer diskettes published by the Mathematical Association of America. These problems can often be extended or modified by teachers and students in order to emphasize their interests. Problems of interest for teachers and their students can also be developed through the use of *The Challenge of the Unknown* materials (1) developed by the American Association for the Advancement of Science. These materials consist of tapes providing real situations from which mathematical problems arise and a handbook of ideas and activities that can be used to generate other problems.

Suppose one had 100 yards of fencing to enclose a garden. What shapes could be enclosed? What are the dimensions of each and what is the area? Make a chart.

What triangular region with $P = 100$ has the most area?

Find all five triangular regions with $P = 100$ having integer sides and integer area (such as 29, 29, 42).

What rectangular regions could be enclosed? Areas? Organize a table? Make a graph?

Which rectangular region has the most area? From a table? From a graph? From algebra, using the arithmetic mean–geometric mean inequality?

What is the area of a regular hexagon with $P = 100$?

What is the area of a regular octagon with $P = 100$?

What is the area of a regular n-gon with $P = 100$? Make a table for $n = 3$ to 25. Make a graph. What happens to $1/n(\tan 180/n)$ as n increases?

What if part of the fencing is used to build a partition perpendicular to a side? Consider a rectangular region with one partition? With 2 partitions? With n partitions? (There is a surprise in this one!) What if the partition is a diagonal of the rectangle?

What is the maximum area of a sector of a circle with $P = 100$? (Here is another surprise: Could you believe it is r^2 when $r = 25$? How is this similar to a square being the maximum rectangle and the central angle of the maximum sector being 2 radians?)

What about regions built along a natural boundary? For example, the maximum for both a rectangular region and a triangular region built along a natural boundary with 100 yards of fencing is 1250 square yards. But the rectangle is not the maximum area four-sided figure that can be built. What is the maximum-area four-sided figure?

Beliefs about Mathematics Problem Solving

The importance of students' and teachers' beliefs about mathematics problem solving lies in the assumption of some connection between beliefs and behavior. Thus, it is argued, the beliefs of mathematics students, mathematics teachers, parents, policymakers, and the general public about the roles of problem solving in mathematics become prerequisite or corequisite to developing problem solving. The *Curriculum and Evaluation Standards* makes the point that "students need to view themselves as capable of using their growing mathematical knowledge to make sense of new problem situations in the world around them" (24, p. ix). We prefer to think of developing a sense of "can do" in our students as they encounter mathematics problems.

The first rule of teaching is to know what you are supposed to teach. The second rule of teaching is to know a little more than what you are supposed to teach. . . . Yet it should not be forgotten that a teacher of mathematics should know some mathematics, and that a teacher wishing to impart the right attitude of mind toward problems to his students should have acquired that attitude himself. Polya (26, p. 173).

Schoenfeld (36, 37) reported results from a year-long study of detailed observations, analysis of videotaped instruction, and follow-up questionnaire data from two tenth-grade geometry classes. These classes, in select high schools, were highly successful as determined by student performance on the New York State Regents' examination. Students reported beliefs that mathematics helped them to think clearly and that could be creative, yet they also claimed that mathematics was learned best by memorization. Similar contrasts have been reported for the National Assessment (5). Indeed, both our conversations with teachers and our observations portray an overwhelming predisposition of secondary school mathematics students to view problem solving as answer getting, see mathematics as a set of rules, and be highly oriented to doing well on tests.

Schoenfeld (37) is able to tell us much more about the classes in his study. He makes the following points.

> The rhetoric of problem solving has become familiar over the past decade. That rhetoric was frequently heard in the classes we observed—but the reality of those classrooms is that real problems were few and far between. . . . Virtually all problems the students were asked to solve were bite-size exercises designed to achieve subject matter mastery: the exceptions were clearly peripheral tasks that the students found enjoyable but that they considered to be recreations or rewards rather than the substance they were expected to learn. . . . The advances in mathematics education in the [past] decade . . . have been largely in our acquiring a more enlightened goal structure, and having students pick up the rhetoric—but not the substance—related to those goals. (pp. 348–349)

Each of us needs to ask if the situation Schoenfeld describes is similar to that in our own school. We must take care that espoused beliefs about problem solving are consistent with a legitimately implemented problem solving focus in school mathematics.

Technology and Problem Solving

For many people the appropriate use of technology has significant identity with mathematics problem solving. This view emphasizes the use of technology as a *tool* for mathematics problem solving rather than the use of technologies to deliver instruction or to generate student feedback.

Programming as Problem Solving

Problem-solving research involving technology has often dealt with programming as a major focus—but has often provided inconclusive results. Indeed, the development of a computer program to perform a mathematical task can be a challenging mathematical problem that can enhance the programmer's understanding of the mathematics being used. Too often, however, the focus is on programming skills rather than on using programming to solve mathematics problems. Most assuredly there is a place for programming within mathematics study, but the focus ought to be on the mathematics problems and the use of the computer as a tool for mathematics problem solving.

A ladder 5 meters long leans against a wall, reaching over the top of a box that is 1 meter on each side. The box is against the wall. What is the maximum height on the wall that the ladder can reach? The side view is:

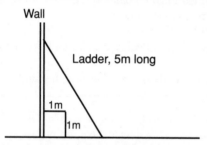

Assume the wall is perpendicular to the floor. Use your calculator to find the maximum height to the nearest .01 meter.

Iteration

Iteration and recursion are mathematical concepts made accessible to the secondary school level with the aid of technology. Students may implement iteration by writing a computer program, developing a procedure for using a calculator, writing a sequence of decision steps, or developing a classroom dramatization. The approximation of roots of equations can be operationalized with a calculator or computer carrying out the iterations. For example, the process for finding the three roots of $2^x = x^{10}$ is not very approachable without iterative techniques. Iteration is also useful when determining the maximum height, h, between a chord and an arc of a circle when the length S of the arc and the length L of the chord are known. This problem may call for solving $S/2 = r\theta$ and $L/2 = r \sin \theta$ simultaneously, and using iterative techniques to find r and θ in order to evaluate $h = r - r \cos \theta$. Fractals can also be explored through the use of iterative techniques and computer software.

Exploration

Technology can be used both to make possible and to enhance exploration of conceptual or problem situations. For example, a function-grapher computer program or a graphics calculator can allow student exploration of families of curves such as $ax^2 + bx + c = 0$ for different values of a, b, and c. A calculator can be used to explore sequences such as $x_{n+1} = \sqrt{a + x_n}$ where $x_0 = \sqrt{a}$ for different values of a. In this way, technology introduces a dynamic aspect to investigating mathematics.

Thomas (46) studied the use of computer graphic problem-solving activities to assist in the instruction of functions and transformational geometry at the secondary school level. The students were challenged to create a computer graphics design of a preselected picture, using graphs of functions and transformational geometry. Thomas found that these activities helped students to better understand function concepts and improved student attitudes.

Evaluation of Problem Solving

As the emphasis on problem solving in mathematics classrooms increases, the need for evaluation of progress and instruction in problem solving becomes more pressing. It no longer suffices for us to know which kinds of problems are correctly or incorrectly solved by students. As Schoenfeld (36) describes:

> All too often we focus on a narrow collection of well-defined tasks and train students to execute those tasks in a routine, if not algorithmic fashion. Then we test the students on tasks that are very close to the ones they have been taught. If they succeed on those problems, we and they congratulate each other on the fact that they have learned some powerful mathematical techniques. In fact, they may be able to use such techniques mechanically while lacking some rudimentary thinking skills. To allow them, and ourselves, to believe that they "understand" the mathematics is deceptive and fraudulent. (p. 30)

Schoenfeld (31) indicates that capable mathematics students, when removed from the context of coursework, have difficulty doing what may be considered elementary mathematics for their level of achievement. For example, he describes a situation in which he gave a straightforward theorem from tenth-grade plane geometry to a group of junior and senior mathematics majors at the University of California involved in a problem-solving course. Of the eight students solving this problem only two made any significant progress.

We need to focus on the teaching and learning of mathematics and, in turn, problem solving using a holistic approach. As is recommended in the NCTM's *An Agenda for Action* (23), "the success of mathematics programs and student learning [must] be evaluated by a wider range of measures than conventional testing" (p. 1). Although this recommendation is widely accepted among mathematics educators, there is a limited amount of research dealing with the evaluation of problem solving within the classroom environment.

Some research dealing with the evaluation of problem solving involves diagnosing students' cognitive processes by evaluating the amount and type of help needed by an individual during a problem-solving activity. Campione, Brown, and Connell (4) term this method of evaluation as dynamic assessment. Students are given mathematics problems to solve. The assessor then begins to provide as little help as necessary to the students throughout their problem-solving activity. The amount and type of help needed can provide good insight into the students' problem-solving abilities, as well as their ability to learn and apply new principles. Trismen (47) reported the use of hints to help diagnosis student difficulties in problem solving in high school algebra and plane geometry. Problems were developed such that the methods of solutions were not readily apparent to the students. A sequence of hints was then developed for each item. According to Trismen, "the power of the hint technique seems to lie in its ability to identify those particular students in need of special kinds of help" (p. 371).

Classroom research: Ask your students to keep a problem-solving notebook in which they record on a weekly basis:

1. their solution to a mathematics problem
2. a discussion of the strategies they used to solve the problem
3. a discussion of the mathematical similarities of this problem with other problems they have solved
4. a discussion of possible extensions for the problem
5. an investigation of at least one of the extensions they discussed

Use these notebooks to evaluate students' progress. Then periodically throughout the year analyze the students' overall progress as well as their reactions to the notebooks, in order to assess the effectiveness of the evaluation process.

Campione and his colleagues (4) also discussed a method to help monitor and evaluate the progress of a small cooperative group during a problem-solving session. A learning leader (sometimes the teacher, sometimes a student) guides the group in solving the problem through the use of three boards: (1) a Planning Board, where important information and ideas about the problem are recorded, (2) a Representation Board, where diagrams illustrating the problems are drawn, and (3) a Doing Board, where appropriate equations are developed and the problem is solved. Through the use of this method, the students are able to discuss and reflect on their approaches by visually tracing their joint work. Campione and his colleagues indicated that increased student engagement and enthusiasm in problem solving, as well as increased performance, resulted from the use of this method for solving problems.

Methods such as the clinical approach discussed earlier, used to gather data dealing with problem solving and the individual's thinking processes, may also be used in the classroom to evaluate progress in problem solving. Charles, Lester, and O'Daffer (7) describe how we may incorporate these techniques into a classroom problem-solving evaluation program. For example, thinking aloud may be canonically achieved within the classroom by placing the students in cooperative groups. In this way students may express their problem-solving strategies aloud, and thus we may be able to assess their thinking processes and attitudes unobtrusively. Charles and his colleagues also discussed the use of interviews and student self-reports during which students are asked to reflect on their problem-solving experience, a technique often used in problem-solving research. Other techniques they describe involve methods of scoring students' written work.

Figure 4.3 illustrates a final assignment used to assess teachers' learning in a problem-solving course modified to be used with students at the secondary level.

Unfortunately, testing often drives the mathematics curriculum. Most criterion-referenced testing and most norm-referenced testing is antithetical to problem solving. Such testing emphasizes answer getting. It leads to pressure to "cover" lots of material, and teachers feel pressured to forego problem solving. They may know that problem solving is desirable and that developing understanding and using appropriate technology are worthwhile, but—there is not enough time for all of that, plus getting ready for the tests. Teachers dedicated to problem solving, however, have been able to incorporate it into their mathematics curriculum without bringing down students' scores on standardized tests.

Although test developers, such as the designers of the California Assessment Program, are beginning to consider alternative test questions, it will take time for these changes to occur. By committing ourselves to problem solving within our classrooms, we will further accentuate the need for changes in testing practices while providing our students with invaluable mathematics experiences.

Looking Ahead . . .

We are struck by the seemingly contradictory facts that there is a vast literature on problem solving in mathematics, yet there also is a multitude of questions to be studied, developed, and written about in order to make genuine problem-solving activities an integral part of mathematics instruction. Further, although many may view this as primarily a curriculum question, and hence call for restructured textbooks and materials, it is the mathematics teacher who must create the context in which problem solving may flourish and students become problem solvers. The first one in the classroom to become a problem solver must be the teacher.

James W. Wilson
Maria L. Fernandez

Thus a teacher of mathematics has a great opportunity. If he fills his allotted time with drilling his students in routine operations he kills their interest, hampers their intellectual development, and misuses his opportunity. But if he challenges the curiosity of his students by setting them problems proportionate to their knowledge, and helps them to solve their problems with stimulating questions, he may give them a taste for, and some means of, independent thinking. Polya (26, p. v)

The primary goal of most students in mathematics classes is to see an algorithm that will give them the answer quickly. Students and parents struggle with, and at

FIGURE 4.3   Final assignment from a teacher's mathematics problem-solving
              course modified for use with secondary students

1. (20 points)
     Select a problem that you have worked on but not yet solved, and that you
     feel you can eventually solve. Present the following:
        a. Show or describe what you have done so far (it could be that you tell me
           where to find your work in your notebook).
        b. Assess how you feel about the problem. Is the lack of closure a concern?
           Why?
        c. Assess what you may have learned in working on the problem so far.
2. (20 points)
        a. Select a mathematics theorem or rule from class and make a list of its
           attributes.
        b. Generate at least three new problems by considering the question: "What
           if some or all of the given attributes are not true?"
        c. Thoroughly investigate one of the problems generated above.
3. (10 points)
     Find the maximum area of a trapezoid inscribed in a semicircle of radius 1.
     Hint: Use the arithmetic mean-geometric mean inequality.

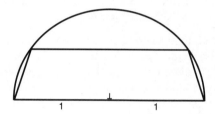

        a. Describe your solution.
        b. Discuss possible extensions.

times against, the idea that mathematics class can and should involve exploration,
conjecturing, and thinking. When students struggle with a problem, parents often
accuse them of not paying attention in class: "Surely the teacher showed you how
to work the problem!" How can parents, students, colleagues, and the public become more informed about genuine problem solving? How can I as a mathematics
teacher in the secondary school help students and their parents to understand what
real mathematics learning is all about?

                                                                    Nelda Hadaway

About the Authors

James W. Wilson is a professor and head of the Department of Mathematics Education at The University of Georgia. He has a B.S. and M.A. from Kansas State Teachers College, an M.S. from Notre Dame, and an M.S. and a Ph.D. from Stanford University. Interested in problem solving for many years, his doctoral research dealt with that subject, and his Problem Solving in Mathematics course is a regular offering at The University of Georgia. Over the years he has also been involved in various problem-solving projects, including the U.S.–Japan Joint Seminar on Problem Solving in School Mathematics.

Maria L. Fernandez is a doctoral candidate in the Department of Mathematics Education at The University of Georgia. She completed both a B.S. and an M.S. in mathematics education at Florida International University in Miami, and is interested in the incorporation of problem solving into the mathematics curriculum at all levels. While teaching mathematics at the secondary level in Miami, Ms Fernandez integrated problem solving into the curriculum using various strategies. Her research interests include mathematics visualizations in problem solving.

Nelda Hadaway received a B.S.Ed., an M.Ed., and an Ed.S. from The University of Georgia, Athens, and is a doctoral candidate at Georgia State University in Atlanta. She has taught mathematics at Hunter College High School in New York City and currently teaches mathematics at South Gwinett High School in Snellville, Georgia. Ms Hadaway is interested in integrating writing into the teaching of mathematics in order to enhance problem solving.

References

*1. American Association for the Advancement of Science. (1986). *The challenge of the unknown*. New York: Norton.

2. BOBROW, D. G. (1964). *Natural language input for a computer problem solving system*. Unpublished doctoral dissertation, Massachusetts Institute of Technology, Cambridge, MA.

*3. BROWN, S. I., & WALTER, M. I. (1983). *The art of problem posing*. Hillsdale, NJ: Erlbaum.

*4. CAMPIONE, J. C., BROWN, A. L., & CONNELL, M. L. (1988). Metacognition: On the importance of understanding what you are doing. In R. I. Charles & E. A. Silver (Eds.), *The teaching and assessing of mathematical problem solving* (pp. 93–114). Reston, VA: Erlbaum/National Council of Teachers of Mathematics.

5. CARPENTER, T. P., LINDQUIST, M. M., MATTHEWS, W., & SILVER, E. A. (1983). Results of the third NAEP mathematics assessment: Secondary school. *Mathematics Teacher*, 76(9), 652–659.

6. CARPENTER, T. P., MOSER, J. M., & ROMBERG, T. A. (Eds.) (1982). *Addition and subtraction: A cognitive perspective*. Hillsdale, NJ: Erlbaum.

*7. CHARLES, R. I., LESTER, F. K., & O'DAFFER, P. (1987). *How to evaluate progress in problem solving*. Reston, VA: National Council of Teachers of Mathematics.

8. DEWEY, J. (1933). *How we think: A restatement of the relation of reflective thinking to the educative process*. Boston: Heath.

9. FREDERIKSEN, N. (1984). Implications of cognitive theory for instruction in problem solving. *Review of Educational Research*, 54, 363–407.

10. GAROFALO, J., & LESTER, F. K. (1985). Metacognition, cognitive monitoring, and mathematical performance. *Journal for Research in Mathematics Education, 16,* 163–176.

11. HENDERSON, K. B., & PINGRY, R. E. (1953). Problem solving in mathematics. In H. F. Fehr (Ed.), *The learning of mathematics: Its theory and practice* (21st Yearbook of the National Council of Teachers of Mathematics, pp. 228–270). Washington, DC: National Council of Teachers of Mathematics.

12. JENSEN, R. (1984). *A multifaceted instructional approach for developing subgoal generation skills.* Unpublished doctoral dissertation, The University of Georgia, Athens.

13. KANTOWSKI, M. G. (1974). *Processes involved in mathematical problem solving.* Unpublished doctoral dissertation, The University of Georgia, Athens.

14. KANTOWSKI, M. G. (1977). Processes involved in mathematical problem solving. *Journal for Research in Mathematics Education, 8,* 163–180.

15. KAPUT, J. J. (1979). Mathematics learning: Roots of epistemological status. In J. Lochhead and J. Clement (Eds.), *Cognitive process instruction.* Philadelphia: Franklin Institute Press.

16. KILPATRICK, J. (1987). Problem formulating: Where do good problems come from? In A. H. Schoenfeld (Ed.), *Cognitive science and mathematics education* (pp. 123–147). Hillsdale, NJ: Erlbaum.

17. KULM, G. (Ed.) (1990). *Assessing higher order thinking skills.* Washington, DC: American Association for the Advancement of Science.

18. LARKIN, J. (1980). Teaching problem solving in physics: The psychological laboratory and the practical classroom. In F. Reif & D. Tuma (Eds.), *Problem solving in education: Issues in teaching and research.* Hillsdale, NJ: Erlbaum.

19. LESH, R. (1981). Applied mathematical problem solving. *Educational Studies in Mathematics, 12*(2), 235–265.

20. LOCHHEAD, J. (1979). An introduction to cognitive process instruction. In J. Lochhead & J. Clement (Eds.). *Cognitive process instruction.* Philadelphia: Franklin Institute Press.

*21. MATHEMATICAL ASSOCIATION OF AMERICA (1986). *Applications in mathematics* (AIM Project materials). Washington, DC: Author.

22. NATIONAL COUNCIL OF SUPERVISORS OF MATHEMATICS (1978). Position paper on basic mathematical skills. *Mathematics Teacher, 71*(2), 147–52. (Reprinted from position paper distributed to members January 1977.)

23. NATIONAL COUNCIL OF TEACHERS OF MATHEMATICS (1980). *An agenda for action: Recommendations for school mathematics in the 1980s.* Reston, VA: Author.

24. NATIONAL COUNCIL OF TEACHERS OF MATHEMATICS (1989). *Curriculum and evaluation standards for school mathematics.* Reston, VA: Author.

25. NEWELL, A., & SIMON, H. A. (1972). *Human problem solving.* Englewood Cliffs, NJ: Prentice–Hall.

*26. POLYA, G. (1973). *How to solve it.* Princeton, NJ: Princeton University Press. (Originally copyrighted in 1945)

27. POLYA, G. (1962). *Mathematical discovery: On understanding, learning and teaching problem solving (Vol. 1).* New York: Wiley.

28. POLYA, G. (1965). *Mathematical discovery: On understanding, learning and teaching problem solving (Vol. 2).* New York: Wiley.

29. REITMAN, W. R. (1965). *Cognition and thought.* New York: Wiley.

30. RILEY, M.S., GREENO, J. G., & HELLER, J. I. (1983). Development of children's problem-solving ability in arithmetic. In H. Ginsburg (Ed.), *The development of mathematical thinking* (pp. 153–200). New York: Academic Press.

31. SCHOENFELD, A. H. (1979). Can heuristics be taught? In J. Lochhead & J. Clement (Eds.) *Cognitive process instruction*. Philadelphia: Franklin Institute Press.

32. SCHOENFELD, A. H. (1983). Episodes and executive decisions in mathematics problem solving. In R. Lesh & M. Landau, *Acquisition of mathematics concepts and processes*. New York: Academic Press

33. SCHOENFELD, A. H. (1985). *Mathematical problem solving*. Orlando, FL: Academic Press.

34. SCHOENFELD, A. H., (1985). Metacognitive and epistemological issues in mathematical understanding. In E. A. Silver, *Teaching and learning mathematical problem solving: Multiple research perspectives* (pp. 361–379). Hillsdale, NJ: Erlbaum.

35. SCHOENFELD, A. H. (1987). Cognitive science and mathematics education: An overview. In A. H. Schoenfeld, *Cognitive science and mathematics education*. Hillsdale, NJ: Erlbaum.

36. SCHOENFELD, A. H. (1988). When good teaching leads to bad results: The disasters of "well taught" mathematics classes. *Educational Psychologist, 23*, 145–166.

37. SCHOENFELD, A. H. (1989). Explorations of students' mathematical beliefs and behavior. *Journal for Research in Mathematics Education, 20*, 338–355.

38. SCHOENFELD, A. H., & HERRMANN, D. (1982). Problem perception and knowledge structure in expert and novice mathematical problem solvers. *Journal of Experimental Psychology: Learning, Memory and Cognition, 8*, 484–494.

39. SILVER, E. A. (1979). Student perceptions of relatedness among mathematical verbal problems. *Journal for Research in Mathematics Education, 10*(3), 195–210.

40. SILVER, E. A. (1987). Foundations of cognitive theory and research for mathematics problem-solving instruction. In A. H. Schoenfeld (Ed.), *Cognitive science and mathematics education* (pp. 33–60). Hillsdale, NJ: Erlbaum.

41. SILVER, E. A., BRANCA, N., & ADAMS, V. (1980). Metacognition: The missing link in problem solving? In R. Karplus (Ed.), *Proceedings of the fourth international conference for the psychology of mathematics education*. Berkeley, CA: The Conference.

42. SMITH, J. P. (1974). The effects of general versus specific heuristics in mathematical problem-solving tasks (Doctoral dissertation, Columbia University, 1973). *Dissertation Abstracts International, 34*, 2400A.

43. STANIC, G., & KILPATRICK, J. (1988). Historical Perspectives on Problem Solving in the Mathematics Curriculum. In R. I. Charles & E. A. Silver (Eds.), *The teaching and assessing of mathematical problem solving* (pp. 1–22). Reston, VA: National Council of Teachers of Mathematics.

44. SUYDAM, M. (1987). Indications from research on problem solving. In F. R. Curcio (Ed.), *Teaching and learning: A problem solving focus*. Reston, VA: National Council of Teachers of Mathematics.

45. STEFFE, L. P., & WOOD, T. (Eds.) (1990). *Transforming Children's Mathematical Education*. Hillsdale, NJ: Erlbaum.

46. THOMAS, E. J., JR. (1990). A study of the effects of a computer graphics problem-solving activity on student achievements, attitudes, and task motivation (Doctoral dissertation, Georgia State University, 1989). *Dissertation Abstracts International, 51*, 102A.

47. TRISMEN, D. A. (1988). Hints: An aid to diagnosis in mathematical problem solving. *Journal for Research in Mathematics Education, 19*, 358–361.

48. VON GLASERSFELD, E. (1989). Constructivism in education. In T. Husen & T. N. Postlethwaite (Eds.), *The international encyclopedia of education*. (Suppl. Vol. 1, pp. 162–163). New York: Pergamon.

49. WATERS, W. (1984). Concept acquisition tasks. In G. A. Goldin & C. E. McClintock

(Eds.), *Task variables in mathematical problem solving* (pp. 277–296). Philadelphia: Franklin Institute Press.
50. WILSON, J. W. (1967). *Generality of heuristics as an instructional variable.* Unpublished doctoral dissertation, Stanford University, San Jose, CA.
51. WILSON, J. W. (1990). *Report of the Georgia Plan problem solving workshop, 1989–90.* Unpublished document, The University of Georgia, Athens.

CHAPTER 5

Mathematical Symbols and Representations

Claude Janvier, Catherine Girardon, and
Jean-Charles Morand

*Is a picture worth a thousand words? How many words do you need to decipher
a picture?*

Students often interpret representations in unintended ways. Take for
example Figure 5.1 (p. 80). Upon studying this, many have viewed the curve drawn
in the Cartesian plane as the track on which the car is driven. Indeed, asking the
students why they answer "nine" will prompt them to move their finger along the
curve, counting the bends. If students are familiar with Cartesian graphs, they can
be talked out of this interpretation. However, for at least some students, the fact that
"the track" does not appear as a closed curve does not challenge their initial interpretation. This well-known example in the research community involves several issues related to the use of representations in mathematics. Representations are om-
nipresent in mathematics, but they create many subtle problems that teachers must
consider. We cannot assume that students can readily create or interpret representations. They need instruction on how to use them.

Are examples of this kind more frequent in today's textbooks? A few generations
ago, written material was the main component of mathematics textbooks. Over the
years, authors have progressively emphasized the roles of different kinds of representations—graphs, tables, diagrams, charts, and figures—as well as the importance of
working on activities with concrete materials, illustrated in several ways. The recent
introduction of microcomputers, with their powerful image-processing capability, has
strongly catalyzed this trend. This growing concern for the importance of representations is taken into account by the NCTM's *Curriculum and Evaluation Standards*
(27).

FIGURE 5.1   The graph shows how the speed of a racing car varies during the
second lap of a race.

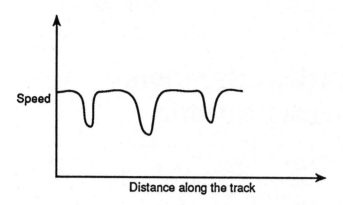

Querstion: How many bend are there on the circuit?

Age \ Answers	3	9	others or none
12–13	46%	26%	28%
14–15	68%	17%	15%

Results

Sample: age 12–13: 224 students; age 14–15: 156 students from a Montreal suburban middle-class school (17, p.8)

C. Janvier (1981). Les graphiques cartésians comme mode de représentations: rôle du language et nature des traductions. *Séminaire de didactique et pédagogie des mathématiques*, n° 25, mai (p. 8). Laboratoire de Structures, Discretes et de Didactique, Grenoble, France. Used by permission.

NCTM Curriculum Standards for Grades 9–12
Standard 5. Algebra
Represent situations and number patterns with tables, graphs, verbal rules, and
equations.
Standard 6. Functions
Represent and analyze relationships using tables, verbal rules, equations, and
graphs. Analyze the effects of parameter changes on the graphs of functions.
(27, pp.150, 154)

However, representations are not a panacea. The objective of this chapter is to show how research, with its theoretical framework and results, can help teachers (a) know better the role of representations in their students' reasoning, (b) be aware of the difficulties involved, and (c) plan and conduct their teaching more efficiently.

Representations

Many researchers (Kaput, Goldin, von Glaeserfeld, Janvier, Vergnaud, etc.) have sought to make the term "representation" more precise. Basic reflections on the topic lead all authors to stress the importance of distinguishing between the material sign (signifier, referent) and the idea—the concept (signified, referenced). The fact that a material sign (such as the graph in Fig. 5.1) has a counterpart in the mind of the thinkers brings about a distinction between the notion of *external representations* and that of *internal representations*. *External* representations act as stimuli on the senses and include charts, tables, graphs, diagrams, models, computer graphics, and formal symbol systems. They are often regarded as embodiments of ideas or concepts. The nature of *internal* representations is more illusive, because they cannot be directly observed. The presence of internal representations in the mind must be inferred from the observation of students at work. They are regarded as cognitive or mental models. They are also referred to as schemas, concepts, conceptions, and mental objects.

The key terms in any theory of representation are "to mean" or "to signify," as they are used to express the link existing between external representation (signifier) and internal representation (signified). However, as Goldin (15) suggests, representations can be more usefully regarded as a system in which elements are combined according to precise rules.

The short analysis we have just made allows us to distinguish the syntax from the semantics. The set of rules for organizing the external representations is referred to as the *syntax*, hence the syntactic level for using representations. In the example of the racing car, the way to read the "value" of each point on the corresponding axis, the conventional orientation of the axis belongs to the syntax. On the other hand, the notions of speed, space, time, the usual car slow-down in a curve—and the way they relate to one another—belong to the semantics. The particular shape of the graph will support the semantics of the representation. Skemp (31) and others make a similar analogical distinction in contrasting the deep structure (internal) of a signifier with its surface level (external).

Uses of external representations can thus be *syntactically driven* in the sense that they can be achieved solely on the symbols themselves, without reference to the internal representations involved (20). This is the case when the algebra exercise "solve $X + 4 = 7$" is solved, using the rules of the external representations such as "move 4 to the other side and change the sign." They can also be considered as *semantically driven* when internal representations are called into play. In the example given above, 4 would be subtracted from both sides of the mental version of the equation in order to keep a balance in the quantities.

Most important, as von Glasersfeld (34, p. 216) mentions, "A representation does not represent by itself—it needs interpreting; to be interpreted, it needs an interpreter." This observation contradicts the view that representations *contain* the knowledge they are meant to convey, a view often described as the container paradigm. According to this view, internal representations are assimilated to information put into external representations and, in this way, they are made "transmittable." The receiver has only to "open up" the message. This view conceals the fact that in knowledge acquisition through the use of representations, *learners are active in a process of interpretation* that depends on the state of their prior knowledge at that instant.

Classifying Representations

External representations can be more or less iconic in the sense that they can more or less suggest in their arrangement or configuration the internal representation to which they relate. (The word "iconic" comes from the Greek *ikon*, which means "image" and has been popularized by user-friendly computer displays.) In that sense, II and III as Roman numerals are more iconic than 2 and 3. The "No Smoking" sign contains both an iconic part (the smoking cigarette) and a noniconic part (the circle with a bar diagonally across it). We shall consider the word "*symbolic*" as equivalent to the word "*noniconic*." The "symbolicity" of an external representation depends mainly on the fact that its arrangement, or the selection of elements constituting it, is done *arbitrarily*. Thus, for noniconic representations, the interpretation process is not helped by any particular feature of the signifier that points to a particular notion or idea. Most mathematical representations are noniconic. Von Glasersfeld (34, p. 221) notes: "It was an arbitrary choice that instituted x as a symbol for an unknown quantity in mathematical notation." However, some mathematical representations turn out to be more *suggestive*, and ease the interpretation. They are then more iconic. For instance, the function-machine encapsulates with arrows and graphical tricks the idea of transformation, and the symbolic combination dy/dx evokes the process behind the notion more than does the configuration y'.

This first distinction was implicitly used by Bruner (5), who can be considered a pioneer in the study of the uses of external representations in learning and reasoning. Piaget insisted on the role of actions in the acquisition of abstract ideas, but is often criticized for having downplayed the importance of the modes of representations. In his systematic discussions of external representations, Bruner distinguishes between enactive, iconic, and symbolic modes of representation, and even suggests that they be regarded as a kind of developmental sequence. (The term *enactive* refers to the activity content of a notion.)

Starting from a different analysis of external representations, Bertin (3) created a useful classification. Generalizations he made from his own domain of research (geography) led him to introduce three main categories of external representations.

The first category, *maps* (see Fig. 5.2), includes the representations that keep a fair degree of similarity with the spacial properties of the objects they represent.

In the second category, external representations exhibit the nature of the relations between two or more variables (in the mathematical sense). Figure 5.3 illustrates representations referred to as *diagrams*. Pie charts, histograms, bar charts, and Cartesian graphs belong to this category (21). The essential idea is to recognize in the

FIGURE 5.2   Map problem

Find the polar coordinates of the town hall of the school

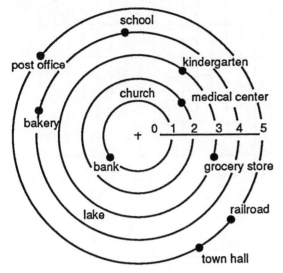

representation two or more curved or straight axes (present or suggested) that relate the variables.

In the third category we have the networks, one of which is illustrated in Figure 5.4 (p. 85). The representations of this class illustrate the relations between events, factors, or individuals. They often show order and level. They may involve time (as in flowcharts) or simply the different steps of an analysis (such as the one done in tree diagrams used in probability).

As may be noted, the criteria behind this classification stem from a study of the pictorial properties of the representations. It is useful to find equivalent ways to depict the same idea and to compare features of diagrams belonging to the same category. Trying to fit a textbook diagram into a specific category is beneficial, in the sense that it gives a tool to examine its properties further. However, classification is of limited use in mathematics education; we must also study more closely the mental processes through which relations between external and internal representations are achieved.

Relating Internal and External Representations

Homonymy.   Distance–time graphs, such as Figure 5.5 (p. 86), appear frequently in textbooks. Students' interpretations of these graphs can be surprising. In the introductory example, the variation of speed or the shape of a track could be associated with the Cartesian graph. Here, the graph can also refer to two different mental objects: a picture of the trip "trajectory" or the change in time of the distance variable. Multiple-referencing features of many graphical representations tend to confuse students.

FIGURE 5.3   Diagrams

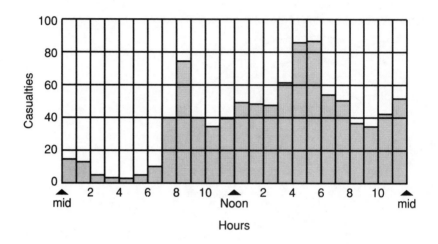

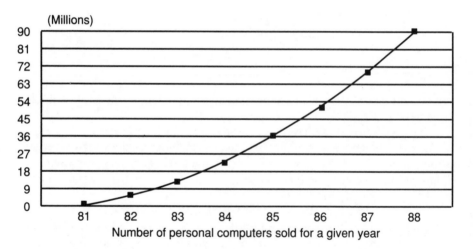

Number of road casualties per hour during a weekday (Monday to Thursday) (33, p. 195)

M. Swan (1985). *The language of functions and graphs* (p. 195). Shell Centre for Mathematical Education, University of Nottingham. Used by permission.

Such a representation behaves like a homonym—a single word having several different meanings, such as bear, bill, club, or close. Hence, this phenomenon is called a homonymy. Note that in Figure 5.6 (p. 86) each arrow stands for exactly one interpretation.

Lay (22) presents several basic examples. He notes that "+" in 3 + 2 may refer to "adding 2 *to* 3" or to "adding 3 and 2 together" (combining 2 and 3). Similarly, Figure 5.7 (p. 87) illustrates the variety of mental objects to which numbers may refer. Solving the equation $2x + 3 = 4$ may refer to finding the "x" for which the

FIGURE 5.4   Network

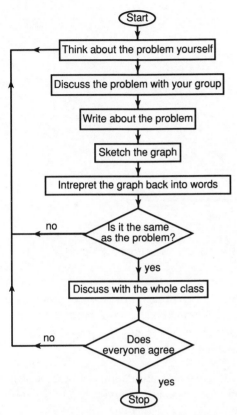

In this lesson, and in several following lessons, the children found that this chart helped them considerably in achieving profitable discussions. (33, p. 220)

M. Swan (1985). *The language of functions and graphs* (p. 220). Shell Centre for Mathematical Education, University of Nottingham. Used by permission.

equality is verified. In that case, x is regarded as an unknown. However, it is also possible that $2x + 3 = 4$ be considered as $2x + 3 = y$ while x varies. In that case, the resulting variable y is likely to take the value 4 for some values of x. Note that in the first interpretation, as Freudenthal (13) judiciously points out, "x" does not vary; it can take only correct values provided the equation can be verified.

Examples of homonymy are numerous in mathematics. The fact that (x, y) stands for a complex number, a point in the plane, or a rational number often brings about confusion in the algorithms performed by students. Similar conditions apply to the "fraction bar" referring ambiguously to a quotient, a fraction, and a ratio. The expression $x^2 + y^2 = r^2$ may describe a Pythagorean relation or define the property of each point (x, y) belonging to a circle of radius r centered at the origin (Fig. 5.8 [p. 88]).

The double referencing of external representations can often be controlled by teachers and mathematicians without their being aware of the rich underlying do-

FIGURE 5.5   Example of homonymy confusion

Describe what happens in this journey.

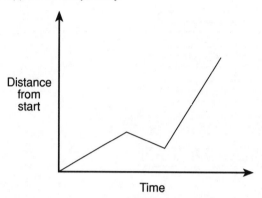

The journey is often interpreted as "going uphill, then downhill, then uphill again" or "climbing a mountain" rather than moving toward and away from the trip origin.

main of internal representations. Teaching is often done on the basis of prominent possible ambiguities such as "x" standing for the variable unknown or for the multiplication. However, the fact that $2x$ can be interpreted geometrically as $x + x$ or 2 times x can be more easily overlooked (see Fig. 5.9 [p. 88]).

Synonymy.   We have considered the case wherein a representation can be associated with different mental objects. The opposite is also possible. Figure 5.10 (p. 89) illustrates the fact that one mental object may be denoted by many representations, just as one idea can be expressed by many synonyms. This special relationship between signifiers and signified ideas is called a *synonymy.*

Synonymy arises from the existence of "equivalent" notations, interchangeable symbols, or representations. For instance, $y = x^2$ defines the function $f(x) = x^2$ that is also written $y(x) = x^2$ or $f : x \rightarrow x^2$. Once a notation is selected for the notion of function, a variety of symbolic representations are available to denote the derivative,

FIGURE 5.6   Homonymy

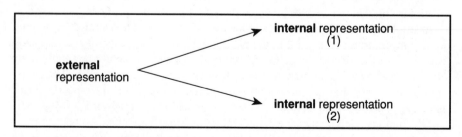

FIGURE 5.7   Representations of number (22, p. 273)

Basic numeral: 5

Array on counters:

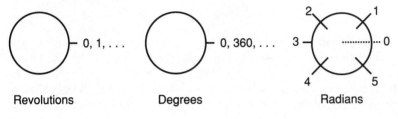

Cardinal number of a set: S = {a, b, c, d, e}   # (S) = 5

Sequence in consecutive order   0 1 2 3 4

Scale for length Measure:

Scale for arc measure:

Revolutions   Degrees   Radians

Ratio of lengths:

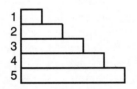

L. C. Lay (1982). Mental images and arithmetical symbols. *Visible Language*, XVI(3), 273. Used by permission.

such as Df, f', dy/dx. The two graphs presented in Figure 5.11 (p. 89) both refer to the inequality $|x - 3| < 5$. Figure 5.12 (p. 89) shows two synonymous ways to denote the set of integers.

As we have mentioned before, the difficulties related to homonymy are easy to overlook, since often the selection of the correct signified idea leading easily to the right answer is done implicitly and from a set of mental objects that teachers may be unaware of.

As Mason (24) mentions, certain uses of symbols become routinized, and the very nature of certain symbols belongs to the routine. Controlling this automaticity is a necessary ingredient to becoming proficient in mathematics. This explains why changing x for t or w in algebraic expressions often causes difficulties for students. The case is even worse when the axes of the Cartesian plane are no longer denoted by x and y. For these reasons (among others), students in the classroom very often show preferences for one particular external representation.

FIGURE 5.8   Example of homonymy, $x^2 + y^2 = r^2$

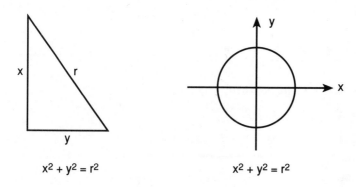

In the case of homonymy, the unicity of the external representation is very easy to check on paper. However, the underlying internal representation in the case of synonymy can only be assumed to be unique. We believe that teachers could at times question the unicity of the mental representations involved, since the aspects that are captured by each external representation are so different in terms of the actions made possible by each.

The situation cannot be made simple, since neither homonymy nor synonymy can be avoided in mathematics: They belong to it per se. Indeed, in the construction of mathematics, relations are established between concepts. Similarity of roles brings about the use of identical external representations; generalization often is achieved by extending the use of internal representations to new objects. For instance, adding real numbers, complex numbers, and matrices can be denoted the same way, but mental operations to which the " + " sign refers are concomitantly different *and* similar. Alternatively, due to different approaches, the richness of certain concepts may lead to the introduction of a diversity of notations: We mentioned: *Df, f'*, and *dy/dx* for derivatives. Symbols are used to distinguish and to unify (22). Distinguishing is done through synonymy, and unifying is achieved through homonymy.

Suggestions from the Researchers

Researchers agree on the objective: Help students by enriching the world of their internal representations so they can more efficiently relate signifiers to corresponding mental objects, and consequently better control their automatic processing of external representations. To put it simply, *go for the meaning, beware of the syntax* can

FIGURE 5.9   Example of homonymy, $2 \times$

FIGURE 5.10   Synonymy

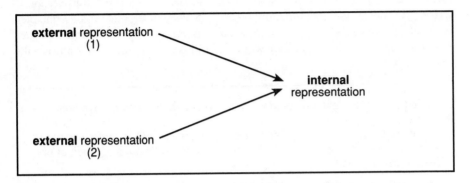

FIGURE 5.11   Different interpretations of absolute value (2, pp. 50–51)

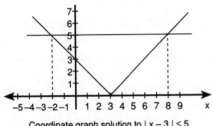

Coordinate graph solution to | x – 3 | ≤ 5

Line graph solution to | x – 3 | ≤ 5

FIGURE 5.12   Different interpretations of the set of integers

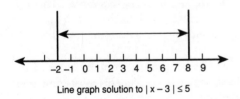

$$Z = \{0, 1, -1, 2, -2, 3, -3, \dots\}$$
$$Z = \{\dots -3, -2, -1, 0, 1, 2, 3, \dots\}$$

D. Ben-Chaim, G. Lappan, R. T. Houang (1989). The role of visualization in the middle school mathematics curriculum. *Focus on Learning Problems in Mathematics* (*Visualization and Mathematics Education, Part One*), 11(1), 50–51. Center for Teaching/Learning Math, Inc. Used by permission.

be regarded as a common guideline. Researchers do not contradict one another; they insist on different aspects of the problem and come up with a variety of principles. Mason (25) and Hiebert (16) are more systematic: They incorporate those principles in global schemes involving precise steps. The accompanying illustration describes Hiebert's scheme. In this chapter we will further illustrate its principles, starting with Mason's scheme.

Hiebert Scheme: How Competence with Written Mathematical Symbols Develops

The theory proposes a succession of cognitive processes that cumulate to yield competence with written mathematical symbols. Five major types of processes are identified.

1. *connecting* individual symbols with referents
2. *developing* symbol manipulation procedures
3a. *elaborating* procedures for symbols
3b. *routinizing* the procedures for manipulating symbols
4. using the symbols and rules as referents for *building* more abstract symbol systems

The third and fourth processes are numbered together because they operate concurrently. (16, p. 335)

Some Basic Principles.   Mason suggests organizing teaching schemes around the idea of a spiral movement based on the enactive–iconic–symbolic distinctions of Bruner. In each loop of this spiral, the students will go from using confidently "manipulable" *external* representations to gain a sense of the *internal* representation, to using the symbolic representation through "*a symbolic record of that sense.*" The next step in the process of instruction is not necessarily going into the next loop of the spiral, but "*at any stage, a question or surprise may induce movement back down the spiral to restore confidence*" (24, p. 75).

We note a progression in the scheme that is based on the iconicity levels of the external representations used. The activities proposed to the students must come from a careful "representational analysis" of the content. The fact that these activities will guide the students to *engage in actions* also characterizes the scheme. Indeed, the student must be active in a planned setting constructed in order to prevent premature introduction of external representations.

This progression stressed in Mason's scheme is aimed at helping students construct internal representations compatible with external representations with which they feel confident. It is mainly achieved by resorting to more primitive representation (enactive and iconic). A greater range and variety of representations in the early stages is recommended (12); they can serve to distinguish and to unify. Skemp (31, p. 287) expresses the same idea: "It is often helpful to use informal, transitional notations as bridges to the formal, highly condensed notations of traditional mathematics". The introduction of the place-holder notation for an unknown, and the use of a sign other than " − " to distinguish negative from positive integers illustrates the application of this principle.

Some researchers insist more on the fact that representations must by *constructed by the students* with the help of the teachers.

> The imposition of external representations that are too distant from the child results in having the child react negatively or causes him difficulties. If one wants to use an external representation in teaching, one needs to take into consideration that it should be as close as possible to children's internal representations. [One frequently overlooks] the large gap that can exist between those used and the one envisaged by the child of the problem situation. (12, pp. 117–118)

Skemp (31), totally in line with this position, adds: "By allowing children to express their thoughts in their own ways to begin with, we are using symbols which are already well attached to their associated concepts (p. 287)."

They both emphasize the fact that the teacher has a lot to learn from this confrontation with the external representations invented by the students: They reveal the nature of the internal representations as they evolve and provide guidelines for further interventions. However, as Dufour-Janvier (12) lucidly mentions: "*Such teaching is very different from traditional teaching . . . it calls for a change of attitude*" (on the part of the teachers) (p. 121).

Multiple Embodiment Principle.   Introduced by Dienes (11), another pioneer in the domain, the notoriety of this principle has made it into a well-established creed, which we will examine in this section. Its common interpretation differs slightly from Dienes's structural view, relating to the "evident" pedagogical fact that to learn any abstract notion, several different embodiments for this abstract concept should be considered, and the student should play with them.

The spiral feature of Mason's approach accounts for this "revisiting." Nowadays, researchers are somewhat divided as to how it should be applied. Many think that the multiple "embodying" should come late. They believe that students should first be allowed to explore a new representational system until it becomes meaningful. Otherwise, students may develop the impression, for example, and that there are abacus calculations and counter calculations, and that they are both different from pencil-and-paper ones (12). Students do not always fully appreciate the fact that two external representations belong to the same concept. In fact, they tend to work on a one-to-one correspondence basis. Furthermore, each iconic representation may refer to one aspect of a notion, and an essential one may go unnoticed.

To summarize: Protesters argue that adding more embodiments does not guarantee a better, more meaningful internal representation of the concept; on the contrary, it keeps the process at the surface level. Teachers should perhaps gather from this debate that there is no royal road to using mathematics representations, and should further attempt to achieve a balance between the *multiple embodiment principle* and the *need for meaningful* (and lengthy) explorations. Sometimes meaningful explorations will take the form of translations.

Translations

As a result of the synonymy phenomenon, very often a concept, a process, or a mathematical object can be represented in different ways. When this is the case, *translations* from one representation to another are possible. As is acknowledged by NCTM standards, such processes are important in mathematics education.

Systematic studies of translations involving the notion of "variable" are reported by Burkhard (6), Swan (32) and Janvier (19). Burkhard uses a translation table, as shown in Figure 5.13, that exemplifies the diversity of translation skills. Each representation (or mode of representation) is listed in the first line and in the first column. Each cell refers to a particular translation: *from* the heading of the line *to* the heading of the column. We shall concentrate on interpretation (first line) and modeling (first column), processes whose importance is emphasized in the NCTM's *Curriculum and Evaluation Standards* (27).

Both processes depend on the ability of the students to associate, using their own words, situation facts with the corresponding graphical features. For Swan (33), *interpretation* amounts to *listening to what graphs say*; and *modeling* corresponds to *how to talk with them*. The introductory example and the time-distance graph (see Fig. 5.4) introduced earlier are interpretation tasks. In the latter case, the ordinate axis refers to the distance from Peter's home. The highest point (with respect to the others) corresponds to the greatest distance away from home, and the steepest segment should be associated with the stretch along which Peter ran the fastest. In each case, what is required from the students is more than being capable of focusing on one single point. Indeed, they must attend to the steepness of the segments and compare top points with the rest of the graph. The students' ability to deal with such processes depends on the familiarity they would have developed with *global features*

FIGURE 5.13   Translation table involving the notion of variable (19, pp. 3.2–3.4)

To / From		Situations Pictures and Verbal Descriptions	Tables	Graphs	Formulas
Situations Pictures and Verbal Descriptions			Modeling Skills (Measuring)	(Descriptive modeling or sketching)	(Analytical modeling)
Tables	Interpretation Skills	Reading		Plotting	Fitting
Graphs		Interpretation	Reading Off		Curve Fitting
Formulae		Parameter Recognition	Computing	Sketching	

NCTM curriculum standards for grades 9–12
Standard 6. Functions
Translate among tabular, symbolic, and graphical representations of functions.
Analyze the effects of parameter changes on the graphs of functions. (27, p. 154)

NCTM curriculum standards for grades 5–8
Standard 2. Mathematics as Communication
Model situations using oral, written, concrete, pictorial, graphical, and algebraic methods.
Standard 10. Statistics
Construct, read, and interpret tables, charts, graphs. (27, pp. 78, 105)

---

of graphs (see Fig. 5.14)—those involving more than one point to be comprehended (19, 32).

If they are not specially trained to handle graphs and their global features at school, it is no surprise that students meet difficulties in interpretation or modeling tasks.

In an *interpretation task*, students start with an external representation (a graph, for example) and try, using words, to specify a situation that fits the representation. *Graphical interpretation is a progressive integration of the various pieces of information conveyed by the graph with the underlying situational background* (29). This

FIGURE 5.14   Description of global features (32, p. 89)

Global Features

1. Maxima and minima
2. Rises, drops, and plateaux
3. Periodicity and symmetry
4. Discontinuity
5. Extrapolation and interpolation
6. Intervals (horizontal and vertical) over which the function image increases/decreases.
7. (Comparison of) two intervals
8. (Comparison of) two gradients
9. Area under graph
10. Translation of a curve (or part of a curve)

M. Swan (1980). *The language of graphs* (first draft) (p. 89). Shell Centre for Mathematical Education, University of Nottingham. Used by permission.

means that the situation guides the interpretation, and this is where we must look for mistakes. Indeed, situations are often characterized by objects or pictures suggested by the verbal descriptions introducing the graphs. Concrete elements belonging to or associated with the situations often *contaminate* the interpretation in the sense that they will determine the meaning attached to parts of the graphical representation. Results on the racing car speed–time problem (introductory) and on the distance–time graph (Fig. 5.5) have already been presented. The tide graph (Fig. 5.15) can be misinterpreted as the actual shape of the wave. In fact, in the introductory (racing-car) example, students sometimes switch from the track interpretation to the speed interpretation and vice-versa (17).

When the difficult notion of rate of change is involved, pictures or real-life features are likely to surface in the reasoning. This sort of contamination may induce other kinds of subtle errors, such as height-for-slope, height-for-difference, or slope-for-curvature (7). A well-known example of the height-for-slope error is the identification of the tide's being high with the fact that it goes up fast.

An alternative presentation for interpretation problems is asking students to select, from a multiple-choice setting, an element that would have produced the graph. The introductory example could have provided a selection of tracks from which to choose (see Fig. 5.16). Problems of this kind can be confusing, since the multiple-choice display can induce the contamination expected. In the bottle problem, Figure 5.17, one notes that one graph "reproduces" the shape of the bottle.

With *modeling* exercises, students are given a description of a situation and then are required to produce a "more abstract" external representation that characterizes it. Sometimes the situation is defined with the help of a drawing or a photograph. The introductory example can be turned into a modeling exercise if the shape of the track is provided and sketching a graph is required (see Fig. 5.18 [p. 96]). Difficulties with modeling problems are easy to imagine: Parts of the bottle or the track will show up in the graphs sketched by the students.

Modeling requires that the convention for producing the target representation be respected. Common mistakes include "forgetting" (because of the motion suggested by the situation), the left-to-right or upward direction used in sketching graphs.

FIGURE 5.15   The harbor tide (19, p. 3.20)

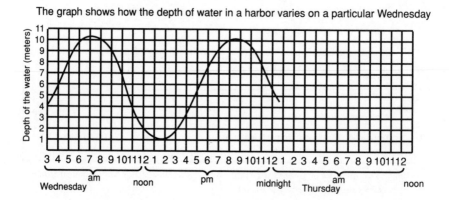

The graph shows how the depth of water in a harbor varies on a particular Wednesday

FIGURE 5.16 The racetrack problem with possible tracks (33, p. 88)

The graph shows how the speed of a racing car varies during the second lap of a race.

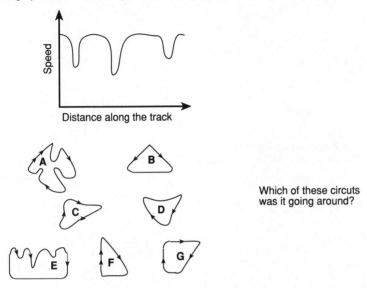

Which of these circuts
was it going around?

M. Swan (1985). *The language of functions and graphs* (p. 88). Shell Centre for Mathematical Education, University of Nottingham. Used by permission.

The process "written description→formula" has been widely researched (8, 30, 35). The following problem has become a legend in the research community: Write an equation using the variables S and P to represent the following statement: *There are six times as many students as professors at this university.* Use S for the number of students and P for the number of professors. Contaminations coming from the initial mode of representation have been discovered. The predominant wrong answer is the formula $6S = P$. More than a third of engineering undergraduates tested made this error. The formula $6S = P$ is the result of changing "six times as many students" into "six times the number of students" (8).

This kind of response leads us to believe that the contamination, in this case, comes from the transposition into the formula of written linguistic patterns that conflict with the analysis of the exact relation. We think that linguistic structures appear to be important since, with the same problem, the expression "as many as" has led students with Spanish as their primary language (and having a questionable command of the English language) to prefer the answer $6S = 6P$ (8). However, some students are less attracted by linguistic patterns and they simply base their reasoning on matching a set of one P with a set of 6S (34). Reports indicate that most students can easily be prompted out of this mistake (34).

Artigues and Sweed (1), looking at the French curriculum, and Janvier (18), for the British School Mathematics Project (SMP) program, have found that translation skills involving the notion of "variable" are practically absent from these programs.

FIGURE 5.17   The bottle problem (33, p. 94)

Filling Bottles
The graph below shows how the height of liquid in a bottle
varies as water is steadily dripped into it.

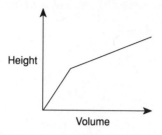

Here are 6 bottles.
Choose the correct bottle corresponding to the graph.

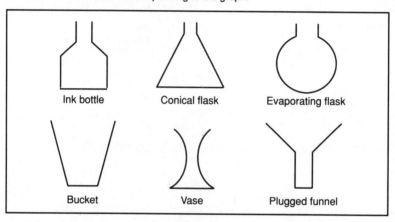

M. Swan (1985). *The language of functions and graphs* (p. 94). Shell Centre for Mathematical
Education, University of Nottingham. Used by permission.

FIGURE 5.18   Sketching the speed of a racing car as a modeling exercise
(19, p. A 3.6)

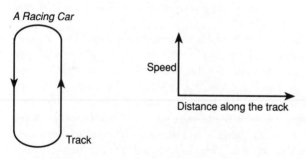

Sketch a graph to show how the speed of a racing car varies during the second lap of a race.

R. Lesh, M. Behr, T. Post (1987). Rational number relations and proportions. In C. Janvier (Ed.),
Problems of representation in the teaching and learning of mathematics (pp. 45, 47). Lawrence
Erlbaum Associates, Inc., Hillside, NJ. Used by permission.

96

On the other hand, translations involving the notions of fractions and rational numbers are numerous in most textbooks. Lesh, Post, and Behr (23) report that (1) the easiest translations go from a written fraction or a ratio to the same one written in a different form; (2) translations involving written language are easier than translations involving symbols; and (3) translations to pictures are easier than translations from pictures (Fig. 5.19). However, these observations are not corroborated by Clements and Del Campo (9), who insist on distinguishing between the translations in which students are given a set of representations to select from and the translations in which the students are asked to produce their own external representations.

FIGURE 5.19   Translation problems on fractions and rational numbers
(23, pp. 45–47)

Translation from Written Symbols

What picture shows 2/3 shaded?

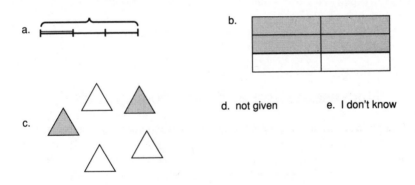

a.

b.

c.

d. not given   e. I don't know

Translation from Static Picture

What fraction is shaded in the picture below?

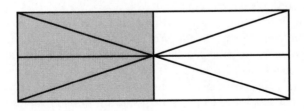

a. 4/4   b. 1/2   c. 1/1   d. not given   e. I don't know

Suggestions from the Researchers

In the case of fractions and rational numbers, spoken language (often as internal speech) is used to control the translations and select the appropriate elements; manipulative models also play a central role (23).

• Exercises must be talked through.
• Teaching should stress the importance of manipulatives.

An efficient teaching of translation skills implies that students must view the translations from both directions (18).

• Opposite translations ("graph→formula" and " formula→graph") should be tackled in pairs.
• Modeling skills can develop only when combined with the corresponding interpretation skills.

Teaching practices and curriculum design must take into account the fact that the "act of representing" is plural, unstable, and evolving (23).

• Students seem to handle simultaneously several representations when reasoning— at least on most problems.
• The particular procedure that students use in combining those representations may vary from problem to problem.
• As students become more familiar with the representations, the set of heuristics they use is likely to evolve.

Representation and Microcomputers

The introduction of microcomputers has altered mathematics content and teaching methods alike. Numerous journals and books now regularly cite the latest innovations and discuss new teaching schemes, as well as experimental projects. Research on the use of technology is discussed in Chapter 11; here our focus is on representations research that provides guidelines for software and computer use.

Because conventional graphs invite misinterpretation, manipulating pieces of a graph on a computer screen can lead to further problems. Using the right scale is necessary in identifying specific features of a curve representing a given equation (10, 14, 28). Although knowing where to look on a graph, and what to ignore, depends on prior knowledge, we need to develop less ambiguous representations and learn more about students' misinterpretations (10).

Today, sensing devices that plug into computers can collect data such as temperature or rate from scientific experiments. Yet research investigating students' abilities to execute experiments and interpret the computer-displayed graphical representations has shown inconsistent results (26, 4). Researchers nevertheless continue to try to track down the "right" pedagogical approach—one combining teachers' interventions and computer support in efforts to help students develop abilities to translate among modes of representation.

On the whole, research on computer use has neglected to start from a sufficiently developed theoretical foundation on representations. As a consequence, we note an absence of general criteria for assessing uses of software and for identifying the essential feature that make it successful.

Conclusion

Is a representation really worth a thousand words? We hope that the reader is now convinced that reality is not so simple: Several conditions must be met for representations to become meaningful. The thousand words in or behind a representation should be viewed as a seed that "contains" a plant. The ground must be rich to welcome it, and then there is the inevitable time factor. The understanding of external representations by students requires that teachers take into account the relevant intellectual or mental experiences that accompany the external representations.

Looking Ahead . . .

The more I think about this duality of corresponding internal and external representations, the more I wonder about the concepts or notions belonging to mathematics. How do they exist per se? Are they really independent of their external representations? Do scientists, engineers, and statisticians have their own internal representations, even though they use more or less "our" external representations? I believe that a central goal for research in mathematics education should be this: probing further the nature of internal representations in mathematics reasoning.

Claude Janvier

Writing this article has led us to look closer at and delve deeper into our students' understanding of the numerous external representations presented in textbooks or used in the classroom. We have found, on many occasions, that a multiplicity of approaches is required to make sure that more students understand. We have been surprised to find that a slight change in the form of an external representation, such as writing $y = mx + b$ rather than $f(x) = mx + b$, makes such a difference, and this encourages us to be more sensitive to the differences in students' methods and answers. In practice, before tackling the solution of a problem with the class, we like to ask students for a reformulation of the problem in words, with a diagram and/or whatever else they like. This helps us discover new representations that are potentially more meaningful to our students. Our conviction is that good teaching on our part depends on how we listen to and interpret everything that comes from our classes, and that mistakes *can* be pedagogically be useful.

Catherine Girardon
Jean-Charles Morand

About the Authors

Claude Janvier is professor and researcher at Université du Québec à Montréal (Mathematics and Computer Science Department) where he is also involved in the training of secondary level mathematics teachers. After his PhD work was completed in Nottingham (England), Dr. Janvier conducted several subsidized research projects on the use of graphical representations in mathematics and science reasoning. He has published and presented several technical papers on representations at international conferences.

Catherine Girardon has many years' experience teaching mathematics at the secondary level. Understanding how students comprehend is a lifetime endeavor for her. She believes that keeping in touch with research is basic to performing the best one can in class. She has recently completed a degree with a research study on students' conceptions of transformations. Her end-of-career challenge: supervising university students in practice teaching.

Jean-Charles Morand is a teacher of mathematics with 25 years of experience. As he says: "I kept the *feu sacré* (enthusiasm) after all those years because I like mathematics and the contact I have with students through it." He has taught all grades at the secondary level, with students of all abilities, and has been involved as a textbook writer. He believes that keeping the spirit of a researcher is important. Recently, he completed a graduate program involving an investigation of students' conception of circle.

References

1. ARTIGUE, M., & SWED, T. (1984). Programmes et manuels de mathématiques. Représentations graphiques. *Publication no 30 de l'IREM de Paris VII.*
*2. BEN–CHAIM, D., LAPPAN, G., & HOUANG, R. T. (1989). The role of visualization in the Middle School Mathematics Curriculum. *Focus on Learning Problems in Mathematics (Visualization and Mathematics Education, Part One),* 11(1), 50–51.
3. BERTIN, J. (1967). *Sémiologie graphique: les diagrammes, les réseaux, les cartes.* Paris: Mouton.
4. BRASELL, H. (1987). The effect of real-time laboratory graphing on learning graphic representations of distance and velocity. *Journal of Research in Science Teaching,* 24(4), 385–395.
5. BRUNER, J. S. (1966). *Toward a theory of instruction.* Cambridge, MA: Belknap Press of Harvard University Press.
6. BURKHARD, H. (1977). *Seven sevens are fifty? Mathematics for the real world. Inaugural lecture.* Shell Centre for Mathematics Education Publication, University of Nottingham.
7. CLEMENT, J. (1989). The concept of variation and misconceptions in cartesian graphing. *Focus on Learning Problems in Mathematics,* 11(1–2), 77–87.
8. CLEMENT, J., LOCKHEAD, J., & MONK, G. (1981). Translation difficulties in learning mathematics. *American Mathematical Monthly,* 88, 289–290.
9. CLEMENTS, M. A., & DEL CAMPO, G. (1989). Linking verbal knowledge, visual images, and episodes for mathematical learning. In *Focus on Learning Problems in Mathematics,* 11, 25–33.
10. DEMANA, F., & WAITS, B. K. (1988). Pitfalls in graphical computation, or why a single graph isn't enough. *College Mathematics Journal,* 19, 177–185.
11. DIENES, Z. P. (1964). The power of mathematics. London: Hutchinson Educational.

12. DUFOUR–JANVIER, B., BEDNARZ, N., & BÉELANGER, M. (1987). Pedagogical considerations concerning the problem of representation. In C. Janvier (Ed.), Problems of representation in the teaching and learning of mathematics (pp. 109–122). Hillsdale, NJ: Erlbaum.

13. FREUDENTAL, H. (1982). Variables and functions. In G. van Barneveld & H. Krabbendam (Eds.), Conference on Functions (pp.7–20). Enschede, The Netherlands: Mathematics Department of the "National Institute for Curriculum Development."

14. GOLDENGERG, E. P., HARVEY, W., LEWIS, P. G., UMIKER, R. J., WEST, J., & ZODHIATES, P. (1988). Mathematical, technical, and pedagogical challenges in the graphical representations of functions. Newton, MA: Education Development Center Inc.

15. GOLDIN, G. A. (1987). Cognitive representational systems for mathematical problem solving. In C. Janvier (Ed.), Problems of representation in the teaching and learning of mathematics (pp. 59–65). Hillsdale, NJ: Erlbaum.

16. HIEBERT, J. (1988). A theory of developing competence with written mathematical symbols. Educational Studies in Mathematics, 19, 333–355.

17. JANVIER, C. (1981). Les graphiques cartésiens comme mode de représentations: rôle du langage et nature des traductions. Séminaire de didactique et pédagogie des mathématiques, n° 25, mai. I.M.A.G. Université de Grenoble.

18. JANVIER, C. (1978). The interpretation of complex Cartesian graphs representing situations-studies and teaching experiments (Doctoral dissertation, University of Nottingham, England).

19. JANVIER, C. (1987). Translation processes in Mathematics education. In C. Janvier (Ed.), Problems of representation in the teaching and learning of mathematics (pp. 27–32). Hillsdale, NJ: Erlbaum.

20. KAPUT, J. J. (1987). Toward a theory of symbol use in mathematics. In C. Janvier (Ed.), Problems of representation in the teaching and learning of mathematics (pp.159–195). Hillsdale, NJ: Erlbaum.

21. KERSLAKE, D. (1977). The understanding of graphs. Mathematics in Schools, 6(2).

22. LAY, L. C. (1982). Mental images and arithmetical symbols. Visible Language, XVI(3), 259–274.

23. LESH, R., POST, T., & BEHR, M. (1987). Representations and translations among representations in mathematics learning and problem solving. In C. Janvier (Ed.), Problems of representation in the teaching and learning of mathematics (pp. 33–40). Hillsdale, NJ: Erlbaum.

24. MASON, J. H. (1987). What do symbols represent? In C. Janvier (Ed.), Problems of representation in the teaching and learning of mathematics (pp. 73–81). Hillsdale, NJ: Erlbaum.

25. MASON, J. H. (1980). When is a symbol symbolic? For the Learning of Mathematics, 1 (2), 8–12.

26. MOKROS, J. R., & TINKER, R. F. (1987). The impact of microcomputer-based labs on children's ability to interpret graphs. Journal of Research in Science Teaching, 24(4), 369–383.

*27. NATIONAL COUNCIL OF TEACHERS OF MATHEMATICS (1989). Curriculum and evaluation standards for school mathematics. Reston, VA: Author.

28. PREECE, J. (1985). Interpreting trends in a graph: A study of 14 and 15 year olds. Unpublished doctoral dissertation, Open University, England.

29. PREECE, J., & JANVIER, C. (1992). Interpreting trends in multiple-curve graphs of ecological situations: the role of context. International Journal of Science Education, 14.

30. SIMS–KNIGHT, J. E., & KAPUT, J. (1983). Exploring difficulties in translating between

natural language and image based representations and abstract symbols systems of mathematics. In D. R. Rogers and J. A. Sloboda (Eds.), *The acquistion of symbolic skills*. New York: Plenum.

31. SKEMP, R. R. (1982). Communicating mathematics: Surface structures and deep structures. *Visible Language*, XVI(3) 281–288.

*32. SWAN, M. (1980). *The language of graphs* (First Draft). Shell Centre for Mathematical Education, University of Nottingham.

*33. SWAN, M. (1985). *The language of functions and graphs: An examination module for secondary schools*. Shell Centre for Mathematics Education. University of Nottingham, Joint Matriculation Board of Manchester, England.

34. VON GLASERSFELD, E. (1987). Preliminaries to any theory of representation. In C. Janvier (Ed.), *Problems of representation in the teaching and learning of mathematics* (pp. 215–225). Hillsdale, NJ: Erlbaum.

35. WOLLMAN, W. (1983). Determining the sources of error in a translation from sentence to equation. *Journal for Research in Mathematics Education, 14*, 169–181.

CHAPTER 6

Improving the General Mathematics Experience

Harold L. Schoen and David Hallas

Most nights, Myrna remembered something interesting or enjoyable that had happened in school that day, but this was the first time she could recall being excited about her general mathematics class. The class had worked in small groups on some very challenging problems that had to do with a salesman going to four towns connected by some roads (Fig. 6.1). The problem was to find a way for the salesman in town A to visit all four towns and return without going over a road twice. It was fun to try different ways and to talk to her classmates as they attempted to solve the problem, too. Once they had a solution they tried starting at a different town, adding or removing a road, and then adding a town with another road or two. In some cases, but not others, there was a way for the salesman to get to all the towns, traveling no road twice. Her group had talked for a long time about a rule for when it could be done. Myrna was sure there was one, but she was still trying to get it straight in her mind.

It was too bad, Myrna thought, that general mathematics was not like that every day. Her first-year teacher, Ms. Wayne, did not usually seem to enjoy her general mathematics class, and neither did most of the students. Most days, Ms. Wayne briefly reviewed some computational methods, like operations with fractions, and then the class practiced at their seats. Myrna found that to be very boring and frustrating. She had been practicing these same operations in her mathematics classes for several years, but she had no idea why the operations worked and why she seemed to make the same mistakes over and over. Like most of her general mathematics classmates, she thought of herself as very inept at mathematics. Today had been great, because she had a chance to think and talk with her classmates about interesting problems. She even forgot that she was poor at mathematics, and Ms. Wayne seemed to enjoy the class, too.

In this chapter we summarize the research on secondary school general mathematics courses like the one just alluded to. We also describe the characteristics of the students and make research-based recommendations for both the curriculum of and instruction in these courses.

Present Practice

At present, significant numbers of U.S. students as young as 12 or 13 years are being sorted into mathematics curricula that offer little intellectual challenge, seriously limit their chances for success in many fields of study (in high school and beyond) and greatly restrict their career choices in today's society. (19, p. xiii)

Not only are students in the United States not achieving up to our expectations in mathematics (5), but their average achievement level pales by comparison to that of age-mates from many other countries (31). Although these facts have been highly publicized by the popular media, by themselves they offer little guidance toward a solution to the problem. It is fortunate (though less newsworthy) that both the National Assessment of Educational Progress (NAEP) and the Second International Mathematics Study (SIMS) go beyond a simple reporting of achievement levels by attempting to relate achievement to curriculum characteristics and course-taking patterns. Such information at least provides some direction for addressing the achievement deficiencies.

Sample NAEP item with grade 11 data:

Jane rode 8 miles east, then 6 miles north, from her home to school. If she had ridden straight from home to school, how far would she have ridden?

Miles	Percent
6	19%
8	32%
10*	35%
14	13%

(*correct answer)

FIGURE 6.1   Network of towns

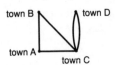

In grade eight in the U.S., SIMS researchers identified four dramatically different types of curricula, which they roughly categorized as *remedial, typical, enriched,* and *algebra* (19). These researchers also found a clear correspondence between mathematics courses completed by students, and their mathematical proficiency—a finding verified by the 1986 NAEP data (5). The curriculum in the remedial courses is dominated by grade school arithmetic, such as common and decimal fractions and percentages. Little instructional time is devoted to topics in other areas of mathematics.

This course description is further detailed by Madsen-Nason and Lanier (18), who report that the high school general mathematics course they studied was virtually a repeat of content covered in middle school. These researchers also found that in general mathematics, compared to algebra in the same school, teachers expected much less of the students, and students exhibited a more negative attitude, a higher absentee rate, and more disruptive behavior. General mathematics classes also lack the "ripple effect" seen in algebra classes, where a core group of students often grasp content quickly and respond to the teacher at critical moments, in these ways, helping the noncore students to learn the content more readily. Perhaps this is to be expected if, as one might suppose, the students in general mathematics are less able than those in algebra. However, in Madsen-Nason and Lanier's sample, many of the general mathematics students had scored as well as or better than some of the algebra students on a standardized achievement test administered during the previous year.

What percent of high school students enroll in general mathematics? According to nationally representative data from NAEP in 1986, 19% of 17-year-olds reported that they had completed *no* mathematics course beyond general mathematics. The percent of students in this category differed significantly by ethnic group (25% of Hispanics, 31% of African Americans, and 17% of whites), and by the nature of the student's high school program. Forty-eight percent of all 17-year-old students reported being in a high school program that was not college preparatory. Most of these students completed a general mathematics course, but over 30% of them completed no mathematics beyond that (5).

Like Hispanics and African Americans, students from families below the poverty level are overrepresented in remedial mathematics programs. For example, as Slavin (28) points out, federal Chapter I funds are used within schools to provide remediation for students according to their educational needs and with no reference to their family's income. Yet, 42% of Chapter 1 students are from poverty-level families, a representation that is fully twice the percent of all students from families below the poverty level.

Discussions of the consequences of such a low level of mathematical sophistication for not merely the individual student but American society as a whole abound in the literature. For the students, often poor and/or minority, consequences range from exclusion from many career options to inability as an adult to make sense of the barrage of data from the media and other sources (21). "The study of mathematics can help develop critical habits of mind—to distinguish evidence from anecdote, to recognize nonsense, to understand chance, and to value proof" (22, p. 8). In fact, because of the relatively low level of mathematical literacy of our citizens (and perhaps of our journalists, as well), the quantitative content of popular media reports in this country is kept simpler than that in Japan (29).

The final and perhaps most disturbing consequence of the present crisis in mathematics education is beyond the scope of this article but needs to be mentioned anyway. America is facing a severe shortage of mathematicians, scientists, engineers, and mathematics teachers—especially among women, African Americans, and Hispanics. The political and economic ramifications of this shortage could be devastating, especially since the proportion of our population in these underrepresented minority groups is growing rapidly (22).

In summary: The prevailing approach in U.S. high schools to accommodating low-achieving or slow-learning students in mathematics is tracking. The typical remedial track, general mathematics course repeats many ideas from sixth-grade arithmetic, focusing primarily on computing with paper and pencil and solving routine word problems. The population of low achievers contains an overrepresentation of poor, Hispanic, and African American students. Teacher expectations and student outcomes are much lower in these courses, as compared to such academic or college preparatory courses as algebra. There are exceptions to this approach to teaching mathematics to low achievers, both in this country and abroad. Some of the more promising, research-based practices will be discussed in later sections. But first, in the next section, we will describe these learners in more detail.

Learner Characteristics

Slow learners, no less than other human beings, are unique individuals. Each has his own set of strengths and weaknesses; each defies a stereotype. Yet in some respects they are alike; for it is common to find them deficient in affective functioning as well as in cognitive functioning. In fact, if slow learners in mathematics do share any common characteristic, it is probably that of a poor self-image with respect to mathematics. (25, p. 22)

In this section we discuss both affective and cognitive characteristics of general mathematics students.

Affective Characteristics

Affective issues are related to cognitive ones for all learners in any learning environment, but the nature of that relationship differs from student to student. For many slow learners, affect appears to be particularly important in explaining inadequate cognitive outcomes (25, 28). Knowing that slow learners tend to have a poor self-image with respect to mathematics, however, says nothing about why the problem exists or how to address it.

Some of the cause lies with factors that are unrelated to the school environment. Family poverty and its social and emotional consequences certainly contribute to the affective problems of some low achievers in mathematics. Schools cannot be blamed for problems in the students' home lives, but their experiences in school often have been part of the problem rather than of the solution. Repeated failure and endless frustrations lead them to a sense of powerlessness, fear, and shame. Identification as a low achiever, placement in the lower track, and the accompanying lowered expectations of teachers and the inevitably repetitious, boring curriculum all contribute to the students' low self-esteem (6, 20, 25). For minority students, this situation is often compounded by a cultural mismatch between home and in-school environments (26, 30).

Have your students complete sentences like these:
I like best the kind of teacher who . . .
When faced with a difficult math problem, I . . .
One thing I would like to learn how to do better is . . .

Especially pertinent for mathematics teachers are their students' emotions and beliefs *about* mathematics and their ability to *do* mathematics. Concerning emotions, there has been some publicity in the past twenty years about a condition called "mathematics anxiety," a strong reaction of panic to any mathematical task (1). Mathematics anxiety appears to be closely related to other affective and cognitive variables and, for the most part, has been studied in connection with them (20).

Students' beliefs about the nature of mathematics (especially school mathematics) are powerful affective forces in any mathematics class, but especially in a general mathematics class. Borasi (1) has identified several such commonly held beliefs. For example, general mathematics students are likely to believe that learning mathematics is a matter of practice alone, so they resist attempts by the teacher to get them to reason about or understand mathematical ideas. Most general mathematics students believe that a mathematics problem should be solvable in a few minutes by a single method that yields one right answer, so they give up on any problem that they cannot solve quickly. They are also likely to believe that a good teacher should make everything crystal clear for them, so they resist those teaching methods that include some ambiguity.

Another affective area that has received a great deal of attention from researchers is causal attribution. Attribution theorists examine the explanations that students give for their success or failure and relate these attributions to their motivation to achieve (12). For example, students who think that their success in mathematics is due to high ability or effort will be motivated to learn mathematics. On the other hand, students who think that their failure is due to low ability or the difficulty of the material will not expect to learn mathematics and will not be motivated to study the subject (12). Unfortunately, many low achievers in mathematics fall into this last category. (More information on attribution theory can be found in Chapter 2.)

Cognitive Characteristics

Developmental researchers, drawing primarily from the work of Jean Piaget and his followers, describe adolescence as the period when children grow out of the stage of concrete operations in which their thinking has been totally dependent on perceptions and specific experiences. In the stage that follows (namely, formal operations), students "can internalize thought, think about thinking, keep two or more variables in mind at one time, and see a concept as part of a larger system" (6, p. 15).

One of the most fundamental characteristics of formal operational thinking is the ability to deal with hypothetical problems—that is, to consider the possible, rather than being restricted to tangible reality. For example, when confronted by a statement prefixed by "Suppose coal is white . . ," a concrete operational student will declare that coal is black, and cannot proceed. A formal operational student, on the other hand, is able to accept the hypothesis that coal is white, and reason from it.

Ask yourself: Do your students follow an inductive or deductive argument more easily? Do you use more inductive or deductive arguments?

A majority of students enter the formal operations stage between the ages of 12 and 14, but for many students, and especially low achievers, the process is much slower and indeed may never be completed. Some of the thinking that is required to understand fully ideas of variable, geometric properties, and proof as they are presented in the usual courses for college-intending students surely requires formal thought. Before arguing for no algebra or geometry for general mathematics students, however, two points need to be considered. First, algebraic and geometric topics can be addressed much more concretely than they are in present courses, and we argue for precisely that later in this chapter. Second, the Piagetian development theory should not be viewed as a reason to limit students' experiences. Rather, it suggests that enriched concrete experiences should be provided in order to enhance cognitive development (3).

Researchers disagree about the direct implications of Piaget's work for curriculum and instruction, but it has surely had a profound effect on the direction of research in mathematics education. It has changed the focus of research from statistically comparing the achievement test outcomes of two contrasting programs of instruction to analyzing students and teachers as they learn and teach particular mathematical concepts and processes (3). More information on theories of cognition can be found in Chapter 1.

A stage theory of the development of student thinking in geometry has received a great deal of attention recently. The van Hiele stages are based on the work of the Dutch educators P. M. van Hiele and D. van Hiele-Geldof. The van Hiele theory describes the development of key concepts and modes of thinking required in synthetic, Euclidean geometry—that is, in the traditional high school course in this country. The model proposes a means for identifying a student's level of geometric maturity and suggests ways to help students to progress through the levels. The emphasis is on instruction rather than maturation, a characteristic that clearly distinguishes it from Piaget's work (4). The details of van Hiele theory are given in Chapter 8. For purposes of this chapter, we note that low achievers are likely to be at lower levels of geometric thinking and, therefore, that they will require many concrete experiences in geometry. The van Hiele theory is a guide for providing such experiences.

By definition, low achievers also have more misconceptions about, and make more errors when dealing with, mathematical content. Describing and interpreting students' misconceptions and errors in specific content domains has been the focus of much recent research—research helpful for guiding remediation plans, and so particularly pertinent for teachers of low achievers. Some topical areas of interest for secondary school in which a great deal is known about student misconceptions are algebra, including variables, equations, functions, and graphs (9), geometry (4), and probability (27). Since most of the results in these areas are described in other chapters, we will not include a general discussion here. However, as an example, we will cite some of the pertinent results on misconceptions in graphing, in our section on research-based teaching suggestions.

In summary: Low achievers in mathematics are likely to have low self-esteem, at least with regard to their ability to do mathematics. Their beliefs about the nature of mathematics and how it is taught and learned are very narrow and rule-bound. In the cognitive domain, they often are concrete operational. In specific content areas, they are likely to have many misconceptions and little technical proficiency. Recent research has resulted in descriptions and explanations of students' most common misconceptions and errors. This research provides a basis for our next-section suggestions for revising current practice in general mathematics courses.

New Directions for General Mathematics

It is pointless to give these (slower) pupils the same diet of elementary mathematics again and again which they then fail to master again and again. On the contrary, it is possible for such pupils to make progress and to gain in competence. (17, p. 232)

This section comprises two parts. The first describes a recommendation for a core curriculum for all students, giving several content examples of this curriculum as it pertains to low achievers. This first part also provides the framework with which to interpret the content of the second part, which concerns remediation.

A Core Curriculum for All Students

The NCTM *Curriculum and Evaluation Standards for School Mathematics* (21) recommends that all students in grades 9–12 be required to complete at least three years of mathematical study that revolves around a core curriculum differentiated in terms of depth and breadth of treatment and the nature of applications. Other recent curriculum recommendations lend strong support to this recommendation (e.g., 22, 23). Implementing a core curriculum would dramatically change the nature of the differentiation that now occurs in high school mathematics. Instead of the present general mathematics that is a repeat of much of the paper-and-pencil computation in sixth-grade mathematics, all students would study a central core of mathematical thinking and processing. They all would thus experience the full range of topics in the high school curriculum (algebra, geometry, trigonometry, probability, statistics, and discrete mathematics), although for those not intending to go to college the treatment would be more concrete, the symbolism and reasoning less formal, and the applications less complex.

Visa accounts paid approximately $6 billion in finance charges in 1985. Have your students investigate how the finance charges are computed.

Next, several examples of this approach to topics from different mathematical areas are sketched. These topics would be presented in such a way as to promote at least one of the three transitions to high school mathematics as described by Hirsch and Lappan (10)—namely, from number to variable, from specific to general, and from description to proof. Noting that most low achievers still need to complete these transitions, Hirsch and Schoen (11) present the following example of a concrete treatment of a problem involving recurrence relations:

> In a planned-growth community the population increases by 100 each year. If the current population is 8,000, what will be the population five years from now? Ten years from now? What will it be n years from now? (p. 698)

The first two questions serve as an experiential base from which students can formulate the recurrence relation $P(n) = P(n-1) + 100$, where $P(0) = 8,000$. Variations on this linear growth model furnish students at this level with further settings for thinking recursively. An extension to geometric growth for somewhat more able students follows:

> Suppose the aforementioned population of 8,000 is not controlled but increases at an average growth rate of 3 percent per year. What will be the population five years from now? Ten years from now? What will it be n years from now? (11, p. 698)

Again, experiences in answering the first two questions will lead to the general recurrence relation: $P(n) = P(n-1) + 0.03P(n-1)$ where $P(0) = 8,000$.

The next example would help facilitate the transitions from number to variable and from specific to general. Consider the following problem:

> In a city with two newspapers, the *Bugle* pays 10 cents a paper for delivery, whereas the *Planet*, pays a daily fee of 75 cents plus 8 cents per paper. Which is the better deal?

This is the sort of situation that invites exploration (13). Students should begin by trying specific numbers and organizing the results in a table.

Number of papers	"The Bugle"	"The Planet"
10	10(10) = 100	75 + 8(10) = 155
20	10(20) = 200	75 + 8(20) = 235
30	10(30) = 300	75 + 8(30) = 315
40	10(40) = 400	75 + 8(40) = 395
50	10(50) = 500	75 + 8(50) = 475

Students should be required to write numerical expressions for their calculations. It is from repeating the same calculations in different specific instances that students are able to discern patterns and to generalize. Once students are able to use variables to express numerical relationships, they can learn to use a computer spreadsheet to do the arithmetic. The following question is a natural extension.

> For what number of papers is the pay less for delivering the *Bugle* than for delivering the *Planet?* For what number of papers is the pay the same?

Students who investigate problems using computer-generated tables see the value of expressing relationships using variables, and they learn that variables and variable expressions really *do* vary (8).

Concerning the concepts of variable and equation: There is a great deal of research about common misconceptions and concrete ways of developing these ideas that are appropriate for low achievers. These are described in detail in the Chapter 7 in this book, and in Driscoll (6).

A geometry topic that can be addressed in a very concrete way is the "shortest path" problem. This particular version comes from *Geometry: A Guided Inquiry*, published by Sunburst Communications, Inc. It is illustrated by Figure 6.2.

> A camper has a campsite in a clearing next to a straight river. He is at point A and his tent is at point B. He sees a spark leap from his campfire and set his tent aflame. Fortunately he is carrying a pail. At what point P on the river should he fill his pail so as to make his path to the fire as short as possible?

Students can use centimeter graph paper to make a scale drawing of the situation, using a scale of 1 cm = 100 ft. They should try various positions for point P along the river, starting at C and moving to D in increments of 100 ft. Besides measuring the total distance of the path from A to P to B, they should also measure the angles of approach and departure at P. Students should record their results in a table. Using that table, they should be able to tell approximately where P should be located so that AP + PB is minimized and how the angle measures compare at that point P. Perhaps working in small groups, they should then make conjectures about a general method of locating P. (This problem could also be solved using the *Geometric Supposer* software from Sunburst.)

FIGURE 6.2   Locating P to minimize AP + PB

(two points off a line or river, with distances marked)

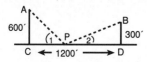

Many probability and statistics topics can be presented in interesting yet concrete ways, too. An example is the following problem (2).

> The Cookie Bin is a small shop that bakes and sells cookies at an indoor shopping mall. The owner plans to introduce a new bite-sized chocolate chip cookie, to be called "Chippies," to her line of products. She would like to have each cookie contain at least five chocolate chips. To minimize the cost of ingredients, she wants to determine the least number of chocolate chips that needs to be mixed into a batch of dough for a dozen Chippies so as to meet the five-chip-per-cookie minimum. How many chocolate chips should she use for each batch?

One approach is to gather data using a computer program provided by Channell (2) that simulates the process of randomly distributing chips to the twelve cookies until each has at least five chips, and then recording the number of chips it took. Groups of students can run the program a large number of times to gather data. The next step is to organize the data. A stem-and-leaf plot is a good way to do this. Figure 6.3 shows such a plot of the distribution of the number of chips required until each of the twelve cookies had at least five chips in over 100 runs of the computer simulation program.

Students can use the stem-and-leaf plot to answer such questions as the following:

> What number of chips will ensure that 75% of the time each cookie will have five or more chips? 90% of the time? 100% of the time?

Have your students find the number of times each major league baseball team plays another team in its league. Investigate alternatives to the present numbers of games, given the number of teams in each division. J. F. Kurtzke (14)

These examples suggest the nature of the curriculum for low achievers if the core curriculum were to be adopted. Notice that we included examples in discrete mathematics, geometry, algebra, probability, and statistics. However, the approach was both concrete and straightforward. Consistent with the NCTM *Standards*, the examples also involved technology as appropriate, problem-solving, group work, conjecturing by students, and student discussion and communication. An entire curric-

FIGURE 6.3   A stem-and-leaf plot

```
 6 |
 7 | 7
 8 | 0335578889
 9 | 0224455666666777778899999
10 | 0111223344455666677789
11 | 0001112223455899999
12 | 1112333344579
13 | 234669
14 | 567
15 | 09              12/3 represent 123 chips
16 | 2
17 |
```

ulum for low achievers would parallel, to a large extent, the college preparatory curriculum, but at a more concrete level. One curriculum already designed to accommodate this sort of differentiation is the new School Mathematics Project in England (17).

> "Making calculators available on tests has the power to transform school mathematics." K. M. Heid (7, p. 712)

There are many arguments in support of the core curriculum recommendations. The failure of the present approach has already been well documented in earlier sections. The present approach in general mathematics seems to be predicated on a belief either that a high level of proficiency in paper-and-pencil computational skills is prerequisite to more interesting and challenging mathematics or that the low achievers simply are not capable of succeeding at more interesting and challenging mathematics. Research and experiences with innovative curricula in this country and abroad refute both of these premises (24). A case of students labeled as low achievers succeeding at very challenging mathematics (in particular, advanced placement calculus) is dramatized in the movie *Stand and Deliver*, which is about Los Angeles mathematics teacher Jaime Escalante and his students.

At present, then, general mathematics is a form of restricting the mathematical environment and career options for certain (disproportionately poor and minority) students, based on criteria that are shown by research to be invalid. Special educators have argued very effectively that students with handicaps or special needs should be placed in the least restrictive educational environment. To do otherwise would be an unethical infringement on the human rights of the students (28). It would seem that a similar argument could be applied to general mathematics in its present form.

Furthermore, there is evidence that the core curriculum is a feasible approach. Many other countries (e.g., England, Japan, Bulgaria, Sweden, Israel, and Hungary) have a core curriculum similar to the one proposed in the NCTM *Standards*. In this country, too, there are a growing number of success stories (24). Given all this, the greater flexibility and more balanced opportunity provided by an up-to-date core curriculum surely warrant its development and widespread adoption.

Remediation

General mathematics, with its focus on paper-and-pencil computation, has traditionally been taught as a remedial course, meaning that although the students had previously been in courses in which most of the content of general mathematics was included, these students had failed to master it. To "remediate" meant to spend another year of drill and practice on these computational skills in hopes that this time mastery would come. Unfortunately, remediation of this sort has almost no positive effect: Students are not much better at the skills at the end of the year than they were at the beginning. To make matters worse, student attitudes are likely to become increasingly more negative as the year of boring repetition progresses (6).

> Have students write word problems from items they find in newspapers or magazines. For example: "The tax levy is projected to cost property owners just 51 cents per thousand dollars of assessed valuation."

Adoption of a core curriculum would greatly reduce remedial drill of this sort. The practice of repeating arithmetic skill courses would be entirely eliminated. Paper-and-pencil skills would rarely be practiced in isolation. Students would proceed to new topics, albeit in concrete presentations, and use calculators as needed. Paper-and-pencil skills would not be an instructional focus, yet it is unlikely that they would deteriorate to even lower levels. On the contrary, research suggests that arithmetic skills are maintained (and often improved) in the absence of isolated drill and practice as students learn more mathematics, probably as a byproduct of improved conceptual understanding. Evidence of this can be seen in NAEP data that show that arithmetic computation skills improve for students from age 13 to age 17, even though this computation is not the focus of the mathematics courses that most students are completing during those years (16).

One reason traditional remedial methods have not worked is that they focus on drill and not on the underlying cause of most students' difficulties, inadequate conceptual understanding (5). Research in mathematics education provides a great deal of guidance concerning the kinds of misunderstandings and errors that students exhibit in various content domains, findings that in turn suggest strategies for teaching and remediating.

Discussions of useful findings concerning misconceptions in algebra and geometry can be found in other chapters of this book, and fractions, decimals, and percents are presented in detail in the other books in this project. We will now discuss some of the research on students' difficulties with graphing as an example of how such research might be helpful for remediation.

Data from NAEP indicate that many students are unaware of the relationship between equations and their graphs.

- When given a ruler and a sheet of paper with labeled axes, only 18% of the 17-year-olds tested were able to produce a correct graph corresponding to a linear equation. Moreover, about 25% of the students with one year of algebra, and less than 50% of those with two years, were successful.
- The reversal of the problem proved to be even more difficult. Given a graph of a straight line with indicated intercepts $(-3,0)$ and $(0,5)$, only 5% of the 17-year-olds, and about 20% of the students with two years of algebra, could write the equation (9, p. 68).

One area of difficulty in graphing is the construction of axes and scales. Many students, through junior high and beyond, graph magnitudes (such as weights or distances) as segments rather than as points. Thus, many students would place three magnitudes (say 5 feet, 7 feet, and 10 feet) on a number line end-to-end, as on the left in Figure 6.4. Other students would graph each magnitude as a segment that starts from the left end of the number line—see the drawing on the right (9).

FIGURE 6.4 Difficulty with marking axes

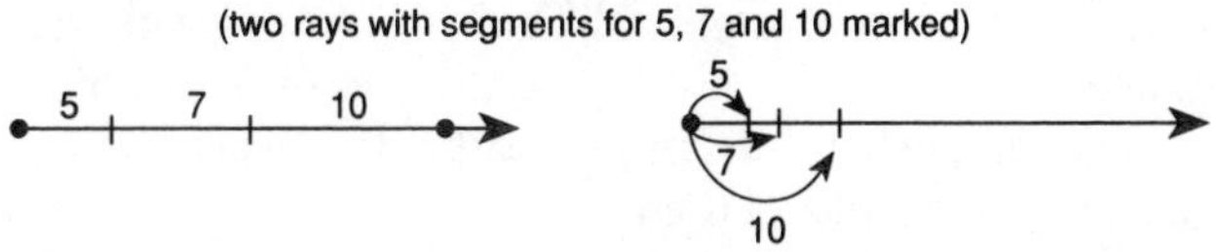

(two rays with segments for 5, 7 and 10 marked)

Many research studies verify that students misinterpret graphs when they represent physical motion or distance–time (15). Among the most common misconceptions concerning graphs are the following:

- Use of different scales for the positive and negative parts of the line
- Placement of axes to intersect at a point other than the origin
- Difficulty with continuity—for example, viewing a line as having a finite number of points

Leinhardt, Zaslavsky, and Stein (15) have also found that most of these "misconceptions" are actually taught, or at least implied, by the kinds of graphing experiences in most elementary school textbooks. For example, students rarely construct a set of axes themselves; mostly they work with line graphs and bar graphs that use discontinuous axes. The activities they mainly engage in are plotting ordered pairs, and perhaps joining the resulting points with lines, or interpreting already constructed bar graphs and line graphs within given "real-world" situations. Students need more experience in constructing graphs, including drawing and marking the axes. Instruction must also emphasize the connection between an equation and its graph and the continuity of most graphs in algebra. Chapter 5 on representation offers additional research and examples.

Looking Ahead . . .

As teachers make heavy use of published instructional materials, there is an immediate need for careful development and evaluation of curriculum materials that reflect the core curriculum recommendations outlined in this article. The NCTM Addendum Project recently produced a monograph that provides classroom examples to guide this development. Some curriculum developers and publishers are attempting to respond to this need, and their materials should begin to appear in 1991 as well.

There is also a pressing need for research that addresses the mathematics education of underachieving, and especially disadvantaged and culturally diverse, students. Some important questions to address are the following: What kinds of learning environments are best for changing students' negative attitudes toward, and beliefs about, mathematics? Do underachieving students benefit from intensive individual treatments focused on uncovering conceptual barriers and voids? How do we prepare teachers to become expert at such treatment?

Harold L. Schoen

This chapter is likely to raise some practical questions for classroom teachers. For example: Should students be tracked by mathematical ability if a core curriculum is adopted? If not, won't the weaker students have great difficulty competing with the better students? To what extent can cooperative learning techniques solve that problem? How can students' attitudes and beliefs be changed, particularly when they are reinforced in typical general mathematics classes?

In the usual tracked general mathematics class, classroom management is a major concern. What new management techniques will a teacher have to learn in order to implement such changes as using technology, more challenging content, and small-group teaching methods? Will the risks be worth it for the teacher? Will the necessary teacher education and administrative support be provided? How?

David Hallas

About the Authors

Harold Schoen is a professor of mathematics and education at the University of Iowa. His current area of interest is in strategies for attaining widespread improvement of the secondary school mathematics curriculum. A former high school mathematics teacher, he was a member of the writing team for the 9–12-grade NCTM *Curriculum and Evaluation Standards*.

David Hallas teaches mathematics at City High School in Iowa City, Iowa. During 1990–91, he was also a visiting lecturer in Curriculum and Instruction at the University of Iowa. He taught mathematics at the middle-school level for many years.

References

*1. Borasi, R. (1990). The invisible hand operating in mathematics instruction: Students' conceptions and expectations. In T. J. Cooney (Ed.), *Teaching and learning mathematics in the 1990s* (1990 Yearbook, pp. 174–182). Reston, VA: National Council of Teachers of Mathematics.

*2. Channell, D. E. (1989). Problem solving with simulation. *Mathematics Teacher*, 82(9), 713–720.

3. Confrey, J. (1990). A review of the research on student conceptions in mathematics, science, and programming. In C. B. Cazden (Ed.), *Review of research in education* (pp. 3–56). Washington, DC: American Educational Research Association.

*4. Crowley, M. L. (1987). The van Hiele model of the development of geometric thought. In M. M. Lindquist (Ed.), *Learning and teaching geometry, K–12* (1987 Yearbook, pp. 1–16). Reston, VA: National Council of Teachers of Mathematics.

5. Dossey, J. A., Mullis, I. V. S., Lindquist, M. M., & Chambers, D. L. (1988). *The mathematics report card: Are we measuring up?* Princeton: Educational Testing Service.

*6. Driscoll, M. (1983). *Research within reach: Secondary school mathematics*. Washington, DC: National Institute of Education.

*7. Heid, M. K. (1988). Calculators on tests—one giant step for mathematics education. *Mathematics Teacher* 81(9), 710–713.

*8. Heid, M. K., & Kunkle, D. (1988). Computer-generated tables: Tools for concept development in elementary algebra. In A. Coxford (Ed.), *The ideas of algebra, K–12* (1988 Yearbook, pp. 170–177). Reston, VA: National Council of Teachers of Mathematics.

9. HERSCOVICS, N. (1989). Cognitive obstacles encountered in the learning of algebra. In S. Wagner & C. Kieran (Eds.), *Research issues in the learning and teaching of algebra* (pp. 60–86). Reston, VA: National Council of Teachers of Mathematics.

*10. HIRSCH, C. R., & LAPPAN, G. (1989). Transition to high school mathematics. *Mathematics Teacher, 82*(9), 614–618.

*11. HIRSCH, C. R., & SCHOEN, H. L. (1989). A core curriculum for grades 9–12. *Mathematics Teacher, 82*(9), 696–701.

*12. HOLMES, E. E. (1990). Motivation: An essential component of mathematics instruction. In T. J. Cooney (Ed.), *Teaching and learning mathematics in the 1990s* (1990 Yearbook, pp. 101–107). Reston, VA: National Council of Teachers of Mathematics.

*13. KIEREN, T. E., & OLSON, A. T. (1989). Imagination, intuition, and computing in school algebra. *Mathematics Teacher, 82*(1), 14–17.

*14. KURTZKE, J. F. (1990). The baseball schedule: A modest proposal. *Mathematics Teacher, 83*(5), 346–350.

15. LEINHART, G., ZASLAVSKY, O., & STEIN, M. K. (1990). Functions, graphs, and graphing: Tasks, learning, and teaching. *Review of Educational Research, 60*(1), 1–64.

16. LINDQUIST, M. M. (Ed.) (1989). *Results from the fourth mathematics assessment of the National Assessment of Educational Progress.* Reston, VA: National Council of Teachers of Mathematics.

17. LING, J. (1987). SMP 11–16: The most recent work in curriculum development by the school mathematics project, and its relation to current issues in mathematical education in England. In I. Wirzup & R. Streit (Eds.), *Developments in school mathematics education around the world* (pp. 225–236). Reston, VA: National Council of Teachers of Mathematics.

18. MADSEN-NASON, A., & LANIER, P. E. (1986). *Pamela Kaye's general mathematics class: From a computational to a conceptual orientation* (Research Series No. 172). East Lansing: Michigan State University.

19. MCKNIGHT, C. C., CROSSWHITE, F. J., DOSSEY, J. A., KIFER, E., SWAFFORD, J. O., TRAVERS, K. J., & COONEY, T. J. (1987). *The underachieving curriculum: Assessing U.S. school mathematics from an international perspective.* Champaign, IL: Stipes.

20. MCLEOD, D. B. (1988). Research on learning and teaching in mathematics: The role of affect. In E. Fennema, T. Carpenter, & S. J. Lamon (Eds.), *Integrating research on teaching and learning mathematics* (pp. 60–89). Madison: Wisconsin Center for Education Research.

*21. NATIONAL COUNCIL OF TEACHERS OF MATHEMATICS (1989). *Curriculum and evaluation standards for school mathematics.* Reston, VA: Author.

22. NATIONAL RESEARCH COUNCIL (1989). *Everybody counts: A report to the nation on the future of mathematics education.* Washington, DC: National Academy Press.

23. NATIONAL RESEARCH COUNCIL (1990). *Reshaping school mathematics: A philosophy and framework for curriculum.* Washington, DC: National Academy Press.

24. SCHOEN, H. L. (1988). *NCTM 9–12 Standards: Reflections from research.* Paper presented at the Research Presession of the meeting of the National Council of Teachers of Mathematics, Chicago, April 1988.

*25. SCHULZ, R. W. (1972). Characteristics and needs of the slow learner. In W. C. Lowry (Ed.), *The slow learner in mathematics* (35th Yearbook, pp. 1–25). Washington, DC: National Council of Teachers of Mathematics.

*26. SECADA, W. G. (1990). The challenges of a changing world for mathematics education. In T. J. Cooney (Ed.), *Teaching and learning mathematics in the 1990s* (1990 Yearbook, pp. 135–143). Reston, VA: National Council of Teachers of Mathematics.

27. SHAUGHNESSY, J. M. (1977). Misconceptions of probability. *Educational Studies in Mathematics, 8*, 295–316.

28. SLAVIN, R. E. (1989). Students at risk of school failure: The problem and its dimensions. In R. E. Slavin, N. L. Karweit, & N. A. Madden (Eds.), *Effective programs for students at risk of student failure* (pp. 3–19). Boston: Allyn & Bacon.

29. STEVENSON, H. W., LEE, S. Y., & STIGLER, J. W. (1986). Mathematics achievement of Chinese, Japanese, and American children. *Science, 231*, 693–699.

*30. STIFF, L. V. (1990). African–American students and the promise of the Curriculum and Evaluation Standards. In T. J. Cooney (Ed.), *Teaching and learning mathematics in the 1990s* (1990 Yearbook, pp. 152–158). Reston, VA: National Council of Teachers of Mathematics.

31. TRAVERS, K. J., & WESTBURY, I. (1989). *The IEA study of Mathematics I: Analysis of mathematics curriculum*. Elmsford, NY: Pergamon.

CHAPTER 7

Advancing Algebra

Sigrid Wagner and Sheila Parker

> *Since Algebra surpasses all human subtlety and the clarity of every mortal mind, it must be accounted a truly celestial gift, which gives such an illuminating experience of the true power of the intellect that whoever attains to it will believe there is nothing he cannot understand.*
>
> G. Cardano

What Is Algebra?   Most people, when they think of "algebra," think of solving equations, factoring polynomials, graphing functions, and other things they did with x and y in their high school algebra classes. Too many people, including some who got good grades in mathematics, may recall that algebra was the point at which mathematics stopped having much connection with the real world.

In the past, many students have gone through algebra memorizing "rituals" (12), those formal procedures for manipulating symbols that have lost their connection to the numbers they represent. Now, hand-held computers can relieve us of the graph-plotting, symbol-manipulating drudgery of doing algebra. We are free to spend more time thinking algebraically. As teachers, we can begin to illuminate the structure of the algebraic forest without asking students to climb every tree.

Rituals often lose something in the translation:
  "When you multiply, you add exponents; when you divide, you subtract."
Students who do not understand the meaning behind this ritual may write:

$$3^2 \cdot 3^3 = 9^5.$$

With this exciting opportunity comes a daunting challenge: We need to reconstitute the algebra curriculum, to shift the emphasis from doing to thinking. Consequently, we have to decide what it means to "think algebraically." We must identify essential concepts and skills and determine, through research, how much conceptual development and skill practice students need to be successful at solving algebraic problems. The NCTM *Curriculum and Evaluation Standards* (32) point some general directions to be followed, but it will be the continuing task of textware authors and classroom teachers to map details of the journey from the algorithmic algebra of yesterday to the problem-solving algebra of tomorrow.

In algebra we need to increase our emphasis on:

* Real-world problems
* Conceptual understanding
* Computer-based methods
* Structure of number systems
* Matrices and their applications

NCTM *Curriculum and Evaluation Standards* (32, p. 126)

Research can help us understand how students construct mature concepts and learn complex procedures. Research can suggest activities for the classroom that foster the connections that build understanding. Research can suggest ways of making algebraic ideas accessible to all students (15), so that algebra becomes part of the mathematical pump that propels students on to higher achievement instead of the filter that holds them back (34). Translating theoretical ideas from research into practical ideas for the classroom can help teachers teach more effectively and students learn more efficiently.

Historical Sketch.   Formal research in the learning of algebra began early in the twentieth century, about the time that psychologists were developing objective methods for measuring intelligence, aptitude, and achievement. Mathematics was a popular vehicle for studying constructs like learning and memory because of the ease of scoring answers. Algebra was often used for studying advanced learning because so few people had yet to understand the subject!

From 1900 to 1930, research on the learning of algebra dealt primarily with the relative difficulty of solving various types of linear equations. In 1923, Thorndike (47) published *The Psychology of Algebra,* in which he applied his "bond" theory to the learning of algebra. Though most of his recommendations focus on such things as the amount of practice students need to acquire certain skills and how the practice should be distributed, Thorndike is credited with bringing a systematic approach to research in the learning of algebra, including a careful analysis of the nature of algebraic tasks.

From 1930 to 1945, research in education declined, as the nation focused on issues of survival surrounding the Great Depression and World War II. After the war, research in algebra rebounded, as a new wave of behavioral psychologists refined some of the earlier methods of investigating skill acquisition. It was in the 1960s that mathematics educators, with academic backgrounds in higher mathematics and teaching experience in secondary schools, began to shift the focus of research toward conceptual understanding. Their work has been complemented by the efforts of cognitive psychologists to analyze the thinking processes involved in problem solving and the acquisition of complex algebraic skills.

> "Algebra to most learners . . . is in large measure forming more or less particular bonds or connections, such as $a \times ab = a^2b$, $a(a + b) = a^2 + ab$, a means $1a$, $-a \times -b = +ab$, learning to operate several of these together as needed, organizing them further into more inclusive habits and insights, summing up what one has learned to do in rules, and thus gradually attaining a sense of what it is right to do with literal numbers and why." Thorndike et al. (47, p. 246)

In this chapter we will discuss the recent research in algebra from three perspectives—that of the learner, of the content, and of the teacher. As we identify major findings, we will propose ideas for teaching certain topics. We will conclude with some general implications for the algebra classroom.

Learning of Algebra

Two theoretical perspectives underlie most of the research on the learning of algebra of the past twenty-five years. Piagetian-style theories of *cognitive development* (see Chapter 1) have provided a theoretical framework for much of the research on conceptual understanding. Written instruments and semi-structured interviews, using nonroutine tasks—that is, tasks that are different from typical textbook exercises—are used to analyze students' concepts of function, equation, and variable. Sometimes tasks are administered using techniques inspired in part by Soviet research methodology, such as asking individual students to think aloud while working on a problem, having pairs of students work together on a problem, or conducting small-group teaching experiments in which tasks are devised to capitalize on responses to previous tasks. Researchers then analyze tapes and transcripts of working sessions to formulate conjectures about students' thinking.

Information processing provides a theoretical framework for much of the current research on skill learning in algebra. Here, researchers study data on such factors as response time or common errors in an effort to identify patterns and infer mental processes students use in carrying out certain algebraic procedures. Sometimes computer models of students' thinking processes are formulated, or computer programs called "intelligent tutors" are developed to remediate student errors (see Chapter 11).

Both cognitive-development and information-processing research can help us understand how students learn. Both kinds of research can alert us to obstacles that arise along the way. Before we consider the mental constructs students need to develop in algebra, let us consider some sources of difficulty they typically encounter.

Research suggests that impediments to learning tend to be of three types: (a) Some are inherent to the subject itself, (b) some are intrinsic to the learner, and (c) some are the unintended consequence of generally good teaching techniques. Most obstacles inherent to algebra stem from notational conventions or the complexity of concepts that arise with the use of letters as variables. Obstacles intrinsic to the learner include such human foibles as the tendency to overgeneralize or to judge on the basis of superficial characteristics. The most common obstacle attributable to teaching is the incomplete mental construct that may result from considering a too-narrow range of simple, special cases of a given concept (46).

Many obstacles to the learning of algebra are inherent to the subject itself:

$$|x| = x, \text{ if } x \geq 0$$
$$|x| = -x, \text{ if } x < 0.$$

We will see examples throughout the next section of obstacles of various kinds. We should keep in mind that cognitive conflict is not necessarily bad for students; in fact, it is an important stimulus to learning. It is our responsibility as teachers to be aware of possible sources of conflict and alert students to differences, as well as similarities, among the various phenomena they study.

Content of Algebra

For convenience, we have divided the discussion of content research into the language, concepts, geometry, and rules of algebra. Generally, research studies reflect a range of ideas and do not fall neatly into a single category. Thus, we will analyze the research by areas of implications, rather than study by study.

Language of Algebra

Algebra is a language for describing actions on, and relationships among, quantities. As with any language, difficulties may arise from features of the language itself or in translating from one language to another. Within the language of algebra, most linguistic difficulties relate to variables and expressions; most translation difficulties arise in translating word problems into equations.

Variables. Research shows that students can work with variables without fully understanding the power and flexibility of literal symbols (51). Because variables operate much like the numbers of arithmetic, and because conceptually they resemble pronouns in ordinary language, most students can acquire some facility in routine algebraic manipulations. On the other hand, variables are different from numerals (e.g., variables can represent many numbers simultaneously, they have no place value, they can be selected arbitrarily), and they are different from words (e.g., variables can be defined in any way we wish and can be changed without affecting the values they represent).

Changing x to y in the equation $2x + 3 = 15$ does not have the same effect as changing *he* to *she* in the sentence, *He was President of the United States.*

Variables are versatile, too. We use them as names for numbers or other objects, as discrete unknowns in equations, as continuous unknowns in inequalities, as indeterminates in polynomials, as generalized numbers in identities, as independent and dependent variables in functions, as parameters in formulas, and so on. Whether we look at variables from the viewpoint of the roles they play in algebra (48) or the ways that students operate with them (24), it is clear that the "concept of variable" is, in fact, a multifaceted idea.

Can you add to this list of ways we refer to literal symbols?

> Unknown
> Variable
> Constant
> Parameter
> Generalized number
> Name
> Placeholder
> Argument
> Indeterminate

However, there is evidence that students' early impressions about variables may impede their construction of a sufficiently general concept. For example, students who first encounter variables as names (as in person A, person B) may assume that letters are like abbreviations. This assumption is reinforced when we use the mnemonic device of choosing as variables the first letter of the name of the objects we are talking about, as in using a to represent some number of $a$pples. Interpreting variables as abbreviations may cause difficulty in translating word problems, as we will see shortly.

Students who first encounter variables as unknowns in equations may assume that letters represent a specific value. When confronted with a letter of indeterminate value, (see Fig. 7.1), they may respond by assigning a value to the variable and computing the answer (24).

A common naive conception about variables is that different letters must have different values. Even students who have been told and are quick to say that any letter can be used as an unknown may, nonetheless, believe that changing the unknown can change the solution to an equation (50). How many of us have unwittingly reinforced this misconception by always picking different values for a, b, and c to illustrate, say, the distributive law $a(b + c) = ab + ac$? If we occasionally pick the same values for different variables, the reactions of our students could be instructive.

Expressions. An algebraic *expression* is a description of some operation involving variables, such as $3a$, $x + 1$, or $x - y$. Because we use two distinct symbol systems (letters and numerals) together in algebra, and because these systems follow different rules, we gain some economy of notation, but at the expense of possible confusion. For instance, many students assume that $-x$ is a negative number (29), as though

FIGURE 7.1   N-gon diagram from CSMS

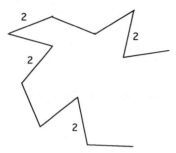

Letter used as a specific unknown.

Part of this figure is not drawn.

There are n̲ sides altogether, each of length 2.

The perimeter p̲ = _____.

Adapted from (24, p. 23)

the variable were a numeral. In this particular case, we should alert students to the three uses of the " − " sign (the subtraction operation "minus," the integer sign "negative," the additive inverse "opposite of") and refer to " −x" as "the opposite of x" rather than "negative x."

The most common notational shortcut in algebra is the omission of the operation sign for multiplication. Because variables have no place value, we can denote multiplication by concatenating (linking) literal symbols with numerals, other literal symbols, or parentheses, as in $3a = 3 \times a$ or $3(1/2) = 3 \times 1/2$. However, students are used to interpreting concatenation in arithmetic as implying addition (29), as in $32 = 30 + 2$ or $3\ 1/2 = 3 + 1/2$. It takes them awhile to internalize these conflicting conventions (10), and of course the fact that both arithmetic and algebraic conventions operate simultaneously in algebra does nothing to alleviate the confusion.

> What do we get if we replace the a in 3a by 2 in arithmetic? What do we get in algebra? Adapted from (10), p. 41

One idea that should, but does not, transfer easily from arithmetic to algebra is the notion of inverse operations. In the elementary grades, a great deal of emphasis is placed on the inverse relation between addition and subtraction, multiplication and division. Yet, these inverse relationships tend to get lost in algebra. For example, most students can multiply $(3x + 2)(5x − 4)$ to obtain $15x^2 − 2x − 8$ readily enough, but if asked in the next breath to factor (the product) $15x^2 − 2x − 8$, surprisingly few students immediately recognize that the factors are the expressions they just multiplied (37). The complexity of algebraic operations can obscure important relationships, and often it is not enough just to remind students that multiplying and factoring are inverse operations—we need to illustrate the implications of a relationship with specific examples.

Just as young students who work with place-value ideas eventually begin to think of ten single units, bundled together, as a single unit of ten, so we expect algebra students who work with polynomial expressions to be able to "unitize" these expressions and treat them as single variables, as in factoring by grouping: $ax + bx + ay + by = (a + b)x + (a + b)y = (a + b)(x + y)$. The tendency of most students to think only of single letters as variables (2, 35, 52) may be partially the consequence of an algebra curriculum that uses only single letters as unknowns. Perhaps occasional use of unknowns like $2n$ or $x + 5$ might help students learn to unitize expressions.

Suppose $5(3z - 1) = 10$.

Then $\dfrac{3z - 1}{2} = ?$

How many of your students see the shortcut?

Adapted from (2)

Parentheses and other bracketing symbols should provide a perceptual aid for unitizing. However, there are three common behaviors that seem to neutralize the suggestive effect of parentheses. Some students apparently ignore or overlook bracketing symbols, as in $4(n + 5) = 4n + 5$ (6). Other students, perhaps in response to the order-of-operations exhortation to "do what's in parentheses first," focus on parentheses to the exclusion of the overall structure of the expression (39). And finally, the equation-solving advice to "clear the parentheses first" may prompt many students to overlook the variable unit in their haste to eliminate grouping symbols. As with any rules of thumb, we need to show students some situations in which the usual rules are not the most efficient way to proceed.

Word Problems.   In their search for well-defined procedures to follow, students may transfer the "key word" approach to solving word problems in arithmetic to a "key context" approach in algebra. That is, they tend to categorize and remember problems according to superficial characteristics—as "distance" problems, "age" problems, or "mixture" problems—rather than according to underlying relations—equal quantities, two quantities added equal a third, and so on (20, 30). We may be able to help students focus more on underlying structures if we do as the *Standards* suggest and increase our use of real-world (not so easily categorized) problems and decrease the number of traditional coin-digit-work type problems (32, pp. 126–127).

Word problems should be integrated throughout the chapter and not given as a separate assignment at the end. (28, p. 423)

Though looking for key words can be a useful problem-solving heuristic, it may encourage overreliance on a direct, rather than analytical, mode for translating word problems into equations. The fact that so many textbook problems lend themselves to direct translation is seductive, and when faced with as simple a real-world situation as "There are six times as many students as professors," even college students translate the statement as $6S = P$ about half the time (40). Though direct translation is not always to blame, certainly the presence of the phrase "six times" and the interpretation of S as an abbreviation for *students*, rather than a representation for the *number* of students, impels many, including some who can draw an accurate diagram for the statement, to write an equation that resembles a literal translation but which is mathematically reversed. This reversal error seems highly resistant to remediation; however, the analysis required to write a computer program to provide the proper output has been moderately successful with some students (43).

A question that needs to be researched for word problems in general is whether using simple, non-mnemonic variables like x and y may wean students away from direct translation toward an analysis of numerical relationships. Moreover, having students write out in words what each variable represents ("x represents the number of students, y represents the number of professors") not only provides a visual reminder that the variables represent numbers, but is also very much in keeping with the increased emphasis on verbalization in the *Standards* (32, p. 140). The interested reader should see (9) for further review of factors related to word problems.

Concepts of Algebra

The two algebraic concepts that have been investigated the most are equations and functions. Conceptually, there is quite a jump from equations, in which a single variable typically represents one or two unknown numbers, to functions, in which two or more variables generally take on infinitely many values in relationship to each other. Inequalities are a conceptual intermediary between these two, in that a single variable represents a whole continuum of numbers, but relatively little research has focused on inequalities.

Equations.   Students typically begin solving simple equations long before they enter a formal algebra course, but a clear vision of the structural differences between equations and expressions may be obstructed by their experience with the equal sign in arithmetic. Students do so much computing of answers in arithmetic, they may come to regard the equal sign as a kind of operation sign—a "write-the-answer" sign—rather than a statement of equivalence (4, 22).

In algebra, the equal sign may still signal writing an answer, as in simplifying an expression: $2x + 5 + 3x - 7 = 5x - 2$. But in solving equations, the equal sign is explicitly a relation sign, and students are asked to operate on the whole relation to find a sequence of equivalent relations. Lingering confusion between simplifying expressions and solving equations is betrayed when students refer to the (often numerical) right-hand side of an equation as "the answer" or when they simplify an expression, look at the "equation" they have thereby written, and begin solving it, only to wonder what happened to x, when all the x terms subtract out.

Have any of your students ever done this?

Simplify: $2x + 5 + 3x - 7$
Solution: $2x + 5 + 3x - 7 = 0$
$$5x - 2 = 0$$
$$5x = 2$$
$$x = \frac{2}{5}$$

Perhaps textbook authors should distinguish between the two uses of the equal sign in algebra by consistently using "≡" to denote identically equivalent expressions (axiomatic properties, simplified expressions, multiplication/factoring identities, equivalent equations, etc.) and " = " to denote the limited equality of an equation or function. Then, for example, students who are wont to solve equations by chaining successive, equivalent equations together with equal signs could quite properly write:

$$7x - 3 = 5x + 5 \equiv 2x - 3 = 5 \equiv 2x = 8 \equiv x = 4$$

Few students fully appreciate the fact that solving an equation is finding the value(s) of the variable for which the left- and right-hand sides are equal (52). Numerical approaches, such as using arithmetic identities to develop the concept of equation (19), or using calculator methods to find or approximate solutions (13), may help students focus more on the relational aspect of an equation and less on the algorithm for solution. Having students reason through a solution instead of always using inverse operations may also help (1; see Fig. 7.2).

Try this with your class:
Find an expression whose value is 17 when $x = 3$.
  Possible response: $5x + 2$.
Find another expression whose value is 17 when $x = 3$.
  Possible response: $7x - 4$.
Now, what is the solution of this equation:
  $5x + 2 = 7x - 4$? How can you tell?
                                          Adapted from (52)

FIGURE 7.2   Solving an equation by reasoning (1, p. 205)

Solve: $14 - \dfrac{15}{7 - \underline{x}} = 9$

Reasoning: 14 minus what equals 9?   (5)

            15 divided by what equals 5?   (3)

            7 minus what equals 3?   (4)

            Solution: $\underline{x} = 4$

Checking numerical solutions *in the original equation*—for word problems, in the problem statement—should be an integral part of the solution process for all types of equations (8), not just for rational or radical equations, where extraneous roots may be introduced. The significance of checking solutions to equations is not intuitively obvious to students (17). The purpose of checking is not just for accuracy, but also for ascertaining the reasonableness of an answer and reinforcing the connection between the original equation or problem situation and the final solution.

Functions. Some early research on concepts related to functions indicates that students construct the formal concept of function in stages, beginning with the notion of a function rule, and progressing through vocabulary and symbolism, graphical representation, operations on functions, and internal properties of specific functions (27). Much research has focused on intuitive ideas about functions and the transition from intuition to formal symbolism (e.g., 14, 36, 49). Research on graphing will be discussed in the next section.

Middle grades students can easily comprehend the basic idea of a function as "a rule of correspondence" either in concrete situations or in two-column tables of numbers. For simple functions, they can identify patterns, fill in missing domain/range elements, and verbally describe rules of association (7; see Fig. 7.3).

The formal $f(x)$ notation, on the other hand, condenses a great deal of information very efficiently but causes difficulty even for advanced students. In the Fourth Mathematics Assessment, for example, success rates of 11th graders evaluating $a + 7$ when $a = 5$ declined 20–40 percentage points (depending on algebra background) when the question was recast as evaluating $f(5)$ when $f(a) = a + 7$ (26, p. 62).

The set-theoretic definition of *function* that appears in many algebra textbooks does not convey the richness of the function concept in a very meaningful way. By and large, students' intuition about what constitutes a function corresponds more to the first functions they encounter than to the formal definition (49). That is, students generally believe that functions should be linear, or at the very least, continuous, smooth, and definable by a single formula. To help students construct a more com-

FIGURE 7.3   Item similar to one used in the Second Mathematics Assessment (7, p. 68)

x	y
1	8
3	
4	11
7	14
n	

What is y when x = 3?   What is y when x = n?

FIGURE 7.4   Items similar to those used by [(49), p. 359]

`Does there exist a graph whose function is:`

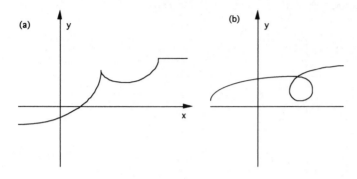

plete conceptualization, we need to augment the introduction of simple examples with a variety of other kinds of functions, as well as nonexamples of functions (see Fig. 7.4). For more discussion of specific types of functions, see Chapter 9.

Geometry of Algebra

Traditionally, algebra and geometry have been regarded as separate subjects in the high school curriculum, with relatively few efforts to draw the connections between them that the *Standards* recommend (32, p. 146ff). Most of the geometry that has appeared in algebra classes has been as graphs of functions, and the treatment of this topic was limited by the practical difficulties of graphing by hand. Computers and graphing calculators enable us to take a much more visual approach to algebra.

Area Models.   The Greeks developed algebraic ideas using geometry. Long before Viète systematized the symbolization of polynomials in the late sixteenth century, the Greeks proved polynomial identities using area models (16; see Fig. 7.5). General learning theory (see Chapter 1) suggests that pictorial representations, together with numerical concretizations,

$$25^2 = (20 + 5)^2 = 20^2 + 2(20)(5) + 5^2 = 400 + 200 + 25 = 625,$$

should help students apprehend the equivalence of algebraic identities in symbolic form. Research is needed to determine the most effective way of incorporating activities with area models into the algebra classroom.

Graphing.   Prerequisites for graphing functions, such as notions of point and line, as well as plotting and naming points on coordinate axes, are standard fare in the elementary grades. Nevertheless, barely 50% of students who have studied algebra can do much more with coordinate systems than simply plot points (26, pp. 62–3). Even students who can graph a function like $x - 2y = 5$ may not be able to look

FIGURE 7.5   Geometric proof of the algebraic identity

$$(a + b)^2 = a^2 + 2ab + b^2$$

as found in Book II of Euclid's *Elements* (16)

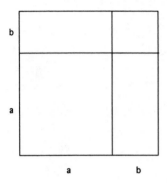

at a given graph and identify a solution of the corresponding equation from the graph (52; see Fig. 7.6).

Some naive conceptions related to graphs seem to reflect naive conceptions in geometry, such as the common notion that the only points on the graph of a function are the points that were actually plotted (21). These kinds of errors can be at least partially attributed to the fact that most representations of geometric concepts have features contradictory to the concepts they represent. That is, representations of points all have size, whereas points themselves do not. When we plot points on a graph, they generally appear "bigger" than the points elsewhere along the line, and this perceptual miscue is misleading to many students. Calculator and computer graphing may alleviate some of these problems but may introduce new problems yet to be identified (46; see also Chapter 11).

FIGURE 7.6   Graph interpretation item from (52)

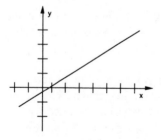

FIGURE 7.7   Graph of the speed of a vehicle with respect to time

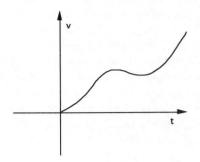

Some misconceptions are not so much geometric in nature as they are idiosyn-cratic to graphing, as when students confuse the picture of the graph with the actual event (5). For example, it is difficult for students to imagine that a vehicle whose speed is graphed in Figure 7.7 could be going uphill when the graph of the speed is going down, and vice versa. A number of researchers (see [25] for a complete review) have asked students to construct stories whose actions could be depicted by a given graph (see Fig. 7.8). This kind of open-ended, multiple-answer problem solving, encouraged by the *Standards* (32, p. 137ff), is easily adaptable to the classroom and could enhance students' graph interpretation skills.

Rules of Algebra

Research on the rules of algebra focuses on describing errors and trying to explain thinking processes. The errors noted in the research literature are generally those familiar to every algebra teacher.

FIGURE 7.8   Graph with multiple interpretations. Students make up stories that could be illustrated by the graph.

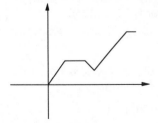

Manipulating Expressions.   Many errors related to expressions seem to involve an interaction between (a) overgeneralizing on the part of the student and (b) the highly abstract nature of the field properties, especially the associative or distributive law. For example, one of the most common errors is to simplify an expression like $4 + 3n$ to $7n$. One explanation for this kind of error is that, in arithmetic, students learn to operate on numbers until they obtain a single number as the answer. Then, in algebra they may feel uncomfortable leaving an expression with a visible operation sign as the final answer, so they perform whatever operations they can on the available numbers to reduce the expression to a single term (11). Of course, in the case of $4 + 3n \rightarrow 7n$, if the first operation were multiplication instead of addition, combining the numbers would be correct, using the associative law:

$$4(3n) = 4 \cdot (3 \cdot n) = (4 \cdot 3) \cdot n = 12 \cdot n = 12n$$

Another common error is to simplify an expression like $\dfrac{x + 2}{2}$ to x by deleting the 2 in the numerator and denominator (8). Again, were the operation in the numerator multiplication instead of addition, dividing above and below by 2 would be correct: $\dfrac{x \cdot 2}{2} = x$. In the case of addition, the distributive law implies $\dfrac{x + 2}{2} = \dfrac{1}{2} \cdot (x + 2) = \dfrac{1}{2} \cdot x + \dfrac{1}{2} \cdot 2 = \dfrac{x}{2} + 1 \neq x$ (unless $x = 2$).

As a third example, the expression $(x + y)^2$ is often converted to $x^2 + y^2$, following the pattern of $(xy)^2 = x^2 y^2$ (29). Of course, writing $(x + y)^2 = (x + y)(x + y)$ and using the distributive law (twice) helps clarify where the missing middle term $2xy$ comes from, in contrast to $(xy)^2$, which converts to $x^2 y^2$ using only the commutative and associative laws.

The frequency and persistence of these kinds of errors clearly show that there is no easy answer to remediating them. Cautioning students to distinguish carefully between multiplication and addition (between factors and terms) undoubtedly helps but is not sufficient. We need to emphasize the importance of structural ideas in algebra by showing how the field properties apply, at the same time using the powerful technological tools at our disposal to clarify and reinforce the structural relationships with numerical examples and visual models.

Standard 14: Mathematical Structure
In grades 9–12, the mathematics curriculum should include the study of mathematical structure so that all students can . . . understand the logic of algebraic procedures. NCTM *Curriculum and Evaluation Standards* (32, p. 184)

Solving Equations.   As with expressions, the errors in solving equations are familiar ones, perhaps the most common being variations of the sign error:

$$x + 37 = 150 \rightarrow x + 37 - 10 = 150 + 10$$

Interviews with students reveal that this error may not always be the result of carelessness or confusion with the transposition rule but may sometimes reflect a belief system that attributes validity to some operations that are not mathematically valid. In the above example, for instance, some students seem to believe in a fairness ("redistribution") principle: Whatever is taken away from one side of an equation should be added to the other side (23).

Just as some students seem more adept at constructing graphs than interpreting graphs already drawn, some students are more adept at solving equations than identifying given transformations that yield equivalent equations. In a recent study (44), about a third of the students who were asked to identify equivalent pairs of equations preferred to compute answers to determine the validity of transformations, even in simple cases like:

$$x + 2 = 5 \quad \text{and} \quad x + 2 - 2 = 5 - 2$$

Judging equivalence of equations was even more difficult when the transformation did not involve a number in the equation, that is, was not a usual step in a standard solution path:

$$x + 2 = 5 \quad \text{and} \quad x + 2 - 99 = 5 - 99$$

Graphing calculators and recent software packages for algebra encourage students to solve equations by graphing the left-hand side and the right-hand side as functions and determining for what x-value the functions are equal (see Fig. 7.9). Students can then perform transformations on the equation and see whether the transformed functions still intersect at the same point or along the same vertical line (same x-value). Explorations of this sort are fun and instructive, and we may find that they help students better understand which transformations preserve the equivalence of equations and why.

FIGURE 7.9   Solving $x - 4 = -2x + 5$ by graphing each side of the equation as a function and finding the value of x for which the two expressions are equal

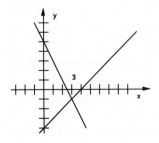

Teaching of Algebra

As promised, we conclude with some general recommendations. Perhaps first and foremost, we need to incorporate more writing in the algebra classroom. The *Professional Teaching Standards* urge more writing throughout the mathematics curriculum (33, p. 52), but writing is especially important in a subject like algebra that is generally viewed as being highly symbolic, almost nonverbal. Journal writing at the beginning of class can provide a mental warm-up for students and improve their attitude toward mathematics (31). Writing during or at the end of class can identify questions, difficulties, or misunderstandings. As much as writing helps students, it can help the teacher even more by providing informal and highly individual feedback in a nonthreatening atmosphere. Students write the most in response to simple, but specific, prompts and particularly when asked to direct their comments to a parent, a friend, or a former teacher (31).

Writing need not be limited to journals, however. Essay test questions that ask students to explain a solution procedure to, say, a younger student not only enhance students' understanding through the process of articulating ideas, but provide the teacher with detailed information about students' conceptualizations. Although supplying students with worked examples of problems, from which to generalize a solution procedure, has met with only mixed success (38, 45), writing might be used in conjunction with incorrectly worked examples to provide students with a context for diagnosing errors and explaining correct procedures.

See if your students can find the error and explain the correct procedure:

$$\text{Solve: } y^2 - 6y = -9$$
$$\text{Solution: } y(y - 6) = -9$$
$$y = -9 \text{ and}$$
$$y - 6 = -9 \text{ so } y = -3$$

Research also shows the value of asking nonroutine questions to ascertain the depth of students' understanding. One technique that has often been used is simply to reverse the standard questions: Give students a graph and ask them to interpret it (5); give students an equation and ask them to make up a word problem for it (39); give students a solution and have them make up an equation or system of equations having that solution (52). Creative questions not only help the teacher/researcher by providing insight into students' thinking, but they also help students become less unidirectional in their thinking and to make those connections between questions and answers, concepts and processes that make learning more meaningful.

Special activities are good motivation for students. "Reversed" questions suggest a game of Jeopardy (3). "What's My Rule" helps clarify the idea of function (41). Bingo can be adapted for all sorts of algebraic activities.

Another theme that underlies much of the research is the importance of applications in algebra—from two perspectives. First, algebra gives us a way of modeling real-world phenomena and predicting outcomes through manipulation of abstract symbols. From this perspective, applied problems give meaning to abstract symbols. But from another perspective, the algebras of polynomials, rational expressions, and equations are themselves concrete examples of more abstract structures like rings, fields, and vector spaces. As such, the algebra of secondary school gives meaning to the abstract structures of higher mathematics. Stressing the importance of applied problem solving in algebra addresses only half of the applications equation. Emphasizing the structural aspects of algebra addresses the other half and balances the equation.

> "When using computing devices in the algebra classroom, choose software or tools that place mathematical decision making in the hands of the students . . . .Tool software, such as function graphers, table generators, and symbolic manipulators, can put students in control of problem-solving decisions." (18, p. 197)

Of all the lessons we learn from research, perhaps the most important is that we must never take for granted that students truly understand a subject just because they are able to operate intelligently within it. We must be careful to explain the "obvious" and ask the questions that are not so obvious. Most of all, we need to listen to our students, to what they say and what they write. Learning, like teaching, is two-way communication. Students will learn more from us, the more we learn from them.

Looking Ahead . . .

Research in the learning and teaching of algebra is maturing to the point that it has important ideas to offer curriculum developers and teachers. New text materials, software programs, and standardized tests (42) are beginning to reflect recent ideas from research. Indeed, several of the writers of these new curriculum materials are researchers eager to share insights with students and teachers. As teachers become increasingly involved in research, communication is enhanced, and cooperation becomes collaboration. We will achieve full partnership when teachers and researchers are as equally involved in formulating the research questions as we are in searching for answers.

Sigrid Wagner

I believe that research can help teachers by providing suggestions for the classroom that help us teach so students will internalize ideas and avoid common misconceptions. Research will be of no use, however, if we do not try some of the ideas. We must heed the message of research into teacher effectiveness and adjust our planning, expectations, and behavior to create a classroom environment in which student input is at the center of every learning experience. I would suggest that every teacher keep a journal that includes general feelings and interesting things that happen in the classroom. You may have questions that can only be answered in your own classroom. If we aren't always looking ahead to how we can become better teachers, then research will be of no value to us.

Sheila Parker

About the Authors

Sigrid Wagner is a professor in mathematics education at The Ohio State University in Columbus, where she works with preservice and inservice middle school and high school teachers. She earned her PhD degree in mathematics education at New York University, and has long been interested in issues and research related to the learning and teaching of algebra.

Sheila B. Parker teaches algebra and geometry at Clarke Central High School in Athens, GA. She earned her Educational Specialist degree in mathematics education at The University of Georgia and has taught high school mathematics for seven years. She is interested in classroom research and speaks to teachers' groups on how to conduct teachers' own classroom investigations.

References

1. ADI, H. (1978). Intellectual development and reversibility of thought in equation solving. *Journal for Research in Mathematics Education, 9*(3), 204–213.
2. ASSAD, S. I. (1978). *Perspectives in mathematics learning.* Unpublished doctoral dissertation, SUNY Buffalo.
3. BARKLEY, C. A. (1988). Math Jeopardy. *Mathematics Teacher, 81*(1), 45–50.
4. BEHR, M., ERLWANGER, S., & NICHOLS, E. (1976). *How children view equality sentences* (PMDC Technical Report No. 3). Tallahassee: Florida State University. (ERIC Document Reproduction Service No. ED 144802)
*5. BELL, A., & JANVIER, C. (1981). The interpretation of graphs representing situations. *For the Learning of Mathematics, 2*(1), 34–42.
6. BOOTH, L. R. (1984). *Algebra: Children's strategies and errors.* Windsor, Berkshire: NFER-Nelson.
7. CARPENTER, T. P., CORBITT, M. K., KEPNER, H. S., JR., LINDQUIST, M. M., & REYS, R. E. (1981). *Results from the Second Mathematics Assessment of the National Assessment of Educational Progress.* Reston, VA: National Council of Teachers of Mathematics.
8. CARRY, L. R., LEWIS, C., & BERNARD, J. (1980). *Psychology of equation solving: An information processing study* (Final Technical Report). Austin: University of Texas at Austin, Department of Curriculum and Instruction.
*9. CHAIKLIN, S. (1989). Cognitive studies of algebra problem solving and learning. In S. Wagner & C. Kieran (Eds.), *Research issues in the learning and teaching of algebra* (pp. 93–114). Hillsdale, NJ: Erlbaum; Reston, VA: National Council of Teachers of Mathematics.
*10. CHALOUH, L., & HERSCOVICS, N. (1988). Teaching algebraic expressions in a meaningful way. In A. F. Coxford (Ed.), *The ideas of algebra, K–12* (1988 Yearbook, pp. 33–42). Reston, VA: National Council of Teachers of Mathematics.

11. COLLIS, K. F. (1975). *The development of formal reasoning.* Newcastle, Australia: University of Newcastle.

12. DAVIS, R. B. (1987, March). Remarks at the Research Agenda Conference on Algebra, Athens, GA.

*13. DEMANA, F., & LEITZEL, J. R. (1988). Establishing fundamental concepts through numerical problem solving. In A. Coxford (Ed.), *The ideas of algebra, K–12* (1988 Yearbook, pp. 61–68). Reston, VA: National Council of Teachers of Mathematics.

14. DREYFUS, T., & EISENBERG, T. (1982). Intuitive functional concepts: A baseline study on intuitions. *Journal for Research in Mathematics Education, 13*(5), 360–380.

*15. EDWARDS, E. (Ed.). (1990). *Algebra for everyone.* Reston, VA: National Council of Teachers of Mathematics.

16. EVES, H. (1953). *An introduction to the history of mathematics.* New York: Holt, Rinehart.

17. GREENO, J. G. (1982, March). *A cognitive learning analysis of algebra.* Paper presented at the annual meeting of the American Educational Research Association, Boston, MA.

*18. HEID, M. K. (1990). Uses of technology in prealgebra and beginning algebra. *Mathematics Teacher, 84*(3), 194–198.

*19. HERSCOVICS, N., & KIERAN, C. (1980). Constructing meaning for the concept of equation. *Mathematics Teacher, 73*(8), 572–580.

20. HINSLEY, D. A., HAYES, J. R., & SIMON, H. A. (1977). From words to equations: Meaning and representation in algebra word problems. In M. A. Just & P. Carpenter (Eds.), *Comprehension and Cognition* (pp. 89–106). Hillsdale, NJ: Erlbaum.

21. KERSLAKE, D. (1981). Graphs. In K. M. Hart (Ed.), *Children's understanding of mathematics: 11–16* (pp. 102–119). London: John Murray.

*22. KIERAN, C. (1981). Concepts associated with the equality symbol. *Educational Studies in Mathematics, 12*, 317–326.

23. KIERAN, C. (1984). A comparison between novice and more-expert algebra students on tasks dealing with the equivalence of equations. In J. M. Moser (Ed.), *Proceedings of the Sixth Annual Meeting of the North American Chapter of the International Group for the Psychology of Mathematics Education* (pp. 83–91). Madison: University of Wisconsin.

24. KUCHEMANN, D. (1978). Children's understanding of numerical variables. *Mathematics in School, 7*(4), 23–26.

*25. LEINHARDT, G., ZASLAVSKY, O., & STEIN, M. K. (1990). Functions, graphs, and graphing: Tasks, learning, and teaching. *Review of Educational Research, 60*(1), 1–64.

26. LINDQUIST, M. M. (Ed.). (1989). *Results from the Fourth Mathematics Assessment of the National Assessment of Educational Progress.* Reston, VA: National Council of Teachers of Mathematics.

27. LOVELL, K. (1971). Some aspects of the growth of the concept of a function. In M. F. Rosskopf, L. P. Steffe, & S. Taback (Eds.), *Piagetian cognitive-development research and mathematical education.* Washington, DC: National Council of Teachers of Mathematics.

*28. MARQUIS, J. (1989). What can we do about the high D and F rate in first-year algebra? *Mathematics Teacher, 82*(6), 421–425.

29. MATZ, M. (1982). Towards a process model for high school algebra errors. In D. Sleeman & J. S. Brown (Eds.), *Intelligent tutoring systems* (pp. 25–50). London: Academic Press.

30. MAYER, R. E. (1982). Memory for algebra story problems. *Journal of Educational Psychology, 74*(2), 199–216.

*31. MILLER, L. D., & ENGLAND, D. A. (1989). Writing to learn algebra. *School Science and Mathematics*, 89(4), 299–312.

32. NATIONAL COUNCIL OF TEACHERS OF MATHEMATICS (1989). *Curriculum and evaluation standards for school mathematics*. Reston, VA: Author.

33. NATIONAL COUNCIL OF TEACHERS OF MATHEMATICS (1991). *Professional standards for teaching mathematics*. Reston, VA: Author.

34. NATIONAL RESEARCH COUNCIL (1989). *Everybody counts*. Washington, DC: National Academy Press.

35. NORMAN, F. A. (1986). Students' unitizing of variable complexes in algebraic and graphical contexts. In G. Lappan & R. Even (Eds.), *Proceedings of the Eighth Annual Meeting of the North American Chapter of the International Group for the Psychology of Mathematics Education* (pp. 102–107). East Lansing: Michigan State University.

36. PIAGET, J., GRIZE, J. B., SZEMINSKA, A., & BANG, V. (1977). *Epistemology and psychology of functions* (F. X. Castellanos & V. D. Anderson, Trans.). Boston: D. Reidel. (Originally published, 1968)

37. RACHLIN, S. L. (1981). *Processes used by college students in understanding basic algebra*. Unpublished doctoral dissertation, University of Georgia.

38. REED, S. K., DEMPSTER, A., & ETTINGER, M. (1985). Usefulness of analogous solutions for solving algebra word problems. *Journal of Experimental Psychology: Learning, Memory, and Cognition*, 11(1), 106–125.

39. RESNICK, L. B., CAUZINILLE-MARMECHE, E., & MATHIEU, J. (1987). Understanding algebra. In J. A. Sloboda & D. Rogers (Eds.), *Cognitive processes in mathematics*. Oxford: Clarendon Press.

40. ROSNICK, P., & CLEMENT, J. (1980). Learning without understanding: The effect of tutoring strategies on algebra misconceptions. *Journal of Mathematical Behavior*, 3(1), 3–27.

41. SAWYER, W. W. (1970). *The search for pattern*. Baltimore: Penguin Books.

42. SCHOEN, H. L., & ANSLEY, T. N. (1992). *Iowa Algebra Aptitude Test*. Chicago: Riverside Publishing.

43. SOLOWAY, E., LOCHHEAD, J., & CLEMENT, J. (1982). Does computer programming enhance problem solving ability? Some positive evidence on algebra word problems. In R. J. Seidel, R. E. Anderson, & B. Hunter (Eds.), *Computer literacy*. New York: Academic Press.

44. STEINBERG, R. M., SLEEMAN, D. H., & KTORZA, D. (1991). Algebra students' knowledge of equivalence of equations. *Journal for Research in Mathematics Education*, 22(2), 112–121.

45. SWELLER, J., & COOPER, G. A. (1985). The use of worked examples as a substitute for problem solving in learning algebra 1. *Cognition and Instruction*, 2(1), 59–89.

46. TALL, D. O. (1989). Different cognitive obstacles in a technological paradigm. In S. Wagner & C. Kieran (Eds.), *Research issues in the learning and teaching of algebra* (pp. 87–92). Hillsdale, NJ: Erlbaum; Reston, VA: National Council of Teachers of Mathematics.

47. THORNDIKE, E. L., COBB, M. V., ORLEANS, J. S., SYMONDS, P. M., WALD, E., & WOODYARD, E. (1923). *The psychology of algebra*. New York: Macmillan.

*48. USISKIN, Z. (1988). Conceptions of school algebra and uses of variables. In A. F. Coxford (Ed.), *The ideas of algebra, K-12* (1988 Yearbook, pp. 8–19). Reston, VA: National Council of Teachers of Mathematics.

49. VINNER, S., & DREYFUS, T. (1989). Images and definitions for the concept of function. *Journal for Research in Mathematics Education*, 20(4), 356–366.

50. WAGNER, S. (1981). Conservation of equation and function under transformations of variable. *Journal for Research in Mathematics Education, 12*(2), 107–118.
*51. WAGNER, S. (1983). What are these things called variables? *Mathematics Teacher, 76*(7), 474–479.
52. WAGNER, S., RACHLIN, S. L., & JENSEN, R. J. (1984). *Algebra Learning Project: Final report.* Athens: University of Georgia.

CHAPTER 8

Restructuring Geometry

William F. Burger and Barbara Culpepper

> *"I have taught geometry to people of thirty years who never had learned anything*
> *of geometry before: they had just the same difficulties as the girls and boys of*
> *twelve. After reading some studies of Piaget, [my wife and I] recognized the gap*
> *of unintelligibleness, and so we discovered the levels of thinking in geometry."*
> —*Pierre van Hiele*

$\mathbf{G}$eometry occupies a special place in the secondary mathematics curriculum, largely because of the rich variety of concepts it comprises. From a psychological point of view, geometry represents the abstraction of visual and spatial experiences—shapes, patterns, measurement, and mappings, for example. From a mathematical point of view, geometry provides approaches for problem solving—drawings, diagrams, coordinate systems, vectors, transformations, and so on. Geometry also is an environment for studying mathematical structure (that is, for the careful development of a collection of theorems in a mathematical system). Euclid's contribution to Western thought is, of course, the mathematization of geometry concepts. Many students find the conceptual and problem-solving aspects of geometry stimulating and useful, but the formal study of geometry mysterious and frustrating. Only in recent years has research begun to shed light on the fundamental conflicts that exist between the psychological and mathematical issues involved in teaching geometry.

Recent research on geometry instruction has focused on a few broad areas: reasoning processes, achievement, approaches to teaching, visualization skills, gender-related issues, and the impact of technology. Research in each area has yielded fruitful results that have direct applications in the classroom.

The van Hiele Model of Reasoning

Intense interest in the van Hiele model of development in reasoning in geometry began in the United States through the efforts of Wirszup (52). As teachers, the van Hieles observed that formal reasoning in geometry does not occur naturally in children, and so must be carefully and systematically nurtured (49).

Levels of Thinking

The van Hieles' efforts led them to conjecture that reasoning in geometry develops through a sequence of levels, beginning with holistic thinking and ending with rigorous mathematical thinking (17). Each new level reflects a refinement of previous reasoning processes. Briefly summarized, the van Hiele model consists of five levels of thinking, each characterized by particular language, symbols, and methods of inference—such as the following from Burger and Shaughnessy (6).

Holistic Level. When thinking primarily holistically, students use imprecise properties to compare drawings and identify shapes. Visual prototypes are used to characterize shapes ("a rectangle is like a door"). Irrelevant attributes, such as orientation on the page, often are included when identifying and describing shapes. For example, a student may insist that two sides of a square be horizontal because when rotated, a square can seem to lose its "squareness." Conversely, relevant attributes may be excluded when identifying shapes (for example, allowing curved sides in triangles). Furthermore, students thinking holistically may not be able to conceive of an infinite variety of types of shapes. They usually do not explicitly focus on properties of shapes when identifying or describing those shapes, but more often rather view each shape as an entire object representing an imprecisely understood class. According to several studies (42, 45, 47), many students enter high school geometry reasoning holistically.

Analytic Level. When thinking analytically, students focus explicitly on properties of shapes. A shape becomes a collection of its necessary properties, which are used to describe, identify, and characterize it. For example, instead of "rectangle" a student may refer to "a four-sided shape with all right angles," even if the term "rectangle" is familiar. Too, class inclusions among types of shapes may be explicitly rejected in favor of personal characterizations. For instance, to some students thinking analytically, parallelograms may not have right angles—thus excluding rectangles as a subclass. And students thinking analytically may view geometry as physics when testing the validity of a proposition, for example, relying on a variety of drawings and making observations about them. At this level, mathematical proof may be explicitly misunderstood and unappreciated.

Abstract Level. Students thinking abstractly form complete definitions that are applied explicitly. Definitions can be modified or used in equivalent forms. Class inclusions among types of shapes then are understood and applied. Also, if–then statements are used explicitly in reasoning about shapes, and students can form correct deductive arguments based on natural logic. (For example, if p implies q and q implies r, then p implies r.) At this level, students can formulate "local" deductions of a few steps—for example, short arguments about properties of shapes that do not explicitly refer to the foundations of the particular geometry in which the student is implicitly operating. A case in point: Students may be able to apply specific axioms (postulates) or theorems without really understanding the logical distinction between them.

Deductive Level.   At this level, the mathematical structure of geometry has completely emerged for the student. Proof is viewed as the final authority in deciding the truth of a conjecture. The roles of the components in a mathematical discourse are understood (undefined terms, axioms, a system of logic, theorems, and proof). Students thus are able to reason mathematically within a particular mathematical system, although perhaps not realizing that different axioms would produce a different system, and hence different theorems.

Rigorous Level.   At this level, students appreciate the investigation of various systems of axioms and logical systems and also are able to reason in the most rigorous way within various systems. This level of reasoning is normally saved for university study.

    Additional descriptions of the van Hiele model have been contributed by Fuys and colleagues (18), Hoffer (21), and Crowley (13).

    As with all other learning hierarchies, there is a temptation to apply the van Hiele model to the reasoning processes of individual students, as a descriptive device. Yet, as Hoffer (23) cautions, we should avoid labeling people by the levels. That is, the model provides a framework for sequencing geometry activities (and those of other disciplines), the implicit objective of which is to enable students to pass unobtrusively from one level to the next. Since reasoning at the deductive level is a traditional goal of high school geometry, teachers can, through carefully sequenced activities, guide their students steadily toward it.

Sequencing Instruction

Using "learning phases," the van Hieles have prescribed a didactic means of sequencing instruction within the level structure. The phases can be described as follows, according to van Hiele (49) and Crowley (13).

> The value of the van Hiele model resides not so much in a stratification of student thought as in a prescription for instruction, not only in geometry but in most structured disciplines. (23)

Information.   New concepts are introduced through a guided dialogue between students and teacher. The teacher of necessity learns the students' vocabulary and interpretations. Through questions and observations designed to familiarize students with the new concepts, the stage is set for further study.

Directed Orientation. Students become familiar with the characteristic features of the new concepts through short, carefully sequenced direct activities.

Explication. Students, with minimal intrusion by the teacher, refine their conceptualizations and vocabulary. They express opinions about the structures observed and begin to observe relations within the structure.

Free Orientation. Students are challenged with more complex tasks of a problem-solving nature. In completing the tasks, they orient themselves within the field of study and discover many new relationships.

Integration. Students review and summarize their observations, forming a synthesis of the new concepts and relationships. The teacher assists by having them reflect on their previous actions and by clarifying observations.

It is clear that the teacher's role is different at each phase. In the *information* phase the teacher introduces new material and "interviews" the students regarding their personal conceptions of the new ideas. In *directed orientation*, the teacher assigns short activities and provides clarification. In *explication*, the teacher moderates a discussion among students and helps them reach consensus. In *free orientation*, the teacher once again clarifies the activities and assists students in discovering solutions and new results. In *integration*, the teacher leads the discussion culminating in summary results. Thus, the teacher's role is primarily indirect during the first four phases. Only during integration is direct explanation provided—but only so far as to assist students in refining and internalizing the concepts and procedures being studied. Research on phase-based instruction is limited, but supports the application of phases to instruction (5).

In applying learning phases to an instructional unit, the teacher may remain in a particular phase for several lessons, and may cycle through phases several times, according to students' needs, before completing the unit. Figure 8.1 gives an ideal-

FIGURE 8.1 Applying learning phases

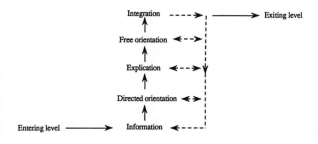

ized diagram indicating the use of learning phases in progressing from one level to the next. The double arrows indicate phases that can be revisited.

An Example Based on the van Hiele Phases

Let's consider an example of instruction using the phases. Suppose that students have holistic familiarity with simple polygons and are beginning to study their properties— angle measure, angle relationships, side relationships, symmetry, and so on. The following is part of a sequence of activities designed to advance students' understanding to the analytic level. (The collection is not intended as a complete sequence, but represents general types of activities at each phase.)

Information Activities

1. Identification of shapes. Students are presented a variety of shapes and are asked to name familiar types (Fig. 8.2).

In the discussion, students identify shapes that are familiar to them and give general descriptions of the types. For example, shapes 1 and 11 may be identified by some students as triangles because they have three "points"; shape 2 as a square because it has "four equal sides and four square corners"; shape 6 as a rectangle because it has "two long sides, two short sides, and four square corners"; shape 8 as a "diamond" (rhombus) because it has "four equal sides." Note the imprecision of these descriptions, characteristic of holistic thinking. Nonexamples of polygons, such as shape 11, are included to draw attention to relevant attributes of examples. Studies on concept formation show that nonexamples provide a useful contrast (51).

FIGURE 8.2   Shapes to identify

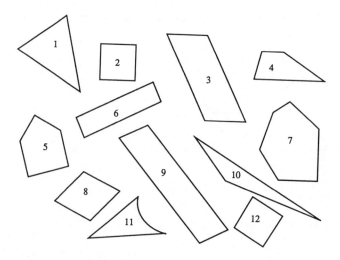

The teacher clarifies the identifications, using suitable language. For example, a right angle ("square corner") is formed by horizontal and vertical lines, or can be turned so that one side is horizontal and the other vertical. Parallel lines point in the same direction, and so on. (The logical difficulties with this approach—i.e., at the analytic rather than the abstract level—may seem troubling at first. They should not be; in fact, approaching the topic at too sophisticated a level can be the source of *far greater* conceptual problems.)

2.   Copying of shapes. Shapes such as those in Figure 8.2 are copied on a geo-board or dot paper. In so doing, students refine their notions of right angle and parallelism. They compare their shapes and resolve discrepancies. Students produce a variety of types of shapes on the geoboard/dot paper, varying irrelevant attributes. Subclasses are identified (e.g., right triangles, scalene triangles, isosceles triangles, and parallelograms).

Directed Orientation Activities

3.   Sorting activities: Students sort a collection of cut-out shapes into groups that are alike in some way. They describe their sortings and then repeat, sorting in as many ways as they can.

4.   Drawing and constructing shapes: Students draw shapes, using a protractor and ruler. They learn basic compass and straightedge and Mira constructions and apply them to constructing familiar shapes. They also construct simple enlargements and reductions of shapes with rulers and compasses. Too, students make models of polygons (e.g., from strips of cardboard and paper fasteners), observing, for example, that a parallelogram model can also make a rectangle.

5.   Students make tessellations with triangles, observing parallel lines, congruent angles, congruent triangles, similar triangles, and the like. For example, in Figure 8.3, the tessellation based on the shaded triangle contains many congruent triangles, congruent angles, parallel lines, and similar triangles.

6.   With Miras, students investigate lines of symmetry in various polygons.

7.   With *Geometric Supposer*, students measure components of shapes and make observations. For instance, using *Geometric Supposer: Quadrilaterals*, students measure sides, angles, and diagonals in parallelograms, observing that opposite sides are congruent, as are opposite angles, and that diagonals bisect each other. Connecting

FIGURE 8.3   A triangle tessellation

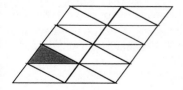

FIGURE 8.4   Connecting consecutive midpoints in a parallelogram

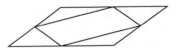

the midpoints of consecutive sides, they discover, seems to produce another parallelogram (Fig. 8.4).

Explication Activities

8.   Students list properties of familiar polygons on cards. On a display board, properties are assigned to all shapes to which they apply. For example, *rectangle* would be assigned such properties as four sides, four right angles, opposite sides parallel, opposite sides congruent, opposite angles parallel, consecutive angles supplementary, diagonals congruent, diagonals bisect each other, can be inscribed in a circle, has rotation symmetry, and has reflection symmetry.

9.   "Clubs" of various shapes are formed by means of membership criteria. Shapes are then assigned membership(s) in clubs based on properties from activity 8. For instance, a square is a member of many clubs, such as parallelograms, rectangles, rhombi, and kites.

Free Orientation Activities

10.   Students identify corresponding parts of congruent figures and simple properties of shapes through Mira investigations.

11.   Students perform nonroutine constructions using *Geometric Supposer*. For example, using *Geometric Supposer: Triangles*, students construct a variety of types of quadrilaterals, such as nonrectangular parallelograms, and kites with exactly two right angles.

12.   In Logo, students write procedures for drawing familiar polygon shapes— for example, a procedure for drawing an arbitrary regular *n*-gon, using inputs. A Logo procedure for drawing an arbitrary parallelogram, with inputs, can be adapted to draw all subclasses of parallelograms.

Integration Activities

13.   As a game, students attempt to identify particular shapes from partial views or from lists of properties that are revealed individually. Scoring includes penalties for premature correct answers. For example, the following list of clues pertains to kites as well as parallelograms: quadrilateral, two long sides and two short sides, a pair of congruent angles, two pairs of congruent sides. Explanations based on properties of known shapes is required.

14. Students critique their initial descriptions of shapes (activity 1), refining all imprecise language and including all relevant attributes. For instance, right angles are now defined in terms of degree measure. Only precise mathematical terminology is acceptable at this time.

Activities such as those described above can be found in several sources, including the New Hampshire Inservice Geometry Program (15), the Visual Geometry Project (26), the Math and the Mind's Eye materials (3), and others (16, 18, 19, 29, 35, 39, 40). More challenging activities are offered by Posamentier and Salkind (36). Research on the van Hiele model of development apparently has influenced several geometry curriculum efforts, particularly those of Hoffer (22); Coxford, Usiskin, and Hirschhorn (12), and Serra (44). In each of these curricula, students' understandings of geometry concepts are developed gradually through a variety of investigative environments.

The Development of Proof

The development of proof remains a primary goal of many geometry curricula. Success at achieving this goal remains mixed, however, with only about half of all geometry students developing some success with proof writing (47). A critical factor in success at proof is the student's van Hiele level upon entering the geometry course (43). Students entering with only holistic thinking skills on many concepts have about a 30% chance of success at proof—that is, only about 30% of such students became successful at writing proofs. Those entering with analytical thinking skills have about a 60% chance. And those entering with abstract thinking skills have nearly a 100% chance. The approximate distribution of students by van Hiele level upon entering and leaving a geometry course is given in Table 8.1.

Senk observed that students who *leave* a geometry course with no more than holistic thinking skills have about a 15% chance of success at proof. Students developing analytic thinking skills have about a 20% chance, and those developing abstract

TABLE 8.1.   Percentages of Students at Each van Hiele Level in Fall and Spring

van Hiele Level	% in Fall	% in Spring
Holistic*	78	31
Analytic	15	34
Abstract	7	28
Deductive	0	5
Rigorous	0	2

*Senk encountered students who may not yet have been operating holistically. To simplify, they are included in the holistic level.

thinking skills have about a 60% chance. Thus, one cannot reasonably hope to develop students' abstract reasoning abilities and facility with proof simultaneously.

These observations clearly call for the development of geometry curricula in elementary and middle schools designed to advance students at least to the level of analytical thinking. Such curricula are essential for the development of conceptual understanding in geometry for *all* students, including the approximately 50% who do not study geometry in high school. Additionally, these observations provide unmistakable warnings against geometry curricula in high schools that begin with the study of proof. Such an approach can be expected to succeed with only about 40% of the students (30% of the 78% entering with at most holistic skills, plus 60% of the 15% entering with analytic skills, plus the 7% entering with abstract skills).

Opportunities Using Technology

The recommendation that extensive conceptual development in geometry precede the study of formal proof is not new (10, 28, 30, 48). Yet until recently there has been relatively little research on alternative approaches, with the possible exception of the transformational approaches of the 1970s. Technology has provided alternatives, though, that have yielded new insights.

Recent research on the effect of Logo on geometry learning gives cause for optimism (4, 8, 9, 27, 33, 38). Using Logo's turtle graphics to assist in teaching about geometric shapes seems to enable children to progress from intuitive, holistic notions about shapes to more analytical conceptions (4, 8, 27). In these studies, children who wrote Logo procedures for drawing polygons and angles developed more mathematically accurate and more general conceptions of these shapes in terms of their necessary components. For example, children who had written a Logo procedure for drawing an arbitrary parallelogram (as in free orientation activity 12) observed that the adjacent angles of a parallelogram must sum to 180°. The study of Logo also seemed to enhance the children's problem-solving abilities in terms of representing problems and applying sophisticated strategies. Interestingly, in the study of Clements and Battista (8), the Logo treatment was designed primarily as computer instruction, not geometry instruction.

> It appears that the use of Logo, *as an environment for geometric investigations*, fosters higher-level thinking.

The study of Logo has been analyzed according to the van Hiele model of development (25, 34). For instance, in sequencing instruction in motion geometry designed to bring students to analytical thinking, the following use of the phases applies.

Information.   The teacher demonstrates a variety of examples and nonexamples of motions, using physical objects, and introduces basic vocabulary.

Directed Orientation.   Using teacher-designed Logo procedures, students create motion images in direct mode. Students complete or debug given procedures.

Explication.   Students design and debug procedures designed to produce motion images of simple shapes.

Free Orientation.   Students extend and generalize procedures, using variables.

Integration.   Students write procedures that will produce given designs that involve motion images. They demonstrate their projects to the class and explain their approaches.

Lessons that we learn from instruction with Logo may well transfer to more sophisticated computer environments.

Another environment for computer investigations in geometry is provided by the *Geometric Supposers* (41). Here, the emphasis is on exploration of shapes via measurement of their attributes, culminating in general observations or conjectures. That is, the *Geometric Supposers* provide a computer environment in which students draw a variety of geometric shapes and measure distances, angles, and areas. In using the *Supposers* to test conjectures, students frequently use some form of deductive reasoning. For example, it appears that the medians of a triangle are concurrent (Fig. 8.5.)

What must a student measure to determine if, indeed, in triangle *ABC* the medians *AQ*, *BR*, and *CP* meet at a single point? That is, the student must determine *sufficient* conditions for their concurrency. In verifying the conjecture, the student cannot rely on the *Supposer's* measuring capabilities, but rather must produce a deductive, general argument.

The use of the *Geometric Supposers* in developing students' conjecturing skills is described in several publications for teachers, including (7) and (24).

The Advanced Computer Tutoring Project has produced the artificial intelligence–based *Geometry Tutor* for developing proof skills in geometry (1). *Geometry Tutor* is designed to model behavior of a human tutor in diagnosing a student's confusion, determining information that a student needs, and providing instruction pertaining to such needs. If a student is proceeding along a successful path to a proof, the tutor does not interfere. If, however, the tutor infers that the student's path is not fruitful, or if the student does not know how to proceed, the tutor provides remedial instruction. While there has been little research on the effectiveness of *Geometry Tutor*, classroom teachers who have used it are most enthusiastic about its versatility and effectiveness. Additional information on the use of computers in teaching geometry can be found in (2).

FIGURE 8.5   Constructing medians in a triangle

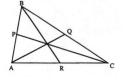

Needed Research

Research often leads to more questions than it answers. In the case of geometry research, we find vast areas left open for further investigation. In researching the van Hiele model of development in geometry, only a relatively narrow spectrum of geometrical ideas has been studied, and that primarily properties of planar shapes. Students' understanding of major topics in geometry needs to be studied in terms of the model—topics such as visualization, measurement, transformations, congruence, similarity, and the relationships between geometry and algebra, all in two and three dimensions. Such research will help clarify our understanding of the model and describe children's basic conceptions of other topics. It is important to keep in mind that the model was initially based on the van Hieles' informal observations of their students' behavior on classroom activities. The model has been refined and analyzed through a variety of research approaches (6, 13, 20, 31). As a result, we now have a more complete "analytic level" understanding of the van Hiele model itself, as applied to properties of planar shapes. It is time to apply the model more widely, as van Hiele has suggested (50).

Technology offers enormous opportunity for curriculum reform in geometry, from the introduction of Logo in elementary grades to investigations on the *Geometric Supposers* in middle and high school grades to computerized tutoring with *Geometry Tutor* in high school. Opportunities for interactive electronic homework using systems like *Geometry Tutor* are imminent. Additionally, utilities for two- and three-dimensional graphics provide unprecedented opportunities for developing visualization skills. All of these areas call for careful research to determine their proper uses. As with all teaching environments, though, each electronic environment has its limitations. For example, examining tessellations is cumbersome with Logo, but much simpler on dot or graph paper. We must make effective use of *all* the teaching environments available to us. Thus, results from research, and particularly from cooperative research with teachers, is beneficial in planning instruction.

In curriculum development, many of the innovations of the past decade remain only lightly investigated. A major unresolved issue is to determine the advantages of integrated curricula and, in particular, eclectic approaches to geometry, as in the Chicago School Mathematics Project (12). In this curriculum coordinates are introduced early, as are transformations and synthetic methods, giving students a variety of heuristics for solving problems. For example, in proving that every angle inscribed in a semicircle is a right angle, we can impose a coordinate system (Fig. 8.6.)

To show that $\angle ABC$ is a right angle, we can compute the slopes of segments AB and BC, and then, using the equation of the circle, show that the product of the slopes is -1. Hence the segments are perpendicular.

Using coordinates in problem solving is very common in calculus. Should it be a central theme in geometry? In the United States, only about 6% of 17-year-olds are proficient at multistep problem solving, according to the 1986 National Assessment of Educational Progress report (14). Only 51% are proficient at *moderately* complex procedures and reasoning. Yet, 96% can do basic operations and beginning problem solving. It appears that we are doing a far better job at teaching computational skills

FIGURE 8.6   An angle inscribed in a semicircle

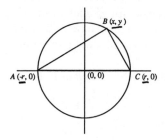

than we are at teaching how to apply them. Approaches to geometry that are computational in nature may help to develop more sophisticated problem-solving skills.

Probably the most comprehensive study of an alternative to traditional Euclidean geometry instruction is Usiskin's investigation of the feasibility of a transformational approach (11, 46). Neither approach was clearly superior overall. On some measures, particularly attitudinal, the transformation approach seemed more successful, while the traditional approach seemed more successful on some measures of achievement.

> One major conclusion of Usiskin's study is that *there are effective alternatives to traditional instruction*. In the intervening twenty years, however, little effort has been made to document such alternatives via research.

The underrepresentation of women in the mathematical sciences indicates the neglect of a critical national resource. In the Cognitive Development and Achievement in Secondary School Geometry study, with a large sample of students and schools, no significant differences were found between girls' and boys' abilities to write proofs in geometry (42). Yet, when career choices of students well prepared in mathematics and science are compared, a disproportionate percentage of boys plan careers in the sciences (37). Perhaps societal forces discourage young women from scientific careers. If so, what are these forces, and what can mathematics teachers do to inspire able students to pursue the advanced study of mathematics and science?

Looking Ahead . . .

As schools implement the *Curriculum and Evaluation Standards* of the National Council of Teachers of Mathematics (32), the state of the geometry program, considering its traditional place in the mathematics curriculum, can be viewed as an indicator of the success of curriculum reform efforts. NCTM recommends a broad-based, exploratory approach to geometry in grades 9–12, including coordinates, transformations, computer investigations, and real-world applications. Areas for deemphasis include the formal study of synthetic Euclidean geometry, two-column proofs, and certain esoteric theorems. What will be the goals for geometry in the year 2000? Will they reflect the research and curriculum development efforts of the last quarter of the twentieth century? Our responsibility as teachers and researchers is to see that they do.

William F. Burger

About the Authors

William Burger was an associate professor of mathematics at Oregon State University, where he was engaged in teacher preparation and research in the acquisition of geometry concepts. He had been a member of the Editorial Panel of the *Arithmetic Teacher*, and was involved in a number of mathematics education projects in Oregon, including efforts to encourage minority scholars to pursue careers in science and mathematics. The untimely death of William Burger, in 1991, is a great loss to the mathematics education community. We are grateful for the many students he conscientiously prepared for teaching and doing mathematics.

Barbara Culpepper teaches geometry at Franklin High School in Portland, Oregon. She has her B.S. in mathematics from Portland State University and has taught high school mathematics for eleven years. She is the past editor of *The Oregon Mathematics Teacher* and has presented state and national workshops for geometry teachers.

References

1. ANDERSON, J. A., BOYLE, C. F., & REISER, B. J. (1985). Intelligent tutoring systems. *Science, 228*, 456–462.
2. BELL, M. (1986). Microcomputer based courses for secondary school plane geometry. In R. Morris (Ed.), *Geometry in schools, studies in mathematics education* (Vol. 5). Paris: UNESCO.
*3. BENNETT, A., MAIER, E., & NELSON, L. T. (1988). *Math and the mind's eye*. Salem, OR: The Math Learning Center.
4. BATTISTA, M., & CLEMENTS, D. (in press). The effects of Logo on children's conceptualizations of angle and polygons. *Journal for Research in Mathematics Education*.
5. BOBANGO, J. (1987). Van Hiele levels of geometric thought and student achievement in standard content and proof writing: The effects of phase-based instruction. Unpublished doctoral dissertation, Pennsylvania State University.
6. BURGER, W. F., & SHAUGHNESSY, J. M. (1986). Characterizing the van Hiele levels of development in geometry. *Journal for Research in Mathematics Education, 17*, 31–48.
*7. CHAZAN, D., & HOUDE, R. (1989). *How to use microcomputers and conjecturing to teach geometry*. Reston, VA: NCTM.
8. CLEMENTS, D., & BATTISTA, M. (1989). Learning geometric concepts in a Logo environment. *Journal for Research in Mathematics Education, 20*, 450–467.
9. COOK, P. (1988). The effects of an instructional unit utilizing Logo and the computer on achievement in geometry and attitude toward mathematics of selected high school general mathematics students. Unpublished doctoral dissertation, Temple University.
10. COXFORD, A. F. (1978). Recent directions in geometry. In R. Lesh & D. Mierkiewicz (Eds.), *Recent research concerning the development of spatial and geometric concepts*.

Columbus, OH: ERIC Center for Science, Mathematics, and Environmental Education.

*11. COXFORD, A. F., & USISKIN, Z. (1971). *Geometry: A transformation approach*. River Forest, IL: Doubleday/Laidlaw.

*12. COXFORD, A. F., USISKIN, Z., & HIRSCHHORN, D. (1987). *Geometry*. Chicago: The University of Chicago School Mathematics Project.

*13. CROWLEY, M. (1987). The van Hiele model of development of geometric thought. In M. M. Lindquist (Ed.), *Learning and teaching geometry, K–12*. Reston, VA: NCTM.

14. DOSSEY, J., MULLIS, I., LINDQUIST, M., & CHAMBERS, D. (1988). *The mathematics report card: Are we measuring up?* Princeton: Educational Testing Service.

*15. FERRINI–MUNDY, J. (1987). *New Hampshire inservice geometry program*. Durham: The University of New Hampshire.

16. FERRINI–MUNDY, J. (1987). Spatial training for calculus students: sex differences for achievement and visualization ability. *Journal for Research in Mathematics Education, 18,* 126–140.

17. FUYS, D., GEDDES, D., & TISCHLER, R. (Eds.). (1984). *English translation of selected writings of Dina van Hiele-Geldof and Pierre M. van Hiele*. Brooklyn: Brooklyn College. (ERIC Document Reproduction Service No. ED 287 697)

*18. FUYS, D., GEDDES, D., & TISCHLER, R. (1988). The van Hiele model of thinking in geometry among adolescents. *Journal for Research in Mathematics Education Monograph No. 3.*

*19. GILLESPIE, N. (1973). *Mira activities for junior high school geometry*. Palo Alto: Creative Publications.

20. GUTIERREZ, A., JAIME, A., & FORTUHY, J. M. (in press). Assessing van Hiele levels in geometry. *Journal For Research in Mathematics Education.*

*21. HOFFER, A. (1981). Geometry is more than proof. *The Mathematics Teacher, 74,* 11–18.

*22. HOFFER, A. (1979). *Geometry: A model of the universe*. Reading, MA: Addison-Wesley.

23. HOFFER, A. (1983). Van Hiele-based research. In R. Lesh & M. Landau (Eds.), *Acquisition of mathematics concepts and processes*. New York: Academic Press.

*24. HOUDE, R., & YERUSHALMY, M. (1988). *Geometry problems and projects*. Pleasantville, NY: Sunburst Communications.

25. KIEREN, T., & OLSON, A. (1983). Linking Logo with learning levels in mathematics. Talk presented at the Northwest Conference on Computers in Education, Oregon State University.

*26. KLOTZ, E. (1989). *Visual geometry project materials*. Berkeley, CA: Key Curriculum Press.

27. LEHRER, R., SANCILIO, L., & RANDLE, L. (1988). Learning pre-proof geometry with Logo. Paper presented at annual meetings of the American Educational Research Association, New Orleans.

*28. LINDQUIST, M. M. (1987) *Learning and teaching geometry* (1987 Yearbook). Reston, VA: NCTM.

*29. MACPHERSON, E. (1985). The themes of geometry: design of the nonformal geometry curriculum. In C. R. Hirsch & M. J. Zweng (Eds.), *The secondary school mathematics curriculum* (1985 Yearbook). Reston, VA: NCTM.

30. MARTIN, J. L. (Ed.) (1976). *Space and geometry: Papers from a research workshop*. Columbus, OH: ERIC Center for Science, Mathematics, and Environmental Education.

31. MAYBERRY, J. (1983). The van Hiele levels of geometric thought in undergraduate preservice teachers. *Journal for Research in Mathematics Education, 14,* 58–69.

32. NATIONAL COUNCIL OF TEACHERS OF MATHEMATICS (1989). *Curriculum and evaluation standards for school mathematics*. Reston, VA: Author.

33. Noss, R. (1987). Children's learning of geometrical concepts through Logo. *Journal for Research in Mathematics Education, 18*, 343–362.

34. OLIVE, J., LANKENAU, C. A., & SCALLY, S. P. (1986). The Atlanta–Emory Logo project: Teaching and understanding geometric relationships through Logo. *Proceedings of the Second International Conference for Logo and Mathematics Education*. London: Institute of Education, University of London.

*35. PEARCE, P., & PEARCE, S. (1978). *Polyhedra primer*. Palo Alto: Dale Seymour.

*36. POSAMENTIER, A., & SALKIND, C. (1988). *Challenging problems in geometry*. Palo Alto: Dale Seymour.

37. RALLIS, S., AHERN, S., & DICK, T. (1987). Blue and pink bootie career choices: Profiles of high school students with strong math and science preparation. Paper presented at annual meeting of the American Education Research Association, Washington, DC.

38. RIEBER, L. (1987). Logo and its promise: A research report. *Educational Technology, 27*, 12–16.

39. SCHATTSCHNEIDER, D. (1987). Resources for teaching geometry in high school and college. In L. Grinstein & P. Campbell (Eds.), *Mathematics education in high school and junior college*. Hamden, CT: Garland Publications.

*40. SCHATTSCHNEIDER, D., & WALKER, W. (1977). *M. C. Escher kaleidocycles*. New York: Ballantine.

41. SCHWARTZ, J., & YERUSHALMY, M. (1986). *The Geometric Supposers*. Cambridge, MA: Education Development Center. (Available from Sunburst Communications.)

42. SENK, S. (1985). How well do students write geometry proofs? *The Mathematics Teacher, 78*, 448–456.

43. SENK, S. (1989). Van Hiele levels and achievement in writing geometry proofs. *Journal for Research in Mathematics Education, 20*, 309–321.

*44. Serra, M. (1989). *Discovering geometry: an inductive approach*. Berkeley: Key Curriculum Press.

45. SHAUGHNESSY, J. M., & BURGER, W. F. (1985). Spadework prior to deduction in geometry. *The Mathematics Teacher, 78*, 419–428.

46. USISKIN, Z. (1969). The effects of teaching Euclidean geometry via transformations on student achievement and attitudes in tenth-grade geometry Unpublished doctoral dissertation, University of Michigan.

47. USISKIN, Z. (1982). *Van Hiele levels and achievement in secondary school geometry*. Chicago: Department of Education, University of Chicago. (ERIC Document Production Ser. No. SE 038813)

48. USISKIN, Z. (1987). Resolving the continuing dilemma in school geometry. In M. M. Lindquist (Ed.), *Learning and Teaching Geometry, K–12* (1987 Yearbook). Reston, VA: NCTM.

49. VAN HIELE, P. M. (1986). *Structure and insight*. Orlando, FL: Academic Press.

50. VAN HIELE, P. M. (1987). A method to facilitate the learning of levels of thinking in geometry by using the levels in arithmetic. Paper presented at the Conference on Learning and Teaching Geometry, Syracuse University.

51. WILSON, P. (1986). Feature frequency and the use of negative instances in a geometric task. *Journal for Research in Mathematics Education, 17*, 130–139.

52. WIRSZUP, I. (1976). Breakthroughs in the psychology of learning and teaching geometry. In J. L. Martin (Ed.), *Space and geometry: Papers from a research workshop*. Columbus, OH: ERIC Center for Science, Mathematics, and Environmental Education.

CHAPTER 9

Teaching and Learning Calculus

Joan Ferrini-Mundy and Darien Lauten

INTERVIEWER: *Does this diagram mean anything to you?*

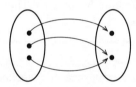

STUDENT: *Sure; it's one of those puddle diagrams. I guess it has something to do with functions. Never knew what it meant.*

The concept of *function* is central to modern mathematics. As teachers of mathematics, we comfortably use various representations of functions as we introduce new concepts and pose mathematical tasks. Yet recent research indicates that the ways in which students think about function may be surprisingly different from what we might expect. In fact, students' ways of thinking about functions seem to parallel the evolution of the modern function concept within the mathematical community.

The present meaning of function has evolved over the past 200 years (44). Originally viewed as a change depending on other changes, function later took on the meaning of an expression with a numerical value. Its modern definition is based on the notion of a special subset of a Cartesian product. Although the concept of function is fundamental to all that we do, students' interactions with this idea are very complex.

The major focus of this chapter is to interpret research on the learning of such precalculus and calculus concepts as function. We look at research-based ideas for the classroom and current curricular innovations. In addition, we present new directions for curriculum development and instruction based on current understandings of how students learn concepts in calculus. We also briefly review additional research that bears upon such precalculus and calculus issues as the participation of young women, the role of advanced mathematics in career choices, predicting success, and the current reform movement to improve the organization, content, and instruction of calculus.

Learning Calculus Concepts

A substantial body of research on student understanding of function, *limit, continuity, derivative,* and *integral* is available. The research has been guided by the researchers' interests in learning more about students' existing understandings and problem-solving approaches. Much of this research is consistent with a constructivist perspective (72) based on the view that students possess their own constructed understandings. Very often, students' understandings are well elaborated and firmly held, yet are unexpected because they are different from the traditional understandings. These nontraditional student views are called misconceptions or alternate conceptions. As we come to understand these we will be able to create a foundation on which to build the kinds of instructions and curriculums by means of which teachers can more efficiently serve as facilitators and guides.

> "If, then, we come to see knowledge and competence as products of the individual's conceptual organization of the individual's experience, the teacher's role will no longer be to dispense 'truth' but rather to help and guide the student in the conceptual organization of certain areas of experience." (72, p. 16)

Function Concepts

> "The role that functions play in mathematics is so extensive that it is impossible to give any summary that is both brief and adequate. There is no branch of mathematics whose developments since 1800 can be studied in their present form without an understanding of the general function concept." (8, p. 252)

There is convincing evidence that the function concept develops over time, and that very young children can learn basic functional ideas (39, 43, 63, 69). Four- and five-year-olds are intrigued by situations embodying one-to-one and many-to-one correspondences (60). Although the topic of function is not heavily emphasized in most elementary textbooks, the NCTM *Curriculum and Evaluation Standards* claims that "The idea of a functional relationship can be intuitively developed through observations of regularity and work with generalizable patterns" (p. 60), in grades K through 4.

Several researchers in mathematics education have been interested in aspects of both secondary school and college students' understanding of function (8, 21, 22, 50, 61). They have studied the subconcepts of function (domain, range, representation, correspondence), representations used for functions (graphs, arrow diagrams, rules, tables), and ways in which students use and conceptualize functions. Collected research in this area has shown that the working definition of function held by most secondary and postsecondary school students is that of function as a rule of correspondence, represented by a formula (33, 44, 45, 70). Students are strongly committed to this view, and believe that a function must have the same rule of correspondence over its entire domain (70). Functions defined differently on different parts of the domain (piecewise functions) present great difficulty (38, 44).

This view of functions as formulas into which values are to be substituted serves students well until they reach problems requiring more sophisticated reasoning. Graphical representations of functions, presented to college students without formulas, are not classified by them as functions, because of the absence of specific formulas (38). Although we knew that students are aware that functions may be expressed in several forms, as we assembled evidence from various studies we saw that connections among these representations are weak and difficult for students (21, 25, 33, 44). For example, finding a function's graph from an algebraic formula is generally easy for students, but working from the graph to produce a formula for the function proves to be difficult. Algebraic and graphical data often are viewed as independent, and students can quite comfortably use contradictory methods of reasoning in each of these settings. As teachers, we need to encourage students to work in both settings and to transfer ideas easily between them.

We find it interesting that a number of researchers have noted that students interpret functions in a point-by-point, or local, way rather than globally (4, 50). Our traditional curriculum may overemphasize local interpretations of functions, both in the graphical sense of examining the behavior of a graph at a single point and in the algebraic sense of evaluating a formula for a single-domain value. Tasks that encourage students to interpret graphs qualitatively , such as the one shown in Figure 9.1, may help build a global interpretation (16, 47, 48).

While real-life problems are useful, familiarity can give rise to other complications (12, 42). An especially interesting confusion in graphing is familiar to all precalculus teachers whose students assume that the actual path of a vertically launched projectile is the parabola representing its height versus time. A calculator capable of graphing parametric equations in real time can demonstrate the fact that a parabolic path results from a projectile launched at a particular angle, as is indicated in Figure 9.2.

Questions that promote deeper understanding of function, help build algebraic and graphical connections, address the "iconic confusion," and (may also) assist with the point-by-point and global distinction are found in research tasks such as those in Figures 9.2, 9.3, and 9.4 (51).

> "*Forwards* questions give a specific value in the domain and ask for the corresponding range value: "How far apart are the cars at time t = 1/4 hour?" Backwards questions ask the student to determine a value in the domain that corresponds to a given value in the range: "At what time are the cars 30 miles apart?"

FIGURE 9.1   Qualitative graphing tasks

Dick plans to study the effect of growing sunflowers in different size pots. The graphs below show four possible outcomes of his experiment.

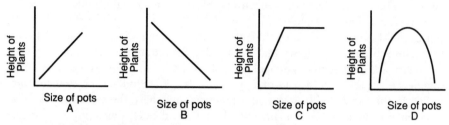

Which graph is *best* described by each of the following statements.

i.   As the pot size increases, the plant height decreases.
ii. As the pot size increases the plant height increases up to a certain pot size. With larger pots, plant height remains the same.

FIGURE 9.2   Parabolic graphs

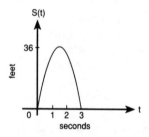

An object is projected directly upward from the ground with an initial velocity v_0 of 48 ft./sec. Its distance s(t) in feet above the ground after t seconds is given by the formula $s(st) = v_0t - 16t^2$.

Determine:
i.   the formula that gives the height of the object relative to the ground after t seconds. (ans. $s(t) = 48t - 16t^2$.

ii. the maximum height of the object. (ans. 36 ft. at t = 1.5 sec.)

iii. the number of seconds the object is in the air. (ans. 3 sec.)

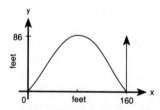

A ball is kicked with an initial velocity of 82 ft./sec at an angle of elevation of 65°.

i.   Create the parametric equations.
     (ans. x = (82 cos 65°)t
           y = (82 sin 65°)t − 16t².)

ii. Determine how far the ball will travel before it hits the ground. (ans. about 160 ft.)

iii. Determine the maximum height of the ball in flight. (ans. about 86 ft.)

FIGURE 9.3   Time versus distance graph

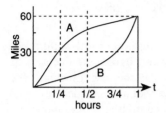

Across time questions ask the student to describe patterns of change in one variable that are related to patterns of change in another variable: "Give an interval over which the distance between the cars is increasing, but at a decreasing rate."

Articulation questions are designed to determine the extent to which students can keep derived quantities separate and yet answer questions that depend on their interaction: "Tell whether the following is true or false. Give an explanation for your answer in terms of the graph. Whenever the speed of car A is greater than the speed of Car B, then the distance between the cars is decreasing."

Multiple representation questions involve translating among the six modes of representations: real phenomenon, verbal rule, diagram, table, graph, and formula, as well as recognizing two representations of the same function: "Draw a pair of axes so that you have distance along the horizontal axis and time along the vertical axis. Then, by plotting points, sketch a graph which indicates, for each distance D the first time the two cars are D miles apart."

FIGURE 9.4   Calculator-generated graphs

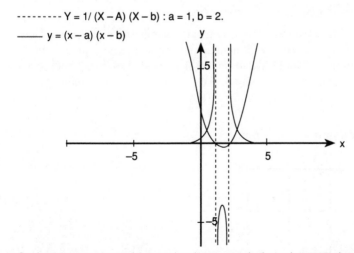

Students are encouraged to note that the two graphs have the same sign, and the reciprocal of $y = 1/(x - a)(x - b)$ has asymptotes where $y = (x - a)(x - b)$ is zero.

> *Change of context* questions require seeing the parallels among distinct embodiments of formally equivalent questions. Such questions might relate an economics question to a graph equivalent to one used earlier in a different context. (pp. 7–14)

Using computer technology, and integrating the investigation of real-world functional situations in the classroom, researchers and teachers have been able to help students develop more powerful intuitive and formal understanding of functions (18, 23, 67, 73). Graphing can become a tool for the discovery of mathematical ideas, or a strategy for problem solving, rather than an arduous end in itself. For example, by graphing $|f(x)|$, $f(x - a)$, and $f^{-1}(x)$ from the graph of $f(x)$, without algebraic representation, students can develop stronger algebraic and geometric connections (23). As is illustrated to some extent in Figure 9.4, by graphing $y = (x - a)(x - b)$ for $a = 1$ and $b = 2$, superimposing the graph of the reciprocal function, considering values of $x < a$, $a < x < b$ and $x > b$, and making conjectures about $y = 1/(a - x)^2$, $y = 1/(a - x)^3$, students' graphical intuitions improved (67).

Superimposing the graphs of $f(x) = \sin(a + x)$ and $g(x) = \sin(a)\cos(x) + \cos(a)\sin(x)$ is a convincing means of demonstrating a trigonometric identity (67). By graphing several functions of the form $y = a^{bx}$ or $y = A\sin(Bx + C) + D$, students begin to formulate rules about the influence of the parameters on the graph (18).

Although technology opens up wonderful new possibilities, we must also be alert to new difficulties that can arise simultaneously: Overall shape, magnitude of a translation, direction of movement, and scale of an object infinite in size all may cause illusions. Some of the confusion results from scale differences, the lack of easily trackable points, and the infinite domain and range of the functions investigated. For example, in teaching vertical translation, we sometimes assume that students see the vertical translation under discussion in the graph on the right in Figure 9.5. In fact, the students may actually see a horizontal shift (16, 37).

Exponential and Trigonometric Functions

In general, function research has not focused on particular classes of functions. However, because of the importance of exponential and trigonometric functions to the precalculus curriculum, we would like to highlight a few studies here. Student understanding of exponential functions may be hampered by traditional approaches to

FIGURE 9.5   Vertical or horizontal shift?

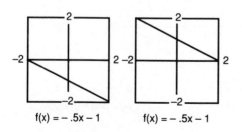

f(x) = −.5x − 1   f(x) = −.5x − 1

multiplication based only on repeated addition (14). The findings suggest that children may construct multiplicative understandings through "splitting" processes (e.g., sharing a cookie first among two children, then among four, etc., via repeated "splits"). Perhaps it is possible to build on this splitting approach in order to help students develop a better intuitive understanding of exponential functions. For example, we can explore recursively defined functions representing exponential growth as a means of introducing functions such as $y = ca^x$. We have found that spreadsheets portraying real-world situations can be especially effective in helping students. Some of the research tasks mentioned below could be used in precalculus settings to enhance understanding of exponential growth.

---

1. Place 1/3, 9^3, 9^{-3}, 2, 9^0, 10, -3, and -1 on the number line.
2. Construct a problem whose answer is 10^{-2}.
3. Venus is 1.1×10^8 km from the sun. Mercury is half that distance. How far is Mercury from the sun? Saturn is 1.4×10^9 km. How many km farther away is Saturn than Venus? (Assume the planets are lined up [14].)

In SIMS, the *Second International Mathematics Study*, (11), ten trigonometry items were administered to U.S. twelfth graders, both at the end of a precalculus course and at the end of calculus. Only 50% of the students could solve correctly the trigonometric equation $\sin x = 1/2$ at the end of a calculus course. An item requiring the students to interpret information from a diagram (see Fig. 9.6) proved difficult, with only 36% of the calculus students able to answer correctly.

Questions involving hypotheses about the Law of Sines, or about the graph of parametric equations, were especially difficult, with success rates of only 20% among calculus students. Evidence from SIMS and anecdotal evidence from college calculus instructors suggest that although students may be able to perfrom fundamental, skill-oriented trigonometric tasks, both their conceptual understanding and their ability to work from diagrams and graphs are less adequate.

Sequences, Series, Limits, and Continuity

Our major conclusion from the rather limited research in these areas is that students' experience conflicts between formal, precise definitions and the informal, natural

---

FIGURE 9.6   Trigonometry task (11, p.59)

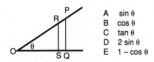

A $\sin \theta$
B $\cos \theta$
C $\tan \theta$
D $2 \sin \theta$
E $1 - \cos \theta$

In the future above, $\overline{PQ} \perp \overline{OQ}$ and $\overline{RS} \perp \overline{OQ}$. If the measures of $\overline{OQ}$ and $\overline{OQ}$ equal 1 and 8 is the measure of $\angle POQ$, then the measure fo segment $\overline{PQ}$ is equal to

language interpretations used conveniently in discourse (13, 38, 68). As an example, consider the standard informal interpretation of the definition of the sequence s_n tending to a limit s, $\lim(n \to \infty) s_n = s$: "We can make s_n as close to s as we please by making n sufficiently large" (68, p. 44). Students frequently believe that s_n cannot *ever* equal s (although it *does* in the convergent sequence 7/8, 1, 9/8, 1, 8/9, . . .). This belief is inconsistent with their acceptance of $\lim(x \to 2) x^2 = 4$ [68]. Although students often can produce correct answers to limit problems, several studies have found that they are uneasy about the mismatch between their intuition and the answers they produce through mathematical manipulation (32, 35, 38).

When college students were asked to judge from graphs (see Fig. 9.7) and formulas whether given functions were continuous, they gave correct answers; yet probing revealed that the responses often were based on incorrect reasoning (71).

Frequently, students would equate a function's continuity with its being defined; for example, the function is discontinuous because it is not defined for every x. Students' conceptions of continuity also are built strongly on natural language descriptions; their use of such descriptions as "it keeps going" or "it continues" as indicators of a function's continuity are quite adequate until problems become more sophisticated (33).

Articles suggesting activities and examples to help students understand sequences, series, and limits can be found in the reference list (5, 26, 58).

Derivative

Our review of literature, together with our experience in the classroom, has convinced us that the ways in which students understand functions relate directly to the ways in which they understand derivatives. Despite relatively good "procedural" per-

FIGURE 9.7   Continuity tasks (71, p. 179)

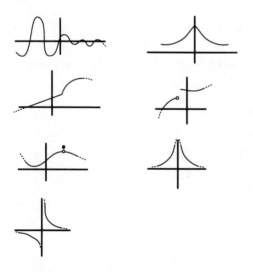

THE FAMILY CIRCUS®   **By Bil Keane**

10-22
© 1990 Bil Keane, Inc.
Dist. by Cowles Synd., Inc.

"What makes hills in the road flatten out when we get there?"

Reprinted with special permission of King Features Syndicate.

formance in computing derivatives, students' ability to work with geometric or physical representations of the derivative is limited (33, 55, 56).

For example, students had difficulty interpreting how secant lines "sliding" along a curve (see Fig. 9.8) lead to the tangent line in the limit (57). Over 40% of the students interviewed were not able to state how the secant lines relate to the tangent

FIGURE 9.8   Tangent as the limit (57, p. 25)

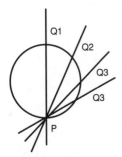

The tangent as the limit

The diagram shows a circle and a fixed point P on the circle. Lines PQ are drawn from P to points Q on the circle and are extended in both directions. Such lines across a circle are called secants, and some examples are shown in the diagram. As Q gets closer and closer to P. What happens to the secant?

line. Typical responses included, "The line gets shorter, it becomes a point, the area gets smaller, and it disappears" (p. 25). A related conception held by students is that the derivative of a function is actually the equation of the tangent line (1, 33).

Prior to the study of calculus in the curriculum, we can help students develop stronger intuitions about the derivative by emphasizing ideas of ratio and proportion. Examining where functional values on a curve are decreasing, increasing, or decreasing *or* increasing most rapidly is an interesting task. The graphical task shown in Figure 9.9 leads students to use the ratio (change in y)/(change in x).

Similarly, "pointwise" and "across-time" understanding (understanding on an interval) (50) can be promoted through problems related to graphs; see Figure 9.10.

Although the questions are basic to the standard calculus curriculum and might be considered straightforward, students tend to have a *pointwise* understanding and are able to answer A and 3/4 in the first question, but lack an *across-time* understanding. They have trouble determining that the cars are farthest apart at time $t = 1$ and move farther apart in the time interval from $t = 1/2$ to $t = 1$ hour.

We can help students to understand rate of change of functions by investigating graphical representation of real-life situations with student-generated data before using more algebraic approaches, as can be seen in Figure 9.11.

The most promising classroom strategies for helping students better understand derivatives seem to involve technology. Several efforts to implement technology-intensive calculus courses have shown that such courses have positive effects on student understanding and interest *without* hindering skill acquisition (3, 19, 40). These approaches have emphasized multiple representations. For example (as Figure 9.12 shows), students examined graphs of the functions to decide under what conditions the rate of change of the function could be determined at $x = 0$, and whether the graph had a tangent at $x = 0$. Although this experience helped the students develop

FIGURE 9.9 Average rate of change (57, p. 26)

The graph of y for a certain equation, for x = 0 to x = 6, is shown below

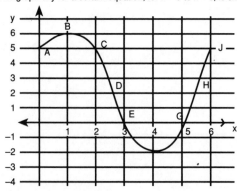

What is the average rate of change of y with respect to x
(i)   from A to B? (ans. 1)
(ii) from B to E? (ans. –3)
(iii) from A t J? (ans.0)

FIGURE 9.10   Pointwise and across-time tasks (50, p. 3)

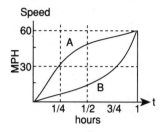

POINTWISE:
Which car is going faster at time t = 3/4?
I s car A going faster at time t = 1/4 or t = 3/4

ACROSS TIME:
Tell whether or not the cars are closest together
at time t = 1. Do the cars get farther apart or closer
together? (Monk, 1987, 50 p. 3)

a better understanding of the concepts, they still exhibited difficulties when the tangent coincided with the graph (66).

By using technology to magnify the graphs of functions, we have found that students can investigate the rate of change of a graph dynamically (67). In Figure 9.13, the chord is drawn from $(x, f(x))$ to $(x + c, f(x+c))$, with c being a small value, and the slope of the chord is plotted as x progresses from left to right, thereby helping students build graphical and algebraic connections.

As already suggested, we found that as students noticed that the slopes generated by $y = x^2$ resulted in approximately a straight line, they could check the algebra and find the slope from (x, x^2) to $(x+c, (x+c)^2)$ to be $2x + c$. As c approaches 0, the slope approaches $2x$. Related investigations for $y = x^3$, $y = \sin(x)$, and other functions lead to an intuitive understanding of the derivative before the formal procedures are introduced.

FIGURE 9.11   Odometer–speedometer task (34, p. 5)

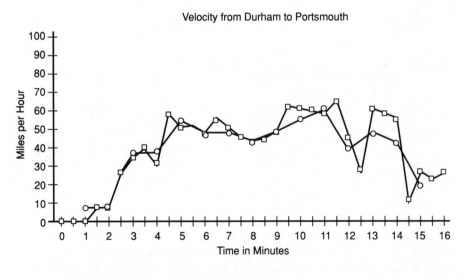

FIGURE 9.12   Rate-of-change tasks (66, p. 71)

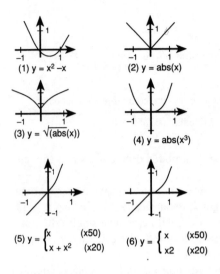

(1) y = x² −x

(2) y = abs(x)

(3) y = √(abs(x))

(4) y = abs(x³)

(5) y = {x   (x50)
         {x + x²   (x20)

(6) y = {x   (x50)
         {x2   (x20)

FIGURE 9.13   A gradient (slope) function interpretation task (67, pp. 161, 162)

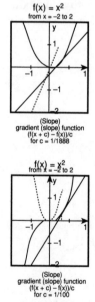

f(x) = x²
from x = −2 to 2

(Slope)
gradient (slope) function
(f(x + c) − f(x))/c
for c = 1/1888

f(x) = x²
from x = −2 to 2

(Slope)
gradient (slope) function
(f(x + c) − f(x))/c
for c = 1/100

Integrals

Students' tendencies to work with function and limit concepts in mechanical ways relate to their difficulty in grasping global notions and interrelationships in integration as well as in differentiation. Sometimes students who can apply basic techniques successfully have fundamental misunderstandings and demonstrate little intuition about the underlying concepts (38, 50, 56). The procedure of dissecting an area or volume using the limit process, and the reasons why such a method works, is not always central to students' understanding of the integral. As is made clear in Figures 9.14 and 9.15, students seemed to lack the understanding of integration as the limit of a sum required to answer the questions precisely.

We believe that the constructs of *across-time* and *pointwise* understanding also are powerful ways of helping students to think about the concepts of integration. The questions used in Figure 9.16 address the area under a curve, and can be used in a classroom situation.

Whereas 85% of the college students gave the correct answer (A(1) = 2, A(3) = 6) to the *pointwise* question, only 53% correctly responded "increase" to the *across-time* question. And although the students in the study had generally been successful in the course, perhaps they still focused on the changing function $f(x)$ rather than on the increasing function $A(p)$. We teachers, influenced strongly by our textbooks, sometimes assume that it is only a small step from reading graphs in a pointwise manner to looking at graphs in a global way. It appears that such a step is not automatic, but must be addressed specifically with examples such as this.

In this context, technology again proves useful. For instance, in a fashion similar to the graphing of numerical values of the derivative, successive cumulative areas can be plotted on a graph simultaneously with a given function so that students may develop the intuitions and insights necessary to understand integration (65). By way of example, see Figure 9.17.

Students plot $f(x) = x^2$ from $x = 0$ to $x = 5$, and then plot the successive cumulative area calculations over the same domain. When the graphs are overlaid, we find that students notice that the graphs cross at the point (3, 9), and that the cumulative area graph appears to be a higher power of x, such as $f(x) = kx^3$. The class is then able to discover that $f(x) = x^3/3$. This activity can lead nicely to a development of the Fundamental Theorem of Calculus.

FIGURE 9.14   Definite integral task (56, p. 16)

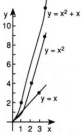

Explain, by means of the diagram or otherwise, why

$$\int_0^a (x^2 + x)\,dx = \int_0^a x^2\,dx + \int_0^a x\,dx.$$

FIGURE 9.15 Solid-of-revolution task (56, p. 17)

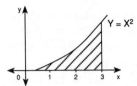

When the area under a curve is rotated through 360°
about the x-axis a solid is traced out.

i Describe the solid traced out when the shaded area above is rotated
   through 360° about the x-axis.

ii. Explain how to use integration to calculate the volume of this solid.
    Why does the method work?

FIGURE 9.16 Area-under-a-graph task (50, p. 3)

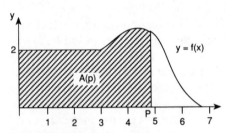

Area under the graph
Pointwise: Determine the values of **A**(1) and **A**(3).

Across-time: The point p moves from 4.5 to 5.0.
Does the area A(p) increase or decrease?

FIGURE 9.17 Cumulative-area task (65, p. 49)

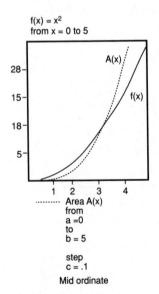

Issues Related to Calculus Learning

Young Women and Mathematics

In addition to the research that examines student understanding of concepts, there are studies concerned more globally with student participation and achievement in calculus. Beginning in the seventies, there was particular interest in the mathematical participation and achievement of young women (27, 36). We were troubled by the underrepresentation of young women in mathematics-related fields, and particularly the engineering areas (2). In addition, young women were not continuing into secondary-school precalculus and calculus courses in numbers comparable with those of young men (7, 59). There has been extensive study of the factors and variables that seem to influence women's participation and achievement in advanced mathematics courses.

Mathematics has been dubbed the "critical filter" (62), because gatekeeping courses such as calculus may limit women's choices of a college major. Although there has been progress in recent years, National Assessment of Educational Progress (NAEP) data from 1986 (20) indicates that whereas 8% of male high school students study mathematics through precalculus or calculus, only 5% of female students do so. There is still reason for teachers to be concerned about the possible differential treatment of males and females in the classroom, their different experiences in their course taking, and the ways in which societal context may be affecting their career plans (6). There is in fact some evidence that college women who elect careers in mathematics and engineering are at least equal to, if not superior to, men in their mathematics achievement (15, 30).

A very specific variable that has been studied with respect to these questions is spatial visualization ability, an area where males typically outscore females on most instruments (9, 28). There is reason to believe that spatial ability is linked to mathematics achievement (6, 29), and that young women in particular can benefit from focused training in spatial activities. There are areas of precalculus and calculus, such as volumes of solids of revolution, where it is quite clear that a spatial or geometric emphasis might be especially helpful to *all* students.

Participation and performance in precalculus and calculus courses are closely related to career choice, more strongly for young women than for young men (49, 59). Research shows that young women are also more significantly influenced by the encouragement of others, including parents, counselors, and teachers, than are young men. In addition, young women's perceptions about the usefulness of mathematics are important influences in their decisions to elect advanced mathematics courses. Finally, the presence of role models, particularly in engineering areas, seems to make a difference in assisting young women toward career choices in mathematics and science.

Predicting Success in Advanced Mathematics

A number of studies have tried to identify predictors of success in advanced mathematical coursework (17, 24, 41). Previous background and performance in mathematics typically are the variables most strongly related to performance in both precalculus and calculus. Although students frequently exhibit weaknesses in the procedural and technical skills of algebra and trigonometry, both of which are important for success in calculus, these skills can be improved through remediation. (A number of colleges provide pretests and assistance.) Nonetheless, calculus still proves difficult for college students. It is entirely possible that student difficulties are related to their concept of function, leading to narrow understandings of concepts such as *derivative, limit,* and *integral.* This is an area in need of more detailed research, for the pretests typically used to predict calculus achievement rarely include the type of "conceptual" items that would help us understand the situation more thoroughly.

Calculus in the Secondary Schools

There has been considerable discussion over the years about the appropriateness of calculus as a secondary school subject. Professional organizations have advised (46) that secondary schools offer only calculus courses comparable to college level courses, and avoid anything less.

> "This standard does not advocate formal study of calculus in high school for all students or even for college-intending students." (52, p. 180)

The research findings on the actual effects of the high school course are mixed at best. The general result seems to be that secondary school calculus has a positive influence on performance in college calculus, at least initially (10). This effect diminishes in the second and third semesters of college calculus, and evidences itself principally in the technical, skill-oriented aspects of the course (31). The secondary school introduction, when it is too cursory and procedural, can provide students with a false sense of security. About 300,000 high school students annually are enrolled in some type of calculus course. Only about 15%–20% of these students are in advanced placement calculus (64). We do not have a very clear understanding of the effects of various types of secondary school calculus courses on continued college work in mathematics.

Calculus Curriculum Reform

There is a national interest in college calculus curriculum reform currently underway. About 600,000 students enroll annually in calculus in the nation's four-year colleges and universities. Approximately half of these students are in "mainstream" engineering calculus courses. Of these, fewer than half finish the course with a grade of D or higher (64). Most college calculus courses are taught in large lecture sections, often by beginning graduate students with little or no teaching experience. The collegiate mathematics community is most concerned about this problem, and with funding from the National Science Foundation and other organizations, a program for "revitalizing instruction in calculus" (54) has been underway for the past several years.

The curriculum development in this area seems to be driven by reorganization of the mathematical content, with, for example, increased emphasis on numerical methods, approximation, and dynamical systems. Most projects are experimenting boldly with technology, using hand-held graphics calculators, symbolic manipulators, and other graphics tools. The availability of technology allows us to reconsider the time and emphasis allocated to traditional calculus topics. For example, many feel that there is less need for extended practice in doing complicated derivatives and using special techniques of integration. Other projects are exploring ways to work more effectively within the constraints of the large-lecture system by using laboratory approaches, projects, and some small-group work. As these projects evolve, their impact will be felt at the precollege level.

Conclusion

The research we have reviewed suggests that students gain technical proficiency with the skills of precalculus and calculus relatively easily, particularly if their technical skill in algebra is strong. Conceptual understanding of certain central themes in both precalculus and calculus is less well developed, although the research provides ideas for both curricular and pedagogical innovation. The concept of function is a central theme that undergirds the precalculus and calculus curriculum. The NCTM *Curriculum and Evaluation Standards* call for the treatment of function at the middle and secondary school levels by isolating it as a separate standard. We should give students the opportunity to relate the concept to real-life contexts (52), and allow them to work with various representations of function, including formulas, graphs, tables, and diagrams. Curricular approaches that encourage students to relate and make connections between symbolic and geometric representations are needed.

By creating problem situations and discussions that relate to the idea of limit into the secondary curriculum earlier, we can help students anticipate certain central ideas of calculus that relate to limit, including continuity. The technology available now, particularly spreadsheets, can help students to play with sequences of numbers and build intuitions that will serve them well as they study limits later on.

We must continue to be concerned about the possibility that young men and young women experience their precalculus and calculus courses in very different ways. The numbers of women electing careers in engineering and physical science areas still are small compared to the numbers of men, despite relatively equal enrollments in calculus.

Finally, we should be mindful of the interesting opportunity for articulation between the secondary schools and institutions of higher education regarding the teaching and learning of precalculus and calculus. Teachers at both levels have much to learn from each other, and much to gain from substantive interaction regarding curriculum development and instructional strategies.

Looking Ahead . . .

Although the research has highlighted the difficulties that students have in coordinating the algebraic and graphical representations of functions, we do not have a collection of curricular strategies that can be useful in classroom settings for enhancing this coordination. I wonder if more research collaboration with secondary school teachers as equal research partners could help us develop the insights we need, within the context of real classrooms. The NCTM *Professional Standards for Teaching Mathematics* charges teachers with "observing, listening to, and gathering other information about students to assess what they are learning" (p. 53). What better way to do so than by collaborating in a research undertaking?

Joan Ferrini-Mundy

As teachers, we try many different approaches to helping students develop a deeper understanding of the topics addressed in this chapter. As I include many of the activities utilizing computers, I notice some students experiencing significant computer anxiety that interferes with their developing the mathematical understanding intended. Research is needed not only to determine how much students' understanding is enhanced by participating in these computer based activities, but also to determine the most effective ways of overcoming students' anxiety about using computers to better understand mathematics. This is certainly an area in which teachers and university researchers can work as partners.

Darien Lauten

About the Authors

Joan Ferrini-Mundy is an associate professor of mathematics at the University of New Hampshire in Durham. She has two years' experience teaching secondary school mathematics. Her research interests include calculus learning, teacher development, and mathematics education reform.

Darien Lauten is a mathematics teacher at Oyster River High School in Durham, New Hampshire. She was a Mathematics Presidential Awardee in 1990 and a member of a Woodrow Wilson National Fellowship Foundation algebra team. Her interests include incorporating technology into teaching mathematics, particularly calculus.

References

1. AMIT, M., & VINNER, S. (1990). Some misconceptions in calculus—Anecdotes or the tip of an iceberg? In G. Booker, P. Cobb, & T. deMendicuti (Eds.) *Proceedings of the Fourteenth International Conference for the Psychology of Mathematics Education* (Vol. I, pp. 3–10), Mexico City: Organizing Committee of the 14th Annual PME Meeting.

2. AUSTER, C. (1984). *Nontraditional occupational choice: A comparative study of women and men in engineering* (Doctoral dissertation, Princeton University, 1984). *Dissertation Abstracts International, 44*, 11-A, 3511.

3. BECKMANN, C. E. (1988). *Effect of computer graphics use on student understanding of*

calculus concepts. Unpublished doctoral dissertation, Western Michigan University, Kalamazoo, MI.

4. BELL, A., & JANVIER, C. (1981). The interpretation of graphs representing situations. *For the Learning of Mathematics, 2*(1), 34–42.

*5. BENNETT, A. B. (1989). Visualizing the geometric series. *Mathematics Teacher, 8*(2), 130–136.

6. BISHOP, A. J. (1980). Spatial abilities and mathematics education—A review. *Educational Studies in Mathematics, 11*, 257–269.

7. BRUSH, L. R. (1979). *Why women avoid the study of mathematics: A longitudinal study* (Contract No. 400-77-0099). Washington, DC: National Institute of Education.

8. BUCK, R. C. (1970). Functions. In E.G. Begle & H.G. Rickey (Eds.), *Mathematics Education, the 69th Yearbook of the NSSE.* Chicago: University of Chicago.

9. BURNETT, S. A., LANE, D. M., & DRATT, L. M. (1979). Spatial visualization and sex differences in quantitative ability. *Intelligence, 3*, 345–354.

10. BURTON, M. (1989, April). The effect of prior calculus experience in introductory college calculus. *The American Mathematical Monthly*, 350–354.

11. CHANG, L. C., & RUZICKA, J. (1985). *Second International Mathematics Study United States, Technical Report 1.* Champaign, IL: Stipes.

12. CLEMENT, J. (1989). The concept of variation and misconceptions in Cartesian graphing. *Focus on Learning Problems in Mathematics, 11*(1–2), 77–87.

13. CONFREY, J. (1980). *Conceptual change, number concepts and the introduction to calculus.* Unpublished doctoral dissertation, Cornell University, Ithaca, NY.

14. CONFREY, J. (1988, February). *The concept of exponential functions: A student's perspective.* Invited address for a conference: Epistemological Foundations of Mathematics Experience, University of Georgia, Athens.

15. DE BOER, G. E. (1984). A study of gender effects in the science and mathematics course taking behavior of a group of students who graduated from college in the late 1970's. *Journal of Research in Science Teaching, 21*(1), 95–100.

*16. DEMANA, F., & WAITS, B. K. (1988). Pitfalls in graphical computation, or why a single graph isn't enough. *College Mathematics Journal, 19*(2), 177–183.

17. DICK, T. P. (1984). *Covariance structural models for mathematics achievement and participation: An investigation of sex differences at the level of college calculus using factorial modeling* (Doctoral dissertation, University of New Hampshire). *Dissertation Abstracts International, 45*, 06-A, 1673.

18. DICK, T. P. (1989, March). *Symbolic/graphical calculators as tools for revitalizing calculus.* Paper presented at the annual meeting of the American Educational Research Association, San Francisco.

19. DICK, T. (1990). *Super calculators as calculus laboratory instruments.* Unpublished manuscript, Mathematics Department, Oregon State University, Corvallis, OR.

20. DOSSEY, J. A., MULLIS, I. V. S., LINDQUIST, M. M., & CHAMBERS, D. L. (1988). *The mathematics report card: Are we measuring up?* Princeton, N.J: Educational Testing Service.

21. DREYFUS, T., & EISENBERG, T. (1983). The function concept in college students: Linearity, smoothness and periodicity. *Focus on Learning Problems in Mathematics, 5*, 119–132.

22. DREYFUS, T., & EISENBERG, T. (1984). Intuition on functions. *Journal of Experimental Education, 52*(2), 77–85.

23. DREYFUS, T., & EISENBERG, T. (1987). On the deep structure of functions. In J. C. Bergeron, N. Herscovics, & C. Kieran (Eds.), *Proceedings of the Eleventh International*

Conference of the International Group for the Psychology of Mathematics Education (Vol. 1, pp. 190–196). Montreal: IGPME.

24. EDGE, O. P., & FRIEDBERG, S. H. (1984). Factors affecting achievement in a first course in calculus. *Journal of Experimental Education, 52*(3), 136–140.

25. EVEN, R., LAPPAN, G., & FITZGERALD, W. (November, 1988). Pre-service teachers' conceptions of the relationship between functions and equations. In M. J. Behr, C. B. Lacampagne, & M. M. Wheeler (Eds.), *Proceedings of the Tenth Annual Meeting of the North American Chapter of the International Group for the Psychology of Mathematics Education* (pp. 283–289). De Kalb: Northern Illinois University.

*26. EGSGARD, J. C. (1988, February). An interesting introduction to sequences and series, *The Mathematics Teacher*. Reston, VA: NCTM.

27. FENNEMA, E. (1977). Influences of selected cognitive, affective, and educational variables on sex-related differences in mathematics learning and studying. In L. Fox, E. Fennema, & J. Sherman (Eds.), *Women and mathematics: Research perspectives for change*, Washington, DC: National Institute of Education.

28. FENNEMA, E., & SHERMAN J. (1977). Sex related differences in mathematics achievement, spatial visualization and affective factors. *American Educational Research Journal, 14*, 51–71.

29. FERRINI–MUNDY, J. (1987). Spatial training for calculus students: Sex differences in achievement and in visualization ability. *Journal for Research in Mathematics Education, 18*(2), 126–140.

30. FERRINI–MUNDY, J., & BALOMENOS, R. (April 1984). *Males and females in college calculus: Relationships among prior, concurrent, and subsequent academic experiences.* Paper presented at the Annual Meeting of the American Educational Research Association, New Orleans.

31. FERRINI–MUNDY, J., & GAUDARD, M. (January 1992). *Secondary school calculus: Preparation or pitfall in the study of college calculus? Journal for Research in Mathematics Education, 23*(1), 56–71.

32. FERRINI–MUNDY, J., & GRAHAM, K. (August–September 1991). An overview of the calculus curriculum reform effort: Issues for learning, teaching, and curriculum development. *American Mathematical Monthly, 98*(7), 627–635.

33. FERRINI–MUNDY, J., & GRAHAM, K. (January 1991). *Research in calculus learning: Understanding of limits, derivatives, and integrals.* Paper presented at the Joint Mathematics Meetings, Special Session on Research in Undergraduate Mathematics Education, San Francisco.

34. FERRINI–MUNDY, J., & ZIA, L. (1989). *Research-based calculus curriculum: Samples.* Unpublished manuscript, University of New Hampshire, Durham.

35. FISCHBEIN, E., TIROSH, D., & MELAMED, U. (1981). Is it possible to measure the intuitive acceptance of a mathematical statement? *Educational Studies in Mathematics, 12*, 491–512.

36. FOX, L. H. (1979). *Women and mathematics: The impact of early intervention programs upon course-taking and attitudes in high school* (Final Report). Washington, DC: National Institute of Education.

37. GOLDENBERG, E. P. (1987). Believing is seeing: How preconceptions influence the perceptions of graphs. In J. C. Bergeron, N. Herscovics, & C. Kieran (Eds.), *Proceedings of the Eleventh International Conference on the Psychology of Mathematics Education* (pp. 197–203). Montreal.

38. GRAHAM, K. G., & FERRINI–MUNDY, J. (1989 March). *An exploration of student understanding of central concepts in calculus.* Paper presented at the Annual Meeting of the American Educational Research Association, San Francisco.

39. GREENO, J. G. (1988, November). The situated activities of learning and knowing mathematics. In M. J. Behr, C. B. Lacampagne, & M. M. Wheeler (Eds.), *Proceedings of the Tenth Annual Meeting of the North American Chapter of the International Group for the Psychology of Mathematics Education* (pp. 481–521). De Kalb: Northern Illinois University.

40. HEID, M. K. (1988). Resequencing skills and concepts in applied calculus using the computer as a tool. *Journal for Research in Mathematics Education, 19*(1), 3–25.

41. HENDERSON, R. W., & LANDESMAN, E. M. (1986). *A preliminary evaluation of student preparation for the study of calculus.* Santa Cruz: California University, Group for Research in Mathematics and Science Education.

42. JANVIER, C. (1981). Use of situations in mathematics education. *Educational Studies in Mathematics, 12,* 113–122.

43. LEINHARDT, G., ZASLAVSKY, O., & STEIN, M.K. (1990). Functions, graphs, and graphing: Tasks, learning, and teaching. *Review of Educational Research. 60*(1), 1–64.

44. MARKOVITS, Z., EYLON, B., & BRUCKHEIMER, M. (1986). Functions today and yesterday. *For the Learning of Mathematics, 6*(2), 18–24, 28.

45. MARNYANSKII, I. A. (1965/1975). Psychological characteristics of pupils' assimilation of the concept of a function. In J. Wilson (Ed.), *Soviet Studies in the psychology of learning and teaching mathematics, XII* (pp. 163–172). SMSG. Chicago: University of Chicago Press.

46. MATHEMATICAL ASSOCIATION OF AMERICA/NATIONAL COUNCIL OF TEACHERS OF MATHEMATICS (1986). *Calculus in the secondary school.* Unpublished paper.

47. MCDERMOTT, L., ROSENQUIST, M., & VAN ZEE, E. (1987). Student difficulties in connecting graphs and physics: Example from kinematics. *American Journal of Physics, 55*(6), 503–513.

48. MCKENZIE, D. L., & PADILLA, M. J. (1986). The construction and validation of the Test of Graphing in Science (TOGS). *Journal of Research in Science Teaching, 23*(7), 571–579.

49. MEECE, J. L., PARSONS, J. E., KACZALA, C. M., GOFF, S. B., & FUTTERMAN, R. (1982). Sex differences in math achievement: Toward a model of academic choice. *Psychological Bulletin, 91*(2), 324–328.

50. MONK, G. S. (1987). Students' understanding of functions in calculus courses. *Humanistic Mathematics Network Newsletter, 2.*

51. MONK, G. S. (1989, March). *A framework for describing student understanding of functions.* Paper presented at the annual meeting of the American Educational Research Association, San Francisco.

52. NATIONAL COUNCIL OF TEACHERS OF MATHEMATICS (1989). *Curriculum and evaluation standards for school mathematics.* Reston, VA: Author.

53. NATIONAL COUNCIL OF TEACHERS OF MATHEMATICS (1991). *Professional standards for teaching mathematics.* Reston, VA: Author.

54. NATIONAL SCIENCE FOUNDATION (1988). *Program announcements & guidelines: Undergraduate curriculum development in mathematics: Calculus.* Washington, DC: Office of Undergraduate Science Engineering, and Mathematics Education (USEME).

55. ORTON, A. (1983a). Students' understanding of differentiation. *Educational Studies in Mathematics, 15,* 235–250.

56. ORTON, A. (1983b). Students' understanding of integration. *Educational Studies in Mathematics, 14,* 1–18.

57. ORTON, A. (1984). Understanding rate of change. *Mathematics in School, 3*(5), 23–26.

58. ORTON, T., & REYNOLDS, C. (1986). Taking maths to the limit. *Mathematics in School, 15*(4), 28–32.

59. PEDRO, J. D., WOLLEAT, P., FENNEMA, E., & BECKER, A. V. (1981). Sex differences in the relationship of career interests and mathematics plans. *Vocational Guidance Quarterly, 29,* 25–34.

60. RUSSELL, S. J., & FRIEL, S. (1989, March). *Dimensions of reality in elementary math problems.* Paper presented at the annual meeting of the American Education Research Association, San Francisco.

61. SCHOENFELD, A. H., SMITH, J. P., & ARCAVI, A. (in press). Learning: The microgenetic analysis of one student's evolving understanding of a complex subject matter domain. In R. Glaser (Ed.), *Advances in Instructional Psychology, Volume IV.* Hillsdale, NJ: Erlbaum.

62. SELLS, L. (1973). *High school mathematics as the critical filter in the job market.* Berkeley: University of California. (ERIC DOC. Repro Service No. ED 080351)

63. SMITH, W. D. (1972). *An investigation of the ability of students in the secondary school mathematics curriculum improvement study to generalize their knowledge of function concepts to other stimulus settings.* Doctoral dissertation, University of Maryland.

64. STEEN, L. A. (Ed.) (1987). *Calculus for a new century.* (Background papers for a National Colloquium). Washington, DC: National Research Council.

*65. TALL, D. (1986, March) A graphical approach to integration. *Mathematics Teaching, 114,* 48–51.

66. TALL, D. (1987). Constructing the concept image of a tangent. In J. C. Bergeron, N. Herscovics, & C. Kieran (Eds.), *Proceedings of the Eleventh International Conference on the Psychology of Mathematics Education* (pp. 69–75). Montreal.

67. TALL, D., & BLACKETT, N. (1986). Investigating graphs and the calculus in the sixth form. In N. Burton (Ed.), *Exploring Mathematics with Microcomputers* (pp. 156–175). London: Council of Educational Technology.

68. TALL, D. O., & SCHWARZENBERGER, R. L. (Eds) (1978). Conflicts in the learning of real numbers and limits. *Mathematics Teaching, 83,* 44–49.

69. THOMAS, H. L. (1975). The concept of function. In M. Rosskopf (Ed.), *Children's mathematical concepts* (pp. 145–172). New York: Teachers College, Columbia University.

70. VINNER, S. (1983). Concept definition, concept image, and the notion of function. *International Journal of Mathematics Education in Science and Technology, 14*(3), 293–305.

71. VINNER, S. (1987). Continuous functions—images and reasoning in college students. In J. C. Bergeron, N. Herscovics, & C. Kieran (Eds.), *Proceedings of the Eleventh International Conference of the Psychology on Mathematics Education* (pp. 177–183). Montreal.

72. VON GLASERSFELD, E. (1987). Learning as a constructive activity. In C. Janvier (Ed.), *Problems of representation in the teaching and learning of mathematics* (pp. 3–17). Hillsdale, NJ: Erlbaum.

73. YERUSHALMY, M. (1988). *Formation of algebraic concepts using multiple representation software environments.* Unpublished manuscript, the University of Haifa, Israel.

CHAPTER 10

Thinking about Uncertainty: Probability and Statistics

J. Michael Shaughnessy and Barry Bergman

"*I have a good math background. I feel in most areas competent, able to answer tall questions in a single bound. Not that everything is algorithmic to me . . . conceptual knowledge and experience help me to quickly sort through strategies and techniques. Probability is another matter. Even after working on a probability question for some time, I am frequently struck with such thoughts as 'Do I have the right interpretation? Have I set it up right? Did I choose a good way to model the situation?' Often I feel a great deal of uncertainty with my answer. I find myself looking for confirmation. It seems to me that probability and statistics is the ultimate problem solving proving ground. This is an area in which we desperately need to improve our intuitive feel for the subject, but simultaneously must remain skeptical of our intuition.*"

—*Confessions of a Teacher*

"*I became fascinated that subjects in those studies could have used elementary probability and statistics concepts to estimate the likelihood of events in the research tasks, but they didn't. Even those who were well schooled in stochastics were caught using certain judgmental heuristics rather than employing their hard earned statistical knowledge. What was even more frightening was that I found myself falling prey to some of the same misconceptions that snared the subjects.*"

—*Confessions of a Researcher*

Although there have been many prior attempts to encourage an increased emphasis on probability and statistics at the secondary level (8, 34, 40), the recent NCTM *Curriculum and Evaluation Standards* document may finally provide the necessary impetus for requiring more probability and statistics of *all* our secondary students (29). At the moment, however, there is a wide gap between the ideals of the *Standards* and what is actually taking place in our schools.

In the United States, stochastics has not yet truly made it into the mainstream of school mathematics.

> The word "stochastics" is commonly used in the literature to refer at once to both probability and statistics.

This is particularly true at the secondary level, where very few secondary schools actually offer a separate course in probability and statistics. If probability and statistics is included in the secondary curriculum at all, it is as a short unit inside of another course. Many students will not have the opportunity to take it and teachers may even be tempted to skip it altogether. This is a very unfortunate situation, since there is perhaps no other branch of the mathematical sciences as important for all students, college bound or not, as probability and statistics.

Until recently, the absence of probability and statistics from our secondary curriculum may have been at least partially due to a lack of appropriate materials.

> A recent study found that only 2% of college bound high school students in the United States had a course in probability and statistics, while at least 90% of these students had a course in algebra. (9)

However, this excuse is no longer valid, because excellent materials to support the teaching of probability and statistics are now available for both middle and secondary schools (15, 26, 27, 30, 31, 41, 44).

For the college bound, the absence of secondary level preparation in stochastics stands in sharp contrast to the demands for both statistical literacy and stochastic reasoning that lie ahead. All of our students, college bound or not, eventually become consumers and citizens at some level of involvement. They will enter a society in which the use of data and graphs to communicate information and to influence decisions is ever increasing.

> A recent survey at a major university discovered that 160 different statistics courses were being taught in 13 different departments. (14)

There is a golden opportunity in mathematics education to begin to implement the NCTM *Standards* recommendations for statistics and probability while informed by the research that has already been done on how students think and react during stochastic tasks. Numerous research studies on stochastics have been conducted over the past twenty years by mathematics and statistics educators and by cognitive psychologists. Much of this research has been done with students, who have had little or no formal training in probability and statistics, in order to uncover their intuitive ideas of stochastics or to study their preconceptions or misconceptions of probability and statistics. As a result, research is beginning to form a picture of the conceptions of probability and statistics that students have *prior* to any formal coursework.

Stochastic Conceptions: Pictures from Research

Since there has been little teaching of stochastics at the secondary level in the United States, much of the research work has been done with college students. These students are only recently graduated from secondary school, and so their conceptions of statistics and probability should give us a fairly accurate picture of how secondary school students think. In other countries, and particularly in Europe, where probability and statistics plays a much more prominent role in the curriculum, secondary level stochastics research is more common. Thus, much of what we have learned about secondary students' thinking in probability and statistics comes from our European colleagues.

Adolecents' Conceptions of Uncertainty

In a three-year study, the largest survey of adolescents' concepts of probability to date, David Green tested over 3,000 students age 11–16 in Great Britain (16, 17). Green was interested both in the probability concepts that these students possessed and in their level of Piagetian development. Green's tasks included tree diagrams, visual representations of randomness, questions on the language of probability, Piagetian marble tasks (see, for example, Fig. 10.1), and spinners with area models of probability (see, for example, Fig. 10.2).

> Two bags have black and white counters.
>   Bag J: 3 black and 1 white   Bag K: 6 black and 2 white
> Which bag gives the better chance of picking a *black* counter?
> A) Same chance
> B) Bag J
> C) Bag K
> D) Don't know
> Why? _____

FIGURE 10.1   Marble task

FIGURE 10.2   Spinner task

Brown   Orange

Half of the students in Green's study chose bag *K* as more likely to yield a black counter, and 39% of all the students gave as their reason that there are just more blacks in bag *K*. The ratio concept, crucial to elementary probability concepts, is not understood by these students. Green found that there was not much improvement with age on this marble task.

> Two discs, one orange and one brown, are marked with numbers. Each disc has a pointer that spins. If you want to get a 1, is one of the discs better than the other, or do they both have the same chance?
> A) Brown is better for getting a 1
> B) Orange is better for getting a 1
> C) Both discs give the same chance
> D) No one can say
> Why did you choose this answer? _____

Only about 50% of the students correctly selected the orange spinner and used the area model to explain their reasoning. Nearly 25% of them—chose brown because it has more regions with a 1. Other students preferred the brown spinner because it had contiguous regions. Although there was some improvement on this item with age, there was not much gain after age 13.

In items designed to test students' conceptions of randomness, Green's subjects were especially poor at distinguishing randomly distributed snowflakes in a rectangular grid from nonrandom distributions or in picking out the random sequences of 0s and 1s from the hand-manufactured sequences. The students believed there should be patterns and symmetry in "random" events. In items designed to examine their understanding of the language of probabililty, Green also found that students' verbal abilities were inadequate for describing probabilistic situations. Certainty and high probability were equated. Students thought either that 50% probability meant that something "might or might not happen," or that all outcomes were equally likely, even when there were more than two events.

Green concludes that (1) the ratio concept, crucial to a conceptual understanding of probability, is not well understood; (2) students are weak when it comes to understanding and using the common language of probability, such as "at least" or "certain" or "impossible"; and (3) students are particularly weak in their concepts of randomness, stabilities of frequencies, and inference. In addition, Green concluded that most of the pupils do not reach the level of Piagetian formal operations by age 16.

"Only an extensive programme of class-based activities is likely to provide the weight of evidence and experience to eliminate fallacious thinking exhibited by pupils and adults alike. The need is for *practical activity* at an early age on which to build adequate experience. . . . (17, p. 41)

In order to improve students' conceptions of chance, randomness, and probability, Green advocates experimental activities, explicit classroom discussion, and mathematical modeling.

Although such a giant survey has not yet been administered in the United States, we might expect the situation to be similar to Green's findings, or even worse, because of the lack of attention to stochastics in our schools. The only large-sample survey data on probability concepts in the U.S. come from a few items on the National Assessment of Educational Progress (NAEP). Carpenter and colleagues (7) report that students do seem to have some intuitive notions of probabilities in very elementary situations and that these notions grow with age. However, many students do not know how to describe their intuitions mathematically.

The NAEP items, much easier than most of Green's items, have dealt primarily with computations rather than with concepts and understanding of stochastic ideas. In the 1986 NAEP study, results indicate that students had difficulty with all but the simplest of probability items.

When items get as "complicated" as predicting the probability of all heads in three tosses of a coin, only 5% of U.S. 17-year-olds made the correct computation.

Students did not recognize an event as certain (the probability of obtaining a penny if you draw from a pocket with three pennies was often given as 1/3), nor did they recognize independent events. The NAEP data on descriptive statistics show that students also lack a working understanding of such concepts as mean, mode, median, and range. While students can compute an average, "their understanding of the concept of average seems rather shallow" (6, p. 244).

Judgmental Heuristics

The research of psychologists Daniel Kahneman and Amos Tversky, and many of their colleagues, has provided mathematics educators with a theoretical framework for researching learning in probability and statistics. Kahneman and Tversky's thesis is that people who are statistically naive make estimates for the likelihood of events by using certain judgmental heuristics, such as *representativeness* and *availability* (19, 20, 21, 43).

Representativeness.   According to the representativeness heuristic, people estimate likelihoods of events based on how well an outcome represents some aspect of its parent population (19). People believe that even small samples, perhaps a single outcome, should either reflect the *distribution* of the parent population or mirror the *process* by which random events are generated. For example, many people believe that in a family of six children, the sequence BGGBGB is more likely to occur than either BBBBGB or BBBGGG (19, 37, 38). In the first case, the sequence BGGBGB may appear more *representative* of the near 50–50 distribution of boys and girls than the sequence BBBBGB. In the second case, the sequence BBBGGG does not appear *representative* of the *random process* of having children. From a normative point of view, all 64 such sequences are equally likely to occur.

Another example of reliance on representativeness occurs in neglect of sample size. People may believe that the chance of getting at least 7 white balls in 10 draws from a population of 50% black and 50% white is the same as the chance of getting at least 70 whites in 100 draws (36). In the extreme case, people may see no difference between the chances of getting at least 2 heads in 3 tosses of a coin, and at least 200 heads in 300 tosses. Thus, the effect of sample size on probability and on variation is *not* a factor for people who are statistically naive.

> Assume that the chance of having a boy or girl baby is the same. Over the course of a year, in which type of hospital would you expect there to be more days on which at least 60% of the babies born were boys?
> A) In a large hospital
> B) In a small hospital
> C) It makes no difference

Kahneman and Tversky's subjects in this study were college freshmen who had not studied probability and statistics (19). The majority of the students chose "C) It makes no difference." Their results were replicated by Shaughnessy, who found that 48 out of 80 students chose "C)," while the remaining students split evenly between the small and large hospital (37). When asked why they chose "C)" in Shaughnessy's study, the students responded that the chance of getting a certain percentage of boys was the same in any hospital. The hidden factor here is the sample size. There is a good chance of getting at least 60% boys in a hospital in which only three babies are born a day. It is much more likely to occur in a small hospital.

Another type of task in which the representativeness heuristic is used by some people to estimate the likelihood of events involves the neglect of given base-rate population percentages. The problem below, called the Taxi problem, has been used by many researchers to examine the phenomenon of base-rate neglect.

> A cab was involved in a hit-and-run accident at night. There are two cab companies that operate in the city, a Blue Cab company and a Green Cab company. It is known that 85% of the cabs in the city are Green and 15% are Blue. A witness at the scene identified the cab involved in the accident as a Blue cab. This witness was tested under similar visibility conditions, and made correct color identifications in 80% of the trial instances. What is the probability that the cab involved in the accident was a Blue cab rather than a Green one?

Results indicate that people tend to neglect the base-rate information (15% Blue cabs), which should suggest that a Blue cab is an unlikely event, and place their faith in the reliability of the witness (80%). One explanation for this is the representativeness heuristic. Many people may feel that the single instance of the accident should be representative of the witness's 80% reliability data. However, many of the responses to the Taxi problem cannot be explained easily by simply appealing to a representativeness argument. For example, subjects who say that the probability that the cab was Blue is 100% clearly are not using representativeness. As a result, the Taxi problem has been at least partially responsible for the current search by researchers for alternatives to representativeness in order to explain people's flawed probability estimates.

Konold offers an alternative explanation, which he calls the "outcome approach" (24). Single-outcome oriented people may believe that their task is to decide correctly for certain which outcome will (or did) occur, rather than to estimate what is likely to occur from among a range of possibilities. This may explain how estimates for the probability that the cab was Blue can reach 100%. The actual mathematical solution of the Taxi problem is a difficult one, even for students who have had training in probability and statistics. A contingency table that models the Taxi problem is presented in Figure 10.3.

Availability. When people base their estimate of the likelihood of an event on how easy it is for them to call to mind particular instances of that event, we say they are employing the availability heuristic. This judgmental heuristic can induce significant bias because of one's own narrow experience and personal perspective. For example, if you have driven into a town and been hit by a car running a stop sign, you are much more likely to give a higher estimate for the frequency of accidents in that town than someone who has driven there accident-free for several years. In fact, *both* of these individual perspectives may be far from realistic. (Consider by comparison that if several of your friends have recently divorced their spouses, you may be led to believe that the local incidence of divorce is on the rise, when in fact it has not changed.)

FIGURE 10.3   Taxi contingency table

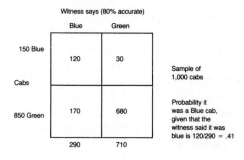

> There is indeed cause for concern in how availability may affect our judgment. When diagnosing a disease, a physician draws on past experience. It may be easier to recall instances in which the symptoms and the disease occur together than to remember counterexamples, where either certain symptoms or the disease occurred separately.

We all have egocentric impressions, based on our own experiences, of the frequency of events. Often these impressions are biased, because even a single occurrence of an event can take on inflated significance when it *happens to us*. We don't think of events that happen to *us* as just one more tally in an enormous, uncaring, objective frequency distribution.

Availability also comes into play when people are asked to give estimates for complex combinatorial tasks. If subjects who are naive about counting techniques are asked if they think it possible to make up more different committees of 2 people, or more committees of 8 people, from a group of 10, they choose committees of 2 people by an overwhelming margin (21, 37). It is easier to construct examples of committees of 2 than committees of 8. In fact, there are the same number of committees of 2 as committees of 8. Thus, availability is a heuristic that affects or reflects our own perception of relative frequency.

Usefulness of Heuristics.   Although we have seen circumstances where reliance on heuristics such as representativeness and availability can result in biased, nonnormative probability estimates, in other contexts both of these heuristics are very useful. If you recall several graphic scenarios of traffic accidents or near misses at a particular intersection, you *will* be more cautious at that intersection, and perhaps avoid an accident. Similarly, the doctor's available diagnostic-frequency experience might help to lead to a correct diagnosis.

Availability is not always such a bad thing. In fact, it often is a very useful organizer for decision making. Likewise, representativeness is really at the very heart of much of statistics. Borovcnik (5) points out that representativeness is "a very statistical idea which should allow transfer of traits of samples to underlying populations." The very reason we try to draw a "random" sample from a population is so that it *will be representative* of the population. We wish to *infer to the population* any traits that we discover in the random sample. Representativeness is therefore fundamental to statistical events; it is the way we claim to "know" something about a population with a certain degree of confidence. Our task as mathematics educators is to distinguish between those circumstances in which judgmental heuristics can adversely affect stochastic thinking and those in which the heuristics are useful and desirable. And we are obliged to point out the differences to our students. It is not that there is "something wrong" with the way our students think. It is just that they (and we) tend to carry useful heuristics beyond their relevant domain.

The Conjunction Fallacy

In probability the chance of two distinct events occurring simultaneously is less than the chance of either one occurring separately. For example, the probability that I am over 35 *and* have red hair is less than the probability that I am over 35. This is expressed in the language of probability by $P(A \cap B) \leq P(A)$, and is called the law of conjunction. Research has discovered that people do not follow this property of probability when they make estimates for the likelihood of events. For example, Kahneman and Tversky (22) found that statistically naive college subjects rated the percentage of people who were 55 *and* had had a heart attack higher than the percentage of people who only had had a heart attack. In fact, on some tasks even graduate students in statistics and decision theory, supposedly statistics experts, gave estimates that violated the conjunction rule about 85% of the time (22).

> When primed with a description of a woman who is "bright, single, 31 years old, outspoken, and concerned with issues of social justice," students rated the statement "She is a bank teller *and* a feminist" as more likely than the statement "She is a bank teller." (22)

There are several possible reasons why people do this. In the heart-attack scenario the two variables—age and incidence of heart attacks—may be strongly (though perhaps falsely) linked in people's minds. This may be either because we see age as a *cause* of heart attacks, or perhaps because in our own experience most of the people we know who have had heart attacks are older. Thus we may be either using the availability heuristic or relying on some causal mechanism to give estimates. There is another possibility here, too. The language "had a heart attack and is over 55" may be interpreted by some people as " had a heart attack *given that* he or she is over 55." Thus, a conjunction may be confused with a conditional.

Trouble with Conditionals

Investigations into the difficulties that students have with conditional probabilities have been done by many mathematics and statistics educators (1,11,12, 33). One of the most prominent misconceptions of conditional probabilities arises when a conditioning event occurs *after* the event that it conditions. Falk (13) discusses this problem, which is now referred to as "the Falk phenomenon" in the literature.

> An urn has two white balls and two black balls in it. Two balls are drawn out without replacing the first ball. (1) What is the probability that the second ball is white, given that the first ball was white? (2) What is the probability that the first ball was white, given that the second ball is white?

In mathematical notation, the first question asks us to compute $P(W_2 \mid W_1)$, and the second question asks us to compute $P(W_1 \mid W_2)$. It is easy for students to see that the first probability is 1/3, because when we draw the second ball, there is one white and two black left in the jar. What is not so easy for students to see, or even to believe, is that the second probability is also 1/3. Students often feel that the answer to the second question is 1/2. In fact, they sometimes believe that you cannot even calculate the second probability, because the outcome of the first draw cannot (in their eyes), depend on the outcome of the second draw. Falk (13) suggests that the reason this problem is so difficult for students is that the first conditional probability can be explained by a causality argument, while it is not possible to infer cause for an event that is conditioned on some other event that has already occurred. The usual method of calculating such probabilities, Bayes's theorem, gives little or no intuitive feel as to why the calculation comes out 1/3 for the second problem as well.

Falk suggests a teaching technique for the urn problem in which one ball is drawn and put aside, then a second ball is drawn. The students are told that the second ball is white, and then are asked what the probability is that the first ball (still hidden) also is white.

One problem that has been used extensively with students to point out the importance of using conditional information is a situation we call Monty's Dilemma (39).

> **Monty's Dilemma:** During a certain game show, contestants are shown three closed doors. One of the doors has a big prize behind it, but the other two have a gag prize behind each of them. The contestants are asked to pick a door. But then the game show host, Monty, first opens one of the remaining *closed* doors, *always* revealing a gag prize. The contestants are then given the option to stick with their original choice or to switch to the other unopened door. What should they do?

To highlight the mathematics of Monty's Dilemma, we usually impose the following problem on the puzzle situation above.

> **Monty's Problem:** If you were the contestant, which strategy below would you choose, and why?
> Strategy 1 (Stick)—Stick with the original door.
> Strategy 2 (Flip)—Flip a coin, and stick if it shows heads, but switch if it shows tails.
> Strategy 3 (Switch)—Switch to the other door.

This problem points out the difficulty with *what* is actually known, *when* it is known, and *how* the new information obtained is used in conditional probability problems. We have administered this task to students from secondary school level through graduate school, thus including preservice and inservice teachers. Most of the students we have shown this task believe that as soon as Monty opens one of the gag doors, the chance of winning the big prize automatically increases from 1/3 to 1/2. They reason that "now you know that one of the doors is no good." However, if *no* action is taken to update the chance of winning in light of this new information, the probability of winning the big prize *remains* 1/3.

A dramatic change occurs in students' understanding of this problem when they actually carry out a simulation of each of the three strategies 100 times with an equal area spinner and a coin. Then they realize that rechoosing after a door has been opened really does make a difference. Furthermore, they discover that it is best for the contestants *always* to *switch*, for the only way to lose in the switch strategy is to pick the correct door the first time. There is only a 1/3 chance of picking the correct door at first, so there is a 2/3 probability of winning the big prize if you switch. The success of a simulation strategy with Monty's Dilemma provides further evidence that the suggestions of Falk (13), Bentz (3), and Shaughnessy (38) to model probability problems via simulations is a promising technique for confronting and overcoming misconceptions.

The Outcome Approach

Judgmental heuristics such as availability and representativeness are rooted in perceptions of random processes. Causal schemas in which subjects believe that one event causes another, as in a chemical reaction for example, reflect *deterministic* processes. We have seen that students may inappropriately infer a causal process in a stochastic situation, as in Falk's black–white marble problem. There is evidence, however, that some of our students might not possess *any* process model for stochastic experiments. Some do not even see the results of a single trial of an experiment as one of many such trials. Konold (23, 24) reports that some subjects perceive each single trial of an experiment as a separate, individual phenomenon, and calls this the "outcome approach." Outcome-oriented people may believe that their task is to decide correctly *for certain* what the next outcome will be, rather than to estimate what is *likely* to occur.

> According to Konold (24), an outcome-oriented student uses a 50% chance as a guide to deciding between a "certain yes" and a "certain no" for an outcome. Events significantly higher than a 50% chance (say 70%) *will* happen, and events with lower than a 50% chance (say 30%) *won't* happen. In the case of exactly 50%, students say they "don't know" or "can't decide."

Konold asked students to predict which side of an irregularly shaped die would land face down. This "die" was actually a seven-sided irregular polyhedron. Several subjects tenaciously maintained their original predictions even when confronted with frequency data from many rolls of the die that refuted their original choice. On any given single roll, they believed they "could be" correct. Thus, belief in a single outcome outweighed all the empirical evidence presented.

> "As long as students believe there is some way that they can 'know for sure' whether a hypothesis is correct, the better part of statistical logic and all of probability theory will evade them." (25)

Konold concludes that subjects are likely to use an outcome approach for predict-ing events if either (1) the outcomes are not all equally likely to occur or (2) the experiment does not appear to be repeatable, as in the Taxi problem.

Misconceptions of the Mean and Variance

Even researchers trained in the use of statistics entertain statistical misconceptions. For example, they may erroneously believe that when conducting a replication studys' even smaller sample sizes than the first study's are sufficient, since samples should be "representative" of the population, regardless of their size (42). If trained researchers have trouble with statistics concepts, it should not surprise us that *students* have misconceptions of some of the most elementary concepts, such as mean and variance.

In an attempt to see if students have a mechanistic approach to computing the mean—such as an active balancing strategy—when they are given new data, Pollat-sek and his colleagues (32) gave statistically naive college students several tasks similar to the following problem.

> The average SAT score for all high school students in a district is
> known to be 400. You pick a random sample of 10 students. The first
> student you pick had an SAT of 250. What would you expect the aver-
> age SAT to be for the entire sample of 10?

Many students who are given this task respond that the average will be 400. These students may be using representativeness as a guide, because they may believe that even such a small sample should mirror the whole population mean. On the other hand, a response of 400 may mean that the student is confusing the population mean with the sample mean. The population mean remains 400, but the expected sample mean changes with the additional information. The normative calculation indicates that we should revise our estimate for the sample mean by *weighting* the nine un-known scores by the population mean, and tossing in our one known score. Thus, the revised mean is $(9 \times 400 + 250)/10 = 385$. Pollatsek and colleagues (32) discuss students' confusion of the sample mean in situations where it must be calculated as a weighted average. Profound misunderstanding of the mean occurs when data must be weighted by sample sizes.

Mevarech (28) found that college students thought that it was possible to "av-erage averages" by the "add them up and divide" algorithm.

Attempts to Change Stochastic Beliefs and Conceptions

So far our discussion of the research in probability and statistics has pointed out that students enter our classes with preconceived notions of chance, randomness, and probabililty. When we teach probability and statistics, we are not "starting from scratch." There have already been a number of "stochastic scratches" etched in our students' minds, based on their experiences (or lack of them). This fact poses big challenges for the teaching of probability and statistics: We wish to give our students opportunities that will allow them to build a working mathematical model of chance. However, we find that their stochastic thought processes already are preoccupied with potentially misleading misconceptions. What should we do?

There have been several documented attempts to teach probability and statistics in such a way as to confront students' misconceptions (2, 37). Shaughnessy (37, 38) conducted an intensive, ten-week teaching experiment in which probability and statistics concepts were introduced to college freshmen in a small-group, activity-based course. The students were first required to make guesses for either the likelihood of outcomes or the number of possible outcomes in an experiment. Then an experiment was conducted to gather, organize, and analyze data. Experimental outcomes were compared to the students' predictions and discussed. Only then was an attempt made to introduce a theoretical or mathematical model of the problem. Thereafter, the students were encouraged to hypothesize and test their own formulas. Some of these activities were specifically designed to confront certain misconceptions. At the end of the instruction, comparisons between the experimental classes and those taught in a traditional lecture format indicated a greatly reduced reliance on representativeness and availability in the experimental classes, with a corresponding increase in correct reasoning. No such change was evident in the traditionally taught classes.

Although Shaughnessy found significant gains in students' probability concepts in the experimental course, there were still some students who clung rather tenaciously to their precourse notions of chance. Other research (10, 23) has also confirmed the fact that misconceptions are sometimes so entrenched, as to be difficult to overcome.

Del Mas and Bart (10) conjectured that unless students are forced to record their predictions, and then to compare those to experimental results, they will tend to look for, and subsequently find, confirming evidence for such concretized misconceptions as availability, the law of averages, and the law of small numbers. The researchers prescribed an evaluative task in which students in an elementary statistics class listed their predictions for a series of one-at-a-time coin tosses, and then watched as their written predictions were listed alongside the randomly generated results. Del Mas and Bart concluded that forcing students explicitly to compare their own predictions to empirical results helps them to employ the frequentist model that they are being taught. On the other hand, results also suggest that students who do not explicitly make predictions may actually rely even more heavily on their misconceptions *after* instruction.

Schrage (36) provides some real life examples of erroneous stochastically-based decisions by members of the legal and medical professions. In one court case, a man was actually on trial for murder because of an erroneous probability argument involving the color of his hair. In another instance, Schrage discovered a faulty question involving probabilities on the German medical school entrance examination. Both these real-life situations involved several misconceptions, including disregard for base-rate data. Schrage was successful at turning the court's attention to the erroneous probability calculations, and the man was acquitted. However, despite his best efforts, the group of "30 medical experts" who constructed the entrance exam failed to see their mistake. Schrage advocates the inclusion of just such real life mistakes in courses on probability and statistics. Only persistent attention to such fallacies, and their social implications, will help focus our students' attention on the importance of correct modeling in stochastics.

Konold provides us with some very salient reflections on the role of instruction in an environment fraught with students' prior stochastic misconceptions. Konold suggests that teachers first ask students to test whether their beliefs coincide with the beliefs of others. Second, ask students whether their beliefs are consistent with their beliefs about other, related things. Third, have students test whether their beliefs are validated by the experimental evidence.

> My assumption is that students have intuitions about probability, and that they can't check these in at the classroom door. The success of the teacher depends on how these notions are treated in relation to those the teacher would like the student to acquire. . . . How students think about probability before and during instruction can facilitate communication between the student and the teacher. (25)

Stochastics Research Needed in the Future

Anyone who has done research in probability and statistics is aware that there are so many exciting possibilities for such research that it is hard to know where to begin. We have chosen to focus on a few topics that are the most important from our perspective as mathematics educators.

Development of Assessment Instruments

We need to develop some standard, reliable tools to assess our students' conceptions of probability and statistics. A real smorgasbord of tasks has been administered in both paper-and-pencil response settings and clinical interviews. We know that the context, the framing, and the wording of stochastic tasks can all affect the types of responses we obtain from our students. Paper-and-pencil instruments as well as structured, repeatable interview scripts are needed so that we can investigate students' conceptions of stochastics across a wide range of grade levels and in a variety of contexts.

What Are Secondary Students' Conceptions and Misconceptions?

With the exception of Green's study (16), which tested large numbers of adolescents on their notions of probability, there is little large-scale information about how middle school and high school students think about chance, random events, and decisions under uncertainty. Do secondary students use heuristics similar to those exhibited by college students? Do they resort to nonstatistical or deterministic explanations of such chance phenomena as Konold's outcome approach? Do their conceptions change under the influence of instruction? As the new NCTM standards are implemented, there will be increased emphasis on probability and statistics at the secondary level. Research efforts at this level are crucial in order to help inform both teachers and curriculum developers.

What Are Teachers' Conceptions of Probability and Statistics?

The success of NCTM's ambitious standards recommendations will ultimately depend on our teachers. What are our elementary and secondary teachers' conceptions of and attitudes toward stochastics? What can we do to change and influence their conceptions and attitudes? We need to gather information from teachers at both the preservice and inservice levels.

> There is currently a wide gap between what many of our secondary teachers know about probability and statistics, and what they will be asked to teach. This gap is only accentuated by the beliefs and misconceptions about stochastics that the teachers are likely to have, just like their students.

Our teachers will be needing more and more inservice experiences in probability and statistics as the standards are implemented. The probability standard for grades 9–12 requires students to understand and use both theoretical and experimental probability to solve problems. It asks that students understand concepts such as random variable, discrete probability distributions, and the normal curve, and that they also use simulations to estimate probabilities. The statistics standard includes recommendations for drawing inferences from graphical data, curve fitting, understanding and applying measures of central tendency and variability, and designing a statistical experiment. Thus, at the preservice level we will need to develop courses that meet stochastic misconceptions and beliefs head-on, and thereby sensitize our prospective teachers to some of the prevalent misconceptions that they can expect to encounter in their own students—as well as in themselves.

What Are the Effects of Instruction?

What can teachers and researchers do to mitigate the twofold problem of (a) a lack of conceptual knowledge in stochastics, accompanied by (b) nonnormative intuitions, beliefs, and misconceptions? We believe it is essential that teachers and researchers form investigative partnerships whereby the teacher is a co-researcher and the researcher is a co-teacher.

> It is crucial that researchers involve teachers in future research projects because teachers are the ultimate key to statistical literacy in our students.

Teaching experiments that include the keeping of careful records of changes in students' stochastic conceptions, beliefs, and attitudes over a long period of time are needed to get a clearer picture of the conceptual and attitudinal development that occurs in those students in an instructional setting. For example, what are the conceptual effects over time on students who are using the Quantitative Literacy Project (15, 26, 27, 30)? How do students' beliefs about probability and their estimations for the likelihood of events change over time when they are constantly doing experiments and using computer simulations?

What Are the Effects of Computer Software?

How can we best use computers to help change students' stochastic beliefs, conceptions, and attitudes? The possibilities for developing interactive representations of statistical concepts are exciting, as can be seen in the *ELASTIC* software in the Reasoning under Uncertainty project (35) and in the interactive package *Hands-on Statistics* (44). The computer provides us with the opportunity to create whole new learning environments for our students, but so far little research and evaluation has been conducted on the effects that these packages have on student conceptions of probability and statistics (4). Computer routines can easily be changed during the developmental stages, using valuable input from researchers and teachers. When the software is in its latter stages, it is often too late for the developers to incorporate suggestions.

Conclusion: Is There a "Right Way" to Teach Stochastics?

It is not uncommon to hear teachers ask questions like these of researchers: So, what is the best way to teach this stuff? Which topics should I include at which grade levels? Should there be a separate course or should I integrate this into the curriculum? Research is an ongoing problem-solving activity, and although the picture becomes clearer as research digs deeper, there are seldom any definitive caveats from research that guarantee the absolute best way to teach a subject or to sequence its topics. We can, however, glean some pretty clear observations and some strong recommendations for the teaching of probability and statistics from research, from curriculum development, and from our own classroom experiences.

1. Our students have many preconceived notions of chance, randomness, and probability. These ideas conflict with the mathematized version of probability and statistics that we are trying to teach.
2. Our teaching must include misuses and abuses of statistics (18), and must be designed to help confront and overcome our students' misconceptions of probability and statistics.
3. To overcome misconceptions of stochastics, it helps to have students working in small groups, with the teaching strategy as shown in Figure 10.4.

FIGURE 10.4 Stochastics via simulation

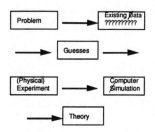

4. The technique of simulation is a tremendous problem-solving tool for situations involving uncertainty.
5. It is important to encourage students to gather data physically, or with concrete simulation objects (spinners, dice, random-number charts), prior to engaging them in computer simulations.

> When computer simulations are used, it is beneficial to have the students write some simulation programs themselves.

6. Students need to be *actively* involved in both statistical investigations and probability explorations. A straight lecture approach to probability and statistics is highly inappropriate for our students.
7. There is no "algorithmic" way to teach probability and statistics. The subject has been referred to as "the ultimate problem-solving proving ground."

> It appears that stochastic problems may closely resemble the type of problem solving that our students will have to do in their own private lives or on their jobs.

8. The stochastic experience of most of our classroom teachers is minimal. Whatever probability and statistics that these teachers have acquired usually was not taught in a way to develop understanding (simulations, activity-based, frequent discussions).

> We have to continue to expand inservice opportunities in probability and statistics for teachers, and for our preservice teachers we must also develop appropriate courses at the college level that model the approach we want them to take with their own students.

9. Probability and statistics must become a mainstay in our secondary curriculum, and must be included in such a way that the topics cannot be passed over. For example, stochastics could replace the traditional catch-all general math course, or an entire semester might be devoted to probability and statistics after a semester of Algebra II.

Looking Ahead . . .

The research we reviewed in this chapter points out just how challenging the teaching of probability and statistics is. Concepts such as random variable, central tendency, dispersion, probability models, and likely versus unlikely events are difficult enough to teach without the excess baggage of students' beliefs and misconceptions confounding the process. On top of that, we as teachers have our own beliefs and misconceptions of stochastics to reckon with when we teach probability and statistics. As the NCTM standards are implemented over the next decade, we must attend to what research tells us about the teaching and learning of stochastics. I hope teachers and curriculum developers will continue to work together with researchers to find better ways to involve our students in stochastics.

J. Michael Shaughnessy

It is truly exciting to find the excellent curriculum materials that have recently been developed. Using them has been a tremendously rewarding experience for students and teachers alike. We will need more of these types of materials as we develop a cohesive stochastics curriculum that spans the years K–12. Can we find ways to lure mathematics teachers, both young and old, into the exciting world of active investigations and simulations? Can we, will we, squeeze the needed time for such activities into an already crowded curriculum? Will the stochastics curricular strand truly become "standard?" The possibilities are there.

Barry Bergman

About the Authors

J. Michael Shaughnessy is a professor of mathematics and mathematics education at Oregon State University. He works extensively with both preservice and inservice mathematics teachers in the Pacific northwest, especially in his favorite areas for both teaching and research: probability and geometry.

Barry Bergman, MTWG (Math Teachers Who Golf), is an instructor of mathematics at Clackamas Community College in Oregon City, Oregon. He taught high school mathematics for twelve years in nearby West Linn. He enjoys many sports and games, including poker, which he prefers to call a probability workshop.

References

*1. BAR-HILLEL, M., & FALK, R. (1982). Some teasers concerning conditional probabilities. *Cognition, 11,* 109–122.

2. BATANERO, MA. C., GODINO, J. D., & CANIZARES, MA. J. (1987). Azar y Probabilidad [Chance and Probability]: Fundamentos didactos y propuestas curriculares [Teaching fundamentals and curriculum recommendations]. From Matematicas: Cultura y aprendizaje, 27. Madrid: Editorial Sintesis, S.A.

3. BENTZ, H. J. (1983). Stochastics teaching based on common sense. In D. R. Grey, P. Holmes, V. Barnett, & G. M. Constable (Eds.), Proceedings of the First International Conference on Teaching Statistics (pp. 753–765). Sheffield: University of Sheffield.

4. BIEHLER, R. (1991). Computers in probability education. In R. Kapadia & M. Borovcnik (Eds.), Chance encounters: Probability in education (pp. 169–211). Dordrecht: Kluwer.

5. BOROVCNIK, M. (1986). On "representativeness"—a fundamental statistical strategy. Unpublished paper, University of Klagenfurt.

*6. BROWN, C. A., CARPENTER, T. P., KOUBA, V. L., LINDQUIST, M. M., SILVER, E. A., & SWAFFORD, J. O. (1988). Secondary school results for the fourth NAEP mathematics assessment: Discrete mathematics, data organization and interpretation, measurement, number and operations. The Mathematics Teacher, 81(4), 241–248.

7. CARPENTER, T. P., CORBITT, M. K., KEPNER, H. S., LINDQUIST, M. M., & REYS, R. E. (1981). What are the chances of your students knowing probability? The Mathematics Teacher, 74, 342–344.

8. DAVIDSON, R., & SWIFT, J. (Eds.) (1988). The Proceedings of the Second International Conference on Teaching Statistics. Victoria, BC: University of Victoria.

9. DEBERES, R. (1988). Statistics for college-bound students: Are the secondary schools responding? School Science & Mathematics, 88, 200–209.

10. DEL MAS, R. C., & BART, W. M. (1987). The role of an evaluation exercise in the resolution of misconceptions of probability. Paper presented at the Annual meeting of the American Educational Research Association, Washington, DC, April.

11. FALK, R. (1981). The perception of randomness. Proceedings of the Fifth Conference of the International Group for the Psychology of Mathematics Education (pp. 222–229). Grenoble, France.

12. FALK, R. (1982). Do men have more sisters than women? Teaching Statistics, 4, 60–62.

13. FALK, R. (1988). Conditional probabilities: Insights and difficulties. In R. Davidson & J. Swift (Eds.), The Proceedings of the Second International Conference on Teaching Statistics, Victoria, B.C.: University of Victoria.

*14. GARFIELD, J., & AHLGREN, A. (1988). Difficulties in learning basic concepts in probability and statistics: Implications for research. Journal for Research in Mathematics Education, 19, 44–63.

*15. GNANADESIKAN, M., SCHEAFFER, R. L., & SWIFT, J. (1987). The art and techniques of simulation. Palo Alto: Dale Seymour.

*16. GREEN, D. R. (1983a). A survey of probability concepts in 3000 pupils aged 11–16 years. In D. R. Grey, P. Holmes, V. Barnett, & G. M. Constable (Eds.), Proceedings of the First International Conference on Teaching Statistics (pp. 766–783) . Sheffield, UK: Teaching Statistics Trust.

*17. GREEN, D. R. (1983b). School pupils' probability concepts. Teaching Statistics, 5 (2) , 34–42.

*18. HUFF, D. (1954). How to lie with statistics. New York: Norton.

*19. KAHNEMAN, D., & TVERSKY, A. (1972). Subjective probability: A judgment of representativeness. Cognitive Psychology, 3, 430–454.

20. KAHNEMAN, D., & TVERSKY, A. (1973a). On the psychology of prediction. Psychological Review, 80, 237–251.

*21. KAHNEMAN, D., & TVERSKY, A. (1973b). Availability: A heuristic for judging frequency and probability. *Cognitive Psychology, 5,* 207–232.

*22. KAHNEMAN, D., & TVERSKY, A. (1983). Extensional versus intuitive reasoning: The conjunction fallacy in probability judgment. *Psychological Review, 90*(4), 293–315.

23. KONOLD, C. (1983). Conceptions about probability: Reality between a rock and a hard place. (Doctoral dissertation, University of Massachusetts, 1983). *Dissertation Abstracts International, 43,* 4179B.

*24. KONOLD, C. (1989). Informal conceptions of probability. *Cognition and Instruction, 6* (1), 59–98.

25. KONOLD, C. (1991). Understanding students' beliefs about probability. In E. von Glasersfeld (Ed.), *Radical constructivism in mathematics education* (pp. 139–156). Dordrecht: Kluwer.

*26. LANDEWEHR, J., & WATKINS, A. E. (1986). *Exploring data.* Palo Alto: Dale Seymour.

*27. LANDEWEHR, J., WATKINS, A. E., & SWIFT, J. (1987). *Exploring surveys: Information from samples.* Palo Alto: Dale Seymour.

28. MEVARECH, Z. (1983). A deep structure model of students' statistical misconceptions. Educational Studies in Mathematics, *14,* 415–429.

*29. NATIONAL COUNCIL OF TEACHERS OF MATHEMATICS (1989). *Curriculum and evaluation standards for school mathematics.* Reston, VA: Author.

*30. NEWMAN, C. M., OBREMSKI, T. E., & SCHEAFFER, R. L. (1987). *Exploring probability.* Palo Alto: Dale Seymour.

*31. PHILLIPS, E., LAPPAN, G., WINTER, M. J., & FITZGERALD, W. (1986). *Probability.* Menlo Park, CA: Addison–Wesley.

*32. POLLATSEK, A., LIMA, S., & WELL, A. D. (1981). Concept or computation: Students' understanding of the mean. *Educational Studies in Mathematics, 12,* 191–204.

33. POLLATSEK, A., WELL, A., KONOLD, C., & HARDIMAN, P. (1987). Understanding conditional probabilities. *Organizational Behavior and Human Decision Processes, 40,* 255–269.

34. RADE, L. (1983). Stochastics at the school level in the age of the computer. In D. R. Grey, P. Holmes, V. Barnett, & G. M. Constable (Eds.), *Proceedings of the First International Conference on Teaching Statistics* (pp. 19–33). Sheffield, UK: Teaching Statistics Trust.

35. RUBIN, A., ROSEBERRY, A. S., & BRUCE, B. (1988). *ELASTIC and reasoning under uncertainty.* (Research report No. 6851). Boston: BBN Systems and Technologies Corporation.

36. SCHRAGE, G. (1983). (Mis-) Interpretation of stochastic models. In R. Scholz (Ed.), *Decision making under uncertainty* (pp. 351–361). Amsterdam: North–Holland.

*37. SHAUGHNESSY, J. M. (1977). Misconceptions of probability: An experiment with a small-group, activity-based, model building approach to introductory probability at the college level. *Educational Studies in Mathematics, 8,* 285–316.

*38. SHAUGHNESSY, J. M. (1981). Misconceptions of probability: From systematic errors to systematic experiments and decisions. In R. Schulte (Ed.), *Teaching Statistics and Probability.* (1981 Yearbook of the National Council of Teachers of Mathematics). Reston, VA: NCTM.

*39. SHAUGHNESSY, J. M., & DICK, T. (1991). Monty's Dilemma: Should you stick or switch? *The Mathematics Teacher, 84,* 252–256.

*40. SHULTE, A. (Ed.) (1981). *Teaching Statistics and Probability.* (1981 Yearbook of the National Council of Teachers of Mathematics). Reston, VA: NCTM.

*41. TRAVERS, K. J., STOUT, W. F., SWIFT, J. H., & SEXTRO, J. (1985). *Using Statistics.* Reading, PA: Addison–Wesley.

42. TVERSKY, A., & KAHNEMAN, D. (1971). Belief in the law of small numbers. *Psychological Bulletin, 76,* 105–110.

*43. TVERSKY, A., & KAHNEMAN, D. (1974). Judgment under uncertainty: Heuristics and biases. *Science, 185,* 1124–1131.

*44. WEISSGLASS, J., THIES, N., & FINZER, W. (1986). *Hands-on statistics.* Belmont, CA: Wadsworth.

CHAPTER 11

Computing Technology

M. Kathleen Heid and Terry Baylor

An onlooker observed: "That contraption is worthless! Look at it—it's hard to start, it breaks down all the time, and where will you buy gas? The roads across the country are muddy. It's easier to get around on a horse. A playtoy for the rich, that's all it is! Don't worry. The automobile won't have much of an effect on society as we know it."

A mathematics teacher observed: "That contraption is worthless! Look at it—it's hard to hook up, it breaks down all the time, and where will you get software? The computer is supposed to be good at mathematical tasks. But it won't solve equations, and I can sketch a curve faster than writing a program to do it. The personal computer is just another educational toy! Don't worry. It won't change the way we teach math."

Limited initial views of the potential of technology are common. Just as the automobile has revolutionized how we live and work, current and future computing technology can shake the very foundations not only of how we teach mathematics but also of what mathematics we teach.

To a greater extent than almost any other educational innovation, computing technology has the potential for wide-ranging and long-lasting impact in the mathematics classroom. A wholehearted incorporation of computing technology in high school mathematics suggests changes in mathematical content as well as in the methods and nature of teaching and learning mathematics. In spite of the apparent inevitability of technologically driven changes in the high school mathematics classroom, the nature and effects of many of these changes are, as of yet, largely undocumented and untested. In this chapter we discuss the current status of research in four areas related to the use of computing technology in high school mathematics: calculators, computers, other technologies, and changing roles in a technologically rich environment.

Current Status and Effects of Calculator Use

Several large-scale studies have addressed the current status of calculator use in class-rooms. The Second International Mathematics Study (SIMS), a twenty-country study of 13-year-olds and terminal secondary college preparatory students, gave an international perspective of the extent of calculator use in 1981 (27). Across nations, twelfth graders used calculators to a greater extent than eighth graders. Indeed the twelfth-grade U.S. population reported a much greater use of calculators both at home and in mathematics classes. The real impact of calculator use on school mathematics will depend on whether their use increases with the general population rather than solely with college-prep twelfth-grade mathematics students. The limited amount of calculator use in mathematics classrooms cannot be blamed on their lack of availability. The National Assessment of Educational Progress in 1985–86 reported that 97% of the eleventh graders (or their families) owned a calculator, but only 26% of the students reported that their school had calculators for use in mathematics class (11).

Just as important as extent of use and availability is the way that calculators are used. The SIMS data tallied only broad categories of calculator use and found that the eighth-grade population, worldwide, used calculators "mainly at home for home-work, checking answers, and recreation," (27, p. 12), while the twelfth-grade popu-lation used them "both at home and school, mainly for problem solving and doing homework" (27, p. 12). More specific information is needed about how calculators are being used in the context of learning mathematics. The NAEP study concluded: "[The mathematics] curriculum continues to be dominated by paper-and-pencil drills on basic computation. Little evidence appears of any widespread use of calculators, computers, or mathematics projects" (11, p. 12).

Effects of Classroom Use of Calculators

With the widespread availability of calculators, what are the implications for their classroom use? Hembree and Dessart (25) identified general trends from seventy-nine calculator studies. The researchers were able to draw several conclusions related to secondary mathematics:

• Students who use calculators in concert with traditional instruction maintain their paper-and-pencil skills without apparent harm (p. 96)
• The use of calculators in testing produces much higher achievement scores than paper-and-pencil efforts, both in basic operations and in problem solving (p. 96)

> Students using calculators possess a better attitude toward mathematics and an especially better self-concept in mathematics than non-calculator students. This statement applies across all grades and ability levels. (25)

The research on calculators shows that there can be great benefit for student achievement in problem solving, especially for low-ability and high-ability students.

"Positive attitudes related to the use of calculators may help to relieve student's traditional dislike of word problems" (25, p. 97). The most sweeping recommendation arising from their meta-analysis is that calculators should be used in all mathematics classes in grades K–12: "It no longer seems a question of whether calculators should be used along with basic skills instruction, but how" (25, p. 97). Hembree and Dessart note, however, that few studies have focused on examining calculator-oriented curricula.

Use of Calculators in Testing

Hembree and Dessart recommend that since calculators greatly enhance student achievement in problem solving, teachers should permit students to use the devices in all problem-solving situations, including testing situations. Some studies have in fact focused on the effects of allowing the use of calculators in mathematics testing.

On the Missouri Mastery and Achievement Tests (MMAT), administered in the spring of 1987 to approximately 240,000 students, calculators were allowed for students in grades 8 and 10, although the machines were neither required nor furnished. The researchers pointed out that "the calculator group showed a clear advantage only when the task was fairly straightforward and required tedious computation" (35, p. 323). Their results showed that "as the complexity of the application [decimal computations] increased, the percentage in both groups who correctly answered the question decreased, and a smaller difference in performance between the calculator and no-calculator groups occurred" (35, p. 322). Based on their results, the researchers made the following observations about the worth and feasibility of calculator use on tests:

1. Calculator use on the test can give test reviewers a clear picture of students' deficiencies
2. Calculator use on the state mathematics test has legitimized the use of calculators
3. Logistics of providing calculators for a large-scale test can be manageable
4. Administrators' reluctance to allow calculators in testing and instruction is decreasing

To investigate the effects of calculator use on standardized mathematics achievement tests, Lewis and Hoover (33) compared eighth-graders' performance on achievement tests done both with and without calculators. Scores with calculators were higher, except for computation problems involving fractions. Noting that students using the calculators omitted many of the fraction problems, the researchers pointed out that pretest instruction did not include specific instruction for computations with fractions using the calculator. The important point is that if students are to use calculators for computations involving particular number types, operations, or functions, they should have prior instruction or experience on related tasks. In a study with general mathematics students, knowledge of the percent key did not seem to improve their performance (1). The study resulted in the following recommendations:

1. Teach concepts independent of calculator usage so that students have something to fall back on

2. Don't rely on the special calculator keys (such as the percent key)
3. Use estimation as a check on the reasonableness of answers
4. Provide practice so students can gain confidence in the use of calculators

---

Introduction to special function keys that provide alternative ways to do computations does not necessarily give students an edge.

A lesson learned from each of the previous studies is that when the calculator is used in testing situations, it has its major effect on questions requiring only straightforward numerical calculations. Acquisition of concepts and ability to solve problems are not automatic with the introduction of computing devices. As ever more sophisticated calculators (e.g., symbolic manipulation and graphing) become available, it will be important to find out what effect they have when students use them on tests of routine algebraic manipulations.

Graphing/Symbolic-Manipulation Calculators

Calculators that display function graphs are a recent innovation affording new problem-solving capabilities. Users can produce a graph on current calculator screens by entering the axes scales and the function rule, and may easily rescale displayed graphs. An important feature of graphing calculators is the "zooming in" facility, a technique for viewing smaller and smaller parts of the graph by using finer and finer axes scales. Using this technique, the user can find solutions to equations like $3x^2 + 4x - 5 = 2x + 4$ (within the accuracy limits of the calculator) by using the "zoom" feature to determine the desired coordinates of the point of intersection of $y = 3x^2 + 4x - 5$ and $y = 2x + 4$ (see Fig. 11.1).

FIGURE 11.1   The grapher is ready to "zoom in" on the intersection of the graphs of $y = 3x^2 + 4x - 5$ and $y = 2x + 4$.

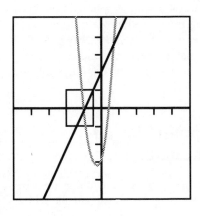

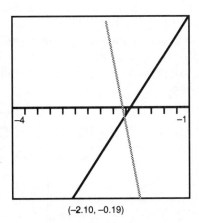

(−2.10, −0.19)

$y = 3x^2 + 4x - 5$
$y = 2x + 4$

The grapher display after "zooming in." The coordinates shown are for the point of intersection.

Demana and Waits (9) integrate the use of graphing throughout a precalculus course. Their curriculum typifies a growing genre of graphing-calculator use that allows for the exploration of realistic applications with multiple representations of solutions. Despite some limitations of screen display and the need to teach new graphing skills, the graphing calculator may well be a promising and cost-effective tool that will further reform in both the content and the pedagogy of school mathematics.

Very little research has been completed on the effectiveness of graphing/symbolic-manipulation calculators. One study (10) analyzed the effects of providing classroom sets of symbolic-manipulation calculators for volunteer high school mathematics teachers. The utility and power of the calculator were more influential in changing the attitudes of male students, while increasing familiarity and comfort with calculator use were more influential in changing the attitudes of female students. Teachers were observed using the calculators more for graphing than for symbolic manipulation. Nevertheless, according to the researchers, "the teachers felt that the use of the calculators brought only minor changes in the dynamics of classroom interaction" (10, p. 333).

A more recent study (14) pointed out a dramatic shift in teacher and student roles when graphing calculators were used in precalculus instruction (see the discussion on changing roles later in this chapter). One important difference was the use of a specially designed calculator-based curriculum in the second study but not in the first. Once again, an important consideration in the use of calculators (graphing/symbolic-manipulation or scientific) is how they change the mathematics that is taught. We need to investigate how instantaneous hand-held access to graphs, equation solutions, matrix manipulations, derivatives, integrals, and trigonometric manipulations would affect the content of school mathematics.

Another study focused on the mathematical performance of upper secondary students who had regular and prolonged access to graphing calculators (42). These students developed specific calculator techniques for finding symbolic rules for graphically represented functions. Interestingly, the graphing-calculator group outperformed students who did not have such access on tasks that required symbolization, but failed to better them on tasks requiring interpretation of function graphs. We need action research (conducted by teachers in order to effect change in their classes) exploring the new techniques and new mathematics that students will generate when graphing calculators become an integral part of their mathematics programs.

The Impact of Computer Use on Secondary Mathematics

A recent survey study suggests that the use of computers in the mathematics classroom may lead to substantial curricular changes. Using an instrument she had developed, Maury (37) found that "high-impact technology" teachers concentrated more on teaching concepts than on teaching arithmetic algorithms, taught a different array of skills, and taught those skills at the same time as they taught the concepts. In lessons taught by these teachers, according to Maury's study, there was more integration of mathematics with other disciplines, and a greater percentage of individualization. It is not clear whether the use of the computer promoted curricular change, or whether those teachers more open to curricular change were more likely to be intense users of computing technology.

There are at least four different ways to use computing technology in the teaching of the concepts and skills of mathematics: *tutor* (teacher), *tool* (assistant), *tutee* (student), and *catalyst* (motivator) (46, 18). Since each of these uses suggests a slightly different perspective on teaching and learning, we will discuss related research results separately.

Use of the Computer as a Tool

Four prominent types of programs have dominated the use of the computer as a tool in the mathematics classroom: as a *grapher*, as a *symbolic manipulator*, as a *geometric construction tool*, and/or as a *catalyst* for the exploration of mathematics. In addition, developers have been working on the multiple use of tools in a single-classroom setting.

Graphing Tools.   In addition to providing dynamic classroom demonstrations of traditional topics, computers as function and relation graphers seem to offer opportunities for significant changes in the content and processes of school mathematics (15, 32). With the capability for computer generation of graphs, and automatic symbolic manipulation, students have earlier access to the graphical representation of a broader range of functions. First-year algebra students using a computer-based curriculum (16), for example, study some polynomial, rational, and exponential functions in their introductory algebra course, analyzing these functions for such properties as rates of change, extrema, and asymptotes.

> Naturally, what seems to make the difference is not the fact that teachers use computer graphics but rather how they use them.

Students are not naturally able to interpret computer-generated graphs. Goldenberg (20) relates misconceptions exhibited by two "bright, successful" second-year algebra students who were using a function grapher to determine the polynomial rule to accompany a given computer-generated graph. For example, the students started out with a reasonable estimate for the function rule but quickly lost sight of the meaning of the y-intercept. Other irrelevant or misleading conclusions can arise from certain computer programs used to generate graphs, depending on the program's treatment of asymptotes, or the idiosyncrasies of the particular graph, or the size of the pixels that the hardware uses (see Fig. 11.2).

When students work with them for a longer period of time, computer graphers can provide arenas in which students can examine a series of exemplars for their

FIGURE 11.2

Consider the impression that students would get about the effect of changing
the value of b in y = mx + b if they were to examine the graphs of y = –2x – 2
and y = –2x + 2 in a window where both x-values and y-values ranged from
–2 to 2. It might appear that as the value of b increases, the graph of y = mx + b
moves further to the right. The intended instructional point might have to
be adjusted.

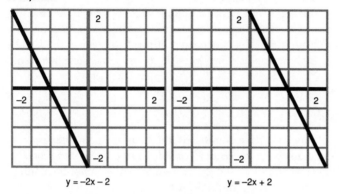

y = –2x – 2   y = –2x + 2

conceptions of mathematical objects (44). Moreover, when students work with a
computer-intensive curriculum over a long period of time (23), these misconceptions
do not seem to dominate students' work with graphs. Although students may not
automatically understand computer-generated graphs, their initial misconceptions
need not be either intractable or long-standing. Even at beginning levels of algebra,
students are able to learn to work with graphical representations of functions prior to
the by-hand symbolic manipulation of function rules.

Symbolic-Manipulation Tools. Symbolic-manipulation programs for microcomputers are rapidly becoming more accessible to secondary schools. Typically, these
programs perform symbolic calculations like equation solving, production of equivalent expressions, symbolic differentiation and integration, and matrix manipulation.
Most of the research on the use of symbolic-manipulation systems so far has centered
on using the systems in the context of college calculus courses. The theme of this
research has been to determine the effects of replacing by-hand symbolic manipulation with computer-generated symbolic manipulation. The message has been fairly
singular: Computer symbolic manipulation is favored.

Heid (22) conducted an exploratory study on the effects of concentrating initial
and primary attention on the concepts and applications of calculus while relegating
execution of routine procedures to the computer. The course delayed the study of
traditional calculus skills (computing derivatives, etc.) until the last three weeks of a
fifteen-week introductory calculus course. Experimental classes showed better conceptual understanding than a traditional class, without noticeable loss in traditional
by-hand skills. In a controlled experimental study, Palmiter (40) found that students
using a symbolic manipulation program for homework assignments and on examinations could learn integration concepts in substantially less time with comparable

or better conceptual understanding. Judson (28) corroborated some of these results in a controlled experimental study and concluded that skill acquisition was not a prerequisite for conceptual understanding.

In a business calculus course, Hawker (21) found that although there was no significant difference between experimental and control groups in achievement, attitude, or dropout data, there were some positive trends favoring the experimental groups in areas of achievement on conceptual problems, performance on algebra items, and attitude toward mathematics. When college calculus students use symbolic-manipulation programs as the technique of choice for some part of the usual by-hand symbolic-manipulation skills, it is possible to maintain traditional skills and make gains in conceptual understanding. A study involving beginning high school algebra students in learning mathematical modeling while using a computer for symbolic-manipulation also suggested conceptual gains without noticeable skill loss (23).

The central feature in each of these studies is that students using the symbolic-manipulation programs were offered a much different mathematics experience than students who performed all of their calculations by hand. In the Heid study (22), distinctive patterns of classroom interaction were noted in the experimental course. The activities that characterized the experimental course included: making, defending, and debating mathematical conjectures; interpreting and reasoning about symbolic and graphical representations; and suggesting and justifying mathematical models. With constant access to automatic algebraic symbol manipulation, students and teachers could concentrate on concepts, problem solving, and mathematical modelling. Although there is a need for much more research about the potential of symbolic-manipulation systems as replacements for the acquisition of manual skills, results like those reported here call into question the traditional high priority given to the refinement of manipulative skills in secondary-school mathematics.

Geometric Construction Tool.   Much of the research on the use of geometric tools in the teaching of geometry has centered on building and testing substantially different approaches to teaching geometry using the *Geometric Supposers*. The *Supposers* are programs that computer-automate geometric constructions. Users can command automatic calculations of lengths of lines, measures of angles, and areas of figures, in order to test conjectures about relationships among figures. The two *Supposer*-based approaches we will discuss here are the reformulation of geometry teaching to correspond to van Hiele's phases of instruction and the effects of an inquiry-based approach to the teaching of geometry. (48)

Bobango (5) found that the *Geometric Supposer*, used in conjunction with van Hiele's five phases of instruction, could increase students' van Hiele levels of understanding geometry from the first level (the visual level, where they see figures only as indivisible wholes) to the second level (the descriptive level, where they can focus on properties). (See the Chapter 8 for information on van Hiele's five phases.) Since many students now enter high school geometry at the first van Hiele level, and since entry at the third van Hiele level seems to be prerequisite to learning to do proofs (45), teachers might profitably engage students in exploratory work with the *Geometric Supposer* prior to work in formal geometry.

What differences in students' reasoning abilities can result from the use of the *Supposers*? Yerushalmy, Chazan, and Gordon (49) studied students' mathematical learning over a period of a year as they used the *Supposers* to engage in a guided-inquiry approach (one that calls on students to gather data, to generate hypotheses to describe that data, and to prove those hypotheses) to learning geometry. They observed that students in the experimental groups produced generalizations at a higher level and were more likely than students in a noncomputer group to produce arguments to support their conjectures, even though they were not asked to support their conjectures. Although the groups did not perform differently on attempts at constructing informal proofs for three theorems, there was a significant difference favoring the experimental group on constructing a formal proof for one of the three theorems.

Students' intensive work with data and generalizations may have enhanced their ability to make arguments. This use of geometric tools suggests a geometry course that resembles real mathematical inquiry to a much greater extent than does geometry as historically delivered. Instead of creating proofs for theorems specified by their text or by their teacher, students design and carry out mini-experiments that allow them to generate and verify their own conjectures. Mathematics as envisioned in the *Curriculum and Evaluation Standards* (39) is epitomized in student activities that center on gathering data, hypothesizing patterns, and verifying their conjectures.

As students engaged in a guided-inquiry approach using the *Supposers*, teachers developed new pedagogical strategies (31) but encountered a new range of pedagogical challenges. In case studies of seven teachers who experimented with the *Supposers* in their high school geometry classes, Lampert (30) noted that teachers had concerns and questions about the sequencing, selection, and coverage of the content, as well as about related pedagogical issues: If content were guided by the students' own questions, would students learn what they were supposed to know? If the course did not follow the text, how would teachers sequence material? How could the inquiry process be guided? What should teachers do if students made conjectures they were not yet ready to prove? What should they do if students got the wrong idea and embarked on a fruitless path? Although teachers in the *Supposer* classrooms came up with partial solutions to these problems, the questions remain ones that many teachers will have to face as they experiment with computer-based curricula allowing students to pursue a variety of different paths.

Catalytic Tools.   Many tool uses of the computer are catalytic, in that they "promote mathematical explorations and discussions and help the building of conceptual understanding" (18, p. 216). When used as catalysts, carefully constructed computer games and simulations can improve targeted skills (8).

Students of different abilities are likely to adopt different goals when they use computer catalysts. When general mathematics and college preparatory students used *Pathfinder*, a computer game in which players use descriptive graphs to reconstruct or to match paths defined by those graphs (12), they chose different tasks and elected different strategies for the same tasks. Teachers using BBN's *Reasoning Under Uncertainty* curriculum (43) and its program *ELASTIC* observed that the curriculum motivated low-level classes to learn some basic skills, and the high-level class to learn about statistical reasoning.

Thompson (47) provides an analysis of current artificial-intelligence (AI) software that engages students in exploring foundational mathematical procedures and concepts (word problems, equation solving, the concept of expression, and the concept of equation). As teachers consider the catalytic use of computers, these emerging AI applications provide fertile ground for action research.

Multiple Use of Tool Software. Frequently, students will use more than one piece of tool software in a mathematics lesson or course. Sometimes the set of software together forms a "toolkit," allowing the user to choose from among several representations and strategies (e.g., tables, graphs, and function rules) when solving a given problem. One example of this type of curriculum is *Computer-Intensive Algebra* (16), a beginning algebra curriculum that uses a mathematical toolkit for the generation of numerical, graphical, and symbolic representations of functions, and that shifts attention from manual skills to mathematical modeling concepts. Traditional algebra topics like by-hand productions of equivalent expressions, of solution of equations, and of factoring are omitted. In one study of this curriculum, Matras (36) found that students in two versions of the experimental curriculum exhibited better problem solving in three out of four comparisons concerning the ability to identify the underlying structure of a problem and the ability to solve problems. Other analyses of this curriculum (23) suggested that students who studied the experimental curriculum for the first eight months of the school year (and studied traditional algebra topics for the last month) performed much better than students in traditional classes on a range of mathematical modeling tasks, with little loss in traditional skills.

Recently developed software is linked in such a way that a change in one representation of a function automatically changes the other representations. Users may, for example, change a function rule and watch its graphical representation change at the same time. There is some evidence, from a study of middle-grades students working in a transformation geometry microworld, that students use graphical or visual feedback from multiple, linked representations to check the results of conjectures they generate (13). There has been some in-depth discussion of the potential of such tools (29). Very little research has been conducted, however, about the effects of using these tools at the high school level (20, p. 136).

The Use of the Computer as a Tutee

Numerous studies have sought to determine the effects of computer-programming instruction on various aspects of mathematics achievement and attitudes. More recent studies have targeted the effects of learning computer programming on particular problem-solving abilities. Liao and Bright (34) reported preliminary results from a meta-analysis of studies that assessed the relationship between computer programming and cognitive skills related to problem-solving abilities. They concluded that computer programming had a slightly positive effect on student problem-solving performance. Blume (3) also reviewed the effects of computer programming on mathematical problem solving. He concluded that the extent to which programming-augmented mathematics instruction influenced student achievement on particular mathematical topics or improved problem-solving performance seemed to depend on the nature of the programming activities. He suggested that programming exercises that required coding routine algorithmic procedures may have little effect on mathematics achievement, and that programming activities that clearly involved problem solving were more likely to have a positive effect on problem-solving performance.

More detailed analyses of strategies used by student programmers may shed light on the effects of learning programming on achievement in various aspects of mathematics. Blume and Schoen (4), for example, found differences in the problem-solving heuristics used by eighth-grade programmers and nonprogrammers. The programmers used more systematic approaches and reviewed their solutions more often. Programmers and nonprogrammers, however, did not differ in their use of equations, in the extent of their planning, or in the number of correct answers they obtained. Further research is needed to determine the exact nature of these differences.

When students learn computer programming as a part of their mathematics instruction, it is common for much time to be spent on computer-specific and language-specific questions rather than on mathematical concerns. Nevertheless, mathematics-related benefits may include increasing student experience with variables, algorithmic thinking, and recursion. The question that teachers need to answer is whether teaching students to program is worth the time and energy cost within the context of teaching mathematics.

The Use of the Computer as a Tutor

Computer tutors have traditionally been used for teaching students to perform paper-and-pencil algorithms, and much of the research on use of the computer as a tutor focuses on these goals. Even the newer "intelligent" computer tutors do not seem to exist for the development of the mathematical concepts for which computer tools are used.

In a meta-analysis of computer-assisted instruction (drill-and-practice or tutorial) used to supplement traditional classroom instruction, Burns and Bozeman (6) found that students achieved better with the CAI supplement than with a curriculum that used only traditional instructional methods. The researchers made no attempt to categorize or describe the nature of the achievement measures, leaving the impression that the results applied to traditional paper-and-pencil routines.

A recent arena for CAI activity has been the development of intelligent tutors. The goals of present intelligent tutors continue to be the refinement of routine symbolic-manipulation skills and their impact on how students learn mathematical ideas is largely untested.

"Intelligent tutors" like Anderson's *Geometry Tutor* (2), BBN's *Algebra Workbench* (41), and McArthur's *Algebra Tutor* (38) monitor students' problem-solving efforts and diagnose and provide feedback on errors. McArthur's tutor capitalizes on multiple representations and has an alternate "boxes and weights" representation for solving equations. In addition, students can command the program to complete the symbolic manipulation. Unfortunately, intelligent tutors, have been focused almost exclusively on the development of routine manipulation skills.

The Effects of Classroom Use of Other Technologies

Research on incorporating other technologies in mathematics instruction has also assumed traditional skill objectives. Recent research in the use of interactive video instruction has demonstrated that the technology combining video and computer can be used effectively (26) to teach traditional secondary mathematics to students who had not made normal progress in learning routine mathematical skills. One group studied the use of videodisc-based instruction in which the teacher selected a video lesson to be shown a group of students. In a comparison, the videodisc program did just as well as a basal text to maintain "high levels of student engagement and foster positive perceptions of competence in fraction skills" (7, p. 50). It often is assumed that individual learning stations comprised of computers connected to videos would be the optimal implementation of video-based technology. "However, other instructional delivery systems that monitor the individual's progress, including group-paced and systems such as peer tutoring, have been shown to be just as effective as some self-paced systems" (7, p. 37). These video-based technologies have not yet been researched as ways to teach to the new goals of mathematics.

Changing Roles in a Technologically Rich Environment

With the advent of computer-intensive teaching and learning environments, new roles emerge for teachers and students alike. In computer-enriched environments, students and computers together tend to assume the roles often executed exclusively by the teacher in the traditional setting. Heid, Sheets, and Matras, for example, describe students occasionally setting their own tasks as they complete explorations designated in the text (24). In an alternate role, the computer often takes over the responsibility for setting the task (19). Lampert describes students challenging one another to "prove it," and responding by generating appropriate examples and nonexamples (31). Farrell (14) observed that students assumed a larger range of roles (including manager, task setter, explainer, consultant, fellow investigator, and resource) with technology.

Fraser has identified the "Fellow Pupil" role for teachers. In this role, the teacher and student are working together to solve the same problem. When teachers assume this role, they can feel particularly threatened, since they are no longer in the familiar role of "expert," but students can benefit from seeing their teachers as believable problem-solving role models. Schoenfeld (44) observes that "with the machine presenting some of the mathematics, the tutor became a colleague, mathematical objects on the screen became 'conversation pieces'."

Farrell (14) reported that teachers more often assumed the role of consultant (and less often the roles of manager and task setter) when graphing utilities were integrated in a precalculus course. She observed students more frequently in a problem-solving mode with technology than without. Observing general mathematics students using a computer-based problem-solving curriculum, Fiber (17) found that when students worked with partners at computer stations, they had especially high (79%) rates of engagement in on-task behaviors. This study showed that general mathematics students could successfully engage in nonroutine problem-solving activities when computer programs provided tools for making related diagrams and tables.

The ability of the computer to influence the fundamental culture of the classroom is readily apparent. In each of the studies reported here, students were involved with specially designed curricula, and the nature of their involvement was investigative and exploratory. The computer seems to foster this type of involvement and investigation.

Conclusion

Recent research has documented the availability and promise of calculators and computers in the high school mathematics curriculum. One of the predominant areas of research is the use of the computer as a tool in the teaching of mathematics. When graphing, numerical, symbolic-manipulation, and/or geometric tools are integrated into the teaching of mathematics at the high school level, content as well as pedagogy can undergo changes that are clearly in the direction of NCTM's *Curriculum and Evaluation Standards* (39).

Research about specific uses of current computing technology is just beginning. The classroom use of graphing and symbolic-manipulation calculators, the effectiveness of intelligent tutors, and the use of artificial intelligence and video-based technology for conceptual learning and problem solving all are awaiting careful study. In many of these areas, it is time for developers to ready themselves for collaborative work in conjunction with researchers and teachers in order to determine and test promising uses of computing technology. We must learn more about the effects of computing technology on what (as well as how) we learn and teach mathematics in a technologically rich environment.

Looking Ahead . . .

With the continuing exponential growth of technology, it is tempting to defer research and evaluation until the dust settles. Worse yet, it is tempting to accept the new technology inherently as good for school mathematics. Neither of these stances can suffice: It is time to test the new computing technologies against the new goals of school mathematics. How well can current and future technologies promote the shared vision of NCTM's *Curriculum and Evaluation Standards?* Research must begin to guide us in the search for the best combinations of content and pedagogy in school mathematics.

M. Kathleen Heid

After looking back at the results of the research reported in this chapter, I wonder how teachers are going to be able to deal with the changes that are taking place in the educational environment. New technologies, ideas, and methods that have an impact on teaching are surrounding the classroom. How will we know what is important in this changing world? Will there be enough research and information to guide us in implementing the changes that need to be made? How will we "get the word out" and implement needed changes? Finding and implementing the answers is a challenge that we all should welcome

Terry Baylor

About the Authors

M. Kathleen Heid is an associate professor in the area of mathematics education at The Pennsylvania State University. She teaches graduate and undergraduate courses in mathematics education. Her research has centered on the content, teaching, and learning of algebra and calculus in technologically rich environments.

Terry Baylor has taught at the secondary level for twenty-two years. His interests include teaching teachers, collecting calculators, and flying airplanes.

References

1. ALLINGER, G. D. (1985). Percent, calculators, and general mathematics. *School Science and Mathematics, 85,* 567–573.
2. ANDERSON, J. R., BOYLE, C. F. & YOST, G. (1986). The geometry tutor. *Journal of Mathematical Behavior, 5,* 5–19.
3. BLUME, G. W. (1984). A *review of research on the effects of computer programming on mathematical problem solving.* Paper presented at the annual meeting of the American Educational Research Association, New Orleans, April.
4. BLUME, G. W., & SCHOEN, H. L. (1988). Mathematical problem-solving performance of eighth-grade programmers and nonprogrammers. *Journal for Research in Mathematics Education, 19*(2), 142–156.
5. BOBANGO, J. C. (1987). Van Hiele levels of geometric thought and student achievement in standard content and proof-writing: The effect of phase-based instruction. *Dissertation Abstracts International, 48A,* 2566. (University Microfilms No. DEV 87–27983)
6. BURNS, P. K., & BOZEMAN, W. (1981). Computer-assisted instruction and mathematics achievement. *Educational Technology, 21*(10), 32–29.
7. CARNINE, D., ENGELMANN, S., HOFMEISTER, A., & KELLY, B. (1987). Videodisc instruction in fractions. *Focus on Learning Problems in Mathematics, 9,* 31–52.
8. DAMARIN, S. K., DZIAK, N. J., STULL, L., & WHITEMAN, F. (1988). Computer instruc-

tion in estimation: Improvement in high school mathematics students. *School Science and Mathematics*, 88(6), 488–492.

9. DEMANA, F., & WAITS, B. (1990). *Precalculus: Functions and graphs.* Reading, MA: Addison–Wesley.

10. DICK, T., & SHAUGHNESSY, J. M. (1988). The influence of symbolic/graphing calculators on the perceptions of students and teachers towards mathematics. In *Proceedings of the Tenth Annual Meeting of the North American Chapter of the International Group for the Psychology of Mathematics Education,* 327–333. De Kalb: Northern Illinois University.

11. DOSSEY, J. A., MULLIS, I. V. S., LINDQUIST, M. M., & CHAMBERS, D. L. (1988). *The Mathematics Report Card: Are We Measuring Up?* Princeton: Educational Testing Service.

12. DUGDALE, S. (1987). Pathfinder: a microcomputer experience in interpreting graphs. *Journal of Educational Technology Systems, 15*(3), 259–280.

13. EDWARDS, L. D. (1991). Children's learning in a computer microworld for transformation geometry. *Journal for Research in Mathematics Education, 22*(2), 122–137.

14. FARRELL, A. (1989). Teaching and learning behaviors in technology-oriented precalculus classrooms. *Dissertation Abstracts International, 51A,* 100. (University Microfilms No. AAD 90–14417)

15. FEY, J. T. (Ed.). (1984). *Computing and Mathematics: The impact on secondary school curricula.* Reston, VA: National Council of Teachers of Mathematics.

16. FEY, J. T. (Ed.). (1991). *Computer-Intensive Algebra.* College Park: University of Maryland Press.

17. FIBER, H. R. (1987). The influence of microcomputer-based problem-solving activities on the attitudes of general mathematics students toward microcomputers. *Dissertation Abstracts International, 48,* 1102A. (University Microfilms No. 87-14816)

18. FRASER, R. (Chief organizer). (1988). Theme group 2: Computers and the teaching of mathematics. In A. Hirst & K. Hirst (Eds.), *Proceedings of the Sixth International Congress on Mathematical Education* (pp. 215–216). Budapest: Malev.

19. FRASER, R., BURKHARDT, H. , COUPLAND, J., PHILLIPS, R., PIMM, D., & RIDGWAY, J. (1988). Learning activities and classroom roles with and without computers. *Journal of Mathematical Behavior, 6,* 305–338.

20. GOLDENBERG, E. P. (1988). Mathematics, metaphors, and human factors: Mathematical, technical, and pedagogical challenges in the educational use of graphical representations of functions. *Journal of Mathematical Behavior, 7,* 135–173.

21. HAWKER, C. M. (1987). The effects of replacing some manual skills with computer algebra manipulations on student performance in business calculus. *Dissertation Abstracts International, 47,* 2934A. (University Microfilms No. 86-26590)

22. HEID, M. K. (1988). Resequencing skills and concepts in applied calculus using the computer as a tool. *Journal for Research in Mathematics Education, 19*(1), 3–25.

23. HEID, M. K., SHEETS, C., MATRAS, M.A., & MENASIAN, J. (1988). *Classroom and computer lab interaction in a computer-intensive environment.* Paper presented at the annual meeting of the American Educational Research Association, New Orleans.

24. HEID, M. K., SHEETS, C., & MATRAS, M. (1990). Teaching and learning algebra in a computer-enhanced environment: New roles and challenges for the teachers and students. In T. Cooney (Ed.), *Teaching and learning mathematics in the 1990s* (1990 Yearbook). Reston, VA: National Council of Teachers of Mathematics.

25. HEMBREE, R., & DESSART, D. (1986). Effects of hand-held calculators in precollege mathematics education: A meta-analysis. *Journal for Research in Mathematics Education, 17,* 83–99.

26. HENDERSON, R. W., LANDSMAN, E. M., & KACHUCK, I. (1985). Computer video instruction in mathematics: Field test of an interactive approach. *Journal for Research in Mathematics Education*, 16, 207–224.

27. JAJI, G. (1986). *The uses of calculators and computers in mathematics classes in twenty countries: Summary report. Second International Mathematics Study*. Urbana: University of Illinois. (ERIC Document Reproduction Service No. ED291589)

28. JUDSON, P. T. (1988). Effects of modified sequencing of skills and applications in introductory calculus. *Dissertation Abstracts International*, 49, 1397A. (University Microfilms No. 88–16484).

29. KAPUT, J. J. (1986). Information technology and mathematics: Opening new representational windows. *Journal of Mathematical Behavior*, 5, 187–207.

30. LAMPERT, M. (1988a). *Teachers' thinking about students' thinking about geometry: The effects of new teaching tools* (Technical report). Cambridge, MA: Educational Technology Center.

31. LAMPERT, M. (1988b). *Teaching that connects students' inquiry with curricular agendas in schools* (Technical report). Cambridge, MA: Educational Technology Center.

32. LEINHART, G., ZASLAVSKY, O., & STEIN, M. K. (1990). Functions, graphs, and graphing: Tasks, learning, and teaching. *Review of Educational Research*, 60, 1–64.

33. LEWIS, J., & HOOVER, H. D. (1981). *The effect on pupil performance of using hand-held calculators on standardized mathematics achievement tests*. Paper presented at the annual meeting of the National Council on Measurement in Education, Los Angeles.

34. LIAO, Y., & BRIGHT, G. W. (1989). Computer programming and problem solving abilities: A meta-analysis. In W. C. Ryan (Ed.), *Proceedings of the National Educational Computing Conference* (pp. 10–13). Boston: International Council on Computers in Education.

35. LONG, V. M., REYS, B., & OSTERLIND, S. J. (1989). Using calculators on achievement tests. *Mathematics Teacher*, 82(5), 318–325.

36. MATRAS, M. A. (1988). The effects of curricula on students' ability to analyze and solve problems in algebra. *Dissertation Abstracts International*, 49, 1726A. (University Microfilms No. 88–18432)

37. MAURY, K. A. (1987). The development of an instrument to measure the impact of calculators and computers on the secondary school mathematics curriculum. *Dissertation Abstracts International*, 49, 755A. (University Microfilms No. AAD 88–08693).

38. MCARTHUR, D., BURDORF, C., ORMSETH, T., ROBYN, A., & STASZ, C. (1988). *Multiple representations of mathematical reasoning*. Santa Monica: Rand Corporation.

39. NATIONAL COUNCIL OF TEACHERS OF MATHEMATICS (1989). *Curriculum and evaluation standards for school mathematics*. Reston, VA: National Council of Teachers of Mathematics.

40. PALMITER, J. R. (1991). Effects of computer algebra systems on concept and skill acquisition in calculus. *Journal for Research in Mathematics Education*, 22(2), 151–156.

41. RICHARDS, J., & FEURZEIG, W. (1988). Intelligent tools for algebra. *Technology and Learning*, 2(3), 1–4.

42. RUTHVEN, K. (1990). The influence of graphic calculator use on transition from graphic to symbolic forms. *Educational Studies in Mathematics*, (21)5, 431–450.

43. ROSEBERY, A. S., & RUBIN, A. (1989). Reasoning under uncertainty: Developing statistical reasoning. *Journal of Mathematical Behavior*, 8, 205–219.

44. SCHOENFELD, A. (1988). *Grapher: A case study in educational technology, research, and development*. Berkeley: University of California Press.

45. SENK, S. (1988). Van Hiele levels and achievement in writing geometry proofs. *Journal for Research in Mathematics Education*, 20, 309–321.

46. TAYLOR, R. P. (Ed.) (1980). *The Computer in the School: Tutor, Tool, Tutee.* New York: Teachers College Press.
47. THOMPSON, P. W. (1989). Artificial intelligence, advanced technology, and learning and teaching of algebra. In C. Kieran, & S. Wagner (Eds.), *Research issues in the learning and teaching of algebra*, (135–161). Reston, VA: National Council of Teachers of Mathematics.
48. VAN HIELE, P. M. (1986). *Structure and insight: A theory of mathematics education.* Orlando, FL: Academic Press.
49. YERUSHALMY, M., CHAZAN, D., & GORDON, M. (1987). *Guided inquiry technology: A year long study of children and teachers using the geometric supposer.* Cambridge; MA: Center for Learning Technology.

PART III

Teaching

CHAPTER 12

Instructional Activities and Decisions

Mary Kim Prichard and Sue Bingaman

What the teacher says in the classroom is not unimportant, but what the students think is a thousand times more important. The ideas should be born in the students' mind and the teacher should act only as a midwife. (29, p. 104)

Good mathematics teaching is an inexact blend of a teacher's knowledge of mathematics, pedagogy, and psychology. Many times we rely on our intuitions about students and on our past experiences to decide what will and will not work in our classes. Research in mathematics education can provide us with some direction about how we can improve and enhance our teaching. This chapter focuses on the research related to the variety of teaching activities that take place in high school mathematics classrooms.

NCTM's *Professional Teaching Standards* (25) and *Curriculum and Evaluation Standards* (24) present a perspective on the teaching of mathematics that may be somewhat foreign to many teachers. Both documents call for changes in current modes of classroom instruction as well as in the roles of teachers and students alike. Most teachers did not experience as students the patterns of teaching that are called for by the *Standards* documents—the kind of teaching that will require many teachers to reexamine their roles in the classroom. With teachers who serve as guides and facilitators of learning, classroom instruction will become more decentralized, so that students will take a more active part in explorations and discussions that help them to build their own knowledge of mathematics.

This chapter focuses on what teachers do when they teach. We look first at the research on specific modes of instruction and then at that on instructional strategies. Rather than describing a variety of models of instruction and discussing the related research, we have chosen one model to use as a framework for discussing the research on teaching. Farrell and Farmer's (12) model for mathematics instruction integrates theory, practice, and research. This model reflects the dynamic nature of mathematics and the view that teaching is a complex problem-solving process. The modes of instruction are the activities that teachers plan and carry out to help their students to learn mathematics. Instructional strategies include the ways in which teachers combine and sequence these modes in their classrooms.

Modes of instruction
1. Lecture
2. Question/Answer
3. Discussion
4. Demonstration
5. Laboratory Activities
6. Individual Student Projects
7. Audiovisual and Technological Activities
8. Supervised Practice

Modes of Instruction

As mathematics students you undoubtedly experienced many of the modes of instruction identified by Farrell and Farmer, and as mathematics teachers you may well have incorporated these activities into your classroom instruction. The following section has three related purposes: (1) to describe the variety of modes of instruction that might be found in a mathematics lesson; (2) to discuss the value of each component, the judgments based on results from research; and (3) to help you implement new activities that reflect the vision of teaching presented in both NCTM *Standards* publications (24, 25).

Teacher Talk

Teacher talk, or a lecture, usually is presented to the entire class, but may take place when the class divides into small groups. Lectures may range in length from a few minutes to the entire class period, the teacher playing the central role in the presentation. Research at the junior and senior high levels of mathematics indicates that several aspects of teacher behavior (including clarity and enthusiasm) during the lecture portion of the lesson are related to student achievement.

McConnell (22) reported that in high school algebra classes clarity and enthusiasm were correlated with student learning. Smith (39) looked at the lecture part of a single lesson taught by twenty teachers on the concept of direct variation, finding that the most effective teachers gave added attention to the objectives of the lesson, used more relevant examples, and offered fewer responses such as "OK" (considered a vague term).

Teacher enthusiasm

Relate mathematics to:	*Express:*
Current Events	Vigor
History	Dynamics
Science	Surprise
Fine Arts	Joy

(13)

Teacher/Student Talk

For a variety of different reasons, teachers ask many questions during a lesson. A great deal of research on teachers' questioning techniques has been conducted in the past twenty-five years, and the findings support the recommendations found in *Professional Standards for Teaching Mathematics* apropos of changes in the current teaching patterns. Teachers should "step back from the role of being the dispenser of knowledge and the confirmer of right answers" (25, p. 4). Research on classroom questioning techniques can offer advice for classroom teachers in the areas of both wait time and the cognitive level of questions.

Helpful questions

"Why are *AB* and *CD* parallel to each other?" may guide students' thinking during a geometry lesson.
"Did anyone solve this problem in a different way?" may encourage students to consider other problem-solving strategies.

Wait Time. In her research on wait time, Mary Budd Rowe (35) found that when elementary science teachers waited three seconds or more for students to reply to questions, students gave more thoughtful responses and classroom discussion increased. She observed eight specific effects when wait times were increased. Longer wait times lead to active classrooms wherein more students are more involved.

Effects when wait times are increased:

1. Length of student responses increases
2. Number of unsolicited, appropriate responses increases
3. Failures to respond decrease
4. Students' confidence in their answers increases
5. Speculative thinking increases
6. Students ask more questions
7. Contributions by slow learners increase
8. Disciplinary actions decrease

(35)

Cognitive Level of Questions.   According to NCTM's *Professional Standards for Teaching Mathematics,* teachers should "orchestrate discourse by posing questions and tasks that provoke and challenge students' thinking [and by] asking students to clarify and justify their ideas" (25, p. 37). In spite of the recommendations from NCTM and other professional organizations, though the results from research on the level of questions has been mixed. Dunkin and Biddle (10) found that "teachers who ask for a higher level of response from pupils are likely to stimulate pupils to a higher level of response. However, the evidence suggesting that this has positive effects on pupil achievement is spotty, if not negative" (p. 396). In their review, Rosenshine and Furst (33) report that the scheme for classifying questions is a critical variable in determining the outcome of the study. Three studies where three or more levels of questions were identified showed a significant positive relationship with student achievement. Significant results were not obtained when only two levels (low and high) were used.

These results are rather surprising to teachers who believe that questions requiring students to think are better than questions that require students simply to recall information. In their meta-analysis of fourteen studies on teachers' use of higher and lower cognitive-level questions, Redfield and Rousseau (31) found that achievement gains could be expected when teachers asked more higher cognitive-level questions. The differences in findings of these reviews may be due to the difficulty in categorizing, identifying, and counting higher-level questions that are asked both during class and on the pre- and postobservation achievement tests.

Tobin (44) studied the use of extended wait time in sixth- and seventh-grade mathematics and language arts classes. He found a relationship between wait time and the cognitive level of questions. When wait time increased to three seconds or more during the math lessons, the number of application-level questions increased. He also found that students' ability to reason also improved.

Helpful discussions on the "art of questioning" can be found in books by Johnson (19), Posamentier and Stepelman (30), and Good and Brophy (13).

Student Talk.   This mode of instruction refers to "planned student-to-student talk with occasional verbal intervention by the teacher" (12, p. 3). Pirie (27) defines discussion as "purposeful talk on a mathematical subject in which there are genuine pupil contributions and interactions" (p. 2). According to the *NCTM Standards* (25), this kind of teaching "requires that students be allowed to talk with their peers, to argue, to experiment, to invent and justify alternatives, and to be wrong" (p. 4). This mode of instruction can be carried out using whole-class or small-group discussion, small-group cooperative learning, or peer tutoring.

Discussion.   Hoyles (17) identified three aspects of discussion that are important to consider. First, the "talking" that takes place forces students to develop their own thoughts about mathematics and to communicate their ideas to others. Second, the situation, problem, or task that engages students must *require* that students communicate. Third, listening for learning should not be passive. As students listen to one another, they should incorporate other ideas into their own and evaluate their own understanding.

Mathematics as communication

Curriculum and Evaluation Standards: In grades 9–12, the mathematics curriculum should include the continued development of language and symbolism to communicate mathematical ideas. (24, p. 140)

Cockroft Report: The ability to "say what you mean and mean what you say" should be one of the outcomes of good mathematics teaching. This ability develops as a result of opportunities to talk about mathematics, to explain and discuss results which have been obtained, and to test hypotheses. (4, p. 72)

Several British mathematics educators have observed classrooms to study student discussions. Hoyles's (17) research indicates that when students working in pairs are learning the computer language Logo, genuine discussion takes place between them. Students collaborate to pose and solve their own problems. Working with one another forces students to communicate their own ideas and take "steps into unknown territory." Discussion also provides students with the opportunity to find out where they might be having difficulties.

Pirie and Schwarzenberger (28) conducted a longitudinal study on whether or not discussion in the mathematics classroom is an aid to understanding. Pirie (27) described a typical lesson with 11- and 12-year-olds by one of the teachers who uses whole-class discussion. Their preliminary analysis has shown no evidence either to support or deny the hypothesis that discussion aids understanding.

"He will start the lesson by offering the pupils an idea, a problem, or a piece of mathematics, pupils are encouraged to offer their thinking to the rest of the class and, frequently, lively open discussion takes place. The teacher virtually excludes himself from this forum, both physically, by sitting unobtrusively to one side, and orally, by deflecting direct questions back to the pupils." (27, p. 2)

Cooperative Learning. Small-group cooperative learning is an alternative to whole-class instruction that facilitates discussion and communication about mathematics. Cooperative learning is an approach whereby a group of students work together to complete a task or solve a problem.

The growing body of research on cooperative learning indicates that this mode of instruction is an effective instructional technique with students of all ability levels and in all areas of mathematics, from remedial mathematics to college calculus and beyond. Slavin (38) has conducted a comprehensive review of research on cooperative learning methods at the elementary and secondary levels. Sixty-eight comparisons were included in the review. Of these comparisons, twenty-three dealt with mathematics—of which only four were at the high school level.

In his review, Slavin discovered that some cooperative learning methods are more effective than others at influencing student achievement. Two features common to the most effective methods are (1) an emphasis on group goals and (2) individual acccountability. The group members must work together to succeed, and the group can be successful only when all members learn and participate.

Cooperative learning

Students' Roles
   Shared responsibility
   Individual accountability
   Group accountability
   Evaluation

Teachers' Roles
   Facilitator
   Role Model
   Observer

According to Slavin (38), the range of outcomes other than achievement that are affected by cooperative learning methods also is impressive. Cooperative learning strategies have been shown to influence positively both student self-esteem and race relations. Cooperative learning activities can also help overcome barriers to friendship and interaction when handicapped students are mainstreamed into regular classrooms. Slavin goes so far as to say "for any desired outcome of schooling, administer a cooperative learning treatment, and about two-thirds of the time there will be a significant difference between the experimental and control groups in favor of the experimental groups (rarely, if ever, will differences favor a control group)" (p. 53).

There are many resources available to teachers that offer suggestions on implementing cooperative learning in high school mathematics classrooms (8, 1, 20).

Ability Grouping. One of the decisions that teachers have to make when using small-group instruction (cooperative or not) is how to divide students into groups. Research indicates that mixed-ability heterogeneous groups have positive effects on learning. These groups can be either randomly assigned or teacher selected. Homogeneous grouping does not work well for the lower-ability students. Mathematics teachers have always had to face the problem of dealing with a wide range of mathematical backgrounds, abilities, and learning styles. Since secondary schools are departmentalized, ability grouping at this level usually is done through course selection.

Ability grouping often results in:

1. Widening gaps in academic performance between high and low achievers
2. Lowering self-esteem and motivation for low-achieving students
3. Restricting friendship choices for minority students

(6)

Peer Tutoring. On the surface, peer tutoring and cooperative learning may look similar: They both involve students working together. However, the two modes of instruction are very different. In cooperative learning, two or more students learn together. In peer tutoring, generally two students work together—but with one as the learner and one as the teacher.

Many teachers and schools have organized programs for peer tutoring wherein more advanced students work either individually or with a small group of students who need remedial assistance. Instruction is planned and paced so that the pupils can master the topic and review and practice necessary concepts and skills.

In peer tutoring programs, there are advantages for both the tutors and the pupils. Cohen, Kulik, and Kulik (5) reviewed 52 studies at the elementary and secondary levels that reported effects of peer tutoring programs on academic achievement. They found positive effects on achievement and attitudes of those who received the tutoring. These students outperformed their peers on examinations, and also showed better attitudes in the subjects in which they were tutored. The review also showed that the student–tutors developed more positive attitudes and a better understanding of the subjects they tutored. Tutors have the opportunity to strengthen and enhance their knowledge of mathematics as they prepare for the lessons and consider alternative teaching approaches. The experience also has affective outcomes for the tutor, such as improved self-esteem and self-concept as a mathematics learner.

An important part of a peer tutoring program is the training phase for the tutors. This includes discussion of the variety of methods and techniques that tutors can use, as well as the resources available to them. The tutors must also be sensitive to the errors that the pupils make, so that they can reteach, or teach differently, when necessary.

Using Instructional Aids in the Classroom

Teachers do much more in the classroom than just talk, of course—and they also use teaching tools and materials other than the overhead projector and the chalkboard. Other modes of instruction range from teacher-centered demonstrations to more student-centered activities in mathematics laboratories. Chapter 11 deals more thoroughly with the use of technology-based activities in the classroom.

Teacher Demonstrations.   The demonstration mode of instruction takes place when the teacher shows a model or uses manipulative materials to demonstrate an idea to the class. A teacher might use algebra tiles on the overhead projector to show that $(x + 2)(x + 3) = x^2 + 5x + 6$. A teacher might also use models of the five regular polyhedra to motivate Euler's formula. Teachers frequently use demonstrations in combination with other modes of instruction, too. The research on effective teaching behaviors provides guidelines for teacher talk as well as teacher demonstration.

Effective classroom demonstrations require:

1. Clarity
2. Enthusiasm
3. Good questioning techniques
4. Student involvement

Laboratory Activities. The laboratory mode refers to student activities rather than to particular places or particular class periods. Suydam and Higgins (43) characterize the range of activities that may be used in the classroom. They vary widely from real-world applications to small-group work. The activity may motivate, introduce, reinforce, or help children apply a mathematical idea. It also may be integrated into the curriculum or stand alone, and it may or may not use manipulative materials. Sobel and Maletsky (40) offer ideas for classroom activities.

Suydam and Higgins (43) reviewed activity-based learning in elementary school mathematics, including grades 7 and 8. They found that students using activity-based programs could be expected to achieve as well as, or better than, students in programs that were not activity-based. The activities appeared to be "effective with children at all achievement levels, ability levels, and socio-economic levels" (p. 84).

More recently, Sowell (41) used meta-analysis to determine the effectiveness of mathematics instruction with manipulative materials. Of the sixty studies reviewed, none was done at the high school level. However, eleven were in grades 7 through 9, and six were at the postsecondary level. She found that mathematics achievement increased and attitudes toward mathematics improved through the use of concrete instructional materials.

Simple manipulative materials should be used:

1. Frequently
2. In conjunction with other aids
3. In ways appropriate to mathematics content
4. In conjunction with exploratory and inductive approaches
5. To aid in organizing content

(43)

Supervised Practice

In guided practice the teacher leads the students, checks for understanding, corrects errors, and reteaches if necessary. Independent practice should help students to develop their understanding of new concepts and skills.

During practice, effective teachers:

1. Give clear instructions and sufficient guided practice before students begin independent practice
2. Circulate around the classroom, explaining, observing, asking questions, and providing feedback
3. Have short contacts of 30 seconds or less with students
4. For difficult material have several segments of practice throughout a single lesson
5. Establish a routine for managing seatwork

(34)

Research indicates that effective teachers should ask many questions, and check for understanding frequently (34). In particular, the more effective teachers ask more process questions. Responses to questions like "Can you explain how you got your answer" help teachers to understand students' thinking and also encourage students to communicate mathematically. Teachers can check for understanding more frequently by calling on students whose hands are not raised and by asking students to summarize and explain in their own words.

Putting It All Together: Instructional Strategies

An instructional strategy is the sequence of modes of instruction that a teacher uses during a class period in order to help students learn mathematics. The particular modes used in a lesson, and their sequence, depend on the objectives of the lesson and the needs of the students. This part of our chapter looks at alternatives for organizing mathematics instruction. (See the 1977 NCTM Yearbook [7] for examples of approaches in more specific mathematical contexts.) The following section has three purposes: (1) to describe instructional strategies ranging from whole-class to individualized instruction; (2) to discuss the value of the strategies based on results from research; and (3) to help you consider alternatives for organizing your lessons.

Direct Instruction

Most of the research on high school mathematics teaching has focused on the teaching approach known as *direct instruction*. Direct instruction has several characteristics (32). Lessons and assignments are supervised by the teacher. There is very little free time or unsupervised seatwork during class. The teacher is the dominant leader, deciding on and directing what takes place. Learning is organized around questions posed by the teacher or materials provided by the teacher. Direct instruction involves in varying amounts several of the modes of instruction discussed earlier—lecture, question/answer, demonstration and laboratory activities, and practice.

Active Instruction. Some researchers have focused on a teaching approach that is called "active teaching." These classes are characterized by whole-group instruction, active student involvement, and teacher–student interaction during practice.

Evertson, Emmer, and Brophy (11) studied the classroom behavior of more and less effective seventh- and eighth-grade mathematics teachers. Teacher effectiveness was determined by student ratings of their teachers and student performance on an achievement test measuring computational and mathematical reasoning skills. The researchers found that effective teaching is characterized not by any single factor, but by many qualities. All of the teachers, both effective and less effective, used direct instruction most of the time. Effective teachers spent more time on the development of the lesson with the entire group than on individual seatwork. They were better classroom managers, they asked more questions; and they displayed greater clarity in their presentations.

Good, Grouws, and Ebmeier (14) extended their Missouri Mathematics Effectiveness Project from elementary mathematics teachers to eighth- and ninth-grade mathematics teachers. Nineteen teachers participated in the study, including eight in the control group. The other eleven were involved in a training program to implement a model for mathematics instruction. The model for direct instruction included a twelve-minute review at the beginning of the class, followed by a ten-minute verbal problem-solving session. The development portion of the lesson was to last approximately twenty minutes. Near the end of the development phase, teachers were to have students work a problem similar to their assignment and then discuss the solution with the entire class. The model called for individual seatwork following the controlled practice.

The researchers found that the development portion of the model was the most difficult part for the teachers to implement. This seems surprising, since most of us would probably consider this to be the heart of the lesson. The teachers varied considerably in the amount of time they spent on both the problem-solving portion of the class and the development portion. However, the average total development time was greater for the teachers involved in the training program than for the teachers in the control group. Also, the students of the training-program teachers did slightly better on a general mathematics achievement measure and significantly better on a problem-solving measure at the end of the project.

Hunter's Instructional Theory into Practice Model.   Another model for direct instruction is Madeline Hunter's Instructional Theory into Practice model. This model has gained widespread use in system-based staff development, and is also used by some school districts as an instrument for evaluating classroom instruction. According to Hunter, "the model is equally effective in elementary, secondary, and university teaching" (18, p. 59). However, several studies at the elementary school level indicate that this model is *not* effective for improving student achievement (42, 9, 21).

Good for What?   Peterson (26) reviewed studies that compared the effects of direct instruction with those of open teaching. Open teaching is characterized by flexibility of space, student choice of activities and materials, and individual and small-group instruction. She concluded that with direct instruction, students tended to do slightly better on achievement tests but slightly worse on tests of creativity and problem solving.

Good for Whom?   Further, according to Peterson (26), the students being taught should also influence a teacher's decision about which instructional approach to take. Low-ability students seem to do better in whole-group direct instruction, while high-ability students do better in a small-group approach. The effectiveness of direct instruction also seems to depend on students' locus of control. Students with an *internal* locus of control (the feeling that they have control over their own success and failure) do better in open teaching approaches than in direct instruction. Students with an *external* locus of control (the feeling that their success and failure are due to fate or luck) tend to do better in direct instruction. It is important to note that we still know very little about how different instructional strategies affect students' locus of control.

Adaptive Instruction

According to Wang and Lindvall (45), "Adaptive instruction refers to educational interventions that are aimed at effectively accommodating individual differences in students while helping each student develop the knowledge and skills required to master learning tasks" (p. 161). Adaptive instructional approaches have taken a variety of forms, employing many different strategies. The most well-known, widely used model for whole-group instruction is the group-based Mastery Learning model developed by Benjamin S. Bloom. Individualized instruction is characterized by F. S. Keller's Personalized System of Instruction, which has been used primarily at the college level.

Mastery Learning. Mastery learning is based on the notion that different students learn different material at different rates and in different ways. A mathematical topic is taught to the class. The class is then tested on the topic, and those students who do not score above a particular level are retaught via the use of different methods and then retested. The role of the teacher is that of "an instructional leader and learning facilitator" (15, p. 10) who uses a variety of instructional techniques and feedback and evaluative procedures.

According to Bloom (3), in the first step of the feedback–correction process, the teacher identifies the errors common to most of the students. The teacher then briefly reteaches the ideas, using illustrations or approaches different from those previously used in the class. In the second pass through the feedback–correction loop, students work together in small groups to help one another on the items missed on the test. If they need to go through the loop again, individual students are referred to specific curriculum materials keyed to the test items they missed.

Research is not conclusive about the effects of mastery learning programs. There is considerable disagreement among researchers about how to measure the programs' effectiveness as well as the instructional time spent in them, and how long instructional treatments should last. For example, Guskey and Gates (16) reviewed and synthesized the results of research on the effects of mastery learning programs, providing evidence that such programs have positive effects on both student achievement and learning retention. But Slavin (37) analyzed studies of mastery learning and found no evidence to support the effectiveness of group-based mastery learning on at least standardized achievement tests.

Individualized Instruction. Guskey (15) characterized the personalized instructional model as "an individually based, student-paced approach to instruction in which students typically learn independently of their classmates" (p. 9). The primary sources of instruction are textbooks and other curriculum materials, occasionally supplemented by individual help from the teacher. The role of the teacher in individualized instruction programs is that of manager and resource for individual help when needed.

Research into individualized systems of instruction at the secondary level is fairly conclusive. These programs produce only a small effect (if any at all) on student achievement (2). Schoen (36) reviewed twelve studies at the secondary level and five at the postsecondary level that compared individualized instruction with traditional instruction. Only one of the secondary studies and one of the postsecondary studies showed significant differences between the two approaches that favored the individualized instruction. In three of the secondary studies, significant differences in achievement favored the control groups.

Individualized instruction

"Over fifty studies in all grade levels aimed at showing the effectiveness of this approach demonstrate no consistent objective evidence that there will be student improvement of any sort. The most consistent result is less mathematics achievement with an individualized teaching approach." (36, p. 356)

Conclusion

The research on modes of instruction and instructional strategies provides suggestions for more effective classroom instruction. The most effective classroom teacher is able to draw from all of these recommendations and make instructional decisions that are based on students' varying interests and abilities, the long-term and short-term instructional goals, and the mathematical content. With a variety of teaching methods at our disposal, we can reach more students and create a more diverse learning environment for them.

"Research findings are useful to teachers when teachers make decisions about adaptations in their classrooms. Teachers, because they know their students and the classroom context, can decide what research findings are relevant and how to bring them to life. Research findings are not helpful when they are turned into rigid directives requiring lock-step implementation." (23, pp. 18, 20)

Looking Ahead . . .

Research on teaching, the methodologies being used, and the theories on which the research is based are changing. Most of the research discussed in this chapter has been experimental in design, using control and experimental groups and gain scores on some evaluation instrument to determine student achievement. Much of this research does not reflect the kind of teaching called for in *Curriculum and Evaluation Standards* (24) and *Professional Standards for Teaching Mathematics* (25). In many cases, researchers make *no* assumptions about how students learn mathematics. There is a tremendous need for further research on teaching mathematics at the high school level. Researchers need to collaborate with classroom teachers in the process of formulating problems, developing studies, and collecting and analyzing data.

Mary Kim Prichard

As you reflect on this chapter, you will again be confronted with conflict as you recall that the research is not conclusive in informing teachers concerning one "best" method for insuring students' mathematical learning. Perhaps it would help to be aware of the larger conflict surrounding various classroom styles and of the fact that you will often be unsure as you make decisions for your classroom teaching.

You have seen from the research that each mode of instruction or instructional strategy has its own benefits. Your task, as the classroom teacher, is to consider the many alternatives and select what seems appropriate for the various objectives and particular groups of students with whom you are working.

Sue Bingaman

About the Authors

Mary Kim Prichard is an assistant professor of mathematics at the University of North Carolina at Charlotte, where she teaches both mathematics and mathematics education courses. Her research interests include the use of technology to teach mathematics and the teaching and learning of calculus. She is a frequent speaker at state and national meetings of professional societies.

Sue Bingaman is head of the mathematics department at Charlotte Country Day School. She studied at the University of Georgia as a GTE GIFT Fellow and is currently on the national selection committee for GTE Fellows. A teacher of geometry and precalculus, Ms. Bingaman is now also exploring ways to incorporate graphing calculators and geometry software into her teaching.

References

*1. ARTZT, A. F., & NEWMAN, C. M. (1990). Cooperative learning. *Mathematics Teacher*, 83(6), 448–452.

2. BANGERT, R. L., KULIK, J. A., & KULIK, C. C. (1983). Individualized systems of instruction in secondary schools. *Review of Educational Research*, 53(2), 143–158.

3. BLOOM, B. S. (1987). A response to Slavin's Mastery Learning Reconsidered. *Review of Educational Research*, 57(4), 507–508.

4. COCKROFT, W. H. (1982). *Mathematics counts: Report of the Committee of Inquiry into the Teaching of Mathematics in Schools*. London: Her Majesty's Stationery Office.

5. COHEN, P. A., KULIK, J. A., & KULIK, C. (1982). Educational outcomes of tutoring: A meta-analysis of findings. *American Educational Research Journal*, 19(2), 237–248.

6. CORNO, L., & SNOW, R. E. (1986). Adapting teaching to individual differences among learners. In M. C. Wittrock (Ed.), *Handbook of research on teaching* (3rd ed.). New York: Macmillan.

*7. CROSSWHITE, F. J. (1977). *Organizing for Mathematics Instruction* (1977 Yearbook). Reston, VA: National Council of Teachers of Mathematics.

*8. DAVIDSON, N. (Ed.). (1990). *Cooperative learning in mathematics: A handbook for teachers.* Menlo Park, CA: Addison–Wesley.

9. DONOVAN, J. F., SOUSA, D. A., & WALBER, H. J. (1987). The impact of staff development on implementation and student achievement. *Journal of Educational Research, 80,* 348–351.

10. DUNKIN, M. J., & BIDDLE, B. J. (1974). *The study of teaching.* New York: Holt, Rinehart. (Reissued by University Press of America)

11. EVERTSON, C. M., EMMER, E. T., & BROPHY, J. E. (1980). Predictors of effective teaching in junior high mathematics classrooms. *Journal for Research in Mathematics Education, 11,* 167–178.

*12. FARRELL, M. A., & FARMER, W. A. (1988). *Secondary mathematics instruction: An integrated approach.* Providence: Janson.

13. GOOD, T. L., & BROPHY, J. E. (1984). *Looking in classrooms* (3rd ed.). New York: Harper & Row.

14. GOOD, T. L., GROUWS, D. A., & EBMEIER, H. (1983). *Active mathematics teaching.* New York: Longman.

15. GUSKEY, T. R. (1985). *Implementing mastery learning.* Belmont, CA: Wadsworth.

16. GUSKEY, T. R., & GATES, S. L. (1986). Synthesis of research on the effects of mastery learning in elementary and secondary classrooms. *Educational Leadership, 43*(8), 73–80.

17. HOYLES, C. M. (1985). What is the point of group discussion in mathematics? *Educational Studies in Mathematics, 16,* 205–214.

18. HUNTER, M. (1985). What's wrong with Madeline Hunter? *Educational Leadership, 42*(5), 57–60.

*19. JOHNSON, D. R. (1982). *Every minute counts: Making your math class work.* Palo Alto: Dale Seymour.

*20. JOHNSON, D. W., JOHNSON, R. T., HOLUBEC, E. J., & ROY, P. (1984). *Circles of learning: Cooperation in the classroom.* Alexandria, VA: Association for Supervision and Curriculum Development.

21. MANDEVILLE, G. K., & RIVERS, J. L. (1988–1989). Effects of South Carolina's Hunter-based PET Program. *Educational Leadership, 46*(4), 63–66.

22. McCONNELL, J. (1977). Relationships between selected teacher behaviors and attitudes/achievements of algebra classes. Paper presented at the Annual Meeting of the American Educational Research Association, New York, NY, April.

23. MYERS, M. (1986). When research does not help teachers. *American Educator, 10*(2), 18–23, 46.

*24. NATIONAL COUNCIL OF TEACHERS OF MATHEMATICS (1989). *Curriculum and evaluation standards for school mathematics.* Reston, VA: Author.

*25. NATIONAL COUNCIL OF TEACHERS OF MATHEMATICS (1991). *Professional standards for teaching mathematics.* Reston, VA: Author.

26. PETERSON, P. L. (1979). Direct instruction: Effective for what and for whom? *Educational Leadership, 37*(2), 46–48.

27. Pirie, S. E. B. (1988). Understanding: Instrumental, relational, intuitive, constructed, formalized . . . ? How can we know? *For the Learning of Mathematics, 8*(3), 2–6.

28. PIRIE, S. E. B., & SCHWARZENBERGER, R. L. E. (1988). Mathematical discussion and mathematical understanding. *Educational Studies in Mathematics, 19*(4), 459–470.

*29. POLYA, G. (1981). *Mathematical discovery: On understanding, learning, and teaching problem solving* (combined edition). New York: Wiley. (Original work published 1962)

*30. POSAMENTIER, A. S., & STEPELMAN, J. (1990). *Teaching secondary school mathematics: Techniques and enrichment units* (3rd ed.). Columbus, OH: Merrill.

31. REDFIELD, D. L., & ROUSSEAU, E. W. (1981). A meta-analysis of experimental research on teacher questioning behavior. *Review of Educational Research, 51*(2), 237–245.

32. ROSENSHINE, B. V. (1979). Content, time, and direct instruction. In P. Peterson & H. Walberg (Eds.), *Research on teaching* (pp. 28–56). Berkeley: McCutchan.

33. ROSENSHINE, B. V., & FURST, N. (1973). The use of direct observation to study teaching. In R. M. W. Travers (Ed.), *Second handbook of research on teaching* (pp. 122–183). Chicago: Rand–McNally.

34. ROSENSHINE, B. V., & STEVENS, R. (1986). Teaching functions. In M. C. Wittrock (Ed.), *Handbook of research on teaching* (3rd ed.). New York: Macmillan.

*35. ROWE, M. B. (1978). Wait, Wait, Wait. . . . *School Science and Mathematics, 78*(3), 207–216.

*36. SCHOEN, H. L. (1976). Self-paced mathematics instruction: How effective has it been in secondary and postsecondary schools? *The Mathematics Teacher, 69*(5), 352–357.

37. SLAVIN, R. E. (1987). Mastery learning reconsidered. *Review of Educational Research, 57*(2), 175–213.

38. SLAVIN, R. E. (1990). *Cooperative learning: Theory, research, and practice.* Englewood Cliffs, NJ: Prentice–Hall.

39. SMITH, L. R. (1977). Aspects of teacher discourse and student achievement in mathematics. *Journal for Research in Mathematics Education, 8*(3), 195–204.

*40. SOBEL, M. A., & MALETSKY, E. M. (1988). *Teaching mathematics: A sourcebook of aids, activities, and strategies.* Englewood Cliffs, NJ: Prentice–Hall.

41. SOWELL, E. J. (1989). Effects of manipulative materials in mathematics instruction. *Journal for Research in Mathematics Education, 20*(5), 498–505.

42. STALLINGS, J., & KRASAVAGE, E. M. (1986). Program implementation and student achievement in a four-year Madeline Hunter Follow-Through Project. *The Elementary School Journal, 87*(2), 117–138.

*43. SUYDAM, M. N., & HIGGINS, J. L. (1977). *Activity-based learning in elementary school mathematics: Recommendations from research.* Columbus, OH: ERIC/SMEAC.

44. TOBIN, K. (1987). The role of wait time in higher cognitive level learning. *Review of Educational Research, 57*(1), 69–95.

45. WANG, M. C., & LINDVALL, C. M. (1984). Individual differences and school learning environments. In E. W. Gordon (Ed.), *Review of research in education* (Vol. 11, pp. 161–225). Washington, DC: American Educational Research Association.

CHAPTER 13

Planning and Organizing Curriculum

Karen Brooks and Marilyn Suydam

"Man, math class was awesome today. Our group planned a trip to the beach— what roads to take and how much gas it would take. Tommorow, we're going to figure the cost of food and stuff. . . ."

Good lessons do not just happen. They take thought and careful preparation. What research has to tell us about effective teachers can help guide us in planning and organizing our curriculum. Good teachers adapt instruction to the needs of the students and the situation, rather than rigidly following fixed "scripts" (21). Effective teachers:

- Are clear about their instructional goals
- Are knowledgeable about the content and teaching strategies
- Communicate their expectations to students
- Use instructional materials expertly in order to devote more time to activities that enrich and clarify the content
- Adapt instruction to student needs
- Teach students metacognitive thinking strategies
- Address higher-level as well as lower-level cognitive objectives
- Offer regular feedback on students' progress and understanding
- Integrate their instruction with that in other subject areas
- Accept responsibility for student outcomes
- Are thoughtful and reflective about their practices

Many of these characteristics are directly related to planning and organizing the curriculum.

Planning What to Teach

In planning what to teach, teachers usually start with the school's curriculum guide and the state requirements. Hare (6) found that the objectives for high school mathematics had changed since the 1977 mandate in North Carolina for minimum-competency testing, and both remedial and advanced courses were added to the mathematics curriculum. In addition to state requirements, teachers should of course consider the needs and interests of their students, including their personal and career needs and their preparation for future mathematics courses. Teachers' beliefs about what needs to be taught will also influence the topics selected (see Chapter 14 and Fig. 13.1). Once the topics are listed in the anticipated sequence they can be grouped into units, along with objectives and the estimated time to teach each one.

The unit plan serves as an outline, but the daily plans put the goals into action. The choices of ways to implement unit plans are virtually endless, and individual teachers have an excellent opportunity to express their creativity and expertise in their daily plans. Most teachers do their daily planning week-by-week as the year progresses, in order to remain flexible—as changes must be made to accommodate such things as student learning, standardized testing, and severe weather.

The Influence of Teachers

Teachers have many opportunities to influence curricular decisions. For example, teachers were involved in creating 1989's *Curriculum and Evaluation Standards* (17), published by the NCTM. Also, publishers put into textbooks content that is mandated by the state and features they believe teachers want. Throughout the country in any given year, groups of teachers are rewriting curriculum guides and selecting

FIGURE 13.1

new textbooks. They also regularly are making suggestions to principals or school boards, concerning new as well as traditional mathematics courses, and helping department chairs and county coordinators select materials and teaching aids to be purchased. Teachers need to utilize these opportunities (and more) to influence the curriculum by making informed decisions. Research findings summarized in this chapter may well provide helpful direction for teachers and other involved decision makers.

Topics to Teach

Surveys, such as the Priorities in School Mathematics Project (16), designed by the NCTM to collect information on beliefs surrounding and reactions to possible mathematics curriculum changes during the 1980s, showed many similarities among various professional and lay groups about appropriate goals for school mathematics. When asked to rank the importance of minimum competencies in mathematics, professional educators and persons in the local community did not differ significantly in their perceptions (23), so it seems that the mathematics necessary for coping in society may be a generally acknowledged set of skills.

Moody (15) gave a list of 46 mathematics topics to department heads in fifty-six colleges and to selected high school graduates. They were asked what topics should be included in Algebra II/Trigonometry and Advanced Mathematics courses. The general agreement was that "as many as possible" of the forty-six topics should be incorporated into the courses. Naturally, the strategy of adding new topics can cause serious problems since, as new topics are added to the curriculum, some topics must either be deleted or have less time devoted to them. Thus making such decisions often can be quite difficult.

Textbooks

Although textbooks play a major role in determining curriculum, only about one-fourth of the mathematics teachers in grades 7–12 indicated, via a national survey reported by Weiss (30), that they "cover" more than 90% of their textbooks, while about half indicated the coverage to be 75% to 90%. Thus, about one in four teachers covered less than 75% of the textbook (see Fig. 13.2).

In the 1986 National Assessment of Educational Progress (NAEP) test in mathematics, 80% of certain groups of students indicated that they used the textbook every day in class (3). It seems clear that the major determinant of a curriculum is the textbook—but it also appears that the teacher ultimately determines what is actually taught to any specific class (12). The selection and omission of certain sections of the textbook may well be based on the teacher's familiarity with the topic and the concepts to be taught. Generally, teachers report that the textbook is the major source of their objectives.

Brown (1) conducted a study on the use of textbooks for Geometry and Algebra II. Results revealed heavy dependence on the textbook by both teachers and students. Teachers followed the textbook very closely with regard to content selection and sequencing, rarely presenting topics not in the textbook. The major objectives of ob-

FIGURE 13.2 Mathematics teachers' (grades 7–12) reported coverage of textbook (30)

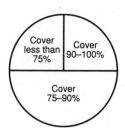

served lessons tended to be completion of the exercises presented at the end of the section of the textbook under discussion. Little use was made of historical and biographical material or enrichment exercises. Mathematics instruction was a repetitious succession of homework/discussion/new homework.

Textbooks differ and as Begle pointed out a number of years ago, can in effect determine not only what is learned, but how. One example of this is provided by Petkovich (19), who sought to determine whether the use of a certain text on strategies, plus a range of examples, could improve the acquisition, retention, and generalization of algebra equation-solving skills of 117 ninth-grade students. Selected because they did not pass a pretest, these students studied one of four sets of worked examples and were then required to do problems—immediately after instruction, after fifteen days, and after thirty days. The strategy text and range of examples did improve acquisition.

In another study of textbooks, Usiskin (28) compared the amount of new material in one textbook series for seventh and eighth grades with the amount of new material the students encountered in algebra. He noted that it is understandable that students have so much trouble in ninth-grade algebra: They have been "lulled" into expecting to learn new ideas and skills only over long intervals of weeks, whereupon in algebra they encounter new skills daily and new ideas monthly.

To follow up on this analysis, Flanders (4) investigated three other K–8 textbook series, plus the algebra books published by the same companies. Overall, students in grades 2–5 encountered about 40% to 65% in new content. By eighth grade this amount dropped to 30%, but in the following year, the algebra students encountered 88% new content (see Fig. 13.3). Difficulties ascribed to the formality of algebra, or its unfamiliarity, may simply be difficulties due to a gross change in the amount of new material to be learned.

Other studies of textbooks that may be helpful include comparisons of different approaches. Han (5) compared an informal geometry textbook, which (consistent with the van Hiele theory) delayed proof until the latter half of the course, with another textbook (having a traditional approach) in which proof was emphasized throughout. Involved in the study were 478 students in two high schools. No significant differences were found on measures of either van Hiele level or attitude toward geometry between students using the two texts. However, significant differences fa-

FIGURE 13.3   New content in textbooks (4)

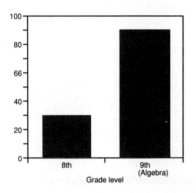

vored the traditional group in both proof-writing achievement and attitude toward proof, perhaps as a result of the greater amount of time spent on proof.

There have been several studies involving the algebra textbook developed by Saxon, which emphasizes mastery of fundamental skills, organization by lessons rather than chapters, an incremental development of concepts, and continuous review. Although Saxon (24) provided data that students using his text outscored students using a traditional text, Pierce (20) and Johnson and Smith (8) challenged these findings. While some of the features of Saxon's textbook, such as continuous review, spaced practice, and an incremental development of concepts are supported by research, other features have been criticized. Namely, Saxon's textbook emphasizes mastery of procedures while neglecting problem solving and understanding and application of concepts. Teachers need to be aware that different textbooks often represent different philosophical orientations toward learning.

International Comparisons

The Second International Mathematics Study (SIMS) in 1982 showed that U.S. students performed at a mean level markedly lower than the mean level of all participating students. Although the calculus classes in the U.S. sample performed at or near the mean level of the international group for most topics, the precalculus classes clearly did not do as well. In most cases, they were close to the 25th percentile. The calculus classes were above the median in most areas, but they were not as high as the 75th percentile in *any* topic. Average Japanese students exhibited higher levels of achievement than the top 5% of American students enrolled in college preparatory mathematics courses (14).

The SIMS report criticizes the repetitive nature of mathematics curricula in the United States, and the NAEP data seemingly support this concern (3). Students appear to concentrate too much on computation (relative to other skill areas) and therefore lack the range of abilities and understandings necessary to take advantage of advanced course offerings. McKnight and colleagues (14) also documented that there exists nonspiral, noncumulative learning in current mathematics curricula.

There is no direct evidence that the quality of classroom teaching in the U.S. was inferior to that in other systems (12). In fact, the data indicated that for most classrooms worldwide, the teaching of mathematics was a "talk and chalk" process. Rather, the differences that seem to explain why U.S. students did not achieve better relate to curriculum construction, expectations, handling of individual differences, and tracking.

> A Student: "My general math class is so boring. We just go over the same things we've been studying for years. . . . "

The structure of the curriculum for U.S. schools clearly falls short at the eighth-grade level when placed next to the curricula of other countries. In most programs, a higher intensity is devoted to a few topics at each level, whereas in the U.S. no more than one-fifth of class periods were focused on any single topic. The curriculum pattern was one of relatively low intensity, with a large number of topics getting a small amount of attention. This diversity was reflected in the broad—but sometimes shallow—content coverage provided in textbooks and classrooms.

Planning How to Teach

Sequencing

The sequence in which topics will be taught during the year is usually decided as the year's planning is done. It tends to depend a great deal on the textbook being used for the course, but teachers do manage to exert their professional judgment on some points.

A decision on which teachers may have some influence has to do with the sequencing of algebra and geometry in secondary school. Nichols (18) reported that few significant differences were found between the effect of teaching two algebra courses before geometry and having geometry taught between Algebra I and II. Apparently both sequences can be effective. This agrees with previous research summarized by Dessart and Suydam (2).

> Advance organizer: "Yesterday we practiced using the Pythagorean Theorem to solve for one of the sides of a triangle. Today we will apply that skill to solve problems related to the construction of buildings."

Advance Organizers

Advance organizers are used to give an overview of a topic to students. Luiten, Ames, and Ackerson (11) did a meta-analysis, which summarized a large number of studies, on the effects of advance organizers on learning (within twenty-four hours) and retention (after twenty-four hours). Using 135 studies, they reported that advance organizers improved both learning and retention. The data indicated that advance organizers were effective with individuals of all ability levels and that the effect on retention increased with time.

Routines and Arrangement of the Room

Planning effective routines for taking roll, collecting and distributing papers, handling make-up work, and so on can save valuable class time and minimize discipline problems. A great deal of research has been done at earlier levels concerning the importance of establishing routines and patterns of behavior, but little reseach attention has been given to this at the secondary level. Weiss (30) found that high school teachers indicated they spent slightly over 10% of class time for instruction on routines.

"Having the students begin to work immediately after the bell has rung is a tremendous aid to classroom control; it gives the teacher meaningful feedback [and] establishes a mathematical atmosphere. . . ." David R. Johnson (9, p. 21)

The arrangement of the classroom can affect such things as the ease with which a teacher can check students' progress, whether all students feel involved in the class activities, and the success of small-group work. This arrangement includes not only how the students' desks are arranged, but also how other furniture, equipment, and materials are placed. If the one computer that a classroom is allotted is to be used also as a display tool, it can be set in a prominent place in the front of the room, but if it will be used more-or-less exclusively for individual practice or exploration, it can be located in a more out-of-the-way area. Books on teaching mathematics at the elementary level often make helpful related suggestions (such as using clear boxes, labeling, arranging by topic on shelves that are easily reached, and similar ideas for storing materials), but this topic has been largely ignored at the secondary level because materials other than textbooks have rarely been used. As activities involving computers and calculators, paper folding, and probability experiments enter the secondary classroom, teachers will have to confront the problem of storing materials so they are readily accessible and take a minimum of time to distribute and collect.

In *Every Minute Counts: Making Your Math Class Work*, Johnson (9) offers some interesting and practical suggestions about routines, room arrangements, and ways to operate efficiently (see Fig. 13.4).

Teaching Techniques

Dossey, Mullis, Lindquist, and Chambers (3) reported that mathematics instruction, as indicated by the 1986 NAEP, continued to be dominated by teacher explanations, chalkboard presentations, and reliance on textbooks and workbooks, as it was in previous assessments. More innovative forms of instruction, such as small-group activities, laboratory work, and special projects, remained "disappointingly rare." Over half of the students indicated that they never work mathematics problems in small groups, while slightly over 80% reported that they "often" listened to a teacher explain

FIGURE 13.4 "The U-shaped arrangement allows me to observe the students' written work more quickly and efficiently . . . every student becomes a part of the group." (9, p. 4)

a mathematics lesson, and 83% said they often watched the teacher work mathematics problems on the board. Weiss (30) reported that 89% of all mathematics lessons in grades 7–12 included lectures.

The picture that emerged from the study of over 200 twelfth-grade mathematics teachers and students in the Second International Mathematics Study was one of an emphasis on orderly, subject matter–oriented classrooms (13). About 40% of a teacher's instructional time in the classroom was spent on developing new material, 20% on reviewing previously taught material, 10% on administrative or managemental tasks, and 30% on supervising students' work in the classroom, including testing (see Fig. 13.5). The SIMS report is in sharp contrast with previous reports from 1955–1975 (27), wherein the typical pattern involved far less time spent on developing new material.

In the SIMS study, students said they spent the major portion of their time listening to teacher presentations (130 minutes a week), doing seatwork (60 minutes a week), and taking tests (45 minutes a week). Although, on the average, little time was spent in small-group work, a great *range* of time was devoted to it, with some classes spending as much as 80 minutes a week, and others spending no time at all.

NCTM's *Standards* calls for a decrease in instruction by teacher exposition and, instead, "the use of a variety of instructional formats" (17, p. 129), including small groups, individual explorations, peer instruction, whole-class discussions, and project work. It also suggests that increased attention be given to "active involvement of students in constructing and applying mathematical ideas" (17, p. 129), problem

FIGURE 13.5 U.S. teachers' reported use of instructional time (13)

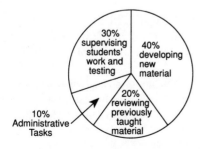

solving as a means as well as a goal of instruction, and effective questioning techniques that promote student interaction. The goal of students being actively involved, so that they "routinely engage in constructing, symbolizing, applying, and generalizing mathematical ideas" (17, p. 129), is supported by research at the elementary and middle school levels, and there is reason to believe that active involvement is equally important at the secondary school level. For information on a variety of teaching techniques see Chapter 5.

A geometry teacher: "I'd like to see more manipulatives used in high school. My students always perk up and pay attention when I use them."

Data from a number of surveys indicate a comparatively low level of use of manipulative materials beyond the primary grades, despite the fact that many studies provide confirmation of the worthwhileness of using them. According to the survey by Weiss (30), manipulative materials were used in only 20% of the classes in grades 7–9, and in only 12% in grades 10–12.

Time

Deciding how to use time is an important aspect of planning effective lessons. Focusing attention quickly, building smooth bridges between and among different topics and activities, and allowing flexibility all are important factors for teachers to consider. Engaged time—the time students spend concentrating on a given topic—also has been found to have an influence on the level of achievement among students (29).

Another study (26) looked at fifteen students in grades 10 and 11 who were in mathematics classes that matched their preference for time of day to take a mathematics class and fifteen who were mismatched. The matched students scored higher.

Another variation on the use of time was provided by a study (7) in which twenty-three students studied algebra for the entire school day for six to eight weeks. Fifty-one students in two control groups studied algebra one hour a day for four days a week for the entire year. While some differences were found on tests during instruction, no significant difference in achievement was found on tests of retention of the material. Thus, saturation learning did not produce an overwhelming achievement or retention gain—nor did it reduce achievement.

Practice

Practice is a necessary concomitant of instruction. The NCTM *Standards* support "the systematic maintenance of student learnings," while decrying "extended periods of individual seatwork practicing routine tasks" and "rote memorization of facts and procedures" (17, p. 129).

Research at all levels provides evidence of the efficacy of spaced or distributed practice. For instance, Walberg (29) reported that spaced practice over several lessons or study periods interspersed with other activities is superior to equal amounts of time spent in massed, concentrated practice.

Homework

In general, regularly assigned homework has been found to improve mathematics achievement (2). Leone (10) used programmed instructional material for Algebra II over a twelve-week period. Having homework assignments resulted in higher achievement than having no homework.

Expedient Ways to Correct Homework

1. Write answers on a transparency
2. Write answers on the board
3. Read answers from the key
4. Ask a student to read answers from the key (9)

However, there also are studies in which no significant differences were reported. In a nine-month study, Siemans (25) found that geometry classes in which homework was emphasized did not achieve significantly better than classes in which homework was not emphasized.

High school teachers reported that students were expected to spend about four hours a week on homework, with calculus classes expected to complete about five hours weekly (13). Seventy-five percent reported that the homework was assigned in the most recent lesson (30). Data gathered in the 1986 NAEP testing showed that students reported having more homework in mathematics than was indicated in previous assessments, perhaps suggesting a growth in academic expectations in schools (3).

Pressman (22) examined student and teacher behavior with respect to the allocation of time for homework. Results from 3,222 students in grades 5, 8, and 10 showed that total homework time is positively related to time in class, time allowed to begin homework in class, the frequency with which homework is reviewed in class, and the perception that homework is given to help.

Parents who provided resources, encouragement, and support for mathematics learning appeared to have a positive effect on performance in mathematics (3). This factor of parental interest, particularly as it interacts with homework, needs clarification. If parental interest is important, then teachers, as well as society in general, need to encourage it—perhaps by giving students homework that will involve their parent or parents.

Thorough planning of what to teach and how to teach it can go a long way toward creating successful lessons, but we must not forget that the teacher is continuously making decisions. For many years it was assumed that the teacher could decide, prior to appearing in the classroom what content was to be covered, and that was the end of the planning process. But increasingly we have come to recognize that such planning is only a beginning. Decisions must be made about adding and omitting content even as instruction is proceeding, with accompanying decisions about revisions in how the content is to be taught, depending on the responses of the students. Myriad other decisions arise from the behavior of the students. Are they disinterested in the lesson? Are they too noisy to continue group work today? How can any particular student be directed into a more profitable activity than making derogatory comments? All these are, as we recognize, just a few of the decisions that most teachers must face throughout each day.

Planning provides a framework within which decisions are made. Sometimes the decision will be to continue to teach the planned content with the method chosen; sometimes the students' responses will indicate that a different direction might be more feasible. The best teachers are flexible, thoughtful, and reflective about their practices.

Looking Ahead . . .

I believe the vision of mathematics teaching set forth in the *Curriculum and Evaluation Standards* will greatly influence research on planning and organizing the curriculum. Our mathematics curriculum will become more integrated, and the teacher will become more a facilitator of learning and less a dispenser of knowledge. Teachers will need help in finding the best ways actively to involve their students. Technology will cause deletions and additions to the curriculum, as well as change the emphasis placed on the topics taught. The increase in cultural diversity in schools and the greater number of minority students will demand that we develop teaching methods that effectively teach *all* our students the skills they need to live happy, productive lives.

Karen Brooks

The NCTM *Curriculum and Evaluation Standards* call attention to many of the points raised by the research cited in this chapter. For example, the need to "unspiral" the curriculum, to include new topics and decrease the amount of attention paid to some old ones, and to approach teaching and learning through small-group explorations with activities and materials. As the *Standards* is implemented, changes will gradually be reflected in how we teach mathematics as well as in what we teach. We can expect to find that research will keep us aware of how effective such changes are, as well as suggesting teacher-tested ways of putting those ideas into practice.

Marilyn Suydam

About the Authors

Karen Brooks a high school teacher for nine years, has taught a wide range of courses, including remedial mathematics, algebra, geometry and precalculus. She is currently on leave from West Hall High School in Gainesville, Georgia, pursuing her doctoral degree in mathematics education at the University of Georgia.

Marilyn Suydam is a professor of mathematics education at The Ohio State University. She has long been interested in the interpretation of research for teachers, and attempts to put research into practice in her work with both preservice and inservice teachers.

References

1. Brown, J. K. (March 1974). Textbook use by teachers and students of geometry and second-year algebra. *Dissertation Abstracts International, 34,* 5795A–5796A. (University Microfilms No. 74-5534)

*2. Dessart, D. J., & Suydam, M. N. (1983). *Classroom ideas from research on secondary school mathematics.* Reston, VA: National Council of Teachers of Mathematics.

*3. Dossey, J. A., Mullis, I. V. S., Lindquist, M. M., & Chambers, D. L. (1988). *The mathematics report card: Are we measuring up?* Princeton: Educational Testing Service.

4. Flanders, J. R. (1987, September). How much of the content in mathematics textbooks is new? *Arithmetic Teacher, 35,* 18–23.

5. Han, T. (1987). The effects on achievement and attitude of a standard geometry textbook and a textbook consistent with the van Hiele theory (Doctoral dissertation, University of Iowa). *Dissertation Abstracts International, 47,* 3690A.

6. Hare, J. D. (1984). Impact of minimum competency testing on the mathematics curriculum in North Carolina (Doctoral dissertation, George Peabody College for Teachers of Vanderbilt University). *Dissertation Abstracts International, 45,* 776A–777A.

7. Hawkins, V. J. (1982). A comparison of two methods of instruction, a saturated learning environment and traditional learning environment: Its effects on achievement and retention among female adolescents in first-year algebra (Doctoral dissertation, University of Connecticut). *Dissertation Abstracts International, 43,* 416A.

8. Johnson, D. M., & Smith, B. (1987, November/December). An evaluation of Saxon's algebra text. *Journal of Educational Research, 81,* 97–102.

*9. Johnson, D. R. (1982). *Every minute counts: Making your math class work.* Palo Alto: Dale Seymour.

10. Leone, A. (1980). Teaching basic statistical concepts to senior high school students using programmed instructional material. *Dissertation Abstracts International, 40,* 3848A. (University Microfilms No. 8000867)

11. Luiten, J., Ames, W., & Ackerson, G. (1980). A meta-analysis of the effects of advance organizers on learning and retention. *American Educational Research Journal, 17,* 211–218.

12. McKnight, C. C. et al. (in press). *Classroom processes in mathematics.* Columbus, OH: ERIC Clearinghouse for Science, Mathematics and Environmental Education.

13. McKnight, C. C., Travers, K. J., & Dossey, J. A. (April 1985). Eighth-grade mathematics in U.S. schools: A report from the Second International Mathematics Study. *Mathematics Teacher, 78,* 292–300, 270.

*14. McKnight, C. C., Crosswhite, F. J., Doosey, J. A., Kifer, E., Swafford, J. O., Travers, K. J., & Cooney, T. J. (1987). *The underachieving curriculum: Assessing U.S. school mathematics from an international perspective.* Champaign, IL: Stipes.

15. Moody, M. (1988). Topics which should be included in college preparatory mathematics courses (Doctoral dissertation, Auburn University). *Dissertation Abstracts International, 48,* 1644A–1645A.

16. National Council of Teachers of Mathematics (1980). *Priorities in school mathematics: Executive summary of the PRISM project.* Reston, VA: The Council.

*17. National Council of Teachers of Mathematics (1989). *Curriculum and evaluation standards for school mathematics.* Reston, VA: The Council.

18. Nichols, B. W. (1987). The effect of different sequences of geometry and algebra II on mathematics education (Doctoral dissertation, University of Missouri–Kansas City). *Dissertation Abstracts International, 47,* 2935A.

19. Petkovich, M. D. (1987). Teaching algebra with worked examples: The effects of ac-

companying text and range of examples on the acquisition and retention of a cognitive skill (Doctoral dissertation, University of Minnesota). *Dissertation Abstracts International, 47,* 4334A.

20. PIERCE, R. D. A quasi-experimental study of Saxon's incremental development model and its effects on student achievement in first-year algebra (Doctoral dissertation, University of Tulsa). *Dissertation Abstracts International, 45,* 443A–444A.

21. PORTER, A. C., & BROPHY, J. (1988). Synthesis of research on good teaching: Insights from the work of the Institute for Research on Teaching. *Educational Leadership, 45,* 74–85.

22. PRESSMAN, E. G. (1980). Allocation of school-related student time. *Dissertation Abstracts International, 41,* 1327A–1218A. (University Microfilms No. 8022147)

23. RAINES, N. E. (1980). Minimum competencies needed for graduation: A comparative case study of perceptions held by professional educators and the local school community. *Dissertation Abstracts International, 40,* 3679A. (University Microfilms No. 8000802)

24. SAXON, J. (1982). Incremental development: A breakthrough in mathematics. *Phi Delta Kappan, 63,* 482–484.

25. SIEMENS, D. W. (1986). The effects of homework emphasis on the time spent doing homework and the achievement of plane geometry students (Doctoral dissertation, Southern Illinois University at Carbondale). *Dissertation Abstracts International, 46,* 2954A.

26. SMITH, S. A. (1988). An experimental investigation of the relationships between and among achievement, preferred time of instruction, and critical thinking abilities of tenth and eleventh-grade students in mathematics (Doctoral dissertation, St. John's University). *Dissertation Abstracts International, 49,* 1052A.

27. SUYDAM, M. N., & OSBORNE, A. (1977). *The status of pre-college science, mathematics, and social science education: 1955–1975. Volume 2: Mathematics education.* Columbus, OH: ERIC Center for Science, Mathematics, and Environmental Education.

*28. USISKIN, Z. (1987, September). Why elementary algebra can, should, and must be an eighth-grade course for average students. *Mathematics Teacher, 80,* 428–438.

29. WALBERG, HERBERT J. (1988, March). Synthesis of research on time and learning. *Educational Leadership, 45,* 76–85.

30. WEISS, I. R. (1987). *Report of the 1985–86 national survey of science and mathematics education.* Research Triangle Park, NC: Research Triangle Institute.

CHAPTER 14

Inside the Teacher: Knowledge, Beliefs, and Attitudes

Catherine A. Brown and Jayne Baird

If we as teachers hope to encourage critical thought in others, we must engage in it ourselves. Throughout our teaching careers we must participate in an ongoing, collaborative process of reevaluation of, and liberation from, our taken-for-granted views. (7)

$\mathbf{A}$s you can tell from reading the previous chapters in this volume, research has quite a bit to say about how students learn mathematics, what good mathematics looks like, and what teachers do to get ready for instruction and to organize their classrooms. The emphasis in this chapter is on the teacher. The teacher is the critical connection between research results and classroom applications of those results or their implications.

Teachers are, as Lampert (18) and others (6) have said, dilemma managers. They cannot, because of the nature of the classroom, always decide to do things that will be the best for all possible reasons. For example, a geometry teacher we know has studied the research on cooperative learning and believes that teaching using cooperative learning activities will enhance students' ability to communicate mathematically as well as increase their understanding of geometry. The teacher is aware that several of the better students in the class have expressed concern that they are wasting valuable time in group work and could learn the material more quickly if the teacher would just teach them. Several other students, apparently intimidated by the group work, are reluctant to talk in the groups. The teacher manages the dilemma by reducing the frequency of her use of cooperative learning activities. She also tries to structure the activities so that it is clearer to students what they are doing, thus reducing some anxiety. Although she would like to do more of such activities, because she believes that they have benefits, she recognizes other constraints on what kind of classroom interaction is best for her students at this time.

From what little research we have on secondary mathematics teachers there is some evidence that teachers' responses to these dilemmas are at least partially based on their knowledge, beliefs, and attitudes related to mathematics, student learning, and teaching. They draw on these to help them make decisions on what action to take in the classroom. Teachers' decisions and actions then influence students' knowledge, beliefs, and attitudes, both about mathematics and about the learning and teaching of it.

> The dilemma manager accepts conflict as endemic and even useful to her work rather than seeing it as a burden that needs to be eliminated. —Magdalene Lampert (18)

> In reality, no one can *teach* mathematics. Effective teachers are those who can stimulate students to *learn* mathematics. (23)

In this chapter we discuss results of some of the research on teachers' knowledge, beliefs, and attitudes, and especially that research related to mathematics, mathematics teaching, and mathematics learning. Although research related to secondary mathematics teachers is still very limited, we believe that what we do know from research is valuable for teachers in general. The results reported here most likely will not match exactly what you know, believe, feel, or do in your own classroom. They may, however, strike a chord of recognition. They may even help you to think again about your own knowledge, beliefs, and attitudes, and relate them in a new way to what you do in the classroom. We believe this is important.

> There's nothing "common" about common sense!

Schoenfeld (30, 31) and others (14) have written extensively about the role of metacognition in mathematics and other problem-solving settings. Metacognition can be thought of as your knowledge concerning your own cognitive processes or anything else related to them, your control or self-regulation of your cognitive processes, and the beliefs and intuitions that you bring to your cognitive processes. We hypothesize that if teachers are to become good at managing classroom dilemmas, a form of problem solving, then knowledge of the factors affecting their decisions is important. Thus, we argue, it is important not only to know the results of research on knowledge, beliefs, and attitudes, but also to understand and monitor your own knowledge, beliefs, and attitudes and to ascertain how they seem to be influencing your thinking and actions in the classroom. In this way, you gain more control over both your teaching and your management of classroom dilemmas.

Mathematics and Mathematics Teaching

Because teachers' knowledge, beliefs, and attitudes influence both their actions in the classroom and their interactions with students, we will focus on research that informs us about what secondary mathematics teachers know, believe, and feel about mathematics and the teaching of it.

Knowledge

Until recently, almost any study of teachers' knowledge of mathematics simply looked either at coursework in mathematics (which we all know is no indication of what a person knows about a subject) or at teachers' scores on standardized tests. There is still very little research that looks in depth at what teachers *understand* about mathematics. Yet the mathematics taught in secondary schools is quite complex. Mathematical ideas, facts, and concepts, and the relationships between and among them, must be taught, but the teacher must also be concerned with the processes of doing and creating mathematics. Clearly, teachers must know mathematics well in order to teach it well.

> "Knowing" mathematics is "doing" mathematics. A person gathers, discovers, or creates knowledge in the course of some activity having a purpose. (21)

Research on what mathematics teachers know about teaching their subject is also scarce. Most studies of teaching have simply looked at what teachers *do* in the classroom, as opposed to investigating what they *know about* what they are doing therein. There is, however, a growing body of research investigating the differences between and among expert and novice mathematics teachers (8) that gradually is providing us with more information about teachers' knowledge of their craft. Other sources of information include studies of teacher decision making (10, 11, 13).

One of the few research programs that has looked at teachers' knowledge of mathematics and of mathematics teaching was conducted by Lee Shulman and his associates at Stanford University. They have studied teachers in various subject areas and have developed a theoretical model of the components of knowledge, based on a three-and-a-half-year program of research investigating Knowledge Growth in Teaching (34, 35, 41). It may be helpful to you to have an overview of the project before the results are discussed.

Shulman and colleagues hypothesize that teachers draw from seven domains of knowledge as they plan and implement instruction: subject matter, pedagogical content, other content, the curriculum, learners, educational aims, and general pedagogy. Their research program focused primarily on the first two domains. Although

Shulman's analysis of knowledge in teaching is a philosophical one, the call for subject-matter knowledge rings true to those who know mathematics teaching. The other kind of knowledge of interest here, pedagogical content knowledge, is an understanding of how to represent specific subject-matter topics and issues in ways that are appropriate to the diverse abilities and interests of learners.

> [It includes] for the most regularly taught topics in one's subject area, the most useful forms of representation of those ideas, the most powerful analogies, illustrations, examples, explanations, and demonstrations—in a word, the ways of representing the subject that make it comprehensible to others. . . . [It] also includes an understanding of what makes the learning of specific topics easy or difficult: the conceptions and preconceptions that students of different ages and backgrounds bring with them to learning. (34, p. 9)

One of the goals of the Stanford project was to determine if knowledge of subject matter and pedagogical content knowledge made any difference in the way that teachers thought about teaching and actually taught in the classroom.

The best teacher will be he who has at his tongue's end the explanation of what it is that is bothering the pupil. These explanations give the teacher the knowledge of the greatest possible number of methods, the ability of inventing new methods and, above all, not a blind adherence to one method but the conviction that all methods are one-sided, and that the best method would be the one which would answer best to all the possible difficulties incurred by a pupil, that is, not a method but an art and talent. —Leo Tolstoy (40)

What Shulman and his colleagues found was that knowledge of subject matter *does* influence the ways in which teachers teach. The study revealed that whereas teachers with greater mathematical knowledge were more conceptual in their teaching, teachers with lower levels of knowledge were more rule based (37). Descriptions of the lessons of the teachers who had a firmer grasp of the subject matter suggested that the lessons were such as those encouraged in the NCTM *Curriculum and Evaluation Standards* (21), exploratory and open, emphasizing relationships and problem solving.

In a study that examined the influence of subject-matter expertise on the pedagogical reasoning of experienced science teachers, Hashweh (16) found that teachers who had more subject-matter knowledge were more likely to notice misleading or poorly articulated themes or explanations in texts. Those teachers were also more likely to reject those textbooks' organization of material when such did not match their own understanding. In addition, teachers with a richer understanding of the content were more likely "to detect student misconceptions, to utilize opportunities to 'digress' into other discipline-related avenues, to deal effectively with general class difficulties, and to correctly interpret students' insightful comments" (p. 305).

The results of these research efforts seem reasonable. If a teacher only knows barely enough about the subject matter to teach the it, then he or she is likely to feel threatened by student questions that might lead to digressions from the prepared lesson. Or a teacher may be unable to pick up on student suggestions that represent a different but equally valid way of thinking about a mathematical concept or solving a problem. Thus, a lack of deep understanding of mathematics may lead to lessons that are teacher directed and school mathematics that is prepackaged and sterile.

Pedagogical Content Knowledge

There are only a few studies specifically investigating pedagogical content knowledge. However, it appears from studies of both expert and novice teachers that experts' systems of pedagogical content knowledge are much more elaborate, interconnected, and easily accessible than those of novices (8, 19). That is, experts have more ways of representing the subject that make it comprehensible to students; more extensive repertoires of explanations, examples, and demonstrations; and more ability to draw on what they know, during instruction, than do novices. Given that much of the research on student learning of mathematics suggests that multiple representations are necessary to encourage conceptual learning in children, it seems particularly important that teachers have *extensive* pedagogical content knowledge.

Beliefs and Attitudes

Closely related to knowledge of mathematics and pedagogical content knowledge are beliefs about what mathematics is and how it should be taught—sometimes referred to as conceptions of mathematics and mathematics teaching, respectively. Research on teachers' beliefs is now a rapidly growing area of investigation that is accumulating hard evidence (10, 13, 29, 38, 39) that teachers' beliefs about mathematics and how it should be taught do indeed influence the way that they teach their subject.

Thompson (38) investigated the conceptions of mathematics held by three junior high school mathematics teachers. She found that there were consistencies between the teachers' professed conceptions of mathematics and the manner in which they typically presented the content. For example, Jeanne, one of the teachers in Thompson's study, seemed to have a narrow view of school mathematics, admitting that she almost never thought about mathematics as a scientific discipline. She said "I don't see how I fit in that picture [mathematics as a science] at all. I see fractions and decimals, those little things. My scope is very narrow" (p. 110). Her teaching was characterized by reliance on mathematical symbols and structural properties in her explanations. She rarely appealed to intuition or spoke of practical applications of mathematics.

Kay, another teacher in Thompson's study, viewed mathematics primarily as a subject that provides the opportunity for high-level mental work. She often used a heuristic approach in presenting content and frequently used problem-solving sessions in which students were encouraged to guess, conjecture, and reason on their own. Furthermore, Kay explained to the students the importance of these processes in the acquisition of mathematical knowledge.

We can see from just these two brief examples the differences in the views of mathematics as manifested in the classroom. Students in classes like Kay's may learn a mathematics "different" from that of students in classes like Jeanne's. A view of mathematics is implicit in the way each teacher teaches, and for this reason the teachers' beliefs about mathematics, often as well as the mathematics itself, are learned by the students. (For examples of what students can unfortunately be helped to learn in a mathematics classroom, see Schoenfeld's [32] article about good teaching leading to bad results.)

Thompson (38) also studied the relationship of certain teachers' conceptions of mathematics teaching to instructional practice. She found that these teachers' views about teaching mathematics influenced what they did in the classroom, even though the tie-in was not always deliberate. For example, Jeanne believed that it was her responsibility to direct and control all classroom activities. She attempted to present the lessons in an orderly and logical sequence, avoiding the kinds of digressions needed to discuss students' difficulties and ideas. Kay, on the other hand, believed that the teacher must create and maintain an open and informal classroom atmosphere in order to ensure students' freedom to ask questions and express their ideas. As Thompson points out (and we can see from our discussions of Jeanne and Kay), at least some teachers' prevailing views of mathematics do seem to correlate with their instructional emphases.

Brown (10) and Cooney (13) have written about the beliefs that Fred, a first-year teacher, had about problem solving and how it should be taught. Fred believed that the teacher's role was to teach students heuristics, so that they could solve mathematical problems. However, he also believed that the teacher's role did not include "forcing" students to learn—rather that *students* should do the job of learning. Fred's perceptions of students and their beliefs and abilities, and his view of the value that mathematics had for these students, seemed to combine to overpower his more general belief in problem solving when he made decisions about what to teach and how to teach it. Frustrated by students' lack of enthusiasm and prerequisite knowledge, Fred frequently resorted to drill and practice lessons on skills, rather than to problem-solving–oriented lessons.

Knowledge and beliefs are difficult to separate from attitudes. Chapter 2 in this volume (McLeod and Ortega on affective issues) makes clear the importance of student attitudes in the mathematics classroom. We suggest not only that teachers' conceptions of mathematics can be learned by students, but also that a teacher's attitudes—such as excitement, curiosity, or anxiety toward mathematics—can be perceived by students and influence them. In fact, according to Aiken (1), "Of all the factors affecting student attitudes to mathematics, teacher attitudes are viewed as being of particular importance" (p. 592).

The *Curriculum and Evaluation Standards* (21) reflect an attitude toward mathematics that is positive, one of interest and curiosity. Often a lack of a deep understanding of mathematics can lead to some anxiety or attitudes toward mathematics that are *not* positive. This connection is discussed in some of the literature on elementary teachers' attitudes toward, and feelings about, mathematics (5, 27). Most often, high achievement is positively correlated with positive attitudes toward mathematics. Secondary mathematics teachers have chosen a mathematics-related career, and thus one might conclude that they have positive attitudes toward mathematics.

We are unaware of any research that has investigated secondary mathematics teachers' attitudes toward mathematics. Some of the studies related to beliefs and knowledge hint that, in general, secondary mathematics teachers seem to like mathematics, but that often their reasons for liking it are basically a reflection either of their beliefs about what mathematics is or of their level of understanding of the subject. You can see in the examples of Jeanne and Kay in Thompson's (38) study that two teachers may both say they like mathematics but may in reality be referring to two different conceptions of it.

Research on teachers' attributions of the reasons for the success or failure of their own teaching is an area of research related to both beliefs and attitudes. Pratt (26) investigated the extent to which secondary science and mathematics teachers assumed responsibility for student successes and failures. Ames (2) reviews the literature on teacher attributions and suggests implications for classroom practices. The conclusions from both of these authors is that teachers who believe that teaching is important, and that student success is generally feasible given the context, have a general value orientation that teachers are "responsible" for their students. That is, they believe that they can make a difference in student success or failure in learning. The implications are that because such teachers closely link the teaching act to student outcomes, they view themselves as trying hard to accomplish student success even in the face of situational obstacles.

Conversely, if teachers do not believe that their teaching is what makes the difference in student success or failure (if they consider success or failure purely a student responsibility), then they are less likely to view teaching as a valuable endeavor and to put time and effort into it. We assume that if teachers do not view instructional techniques as important to student learning, then efforts to be innovative in instruction—to try techniques such as cooperative learning or discovery-oriented teaching—will be minimal.

Studies of teachers' beliefs and attitudes about mathematics and the teaching of it indicate the role that such beliefs and attitudes can play in influencing interactions in the classroom. The NCTM *Curriculum and Evaluation Standards* (21) and the *Professional Standards for Teaching Mathematics* (22) both present a vision of school mathematics curriculum, evaluation, and teaching that is different from what most teachers have experienced in their mathematical education and what is currently found in most textbooks. In order for teachers to choose to teach according to this vision, they must believe that the mathematics and teaching described in these NCTM documents are indeed valuable. If teachers do not share these visions, or even perceive of them as being only minimally influential in effecting learning, it is unlikely that they will implement these standards.

You should do a little acting for the sake of your students who may learn, occasionally, more from your attitudes than from the subject matter presented. — Polya (25)

Student Mathematics Learning

Secondary mathematics teachers' knowledge, beliefs, and attitudes about students and student learning also have a big impact on how these teachers interact with students in the mathematics classroom (12). In this section we discuss some of the research on these topics.

Knowledge

Unfortunately, there is very little research on secondary teachers' knowledge of students and students' mathematical learning that relates teachers' understandings of their students' learning theories or cognitive psychology to their actions in the classroom and student achievement. This is an area that certainly needs to be explored further.

Calderhead (12) suggests that it is important that teachers know their students, at least in a general way. Being aware of such details as home backgrounds, experiences outside of school, and ranges of knowledge, skills, and interests "enables teachers to plan activities, avoiding or coping in advance with many potential instructional and managerial problems" (p. 55). As others reported in earlier chapters, different students may interpret *any* teacher's actions differently. Unless teachers are knowledgeable enough about their students to use that information when deciding on classroom actions, even the best-intended moves may not result in the desired reactions.

As the reader can see from this volume's discussions of learning mathematics, there are quite a number of research programs whose findings could better inform secondary teachers concerning student learning. For example, there is a great deal known about student problems with learning algebra—information that teachers of algebra could use to help design classroom activities more readily and purposefully. With the aid of this information, teachers could (for example) ask questions that might well expose student misconceptions, and could design activities aimed at creating the kinds of interactions that help students recognize and deal with misconceptions.

Beliefs and Attitudes

More subtle than knowledge per se but nonetheless a powerful influence on classroom learning may be teachers' beliefs and attitudes about students and their mathematical learning. The research on gender differences in instruction indicates that teachers often are unaware of the beliefs and attitudes about students and student learning that teachers' classroom actions convey, and the effect that these can have on student learning.

Teacher Expectations. A topic that has received considerable attention over the years is the role of teacher expectations in both classroom teaching and student achievement. Expectations are often a result of beliefs and attitudes. Rosenthal and Jacobson's *Pygmalion in the Classroom* (28) created controversy and interest about the "self-fulfilling prophecy" effect, the kind of sequence whereby an originally erroneous expectation leads to behavior that causes the expectation to be realized. A second type of "expectation" effect is the "sustaining" one according to which teachers expect students to sustain previously developed behavior patterns (15). Research results seem to indicate that the expectations that teachers have of students often *are* an accurate assessment of student ability, and so teacher expectations for student behavior are not necessarily inappropriate.

The problem, Good (15) argues, may not be low teacher expectations but inappropriate knowledge of, and beliefs about, how to respond to students who have difficulty in learning. Teacher beliefs and expectations are responsive to (and perhaps partially determined by) students' beliefs and behavior—and these may interact to affect student performance. For example, Hoyles (17), in her investigation of high school pupils' views of mathematics learning, found that students appeared to want security and structure when studying mathematics; they wanted to "get it right." They appeared to insist on being graded, viewing the grade as a measure of their mathematical ability. Hoyles suggested that, because of pupil behaviors motivated by these views, pupils' views might well influence the approaches that a mathematics teacher can successfully take in the classroom. Metz (20) found that low-ability students often disliked public interaction and classroom lecture, preferring seatwork. Teachers who sense these latter student preferences and entertain low expectations for students will tend to engage in behaviors that maintain both the students' and their own previously formed low expectations—assigning lots of worksheets for seatwork, low level questioning, and the like.

Because teachers express expectations in so many ways (e.g., choice of curriculum topic, performance feedback, differential assignments), it is impossible to suggest a unique combination of behaviors that can lead to the communication of appropriate expectations. This difficulty is magnified because the varied implications of teachers' behavior (praise, criticism, questioning, etc.) are dependent not only on the behavior, but also on the context in which it occurs. Too, the quality or style of the behavior, together with student interpretations of it, will determine the effects of particular behaviors on students.

Teachers must be dilemma managers, applying concepts and research findings to their own classrooms. As we have already mentioned, there have been a number of reviews, both long-standing and recent, of research on the self-fulfilling prophecy effect and the sustaining expectation effect (3, 9, 15) that can help teachers to understand these phenomena and become more knowledgeable with regard to the effects of expectations in their own classrooms.

Ethnicity and Gender.   The expectation literature is closely related to issues particularly evident in research that has investigated differences in teacher–student interactions related to ethnicity and gender differences in students (24). Differential expectations due to gender have been documented (26). For example, Becker (4) found that gender-biased interaction patterns occurred in the ten geometry classes she studied. Teachers interacted with boys more frequently than with girls and encouraged boys more. They were more persistent with boys, with 70% of the interactions coded as persistence involving male students. Becker concluded that teachers have different expectations of students, based on the gender of those students. For example, teachers expected males to need more teacher attention and reinforcement, both to keep them on task and to stimulate them to achieve to their ability. Females were expected to be self-motivated.

> It has become clear to the scientific and education communities that the United States cannot continue to allow vast numbers of its human resources to remain unproductive in what has become a high-technology society. What has not become clear is how to bring women and underrepresented minorities into the educational mainstream so that they can obtain an education equal to that of their white male counterparts and can then compete in society on an equal footing. (27)

Becker hypothesized that these expectations reflect the stereotypical views our society holds of the roles of men and women in mathematics. Second, she hypothesized that teachers then treat students differently on the basis of gender in ways consistent with these expectations. Third, she hypothesized that students respond differentially in class in accordance with these expectations and those of society of their roles. This implies that males continue an active role in class, and that females tend to become even more passive due to perceived teacher indifference. Becker concluded that, in general, teachers behave in ways that involve women less in classroom interactions and thus offer them less encouragement in mathematics because of lower expectations. These findings are supported by the work of Stallings (36), who observed that secondary mathematics teachers both initiated more interactions with boys and provided more specific feedback to them.

Although there is considerable literature on differences in mathematics achievement based on ethnicity, we know of no studies that have investigated differential treatment by ethnicity or of teachers' expectations related to ethnic differences. Secada (33) has argued that, in fact, most of the research on learning and teaching mathematics excludes culturally diverse populations, and that therefore "by definition, their behaviors vary from the norm, their thinking gets treated either as marginal when results are consistent with prior work, or as deviant when results vary from the norm" (33, p. 24). We cannot however assume that all results of gender-difference studies would imply analogous results in ethnic-difference studies (27). We simply do not know (as yet) what teachers expect of various ethnic groups in our nation's classrooms—nor do we understand the impact that such expectations may or may not have on classroom interactions.

NCTM's *Standards* (21) stress that *all* students should have the opportunity to study and learn important mathematics. It is necessary that research seriously begin to address questions concerning the impact of teachers' beliefs and expectations on these opportunities for underrepresented ethnic groups. We also urge teachers to study their own beliefs and expectations—and classroom actions—related to teaching students from diverse ethnic backgrounds. Perhaps in this way we can finally determine precisely where there are unseen (as well as known or suspected) stumbling blocks along the way to answering NCTM's call for mathematics for all students and deal with them swiftly and properly.

Summary and Suggestions

In this chapter we have tried to show that in teaching secondary mathematics, knowledge, beliefs and attitudes about mathematics, teaching, and learners all influence the teacher's classroom decisions and actions. We have discussed some of the limited research done in this area. At the beginning of this chapter we argued that teachers could improve their management of classroom dilemmas by improving their knowledge about, and control over, their cognitive processes—that is, their metacognition related to teaching. We now pose here some questions that we think may help you reflect on your knowledge about, and control of your cognitive processes. We challenge you to improve your metacognition related to your teaching, but we also suggest some ways to do this.

Some Questions about Knowledge

What do you know about mathematics, mathematics teaching, and learners of mathematics? Do you have a deep understanding of the mathematics you are going to teach? Do you know several different ways of approaching the topic? Do you know of topics that students might have difficulties with, or of misunderstandings concerning such that students might already have? How does all this affect what you do in the classroom?

Some Questions about Beliefs and Attitudes

Survey yourself. Do you view secondary mathematics as intriguing, challenging, intuitive, static, safe, rote, or nonsense? If you were to survey your students, asking them the same question, what would they say? Do you think their answers would have anything to do with you? What do you believe is important about mathematics? What *is* mathematics? Do you think that some students are just naturally better than others at it? What makes the difference? Do you like mathematics and find it interesting to study? Is it important that all students study higher-level mathematics? What beliefs and attitudes do your students think you have? What are their beliefs and attitudes? How high are your expectations for students? Do these depend on gender or ethnicity?

Some Classroom Scenarios to Ponder

How might your knowledge, beliefs, and attitudes influence your responses to the following classroom scenarios?

1. A student in class asks, "When are we ever going to use this?" How do you react?
2. A general math student invents an algorithm for dividing fractions. he or she claims you can get a common denominator and then just divide the numerators to get your answer. How do you react?
3. Your principal announces that all teachers are to begin to incorporate cooperative group work in their classes. What do you do to prepare yourself and your students?

4. You are asked by a new teacher what the differences are when one teaches algebra versus general math. How do you respond?

Looking Ahead . . .

We need to continue efforts to understand how secondary mathematics teachers develop knowledge, beliefs, and attitudes, and how these influence classroom activities and student learning. Currently, research on these topics is focused on elementary teachers; research involving secondary mathematics teachers is needed. It is very difficult to study knowledge, beliefs, and attitudes: You can't see them, and teachers often are unable to talk about them. Teachers can help researchers by trying to develop their own metacognitive processes and by becoming more conscious of the impact of their own knowledge, beliefs, and attitudes on the teaching and learning occurring in their classrooms. In collaboration with researchers, teachers could provide a stronger foundation of research results on which to base suggestions for teacher-education activities related to knowledge, beliefs, and attitudes. At the same time this greater awareness can help teachers improve their management of classroom dilemmas.

Catherine Brown

Imagine this scenario: A colleague from another discipline says to you, "The kids love your class! What do you do that could possibly make mathematics interesting?" Some observations might follow. After all, mathematics hasn't changed—or has it? Many students these days are more outspoken than before. They aren't afraid to take a chance or even argue a point. Just wondering: Are they hard-headed? They seem to invest more of themselves in problem solving. Just wondering: Is it the groups? There is even a difference in the way they write. The pencil strokes appear to have more power behind them. Just wondering: Is it because they have had to write so much more than ever? They are completely consumed by the attack on a problem! Just wondering: Is it because they have been conditioned early to stay with a task?

Some self-reflection may occur. Are you enjoying the students' enthusiasm and your desire to feed their curiosity? Just wondering? Where did they get this intense desire? From you? Do you get easily frustrated when a student questions your logic, or do you consider the questioning intriguing? Do you accept the method of instruction as developed by the textbook or do you find other ways to describe the concepts? Just wondering: Is mathematics alive and well in your classroom? The *mathematics* hasn't changed, but maybe *you* have. Your colleague says: "The kids love your class. What do you do that could possibly make mathematics interesting?" What do *you* say? That you love mathematics too?

Jayne Baird

About the Authors

Catherine A. Brown is an associate professor of mathematics education at Virginia Polytechnic Institute and State University in Blacksburg, Virginia. She teaches mathematics and education courses for teachers at all levels. Her research interests include learning to teach mathematics and mathematics teachers' knowledge and beliefs.

Jayne Baird , a Virginia Tech alumna, has been teaching mathematics in both Virginia and Maryland since 1978 and currently teaches geometry and algebra at Chopticon High School in St. Mary's County, Maryland. She is intrigued by the powerful influence that the act of writing has on problem solving.

References

1. AIKEN, L. (1970). Attitudes toward mathematics. *Review of Educational Research, 40,* 551–596.
2. AMES, R. (1983) Teachers' attributions for their own teaching. In J. Levine & M. Wang (Eds.), *Teacher and student perceptions: Implications for learning.* Hillsdale, NJ: Erlbaum.
3. BARON, R., TOM, D., & COOPER, H. (1985). Social class, race and teacher expectations. In J. Dusek (Ed.), *Teacher expectancies* (pp. 251–269). Hillsdale, NJ: Erlbaum.
4. BECKER, J. R. (1981). Differential treatment of females and males in mathematics classes. *Journal for Research in Mathematics Education, 12*(1), 40–53.
5. BENNINGA, J. S., GUSKEY, T. R., & THORNBURG, K. R. (1981). The relationship between teacher attitudes and student perceptions of classroom climate. *The Elementary School Journal, 82*(1), 66–75.
6. BERLAK, A., & BERLAK, H. (1981). *Dilemmas of schooling: Teaching and social change.* London: Methuen.
7. BERLAK, A., & BERLAK, H. (1987). Teachers working with teachers to transform schools. In J. Smyth (Ed.), *Educating teachers: Changing the nature of pedagogical knowledge* (pp. 169–178). New York: Falmer.
8. BORKO, H., & LIVINGSTON, C. (1989). Cognition and improvisation: Differences in mathematics instruction by expert and novice teachers. *American Educational Research Journal, 26,* 473–498.
9. BROPHY, J. (1983). Research on the self-fulfilling prophecy and teacher expectations. *Journal of Educational Psychology, 75,* 631–661.
10. BROWN, C. A. (1986). A study of the socialization to teaching of a beginning secondary mathematics teacher (Doctoral dissertation, University of Georgia, 1985). *Dissertation Abstracts International, 46,* 2605A.
11. BUSH, W. S. (1986). Preservice teachers' sources of decisions in teaching secondary mathematics. *Journal for Research in Mathematics Education, 17*(1), 21–30.
12. CALDERHEAD, J. (1984). *Teachers' classroom decision making.* London: Holt, Rinehart.
13. COONEY, T. J. (1985). A beginning teacher's view of problem solving. *Journal for Research in Mathematics Education, 16*(5), 324–336.
14. FLAVELL, J. (1976). Metacognitive aspects of problem solving. In L. B. Resnick (Ed.), *The nature of intelligence* (pp. 231–235). Hillsdale, NJ: Erlbaum.
15. GOOD, T. L. (1987). Two decades of research on teacher expectations: Findings and future directions. *Journal of Teacher Education, 38*(4), 32–47.
16. HASHWEH, M. Z. (1986). *An Exploratory Study of Teacher Knowledge and Teaching: The Effects of Science Teachers' Knowledge of Subject Matter and Their Conceptions of Learning on Their Teaching* (Doctoral dissertation, Stanford University, 1985). *Dissertation Abstracts International, 46,* 3672A.
17. HOYLES, C. (1982). The pupils' view of mathematics learning. *Educational Studies in Mathematics, 13*(4), 349–372.

18. LAMPERT, M. (1985). How do teachers manage to teach? Perspectives on problems in practice. *Harvard Educational Review, 55*(2), 178–194.
19. LEINHARDT, G., & GREENO, J. G. (1986). The cognitive skill of teaching. *Journal of Educational Psychology, 78,* 75–95.
20. METZ, M. (1978). *Classrooms and corridors.* Berkeley: University of California Press.
21. NATIONAL COUNCIL OF TEACHERS OF MATHEMATICS. (1989). *Curriculum and evaluation standards for school mathematics.* Reston, VA: Author.
22. NATIONAL COUNCIL OF TEACHERS OF MATHEMATICS. (1991). *Professional standards for teaching mathematics.* Reston, VA: Author.
23. NATIONAL RESEARCH COUNCIL. (1989). *Everybody counts.* Washington, DC: National Academy Press.
24. OAKES, J. (1990). Opportunities, achievement, and choice: Women and minority students in science and mathematics. *Review of Research in Education, 16,* 153–222.
25. POLYA, G. (1962). *Mathematical discovery.* New York: Wiley.
26. PRATT, D. L. (1985) Responsibility for student success/failure and observed verbal behavior among secondary science and mathematics teachers. *Journal of Research in Science Teaching, 22,* 807–816.
27. RESEARCH ADVISORY COMMITTEE OF THE NATIONAL COUNCIL OF TEACHERS OF MATHEMATICS (1989). The mathematics education of underserved and underrepresented groups: A continuing challenge. *Journal for Research in Mathematics Education, 20*(4), 371–375.
28. ROSENTHAL, R., & JACOBSON, L. (1968). *Pygmalion in the classroom: Teacher expectation and pupils' intellectual development.* New York: Holt, Rinehart.
29. SCHMIDT, W., & BUCHMANN, M. (1983). Six teachers' beliefs and attitudes and their curricular time allocations. *The Elementary School Journal, 84*(2), 162–171.
30. SCHOENFELD, A. H. (1985). Metacognitive and epistemological issue in mathematical understanding. In E. A. Silver (Ed.), *Teaching and learning mathematical problem solving: Multiple research perspectives* (pp. 361–380). Hillsdale, NJ: Erlbaum.
31. SCHOENFELD, A. H. (1987). What's all the fuss about metacognition? In A. H. Schoenfeld (Ed.), *Cognitive science and mathematics education* (pp. 189–216). Hillsdale, NJ: Erlbaum.
32. SCHOENFELD, A. H. (1988). When good teaching leads to bad results: The disasters of "well-taught" mathematics courses. *Educational Psychologist, 23*(2), 145–166.
33. SECADA, W. G. (1988). Diversity, equity, and cognitivist research. In E. Fennema, T. P. Carpenter, & S. Lamon (Eds.), *Integrating research on teaching and learning mathematics* (pp. 20–59). Madison: Wisconsin Center for Education Research.
34. SHULMAN, L. S. (1986). Those who understand: Knowledge growth in teaching. *Educational Researcher, 15*(2), 4–14.
35. SHULMAN, L. S. (1988). *Knowledge growth in teaching: A final report to the Spencer Foundation.* Stanford, CA: Stanford University.
36. STALLINGS, J. (1985). School, classroom, and home influences on women's decisions to enroll in advanced mathematics courses. In S. F. Chipman, L. R. Brush, & D. M. Wilson (Eds.), *Women and mathematics: Balancing the equation* (pp. 199–223). Hillsdale, NJ: Erlbaum.
37. STEINBERG, R., HAYMORE, T., & MARKS, R. (1985). *Teachers' knowledge and structuring content in mathematics.* Paper presented at the annual meeting of the American Educational Research Association, Chicago, April.
38. THOMPSON, A. G. (1984). The relationship of teachers' conceptions of mathematics and mathematics teaching to instructional practice. *Educational Studies in Mathematics, 15,* 105–127.

39. THOMPSON, A. G. (1985). Teachers' conceptions of mathematics and the teaching of problem solving. In E. A. Silver (Ed.), *Teaching and learning mathematical problem solving: Multiple research perspectives* (pp. 281–294). Hillsdale, N.J.: Erlbaum.
40. TOLSTOY, L. (1967). *Tolstoy on education.* (L. Wiener, Trans.). Chicago: University of Chicago Press. (Original work published 1862)
41. WILSON, S. M., SHULMAN, L. S., & RICHERT, A. E. (1987). "150 different ways" of knowing: Representations of knowledge in teaching. In J. Calderhead (Ed.), *Exploring teachers' thinking* (pp. 104–124). London: Cassell.

CHAPTER 15

Evaluation Issues

Elizabeth Badger, Thomas J. Cooney, and Timothy Kanold

TEACHER: *It looks like we could use the quadratic formula to solve this geometry problem. Who can tell me what the formula is?*

(Silence)

I know you studied it last year in algebra class. Can anyone remember what it is or how to figure it out?

HOLLY: *I remember we studied it last year. But you can't really expect us to know it. We weren't tested on it.*

Although we resist the notion that what we test is identical to what we expect students to learn, Holly is not incorrect in her perception. Deliberately or otherwise, testing signals what is valued. When teachers review the topics that will be on the next test they are saying, in effect, "Of all the material that we've covered in class, *this* is what you will be expected to remember." And, all things being equal, *this* is what students will remember because *this* is what they understand to be important, *this* is what they will review, *this* is what they will practice and think about. There is no doubt that tests serve a useful purpose in student learning, as they motivate, focus, and provide a standard for performance.

It is not surprising that frequent testing is associated with higher achievement (7). Research has shown that classroom testing sends a powerful message to students, not only about the content that is considered important, but also about the kinds of thinking that are valued (20). In his review of the impact of classroom evaluation on students, Crooks (7) emphasizes the potent effect, on their studying and learning, of students' expectations of what will be tested. If students expect to be evaluated on their ability to manipulate numbers, solve equations, or reproduce arguments, rather than on a deeper understanding of a topic, it is the former and not the latter that will be learned.

> Examinations tell them our real aims, at least so they believe. If we stress clear understanding and aim at a growing knowledge of physics, we may completely sabotage our teaching by a final examination that asks for numbers to be put into memorized formulas. However loud our sermons, however intriguing the experiments, students will judge by that examination—and so will next year's students who hear about it. (26, p. 956)

Given the power of testing to influence learning, there is an uneasiness among teachers about their own assessments. For example, despite the fact that as much as 15% of the typical secondary student's time is spent taking tests (9, 14), 85% of the eleventh-grade teachers surveyed expressed concern over the quality and use of the tests they constructed (31).

Is this concern justified? Does the constant testing that apparently takes place in classrooms actually yield useful information about students' learning? Mathematics educators have doubts about this. The authors of the recent NCTM *Curriculum and Evaluation Standards* have argued that "the vision of mathematics education in the *Standards* places new demands on instruction and forces us to reassess the manner and methods by which we chart our students' progress" (24, p. 190). Research can help us in this reassessment of student evaluation. However, in order to understand its relevance, it is necessary to distinguish among the different purposes of evaluation.

Evaluation can be divided into two major types: *formative* and *summative*. Formative evaluations—informal and informative, often the result of a dialogue between teacher and student—are conducted in order to provide information about the effectiveness of instruction. In contrast, evaluations that have a more public aspect, entailing judgments of mastery, fall into the summative category. The latter involves criteria reflecting larger objectives and usually refers to a final product or the culmination of prolonged effort. Because of the considerable difference in the purpose, research implications differ accordingly. We will consider each of these types of evaluation as they are relevant to the teaching of secondary school mathematics.

Two Types of Evaluation

Formative Evaluation

Whether they use the term or not, for most teachers formative evaluation is an integral part of instruction. Whenever teachers seek information about students' understanding in order to modify their instruction, they are conducting formative evaluation. However, formative evaluation is far more than just checking students' progress. Ideally, it goes beyond determining what students can do, focusing on what and how they understand—and, in so doing, providing a basis for diagnosing learning difficulties. It identifies problems in understanding. Questions that require explanation amidst class discussion (such as, "*Why* does the trapezoid have to be isosceles?" or "*Why* does this system of equations have no solution?") exemplify this kind of evaluation.

The research cited in this volume is particularly relevant to formative evaluation. It gives insight on what to expect of students, helps teachers to be sensitive to potential learning difficulties, and can provide a framework for considering students' mathematical development. It demonstrates the complexity that underlies students' understanding of mathematics and, concomitantly, their errors and misconceptions. It also demonstrates that students' errors seldom are arbitrary and easily correctable; rather, they often are the result of rational thinking and, consequently, resistant to change. While sometimes we are prone to interpret mistakes as manifestations of carelessness, in fact often they are a sign of significant misconceptions. Formative evaluation provides a continual basis for identifying and diagnosing these misconceptions.

Summative Evaluation

The second kind of evaluation, summative, is neither continuous nor informal. It is judgmental, presupposing a criterion for success, with standards that are aimed for and must be attained. It can take many forms, including end-of-semester grades, the fulfillment of graduation requirements, and national, state, and local examination results. Its purpose is to provide credentials for the future—whether that means the next grade in school, a new school, or future employment. Here the emphasis is less on evaluation for the purpose of diagnosis and modifying instruction and more on evaluation to determine at what level students can perform. The audience for summative evaluation is the public, for example, parents, future employers, college administrators, students themselves. Because of the importance of these decisions, the research area that is most pertinent to this kind of evaluation is *measurement theory*, and more specifically the concepts of *reliability* and *validity*. These concepts are central to tests created by teachers, as well as to tests created for large-scale assessment. We will consider reliability and validity in both contexts.

The Notions of Reliability and Validity

Reliability

Reliability is the *sine qua non* of testing. Without the strong probability that, all things being equal, the outcomes of a test are consistent, testing is a waste of time. Since reliability is a direct function of the quantity of information obtained, the longer the test the more reliable it is apt to be. However, other factors can affect reliability as well. Whenever variability is introduced into the testing situation, for instance, the results become less reliable. Reliability is particularly problematic in more naturalistic assessments, such as when teachers base assessment on classroom observations or on students' oral contributions. However, even within the confines of more traditional testing, variability in student performance is an issue.

One possible source of variation is the way in which questions are posed. For example, students who are able to choose the correct option when presented with a multiple-choice question often are at a loss when asked to generate correct information covering the same content (3). Even within the relatively narrow domain of geometric proof, Stevenson, Averett, and Vickers (30) report that more than half the students who failed to generate an adequate proof were nevertheless able to answer correctly the majority of multiple-choice items concerning the same proof. In explaining similar results in response to problem-solving tasks, Ward, Frederiksen, and Carlson (32) suggest that more is involved than the obvious advantage in choosing a correct option over creating one. Questions such as the following, while ostensibly measuring the same skill, may trigger different processes and, consequently, may favor or penalize different styles of students' thinking.

1. What is the least common multiple of 8 and 12?
2. What is the smallest whole number that has both 8 and 12 as factors?
3. What is the smallest number of square tiles that can be grouped into 8 equal groups and into 12 equal groups?

In addition to the unreliability that can be attributed to differences in the test questions, research has noted the variation in performance that is due to students themselves. Studies have repeatedly shown the debilitating effects of test anxiety, particularly at the higher grades where summative evaluation is more common (16).

> Among the important factors (affecting reliability) are subtle variations in physical and mental efficiency of the test taker, uncontrollable fluctuations in external conditions, variations in the specific tasks required of individual examinees, and inconsistencies on the part of those who evaluate examinee performance. Quantification of the consistency and inconsistency in examinee performance constitutes the essence of reliability analysis. (11, p. 105)

Crooks (7) notes that although early failures influence the development of anxiety, anxiety arises from more sources than just a lack of knowledge needed to solve problems. If the performance of highly anxious students improves when the same tests are administered under less stressful conditions, test results cannot be considered reliable (17, 18).

Validity

Although correlations among test results often are used as evidence of validity, establishing validity is basically an interpretive process, not a statistical one. This is because validity is not a characteristic of tests per se, but rather refers to the "appropriateness, meaningfulness, and usefulness of specific inferences made from test scores" (1, p. 9). Our examination of validity addresses such questions as "When Dick does poorly on this test, are we correct in inferring that he does not understand?" and "When Marie answers these questions correctly, does it mean that she is capable of applying her knowledge in other situations?" In considering the issue of validity, various questions have to be addressed, the most fundamental of which is *"Does this test measure what it purports to measure?"*

> What is to be validated is not the test or observation device as such but the inferences derived from test scores or other indicators. (23, p. 13)

As we saw in the previous section (on reliability), many factors influence students' behavior when taking tests. These factors act as potential threats to validity. For example, poor performance may be due to anxiety, inattention, low motivation, or fatigue. To draw a valid inference about students' competence from test results one must consider and find grounds for rejecting such alternative hypotheses (23). In addition, the test itself may not constitute an accurate reflection of what is to be measured. If tests are confined to a narrow content range, they will fail to include important dimensions of achievement. On the other hand, if they cast too wide a net, as do many standardized achievement tests, their results will be contaminated by other factors (such as test-wiseness), that are irrelevant to what we want to measure.

An additional question that addresses the issue of validity pertains to the potential utility of the test results in predicting behavior. For example, a problem-solving test with an open-ended format should have greater validity for real-life problems than a series of multiple-choice items requiring the selection of a single answer. On the other hand, while the ability to do proofs in geometry may predict success in doing proofs later in mathematics, it provides little evidence for predicting more global mathematical thinking.

Research has shown the folly of overinterpreting test results. Sleeman (29) provides an example in the area of algebraic substitution. He notes that on most algebra tests in which the focus is on the manipulation of unknowns, the majority of problems have whole-number solutions so that students do not waste time doing arithmetic. Although students may do well in this context, their scores may fail to predict performance when the same type of problem is encountered in a real-life context in which numbers are seldom small and simple. Finally, because our interpretations of tests are not made in a vacuum but have significant social consequences, researchers are increasingly concerned with the question *"Do interpretations of test results reflect significant social values?"*

Researchers who have investigated this aspect of validity have focused on what Frederiksen (12) has called "the real test bias"—that is, the tendency for tests to constrict the curriculum. In contrast, Frederiksen and Collins (13) have proposed the concept of *systemic validity*. Generally, this refers to the extent to which tests are congruent with the larger instructional goals of the curriculum and provide information in attaining those goals. Some researchers (19, 13, 28) argue that there exists a trade-off between the ease with which a test is scored and its instructional relevance. Objective tests that use simple algorithmic scoring methods, such as counting the number of correct items, tend to be reliable and much simpler to score than extended tasks that require judgment, analysis, and reflection on the part of raters. On the other hand, such tests typically consist of low-level items that cannot be used as a basis for valid inferences about higher-level cognitive skills. For inferences about complex thinking, one needs tasks that more clearly reflect what is meant by "mathematical thinking." The difficulty in scoring is balanced by the amount of relevant information gained.

Underlying the very notion of validity is the question "*What does it mean to know mathematics?*" One of the primary emphases in mathematics education today is that mathematics should be seen as a product of human activity in which students' constructions of mathematical ideas capture both the interrelatedness within mathematics and the connections between mathematics and real-world phenomena. The notion of mathematics as a set of abstract principles disconnected from human experience and devoid of meaning save for its own symbolic referents has been increasingly challenged by researchers who have studied the mathematical activities of people outside the confines of the classroom (21). By showing how adults and children alike develop mathematical competence in forms that are distinct from school mathematics, Brown, Collins, and Duguid (4) have argued that mathematics is a product of the activity, context, and culture in which it is developed and used. Furthermore, they point to evidence that school mathematics neither is relevant for most everyday activites nor necessarily predicts success in such activities.

A conception of mathematics as the product of mental constructions suggests that valid measures of students' understanding of mathematics should consider their abilities to represent, to communicate, to translate, to reason mathematically, and to solve problems. This, in turn, calls for alternative methods of evaluating students that both permit and require students to exhibit these kinds of mathematical outcomes.

An issue related to validity that arises from a more constructivist orientation toward mathematics involves standards for achievement. The shift from a conception of mathematics as an invariant and abstract set of rules to one that places increasing value on personal relevance and individual understanding raises the question of what constitutes acceptable standards of achievement. Until there is a public consensus on what it means to "know" or to "do" mathematics, the validity of assessment will continue to be challenged. The more value that is placed on personal construction, the more relative becomes the judgment process, and the greater the role of subjectivity in deciding on students' achievement. These issues will have to be addressed, not only by the mathematics eduation and evaluation communities, but by teachers responsible for making valid decisions regarding their students' understanding and competencies.

> How are we to assess what the student understands if there are no standards in the discipline with which to judge the adequacy of "plausible reasoning"? (25, p. 70)

The issue becomes even more complex when we recognize that the public is not uniform either in its perception about standards for school mathematics or about what constitutes mathematics. Donovan (8) observes that working-class parents are more likely to value their children's *learning* of mathematical facts and procedures than are parents in professional occupations, who tend to place more value in the processes of *doing* mathematics (e.g., solving problems). This difference in perception can be particularly troublesome if parents see their children being evaluated on mathematical outcomes that they neither believe in nor support. This lack of uniformity makes it increasingly difficult to determine what sort of measures are valid indicators of either knowing or doing mathematics.

Implications for Classroom Assessment

Our previous discussion on reliability and validity illustrates the fragility of information based on a single testing format or occasion. In order to accumulate a reliable body of evidence for evaluation, it is important that teachers turn to a variety of sources of information. The NCTM *Curriculum and Evaluation Standards* (24) emphasize that the assessment of students' understanding of mathematics should be based on the convergence of information obtained from a variety of sources. Further, the assessment process should incorporate different kinds of mathematical thinking. The evaluation standards were created with the intent of encouraging teachers to consider a broad array of mathematical outcomes and to use as many sources and means as appropriate when assessing students' understanding. Different sources of information include evaluating students' journals and notebooks, tests, quizzes, essays and oral reports, homework, and class discussions.

It has also been argued that, in order for a test to be valid, it must involve authentic mathematical achievement. This call for authenticity has evoked a cluster of ideas very different from our usual notions of testing. Archbald and Newmann (2) have suggested three features that distinguish authentic forms of achievment: disciplined inquiry, the integration of knowledge, and the presence of an aesthetic or utilitarian value apart from merely determining the competence of the learner. In practice, this implies that evaluation tasks should present mathematical challenges in contexts that hold meaning for the students, rather than isolated either from other mathematical tasks or from disciplines outside the field of mathematics.

To illustrate how an often isolated task of factoring whole numbers or algebraic expressions can be contextualized, consider the following.

> In how many ways can 12 people be seated to form a rectangular array?
> In how many ways can 7 people be seated to form a rectangular array?
> If the number of people seated is represented by $x^2 - 7x - 12$, how can the number of rows and columns be represented?
>
> If the area of a rectangle is 12, what are its possible dimensions if the sides are whole numbers? If the area of a rectangle is 7, what are its possible dimensions if the sides are whole numbers? If the area is $x^2 - 7x - 12$, what are its possible dimensions if the sides are represented by rational expressions?

Students should be encouraged to see that the question "What are the factors of 12 (or 7 or $x^2 - 7x - 12$)?" is mathematically equivalent to the question "How can 12 people be seated in a rectangular array?" or "What are the possible dimensions of a rectangle having an area of 12?" and hence develop the notion that different forms of questions can be rooted in the same mathematical content. This emphasis should be embedded throughout the instructional process and assessed both informally in a variety of contexts and more formally (as when tests are being used). In either case, the students' ability to construct a pictorial representation of factoring numbers or algebraic expressions and to shift from one representation to another is the focal activity rather than the simply factoring 12 or $x^2 - 7x - 12$.

Sensitivity to issues related to scoring is particularly important in ensuring a valid and reliable assessment of student performance. This becomes particularly important when students encounter real-world phenomena that involve complexity and diversity of possible solutions. Consider the task of predicting winning times in future Olympics by constructing graphical representations of the winning times, to the nearest second, in the men's 1,500-meter run in the 1900 through 1984 Olympics. (See Table 15.1.) While the task involves significant mathematics couched in a real-world setting (that is, it has authenticity), an appropriate scoring mechanism is not clear. Scoring considerations should include not only whether the graph is reasonable and accurately reflects the data, but whether inferences drawn from the graphical representation are appropriate and accurate. In other words, scores should reflect students' ability to use mathematics as a tool for making sense of the world about them.

Implications for Large-scale Assessment

Issues concerning reliability and validity are relevant not only to tests created by teachers but also to large-scale testing that is often imposed upon teachers. The traditional and almost universal format for large-scale testing has been multiple-choice, whereby a student chooses a single correct answer from a number of options. With a highly controlled structure, multiple-choice items can be easily translated to numerical form and statistically manipulated to examine how well and reliably they relate to one another, whether they consistently discriminate against groups of students (girls, minorities), and whether—as a group—they relate to other measures of the same construct. Because responses to such items can be examined, monitored, and modified easily, multiple-choice tests are regarded as objective and reliable. Furthermore, scores achieved by students or schools on multiple-choice tests correlate moderately with those obtained on more free response items (3, 30).

It appears that if the goal of assessment is confined to a simple ranking of students or schools, multiple-choice tests are adequate. Objections to such tests have focused

TABLE 15.1. Winning Times in Men's 1,500-Meter Olympic Event

Year	Time	Year	Time	Year	Time	Year	Time
1900	246	1924	234	1952	225	1972	216
1904	245	1928	233	1956	221	1976	219
1908	243	1932	231	1960	216	1980	218
1912	237	1936	228	1964	218	1984	213
1920	242	1948	230	1968	215		

primarily on issues of validity, not reliability, and are related to changing ideas of what it is to know mathematics. When school mathematics is considered to be primarily a set of discrete skills to be applied to highly structured situations, tests that reflect this conception are valid. However, when the mathematical processes of problem solving, communication, reasoning, and making connections—processes emphasized in the NCTM *Standards*—are seen as an integral part of mathematical knowledge, these tests can no longer be considered valid. Romberg, Wilson, and Khaketla's (27) analysis of six commercially available mathematical achievement tests points out that these tests do *not* reflect a more process-oriented conception of mathematics.

As the *Standards* get implemented in the schools, the standardized tests used in those schools will have to change to more accurately reflect the new visions of the mathematics curriculum. (27, p. 3)

On the other hand, the move for more authentic measures of achievement such as performance tasks, extended problems, and open-ended questions poses concerns for the reliability of the results (28). The more open formats are more difficult to monitor and control and thus invite greater sources of variability. For example, it is far more difficult than usual to control sources of measurement error in testing situations that extend over time or when the tasks themselves encourage variability. This trade-off between reliability and validity is only now being addressed by the assessment community.

Implications of Research Methodology for Evaluation

In addition to research findings, research methodology is also relevant to the evaluation of students' mathematical achievement. Whether they are interested in the psychological aspects of students' learning or the mathematical requirements of the tasks themselves, researchers have relied heavily upon interviews, observations, and self-reports, as well as on conventional tests, as means of gathering data. Such techniques, having revealed the complexity of knowledge required to perform seemingly simple tasks, have resulted in rich descriptions of children's mathematical inventions, errors, misconceptions, and methods of solving problems. Although secondary school teachers, sometimes faced with forty students in a classroom rather than one or two subjects in a laboratory, may not be able to incorporate these ideas directly into their instruction, they can adapt them for evaluation purposes.

Interviews

When learning was viewed as primarily a process of stimulus–response, psychologists were wary of personal interpretation. However, the increasing recognition of the influence of perception and understanding on students' ability to use mathematics has led to a greater use of interviews and self-reports. For the classroom teacher, as well as for the researcher, interviewing is an important technique in assessing students' understanding of mathematical concepts and principles and the reasoning behind their actions. There is *no* standard procedure for conducting interviews, nor should there be. Basically, interviewing is a process of coming to understand what a student is thinking. As such, it is nonjudgmental; the teacher's role is to unravel those meanings that mathematics holds for the student.

Each particular child is the authority on what he or she thinks and what makes sense to him or her, not Piaget, not any researcher, no matter how deeply the researcher has probed or how broadly he or she has sampled. (10, p. 27)

Occasions for interviews arise naturally in a problem-oriented classroom. Because problem solving is, by its nature, a very complex type of intellectual activity, written work alone is seldom sufficient to determine students' thinking or strategies for solving problems. In fact, in reviewing work on the assessment of problem solving, Lester and Kroll (22) conclude that what students write is often very different from what they think. Only by questioning are teachers able to understand the rationale for their methods.

Like most good assessment methods, the function of interviews extends beyond evaluation. A discussion of ideas promotes learning—for the teacher, as well as for students. As teachers discover how their students understand mathematical processes, students develop the habit of examining their own thinking and problem-solving strategies.

Observations

Whereas interviews are a deliberate intervention in an attempt to make the implicit explicit, observations permit the gathering of information in an unobtrusive way. They are increasingly appropriate as the mathematics class becomes the focus for discussion among students, particularly when students are asked to convince each other of the validity of their arguments and their processes for solving problems. Students' informal dialogues with one another are more likely to reveal their way of thinking than are their responses to a direct question, as the give-and-take of conjectures, examples, and counter-examples provides a context for them to exhibit their reasoning.

Group problem solving, in which students are given problems to solve jointly, is a natural context for observation. One technique used by researchers is that of paired problem solving (33), in which two students mutually share and contribute to the solution process. Another variation (6) involves one member solving the problem and then explaining his or her solution method to the other student. The explainer is evaluated for clarity and coherence of explanation and the ability to handle questions. The listener is evaluated on listening skills and the quality of questions asked.

As a method of evaluation, observation requires far more than just looking. Decisions must be made about what to look for. Attention must be given to the context in which students are responding and to the many factors that contribute to a given response. In addition, as is the case with the researcher, the teacher must take into account a large number of factors, then focus on those most relevant to understanding how students are thinking about mathematics.

The Role of Calculators in Evaluation

One of the questions often asked in conjunction with evaluating student performance is whether students should have access to calculators when being tested. The NCTM *Standards* (24) clearly emphasize that increased attention should be given to calculator usage during assessment as well as during instruction. However, calculator usage sometimes changes the nature of the information gained when students solve problems. For example, Harvey (15) points out that calculators can affect the difficulty level, the level of thinking, and the objective measured. Consider the following item couched in a multiple-choice format.

$$\text{Solve the equation } 4(x + 15) - 10 = 5 - 5x$$

Use of the calculator encourages a strategy of substitution and evaluation—a different objective than that of using field properties to solve equations. Furthermore, Wilson and Kilpatrick (34) argue that if we are to realize the calculator's potential, we must adopt a different perspective on what it means to know mathematics. The presence of calculators requires us to shift away from assessing students' ability to perform algorithmic processes and toward assessing processes that are more conceptual in nature.

Calculators also facilitate the validation of students' ability to use mathematics in a variety of contexts, for example, identifying multiple ways of solving problems and solving more authentic problems. The *Standards* (24) emphasize that assessment of a student's problem-solving ability should include evidence that the student can "apply a variety of strategies to solve problems" (p. 209). To illustrate how the graphing calculator can facilitate this outcome, consider the following problem that students typically solve using algebraic techniques and the definition of absolute value.

$$\text{Solve } |x + 2| < |x - 1|$$

Generally, students encounter difficulty in considering the different cases involving absolute value. In contrast, the graphing calculator provides at least two other solution strategies that are accessible and easily assessable. One strategy involves graphing two functions: $y_1 = |x + 2|$ and $y_2 = |x - 1|$ and determining the values of x for which $y_1 < y_2$. The graphing calculator can provide a visual stimulus for helping students answer the question "For what values of x is y_1 less than y_2?" (See Fig. 15.1.) A second strategy consists of graphing the equation $y = |x + 2| - |x - 1|$ and determining that part of the graph for which $y < 0$. (See Fig. 15.2.) By providing a context in which a variety of solution methods are encouraged, teachers can

FIGURE 15.1   The graph of $y_1 = |x + 2|$ and $y_2 = |x - 1|$

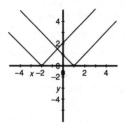

x = -.4736442 y = 1.52631458
The graph of $y_1 = |x + 2|$ and $y_2 = |x - 1|$

gain better information about their students' understanding of what it means to solve inequalities.

The availability of calculators also enables students of all ability levels to solve meaningful and challenging problems. Authentic problems involving buying cars or television sets are cases in point. The calculations involved in such problems often inhibit many students from even attempting a solution and prevent teachers from assessing the students' intuitive understanding of mathematics in everyday contexts.

> You find a car that you like at a local dealership. The price is $9,000 including tax, dealer preparation charges, and all other fees. You have $10,000 in the bank so that you can buy the car for cash if you want to. Paying cash now entitles you to receive a $1,000 rebate. However, the dealer is also offering a two-year, low-interest (3%) loan, with no down payment but no rebate. Which would cost you less in the long run: buying the car for cash or taking out the loan for it? (Problem developed by Harold Baker, Litchfield High School, Litchfield, Connecticut)

Finally, the presence of a calculator introduces the possibility of evaluating facets of understanding that often are taken for granted (e.g., the concept of scaling). Consider a problem in which students are to determine the maximum volume that can be formed by folding a square sheet of paper 25 cm on a side into a box (without a top). The problem involves finding the maximum value of $f(x) = x(25 - 2x)^2$. In order for the maximum value to make sense in the context of this problem, the student must determine that the maximum value must occur for an x value between

FIGURE 15.2   The graph of $y = |x + 2| - |x - 1|$

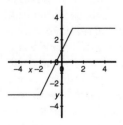

x = -.4736843 y = .05263158
The graph of $y = |x + 2| - |x - 1|$

0 and 12.5. The drawing of an interpretable graph requires identifying a reasonable range of y values as well. Accordingly, an open-ended question could be posed that asks students to identify an appropriate range or, alternately, a multiple-choice item could be presented (see below).

In order to find a maximum positive value of $f(x) = x(25 - 2x)^2$ in the interval $(0, 12.5)$, which of the following intervals for the range values is most reasonable?

      (a) $(0, 10)$ (b) $(0, 1000)$ (c) $(0, 2000)$ (d) $(500, 1000)$

In considering the role of technology in evaluating students' understanding of mathematics, several points should be emphasized. First, if technology is considered integral to instruction, then it should be considered integral to evaluation. Second, technology provides a context for validating not only a student's ability to generate alternate solution methods, but also a flexibility of thinking mathematically by moving from one representation to another. Third, technology permits the evaluation of students' ability to solve more realistic problems. Fourth, while the use of technology can eliminate or reduce the need for some mechanical, algebraic skills, it creates a need for examining other types of concepts and skills, for example, scaling, which can in themselves serve as focal points for evaluation.

Conclusion

The anecdote with Holly at the opening of this chapter represents an exchange between one of the authors and a student in a geometry class. To Holly, a student should not be held responsible for learning a topic if the teacher fails to "test" that topic; she conflated the notions of teaching and testing. But the conceptual fusing of these notions is not limited to students: it pertains to teachers as well (5). Although we should resist Holly's implicit conclusion, it is sheer folly to think that teachers and students do not at least partially embrace it. We should realize that testing is only one aspect of evaluation. We would argue that evaluation, in its broader context, needs as much consideration as teaching. Consequently, we should conceive of evaluation as a means of informing teaching, not of delimiting it.

Evaluation can be informed in the several ways that we have tried to illustrate in this chapter. Certainly it can be informed by research in the field of measurement, thus addressing such issues as reliability, validity, and formative and summative evaluation. But it can also be informed by research conducted on the teaching and learning of mathematics. To have a framework on how students think about mathematics—which factors contribute to their performance or lack thereof—is to have a powerful and generative view of the teaching/learning process and of how we can assess their understanding of mathematics. When evaluation is seen as the flip side of instruction, we realize that it is essential for more effective instruction and as a vehicle to promote learning. Without a map of the terrain of student thinking, we have little chance of knowing where to stop, where to back up, when to slow down, and what the critical sites are for students to concentrate their efforts. The process of evaluation allows us to locate where students are on their map of understanding mathematics, and how we can accommodate their movement along the right path of that understanding through appropriate instruction.

Looking Ahead . . .

Research that has stressed the complexity of the learning process holds strong implications for the evaluation of students' understanding of mathematics. It has underscored the need for a broader range of methods, as well as more challenging and thought-provoking tasks in evaluation. This need has been reinforced by both the psychometric community, wherein validity issues are of paramount concern, and the educational community, in which knowledge of school mathematics is being redefined.

On the other hand, there are many questions still to be answered: What tasks best measure what it means to know mathematics? Indeed, how is "knowing mathematics" defined? To what extent does the ability displayed in one task transfer to another? How can technology expand our ability to evaluate students' understanding and achievement?

Finally, as we look ahead, we would be wise to consider the question of what meanings teachers ascribe to evaluation, and how the above questions are answered in the crucible of the classroom. For it is in the classroom that evaluation takes place, and it ultimately is there that the issues must be resolved.

Elizabeth Badger
Thomas Cooney

There are many questions that teachers wonder about when evaluating students— questions that research can at least enlighten, if not answer. Research can address successful and meaningful alternatives for evaluating students. It can provide insight into what types of assessment best enhance students' achievement (for example, which ones demonstrate improved student performance). It also can (as discussed earlier in the chapter) provide information about the appropriateness and effectiveness of paired problem-solving experiences. Too, it can afford information about how we can better understand what students know about mathematics, and how teachers can improve the diagnostic aspects of their teaching. And it can inform us as to how calculators can be used effectively in assessment activities. Finally, research can grant insight into *how* assessment can *promote* learning rather than remain as a tool confined to determining grades.

Given the current emphasis on evaluation, it is important that both teachers and researchers focus on how we can better assess our students' understanding of mathematics. What is needed are means by which researchers and teachers can come to understand the issues each group faces so that we can all become more fully informed about evaluating students' understanding of mathematics.

Timothy Kanold

About the Authors

Elizabeth Badger is the director of the Massachusetts Educational Assessment Program. She was a member of the task force that wrote the *Evaluation Standards* in the *Curriculum and Evaluation Standards for School Mathematics*. Dr. Badger serves as a consultant to various state and local agencies concerned with evaluation and is the author of numerous articles on evaluation.

Thomas Cooney is professor of mathematics education at the University of Georgia. He was a member of the task force that wrote the *Evaluation Standards* in the *Curriculum and Evaluation Standards for School Mathematics*, and was chairperson of the task force that wrote the *Standards for the Evaluation of Teaching* in the *Professional Standards for Teaching Mathematics*.

Timothy Kanold is chairperson for mathematics and science at Adlai Stevenson High School in Lake County, Illinois. At one time a member of the task force that wrote the *Standards for the Evaluation of Teaching*, he was the 1986 Illinois Presidential Awardee for Excellence in Mathematics Teaching. Mr. Kanold is a consultant to various school systems regarding implementation of the NCTM standards.

References

1. AMERICAN PSYCHOLOGICAL ASSOCIATION, AMERICAN EDUCATIONAL RESEARCH ASSOCIATION, AND NATIONAL COUNCIL ON MEASUREMENT IN EDUCATION. (1985). *Standards for educational and psychological testing.* Washington, DC: American Psychological Association.
*2. ARCHBALD, D., & NEWMANN, F. (1988). *Beyond standardized testing.* Reston, VA: National Associaton of Secondary School Principals.
3. BADGER, E. (1990). *Using different spectacles to look at student achievement: Implicatons for theory and practice.* Paper presented at the annual meeting of the American Educational Research Association, Boston, April.
4. BROWN, J. S., COLLINS, A., & DUGUID, P. (1989). Situated cognition and the culture of learning. *Educational Researcher, 18*(1), 32–42.
5. BROWN, S., & COONEY, T. (1986). Stalking the dualism between theory and practice. In P. F. L. Verstappen (Ed.), *Second conference on systemmatic co-operation between theory and practice in mathematics education* (pp. 21–40). Lochem, The Netherlands: National Institute for Curriculum Development.
6. COLLINS, A., HAWKINS, J., & FREDERIKSEN, N. (1990). *Technology-based assessment.* Paper presented at the annual meeting of the American Educational Research Association, Boston, April.
7. CROOKS, T. (1988) The impact of classroom evaluation practices on students. *Review of Educational Research, 58*(4), 438–481.
*8. DONOVAN, B. F. (1990). Cultural power and the defining of school mathematics: A case study. In T. J. Cooney (Ed.), *Teaching and learning mathematics in the 1990s* (pp. 166–173). Reston, VA: National Council of Teachers of Mathematics.
9. DORR-BREMME, D. W., & HERMAN, J. (1986). *Assessing school achievement: A profile of classroom practices.* Los Angeles: Center for the Study of Evaluation, UCLA Graduate School of Education.
10. EASLEY, J. A. JR. (1977). *On clinical studies in mathematics education.* Information Reference Center of Science, Mathematics, and Environmental Education. Columbus, OH: Ohio State University Press.

11. FELDT, L. S., & BRENNAN, R. L. Reliability. In R. Linn (Ed.), *Educational Measurement* (3rd ed., pp. 105–146). New York: Macmillan.

12. FREDERIKSEN, N. (1984). Implications of cognitive theory for instruction in problem solving. *Review of Educational Research, 54*(3), 363–407.

13. FREDERIKSEN, J. R., & COLLINS, A. (1989). A systems approach to educational testing. *Educational Research, 18*(9), 27–32.

14. HAERTEL, E. (1986). *Choosing and using classroom tests: Teachers' perspectives on assessment.* Paper presented at the annual meeting of the American Educational Research Association, San Francisco, April.

*15. HARVEY, J. (1989). Placement test issues in calculator-based mathematics examinations. *The use of calculators in the standardized testing of mathematics.* New York: College Board and Mathematical Association of America.

16. HEMBREE, R. (1990). The nature, effects, and relief of mathematics anxiety. *Journal for Research in Mathematics Education, 21*(1), 33–46.

17. HILL, K. T. (1984). Debilitating motivation and testing: A major educational problem— Possible solutions and policy applications. In R. E. Ames and C. Ames (Eds.), *Research on motivation in education: Vol. 1. Student motivation.* New York: Academic Press.

18. HILL, K. T., & WIGFIELD, A. (1984). Test anxiety: A major educational problem and what can be done about it. *Elementary School Journal, 85,* 105–241.

19. KANE, M. T. (1983) A sampling model for validity. *Applied Psychological Measurement, 6,* 125–160.

20. KIRKLAND, M. C. (1971). The effects of tests on students and schools. *Review of Educational Research, 41,* 303–350.

21. LAVE, J. (1988). *Cognition in practice.* Cambridge: Cambridge University Press.

22. LESTER, F. JR., & KROLL, D. (1990). Assessing student growth in mathematical problem solving. In G. Kulm (Ed.), *Assessing higher order thinking in mathematics* (pp. 53–70). Washington, DC: American Association for the Advancement of Science.

23. MESSICK, S. (1989). Validity. In R. L. Linn (Ed.), *Educational measurement* (3rd ed., pp. 13–103). New York: Macmillan.

*24. NATIONAL COUNCIL OF TEACHERS OF MATHEMATICS (1989). *Curriculum and evaluation standards for school mathematics.* Reston, VA: Author.

*25. PUTNAM, R., LAMPERT, M., & PETERSON, P. (1989). *Alternative perspectives of knowing mathematics in elementary schools.* Center for Learning and Teaching of Elementary Subjects. East Lansing: Michigan State University.

26. ROGERS, E. M. (1969). Examinations: Powerful agents for good and ill in teaching. *American Journal of Physics, 37,* 954–962.

*27. ROMBERG, T. A., WILSON, L., & KHAKETLA, M. (1990). The alignment of six standardized tests with the NCTM *Standards.* Unpublished manuscript, University of Wisconsin–Madison.

28. SUEN, H. K., & DAVEY, B. (1990). *Potential theoretical and practical pitfalls and cautions of the performance assessment design.* Paper presented at the annual meeting of the American Educational Research Association, Boston, April.

29. SLEEMAN, D. H. (1982). Assessing competence in basic algebra. In D. H. Sleeman & J. S. Brown (Eds.), *Intelligent tutoring systems.* New York: Academic Press.

30. STEVENSON, Z. JR., AVERETT, C., & VICKERS, D. (1990). *The reliability of using a focused–holistic scoring approach to measure student performance on a geometry proof.* Paper presented at the annual meeting of the American Educational Research Association, Boston, April.

31. STIGGINS, R. J., & BRIDGEFORD, N. J. (1985). The ecology of classroom assessment. *Journal of Educational Measurement, 22*(4), 271–286.

32. WARD, W. C., FREDERIKSEN, N., & CARLSON, S. B. (1980). Construct validity of free-response and machine-scorable forms of a test. *Journal of Educational Measurement, 17,* 11–19.
33. WHIMBEY, A., & LOCKHEAD, J. (1980). *Problem solving and comprehension.* Philadelphia: Franklin Institute Press.
*34. WILSON, J. W., & KILPATRICK, J. (1989). Theoretical issues in the development of calculator-based mathematics tests. *The use of calculators in the standardized testing of mathematics.* New York: College Board and Mathematical Association of America.

PART IV

Research

CHAPTER 16

Teacher as Researcher: What Does It Really Mean?

Nina Kay Lankford

To hear the words "I've got it!" and to see a student's face light up after he or she has struggled and finally made sense of a problem or situation is a genuine thrill for me. I love teaching. I especially love teaching mathematics. It's the good days that keep me going, of course. They're the ones that provide enormous satisfaction. Naturally, there are the other days, too. Sometimes I'm tired, frustrated—even angry. I feel overworked and somehow alone. But still I continue to wonder how I could be more effective.

Since these joys and frustrations are shared by my colleagues, I am sure they must seem familiar to you. I have taught middle school and high school mathematics for fourteen years. Although I have gained a great deal of practical knowledge about teaching mathematics, I seldom have had the opportunity to reflect on it—or, more important, to share and integrate my knowledge with that of others. However, when I recently participated with nine other classroom teachers in a project associated with the production of this book, I finally had the chance (as well as the challenge) to reflect on my own effectiveness as a teacher. At long last I had the opportunity to read, to try out new ideas, and to discuss my viewpoints with interested colleagues. For me, the experience was delightful—and similar opportunities are available to you and your colleagues.

NOTE I would like to acknowledge my fellow panel members from urban and rural areas of Georgia who participated in this project: Charlee Goolsby, Oconee High School; Mary Hannon, Oglethorpe County High School; Kay Haugen, Commerce High School; Dwight Love, Greater Atlanta Christian; Barbara Malcom, Carver Junior High; Shelia Parker, Clarke Central High School; Pam Poppe, Shiloh High School; Meg Taylor, Northside High School; Jeff Weeks, Burney–Harris–Lyons Middle School; and Patricia Wilson, University of Georgia, who served as panel director.

Thinking about Research

It goes without saying that research in education has been conducted for many years. However, since I myself had no firsthand experience with it, I had always felt that it was outside the realm of my endeavors as a teacher. I did read research articles occasionally to keep myself informed of current general trends and attitudes, but that was just about the full extent of my involvement with research.

While working on my master's degree in mathematics education, though, I began to change my viewpoint about research and especially its impact on the daily activities of the classroom teacher. After reading several research articles that described classroom teachers using research as a basis for trying new teaching approaches, I began thinking about my own experience. As a professional I wanted to grow, to improve. I realized that this meant being willing to try new ideas—but I didn't want to engage in a haphazard routine of trial and error with my students: I needed something that would provide me with direction. I pondered the idea that research might offer me a very desirable and totally viable opportunity for improving my classroom efforts.

When I was asked to participate on a teacher panel for the Research into Practice Project, I was delighted to be given an opportunity to focus on research and its classroom impact. I felt that perhaps I might even gain better insight into how research could aid me as a teacher. Concurring with the project's main goal (to bridge the gap between research and practice in mathematics education), I was suddenly more than eager to examine research findings, and additionally to benefit from the suggestions of other panel members.

Reading and Discussing Research

At the panel's initial meeting we discussed our roles in the project. Our ten-member panel of teachers was to read a wide range of educational research related to the sixteen broad topics addressed in this book, and (out of our own experience) discuss the implications that research might have on the classroom. After having time to immerse ourselves in reading research, we met to discuss and share information on what we had read and to say how we felt it all related to our mathematics classrooms.

For me, these meetings were most informative and enjoyable. Sharing ideas with peers helped me to gain a broader perspective on what research was reporting, and how that might be useful in my classroom. We then continued to read research articles and later divided into small groups that focused on particular areas of interest.

Designing and Critiquing
Classroom Investigations

As the project progressed, we began to share ideas about conducting our own research projects in our particular areas of interest. We discussed the research base for our projects and gave one another feedback on how best to implement our proposed project in our classrooms. Since we realized that we were all novices in the area of conducting research, panel members seemed to feel comfortable in sharing their ideas without fear of disapproval. Suggestions were encouraged and, with the help of the panel, each of us finally refined our ideas and made plans to implement our projects.

Our final meeting was a time for sharing the results of our first endeavors as classroom researchers. Our projects covered a wide range of topics. As a result, each of us not only benefited from the experience with our own project, but had firsthand accounts of nine other projects as well. I have already found that I have been able to use, in my current teaching assignment, information gained from others' projects.

Classroom Investigations

What now follow are the accounts of various classroom investigations undertaken by our teacher panel. We offer them as examples of projects that you and your colleagues may wish to consider. Note from the start that they are not rigorous research studies conducted according to established methodologies. Rather, they are carefully planned investigations based on a body of research and implemented to investigate the teaching and learning of mathematics in our own classrooms.

Affective Studies

I was particularly intrigued with the projects concerning the affective domain of students' mathematical processing. One panel member noted from his reading of Chapter 2 that although much had been written on the heuristics of problem solving, little had been done in the area of students' feelings and attitudes. He decided to do an investigation with his students that might give him more insight into how their feelings affected their problem solving. His project involved thirty students in two sections of Algebra I who were asked to keep journals of their problem-solving activities for two weeks. A problem was posed each day, with students having sufficient time to discuss the problem in groups of two or three before the period ended. Time at home for working on the day's problem was limited to forty minutes. The next day the problem was addressed by the class as a whole. During this time, students were asked to make journal entries of their feelings about and progress on the problem. After reading these journals, the teacher concluded that students found it difficult to communicate their feelings. Also, several students seemed overly concerned about how the journals would affect their grade, and some students thought that they had not been successful unless they were able to give correct answers for all problems.

As I reflected over his students' comments, I realized how often I had encountered students focusing on the answer to a problem as the only important factor in problem solving. Perhaps we need to balance our emphasis on arriving at a correct solution with an equal emphasis on the thought processes and steps that result in a correct answer. Teachers may have unconsciously been guilty of reinforcing the failure some students feel in problem solving by not acknowledging the importance of the part of the process that has been done correctly. While each of us knows that preciseness is important in mathematics, we may find that we can do more to encourage our students by helping them to "unlearn" the misconception that the grade they receive is the main goal of their mathematics endeavors.

I so much liked this project's use of journals to help establish students' feelings and perceptions about their work that I now have my own students keep daily journals along with their mathematics assignments. Already I feel that I have a better understanding of the individual student's feelings and needs, as well as a better idea of the class attitude as a whole.

Also in the area of affective factors, one colleague investigated fifteen gifted students who were enrolled in various special programs but either did not participate in, or did not perform well in, the "gifted mathematics" program. Each student was profiled as to his or her mathematics achievement from grade 1 to present high school status. A learning-style inventory was administered to each student, and then each was interviewed as to perceptions, feelings, and recollections about personal learning experiences in mathematics.

All of the participants in the investigation indicated a stronger preference for language and visual arts than for mathematics and natural sciences. Paul Torrance's Human Processing Information Survey was used to indicate learning styles. Of those students surveyed, only two showed integrated processing styles, while the remainder reported a leaning toward right-brain dominance.

The students interviewed expressed a common attitude toward mathematics of perceived lack of usefulness, rigidity and absoluteness of the subject matter, too great an emphasis on detail, and a strong dislike for the teacher-centered nature of mathematics classrooms with little room for student expression or interaction.

While we don't want to change the precise nature of mathematics, we would like to dispel the myth that mathematics is rigid. We can try to reach out to those students who are not naturally drawn to the study of mathematics. Two of the students' on-target suggestions were that we more closely relate mathematics to practical uses and also allow more time for sharing ideas and less for the teacher's doing the "telling." They also suggested more small-group work, peer tutoring, and concern for the individual learner. Too, they felt that a check for understanding of prerequisite skills before moving to more difficult concepts should be given greater importance. I was somewhat surprised at some of the students' suggestions, because I felt that the mathematics teachers I know do try to incorporate most of these ideas into their classes. However, the students surveyed did not perceive these areas as being addressed.

Since becoming more aware of students' concerns, I have tried to make a concerted effort to address these areas in my own teaching. I think that the use of student journals is one way to let my charges know that I really do care about what they think. In addition, I want to let them know that I am checking on their understanding of skills even as I prepare my lessons. I do not engrave my lesson plans in stone; they are directly related to my students' understanding of previous skills and I want my students to be aware of this at all times. I also want to help my students view math as exciting and useful rather than as a cold and impersonal subject that they must endure. A positive teacher attitude about mathematics seems to be a prerequisite for student success.

Studies of Preconceived Concepts

Two of our panel members addressed misconceptions that students brought with them to the mathematics classroom. The first project used Chapter 5 as a research base. The teacher distributed a handout composed of terms that students would not yet have studied, although some terms were related to earlier courses. The teacher wanted to know what the "situational background" was for the students relative to their entering the study of trigonometry. They were given a list of eight terms and asked to write a response for each item with the understanding that although they were not yet responsible for these terms, they were nevertheless to write what they knew about each term at this point. Afterward, the students were videotaped as they discussed the terms.

A second class was taped wherein students were given examples of the terms and then asked to respond to them. The tape was reviewed to see if any student's background related on the handout interfered with or contaminated the integration of the concept.

After the first phase of the project, the teacher noted that the students exhibited considerable confusion about the terms both as they initially described them on the handout sheets and later as they discussed them in class. She concluded that background did seem to affect a student's grasp of new concepts, felt that an awareness of her students' misconceptions would aid her in her presentations, and believed that she could now focus on eliminating the confusion that background material might cause in understanding a new concept.

The other project addressing misconceptions used the work (including experiments) on probability in Chapter 10 as a rationale. Recurring misconceptions that students often bring with them to the classroom were to be confronted, the intent being that of working through them to a clear understanding of the concept. Class time was to be used for discussing the experiments, and students were to keep journals of their work. Due to end-of-the-year activities, problems arose that prohibited the conclusion of the project. Although the project was not finalized, the teacher felt that he did gain some valuable information from the project, such as that probability as a small part of a larger course did not seem to be sufficient for students' grasp of the concepts. The teacher had arrived at a better understanding of the proposal to offer probability and statistics as a course of its own.

Studies of Characteristics of Problem Solvers

Two other projects addressed characteristics and learning approaches of successful math students. The first project, which used Chapter 7 (on algebra) as a research base, involved successful and unsuccessful equation-solvers and how they approached a solution. Eight students were questioned about their understanding of an algebraic equation and the pertinent solution process. Later, each was videotaped as he or she solved a series of simple linear equations. Four of these students had shown proficiency on in-class exercises and tests covering multistep linear equations. The other four had not mastered either single or multistep equation solving in the same context.

The results of the project confirmed both the research and the teacher's suspicions. Four of the successful students solved either eleven or all twelve of the equations, doing so by using the inverse operation method presented and discussed numerous times in class. The four unsuccessful equation solvers were not able to solve the six equations, and three of these students would not even attempt the last three (which were multistep) equations. Instead, these students used the arithmetic approach, which utilized trial and error. One of them used the trial-and-error method until he reached the more difficult equations, then attempted the inverse operation method— but could not decide which operation to do first.

The four unsuccessful students had been unwilling to participate in class discussions and group activities about equation solving. The teacher noted that these students seemed content to use the "guess and check" method until it would not work, and then simply say that the other problems were too hard.

I think that this project helps confirm the belief that students must move beyond arithmetic to be successful in algebra. Since, however, other questions arise as to how to motivate students to move from this level, perhaps another project that focuses on motivation might be in order. It seems that each project not only sheds light on its original aim, but also points to new avenues worthy of further investigation.

The second project on characteristics of problem solvers was done by a teacher with five of her eighth-grade Algebra I students, two boys and three girls whose names were randomly drawn from a bowl containing the names of all her Algebra I students. All of the students had been instructed in the use of Polya's problem-solving method. All were given a copy of a rather complex problem situation and asked to solve it, verbalizing their work as they proceeded to work on the solution. The students were individually videotaped. Each worked fifteen to twenty minutes on the problem.

Most of the students identified the correct answer to the problem, but only one went into enough detail to solve it correctly and back up his answer. This student, also the most verbal, appeared the most relaxed and confident in the situation. He was able to sort through irrevelant information and focus on the important aspects of the problem. The girls appeared to be more nervous in the situation, a factor that may account for their lack of success in solving the problem.

The students said that if they had experienced previous problem solving while on camera, they would have been more comfortable and perhaps would have performed more successfully. The teacher felt that it was difficult actually to follow the cognitive processes that each student was using. Perhaps several sessions with each student would reveal more clearly each individual's problem-solving procedures.

Although the aim of this project was to analyze each student's use of sensory modalities and problem-solving techniques, the project also gave us insight into the effect that a student's feelings have on the ability to solve a problem. Some students may simply feel too uncomfortable to verbalize their problem solving correctly. I have found that many of my students do not have enough confidence to work through a problem with the class or teacher as an audience. These students prefer to work on their own until, after thinking through the solution, they are confident enough to explain their work. Likewise, this project seems to indicate that the ability to solve a problem correctly may be hindered by a student's concern about being incorrect. It appears that teachers need to continue to stress that the correct answer is not all there is to learning mathematics. Being incorrect is acceptable if we use what we have done incorrectly to clarify our thinking before trying a new approach. Learning mathematics is a process in which we can make valuable use of our mistakes. We hope that we can reduce the kind of anxieties that may inhibit students' ability to become successful problem solvers.

Study on Homework

Another project focused on whether giving homework assignments in mass or distributed over several days affected students' achievement. Two Algebra I classes of the same approximate number and ability level were used for this project. One class was given individually massed assignments that were due daily. The other class had the same problems assigned, but was given several days to complete the them. The homework grades for the two classes were similar, but the median score for the students who were given distributed assignments were about ten points lower. This result was the opposite of what other research results had indicated. In addition to students' scores, the teacher also used student surveys about homework for her investigation—and felt that the surveys gave her the most helpful information. Surprisingly (to her), she found that her students' perceptions about length of assignments, difficulty, level, and completion rate for homework were very similar to her own views.

This project seems to illustrate the need for caution in our reading a research article and accepting the results as true for our students. This teacher, rather than simply changing her method of assigning homework because of what she had read, investigated how such a change might affect her own students. To her, distributed assignments did not seem to be the best method. This finding does not mean that what worked poorly with the students involved might not work well for other students, however. Research can be a great help to us in pointing to areas of investigation that might result in our improving areas of instruction or (on the other hand) convincing us that a current method is what is best for our students.

Studies of Cooperative Learning

Two of the panel's projects addressed cooperative learning situations. One of these projects was my own. Because I often felt frustrated by the lack of motivation and the poor performance of my high school general math students, I was particularly interested in a statement from Chapter 1 (on cognition), which says that there is some evidence that poor and nonwhite students are more motivated in cooperative, rather than competitive, learning environments. Since this described the general make-up of my general math class, I was eager to develop and implement a project that might aid me in improving both the motivation and the performance of my students.

While reading and planning for my project, I noted that Chapter 5 (on models of learning) suggested that cooperative learning is most effective when individual accountability is combined with a group goal. With this in mind, I developed a two-week plan on problem solving that combined group performance and individual performance into a single grade for each student. Fifteen students were assigned to groups. Three groups had four members, and one group had three members. Care was taken to balance the groups with respect to perceived ability and leadership attributes of their members.

Each group's folder of work was checked daily. Each member received the score awarded to the group's work. At the end of the two-week period, a test was given on the material covered. Half of the test was worked on by each group as a combined effort of its members. The other half was completed by each member working alone. Each student's test score was a combination of the two parts, each having equal weight. For analysis, each student's test score was compared to scores on previous units; students were interviewed individually for their opinions on the group learning experience; and videos were made of the students engaged in their group activities.

Out of fifteen students, twelve showed equal or improved test scores. All three students whose scores did not improve were in the same group; the fourth member showed slight improvement. This particular group had experienced difficulty functioning as a unit. The students seemed to be more distracted by one another and unable to focus on the task at hand. The other three groups, however, functioned very well. These students seemed to enjoy working with others—often one student would carefully explain a problem to another group member. As time progressed these three groups became more self-directed, requiring less help and prodding from the teacher.

In the student interviews, ten students said that they preferred group work to individual learning situations, while five indicated preference for working alone. Two of these five students said that they might like group work in the future if they could work with a different group of students.

One of my colleagues (who also implemented a cooperative learning project) noted that this was a new teaching technique for her. While she had allowed students to work together at times, she had never felt that this had been a beneficial experience. After reading what research said on the subject, she felt that the lack of success of her group work might be due to the absence of a group goal and individual accountability. Because of this, she adjusted her previous procedures to address these points. Her groups were structured in a manner similar to that in my own project, but instead of an extended time frame of only group work, on different occasions she used groups as study teams in preparation for quizzes and tests. After noting which students kept their groups moving and stimulated group involvement, the teacher made changes in the second group assignments, and the new groups functioned more effectively. A side note of interest: Because of being extremely distracting, two students were not allowed to participate in group work at all.

From comparing scores to previous scores, from reviewing students' written opinions of group activities, and from considering her own observations, my colleague concluded that, over all, this cooperative learning situation had been a very positive experience. In particular, students with the lowest base scores seemed to gain the most benefit from group work. This teacher also noted that even though some students used the time to socialize, and some were not enthusiastic, she had heard more mathematics being discussed and explained than ever before. My colleague and I have come to agree that cooperative learning is a valuable teaching technique. Perhaps through continued effort we all can refine it enough to become comfortable with when and how to utilize it best.

Getting Started

I hope that the accounts of our various classroom investigations have helped to convince you that teachers can play an important role in research. In addition, I hope you agree that investigations do offer teachers valuable information about students and their role in the learning and teaching of mathematics. Most important, I hope that you can see yourself in the role of teacher–researcher. Even though you may be an investigator only in your own classroom, and not engaged in the rigor of "hard core" research of mathematics education, it still is important to have direction in both planning and implementing your investigation. Let me offer some suggestions.

Reading and Discussing

Read current research in mathematics education. *Journal for Research in Mathematics Education* and *Mathematics Teacher* are good choices for a beginning. Read an article that interests you and relate its findings to your own classroom experience. Discuss your opinions with a colleague—perhaps your discussions, as well as your readings, will point you to a particular area that you would like to investigate further. Read how other teachers are conducting investigations. A *Teacher's Guide to Classroom Research*, by David Hopkins (1), offers valuable insight into the teacher as researcher and relates several examples of classroom investigations conducted by teachers.

Designing and Critiquing

As you begin to focus on a particular aspect of your students' learning or of your teaching techniques, make notes from your readings in line with your area of interest. Ask your colleagues for their opinions and experiences that relate to your topic. Finally, make a decision on exactly what you would like to explore, and (if in the least possible) seek out all of the research related directly to it that you can.

Conducting Your Investigations

Now that you really know what you want to investigate, the next step is to decide how best to accomplish this task. Ask colleagues for suggestions. From your reading, consider the various methods and tools used by others and write them down: checklists, videos, interviews, tape recorders, outside observers, and so on. Decide whether plans for a particular unit of study need to be developed for the investigation or whether your regular plans suffice. Consider what you hope to learn from your investigation, and then choose from your checklist those methods and tools that would best help you to obtain this information. After developing your plan, assemble your materials and tools. You are now ready to implement your investigation.

Analyzing

Don't be discouraged if things don't proceed as you expected: You still are investigating. You will learn at the very least *something* from your experience that can be useful to you as a teacher. You may come to feel that you haven't obtained information truly pertinent to your goal, but you will nevertheless *have* obtained information. And it may even be that this information will point to a different and more important aspect than what you were targeting.

This can still be useful information. Be sure to organize it in such a way that you can make comparisons and interpretations from it. Information sheets with data per student may be appropriate for your study, or you may then require tally sheets for recording certain types of student responses. Regardless of the form you choose for recording your data, a written response of your interpretation of the results, along with your general feelings about your project, is valuable. Include any numerical comparisons in your conclusion, together with your perception of what the data suggest. For instance, how do your results compare to your research base? What changes could be made to gain more useful information? How can you use your results to be a more effective teacher? Having a written record of your conclusions, you can now begin a file that well may offer valuable reference assistance to you, even in the near future.

Sharing

Finally, share your experience with your colleagues. Encourage them to try an investigation of their own. Perhaps you could work together in your math department, helping one another to develop or implement a project. Departmental meetings could be utilized for a sharing time. Encourage one another to share your experiences with teachers on a county-wide level. I feel that if we actively pursue this avenue of growth, the benefits will be tremendous. There are so many talented and creative teachers in our mathematics classrooms. If we can pool our experiences, share our perspectives, and continue to use research as a springboard for our own classroom investigations, the teaching and learning of mathematics will evolve into a vital area of study in which continuous progress is the standard.

Conclusions

Do I still feel overworked and frustrated at times? Do I think that conducting research investigations in addition to full-schedule teaching is worthwhile? Yes, I emphatically do—in both cases.

Some days I seem simply to get through the day. No doubt you know that feeling too well. But on other days—on some of the most rewarding days—I have been more effective as a teacher not only because of my own investigations, but also because of what I have learned through the shared experiences of others. Through my students' journals, for example, I have come to know some of them in a personal way that otherwise would have been impossible. I have been able to adjust my methods and respond to students' individual needs much more effectively than before because now I know what those needs are. Yes, the extra effort required to investigate methods, topics, student needs, and the rest definitely is worthwhile. I invite you to experience the rewards that such efforts can bring. Become a teacher–researcher.

References

1. HOPKINS, D. (1985). A *teacher's guide to classroom research*. Milton Keynes, Philadelphia: Open University Press.

Research Ideas for the Classroom: Early Childhood Mathematics

Contents

Research Ideas for the Classroom: Middle Grades Mathematics

Contents

293

Index

A

Ability grouping, 222
Abstract level of thinking, 141–42
Accommodation, 6
Achievement tests, 12, 200
Across time questions, 159, 164, 166
Active instruction, 225–26
Activities. *See* specific types of
Adaptive instruction, 227–28
Advance organizers, 237–38
Affect. *See also* Attitudes; Beliefs;
    Emotions
  assessment of, 22
  attitudes and, 29–31
  beliefs and, 25–29
  cognition and, 24
  domain of, 22–23
  emotions and, 31–32
  importance of, 21–22
  investigations of, 281–82
  learner's characteristics of, 106–9
  learning and, 21–22
  psychological theories and, 23–25
  teaching and, 21–22
AI (artificial intelligence) software, 149,
    207
Algebra
  cognition and, 121
  computers for, 119, 133
  concepts of, 126–29
  curriculum, 119–20
  deficiencies in, 5–6
  definition of, 119
  faulty construction of knowledge and,
    10
  geometry of, 129–31
  graphing calculators for, 130, 133,
    201–2

historical sketch of, 120–21
  language of, 122–26
  learning, 121–22
  rules of, 131–33
  teaching, 134–35
  variables in, 122–25
Algebraic expressions, 123–25, 132
Algorithms, 3, 4, 63
Analogical reasoning, 43
Analytic level of thinking, 141
Analyzing investigations, 288
Area models, 129
Arousal, 24–25
Articulation questions, 159
Artificial intelligence (AI) software, 149,
    207
Assessment. *See also* Tests
  of affect, 22
  attitudes of students and, 30
  beliefs of students and, 26
  calculators in, 270–72
  classroom, implications for, 266–67
  formative, 261–62
  large-scale, implications for, 267–68
  of problem solving, 71–73
  reliability and, 262–63
  research methodology and, implications
    for, 268–70
  of stochastics, 190
  summative, 262
  testing-learning relationships and,
    260–61
  types of, 261–62
  validity and, 263–66
Assimilation, 6
Attitudes
  affect and, 29–31
  cognition and, 22–23
  definition of, 29